Syntax

Syntax

Peter W. Culicover

University of California, Irvine

ACADEMIC PRESS   New York   San Francisco   London

A Subsidiary of Harcourt Brace Jovanovich, Publishers

ACADEMIC PRESS, INC.
111 Fifth Avenue, New York, New York 10003

United Kingdom Edition published by
ACADEMIC PRESS, INC. (LONDON) LTD.
24/28 Oval Road, London NW1

Library of Congress Cataloging in Publication Data

Culicover, Peter W
    Syntax.

    Bibliography: p.
    Includes index.
        1.   Grammar, Comparative and general—Syntax.
2.   Generative grammar.   3.   English language—
Syntax.   4.   English language—Grammar, Generative.
I.   Title.
P291.C8   415   75–30466
ISBN 0–12–199250–0

Contents

PREFACE   ix

1 **Introduction**   **1**

The Linguistic Capacity   1
Theory of Grammar   2
The Form of a Grammar   2
The Syntactic Component   3
Methodological Remarks   4
Suggested Further Readings   5

2 **Basic Notions and Notation**   **7**

How to Get Started   7
Categories and Structures   8
Phrase Structure Trees   16
Tree Terms   19
What a Grammar Can Do   21
The Proper Use of Power   24
The Power of Transformations   30
Exercises   33
Problems   5 6 6 4 0   35
Suggested Further Readings   36

3 A Basic Rule of English   38

Preliminaries   38
Some Data: Verbal Sequences   38
The Analysis: Extracting Regularities   47
The Description: Affix Hopping   48
Morphology   55
Syntactic Features   56
Summary   59
Summary of Rules   59
Exercises   60
Suggested Further Readings   61

4 Questions   63

Yes–No Questions   63
A Tranformational Analysis   67
Do Deletion and *Do* Replacement   69
Wh Questions   72
The Deep Structure of *Wh* Words   76
Summary   85
Summary of Rules   86
Exercises   87
Problems   87
Suggested Further Readings   88

5 Aspects of a Theory of Grammar   89

Introduction   89
Some Notions of Rule Ordering   90
A Preliminary Rule Ordering   94
More Rule Orderings   99
A Restriction on Transformational Power   104
The Relationship between the Syntactic and Semantic Components   114
Summary of Rules   116
Exercises   118
Problems   118

6 Negation   120

Introduction   120
Sentential Negation   121
Negative Questions and Contraction   128
Tag Questions   131
Summary of Rules   140
Exercises   141
Problems   141
Suggested Further Readings   142

7

More Transformations   144

Introduction   144
Reflexive Pronouns   144
The Imperative   147
The Dative   153
The Passive   160
Summary   172
Summary of Rules   172
Exercises   174
Problems   175
Suggested Further Readings   177

8

Relative Clauses   178

Introduction   178
Recursion   178
The Structure of the Noun Phrase   183
Locating the Relative Clause   187
Some Remarks on Semantic Interpretation   188
Inside the Relative Clause   191
That in Relative Clauses   198
Related Constructions   201
Summary   208
Summary of Rules   208
Exercises   209
Problems   210
Suggested Further Readings   213

9

Verb Complements I: Infinitival Complements   214

The Varieties of Verb Complements   214
The Understood Subject of the Infinitive   217
Raising   223
Problems with the Analysis   233
Summary   237
Summary of Rules   237
Exercises   238
Problems   238
Suggested Further Readings   241

10

Verb Complements II: *That* Clauses   242

Introduction   242
Moving the *That* Clause   243
An Ordering Paradox   257
Summary   268
Summary of Rules   268

Exercises   269
Problems   269
Suggested Further Readings   272

11 Constraints and Language Learnability   274

The A-Over-A Principle   274
Ross' Constraints   277
Formal Language Learnability: An Introduction   284
The Learnability of Transformational Grammars   288
Evidence for the Freezing Principle   298
Summary   301
Exercises   302
Problems   302
Suggested Further Readings   305

REFERENCES   307
SUBJECT INDEX   313

Preface

This textbook is an introduction to the study of the formal syntax of natural language. The level is one that should be generally comfortable and occasionally challenging to the upper-division undergraduate linguistics major and beginning graduate student in linguistics or a related discipline, such as psychology or anthropology. The book presupposes that the reader has a background at least equivalent to a comprehensive introduction to linguistics that makes some contact with transformational grammar; such introduction appears, for example, in Fromkin and Rodman (1973). More specifically, I assume that the reader does not have to be convinced that the study of linguistics is worth pursuing, and is not unaware that there is much more to linguistics than what is covered in this book. Chapter 1 touches on these points very lightly and is intended as a review.

The book is concerned with four distinct but related aspects of syntactic analysis. One is the notational system and the terminology, which is introduced intensively in Chapters 2 and 3, and more sporadically throughout the book. My aim is to establish the important connection between the phenomena that have to be accounted for and the devices by which one describes them.

I have taken the position throughout that semantic information is not sufficient for the justification and evaluation of syntactic analyses;

only **syntactic** facts will do. A second concern of this book, therefore, is to illustrate the way one goes about constructing descriptions of the syntax of a language, given this criterion.

Another concern has been to acquaint the reader with a selection of the standard phenomena of English syntax that have formed the basis for much of the important work in linguistics in the past 20 years or so. I have not attempted to provide a historical survey; rather, I have chosen the problems and solutions that seem to me to illuminate interesting theoretical points most effectively. Chapters 3–7 deal with syntactic phenomena whose scope is the simple sentence; Chapters 8–10 are concerned with the syntax of complex sentences.

This book emphasizes the relationship between descriptions of the syntax of natural language, the theory of grammar in which such descriptions can be formulated, and the goal of accounting for the phenomenon of language acquisition. Although Chomsky (1957) originally established this goal as a major concern of linguistic theory and has repeatedly emphasized its importance, it has not received as much attention as other aspects of linguistics. The material in Chapters 10 and 11 makes clear the intimate relationship between a theory of grammar and a theory of language acquisition, and shows that providing a formal description of the syntax of natural language is a prerequisite for illuminating this relationship and making it coherent.

There are a number of exercises and problems at the end of each chapter. The exercises take the student through the notations, conventions, and rules established in the text; the problems are intended to take the student beyond the text. The problems that I consider relatively difficult are marked with an asterisk. Those that I feel to be not only difficult but open-ended as well are marked with a double asterisk. These should be viewed as points of departure into questions that the instructor would like to discuss in class, and not as problems for which a complete, neat, and final solution should be expected.

Also at the end of each chapter is a short list of suggested further readings. I have indicated with an asterisk those that I think are most comprehensible to the beginner. The others, while somewhat more difficult, provide illustrations of the variety of approaches to problems of natural language. The student should be encouraged to become familiar with the literature, since the view presented in this book is necessarily a limited one and admittedly idiosyncratic at times.

I would like to acknowledge Janet Dean Fodor's many helpful suggestions for reanalysis, rephrasing, and reorganization. Naturally, all errors that remain are my own.

Also, I am deeply indebted to Kenneth Wexler for the stimulating collaboration that he has provided over the past 5 years. Many of the ideas in this book, particularly in the later chapters, are due entirely to him or are the products of our joint research.

Thanks also to my students, my teachers, and my friends. Much of what is good in this book is theirs.

Finally, I would like to thank my wife, Pam Coker.

1

Introduction

THE LINGUISTIC CAPACITY

The capacity for acquiring and using a language is a property that distinguishes human beings from all other species. The task of the linguist is to explain what it is about human beings that renders them capable of performing this feat, and what it is about human languages that renders them capable of being learned and used by human beings.

Human language learning is a remarkable phenomenon. The child is born into the world with no language at all. Through exposure to a speech community, the child begins to speak at some time during the second year, and in five or six years can be said to know the language quite well, if not completely. This feat of language learning is accomplished by every normal child without fail, and without extensive explicit instruction on the part of adults concerning the "rules" of the language.

Each child in fact reinvents the language of the speech community for himself. In order to acquire a language, the mind of the child must have built into it some notion of what is to be learned. This can be seen from the fact that every speaker of a language is capable of creating and understanding sentences of that language that he has never heard before. Consequently, on the basis of the sentences that he *has* heard the speaker must be able to arrive at a set of rules for creating and understanding new sentences. This ability to project from the sentences actually encountered in the course of language learning to a general set of rules for creating and understanding novel utterances is the human linguistic capacity. It is, essentially, an inborn understanding of what a possible language can be. By studying the characteristics of human languages we study this aspect of human intelligence, for the structure of the languages themselves reflects the nature of the device that created them and recreates them in the mind of every human child.

THEORY OF GRAMMAR

The task of the linguist can be divided into two parts. On the one hand, the linguist must determine what properties various human languages possess. For each human language, we seek a complete and precise description of the properties of that language. Such a description is called a **grammar.** Note that a grammar as we understand it here is not an account of what properties a language *should* have but of what properties a language *does* in fact have.

On the other hand, the linguist must determine what properties are common to all languages. If we find that all human languages share a particular property or are restricted in certain ways, then we may reasonably take this to be a product of the universal human capacity for language.[1] Discovery of universals of language brings the linguist closer to an understanding of the structure and capacities of the human mind. A formal account of what properties a human language must or may have is called a **theory of grammar**. A theory of grammar specifies the necessary and possible properties of grammars of human languages.

THE FORM OF A GRAMMAR

While linguists disagree radically about precisely what form a grammar of a human language may take, there is considerable agreement that the correct theory of grammar must allow for grammars that have the following **components:**

1. A **lexicon,** in which each word of the language is listed along with information about its meaning, its pronunciation, its internal structure and relationship to other words of the language, and the ways in which it may be used in the formation of sentences.

2. A **phonology,** which is a description of what the possible sounds of the language are, and how they may be combined to form words.

3. A **syntax,** which is a description of the various ways in which words of the language may be strung together to form sentences.

---

[1] Unless the universal property happens to be due to a universal of human experience. For example, the fact that all languages have a word for *water* does not reveal anything about the human capacity for language but simply shows that all human cultures have experience with water.

4. A **semantics,** which is a description of how the meaning of a string of words in the language is made up of the meanings of the individual words in the string.

The theory of grammar specifies in precise detail what form each of these components must or may take. The focus of this book will be the syntactic component. We will examine a variety of phenomena in English in order to determine in part the form of the syntactic component of English. From this, we will attempt to form hypotheses about what properties are universal to the syntactic components of all languages.

THE SYNTACTIC COMPONENT

An example should serve to make more concrete the notion of the syntactic component. It was observed earlier that native speakers of a language are not restricted to uttering sentences that they have heard before, but can make up and understand new sentences of the language. Consider the examples in (1.1):

(1.1)   a. *My brother married a native speaker of Classical Latin.*
          b. *Married my brother a native speaker of Classical Latin..*

It is highly unlikely that any native speaker of English has ever heard (1.1a), since there are no speakers of Classical Latin alive today. Nevertheless, all speakers of English recognize that (1.1a) is a sentence of English, while (1.1b) is not. This ability must be explained on the basis of the properties of the words in these examples and the order in which they are strung together. In this case, for example, the verb *married* must appear between the two noun phrases *my brother* and *a fluen speaker of Classical Latin.* This is evidence that the speaker has knowledge of the structure of sentences, and it is this knowledge that the linguist seeks to describe in formulating an account of the syntactic component of a language.

The notion that we will attempt to characterize precisely in the case of English is that of **grammatical sentence of English.** Intuitively, the grammatical sentences are the sentences that sound good to the native speaker; formally, they are the strings of words that can be formed by the rules of the syntactic component. Ideally the two sets should be identical, so that the syntactic component produces all and only the sentences that the native speaker judges to be grammatical.

Notice that the grammaticality of a string of words is quite independent of whether it makes sense or not. For example, (1.1a) is odd to the extent that it asserts something that cannot be true at the present time. The reason for this has nothing to do with English, of course, since it is not a property of English that there are no living native speakers of Classical Latin.

On the other hand, (1.1b) is ungrammatical, and this is independent of whatever we might understand by this string of words. Sentence (1.1a) is made somewhat less odd if we substitute *French* for *Classical Latin*, while (1.1b) is not improved at all by the same substitution.

The syntactic component of a language, then, is the set of rules by which words and groups of words may be strung together to form grammatical sentences of the language. The question of whether a string of words is a grammatical sentence of a particular language is completely independent of whether or not that string of words makes a true statement, is logically consistent, or makes much sense at all. The distinction between the **form** of a linguistic expression and its **content** is a fundamental one and is maintained quite strictly in this book.

The existence of this distinction does not preclude the existence of a **relationship** between the syntactic structure of a linguistic expression and its semantic content. It is obvious, for example, that when the order of words in a sentence is changed the result may be a nonsynonymous sentence:

(1.2)   a. *Horatio hit Porky.*
                         b. *Porky hit Horatio.*

As we proceed to construct precise syntactic descriptions, the question of which aspects of the syntactic structure contribute to the semantic content of an expression will become more meaningful than it might appear to be at this point. Further discussion of this issue is deferred, therefore, to later chapters.

METHODOLOGICAL REMARKS

The learning of a first language is for the most part an unconscious process. While it is necessary for the native speaker to acquire rules of the language in order to speak it correctly, the rules are not explicitly made available to the learner, but are simply exemplified for him by other native speakers. The end result of this is that while it is clear that the native speaker employs rules for forming sentences, it is impossible to ask the native speaker what the rules are. Rather, it is necessary for the linguist to figure out what the rules must be on the basis of what the native speaker judges are grammatical and ungrammatical sentences of the language.

The linguist seeks patterns of grammaticality and ungrammaticality and infers from these what the organizing principles behind these patterns must be. For example, a simple organizing principle that distinguishes between (1.1a) and (1.1b) is that the verb must follow the subject in English. Such a principle is incorporated into a tentative grammatical description of the language, and is subsequently tested against an increasingly wider range of relevant examples. It is important to recognize that the grammar that the linguist proposes is a **hypothesis.** That is, it is a guess as to what is really the case. The hypothesis must be formulated on the basis of good evidence; it must be tested whenever possible.

Finally, it is useful to distinguish between the **competence** of a native speaker and his **performance.**[2] Competence is defined as the native speaker's unconscious knowledge of his language. This knowledge would be reliably revealed in the native speaker's judgments about the grammaticality of sentences and in the sentences uttered by native speakers if they were not subject to limitations of memory, lapses of attention, imperfect understanding of the physical world, and so on. Native speakers do have these performance limitations; they are not ideal (i.e., perfect) speakers and hearers. What we must attempt to do is to abstract from the complex and often contradictory data that result from performance factors. To the extent that this abstraction permits us to discover interesting and important properties of human language and human intelligence, we will have justified the distinction between competence and performance and the decision to treat particular linguistic phenomena as lying within the domain of one or the other.

SUGGESTED FURTHER READINGS

(*Asterisks indicate titles that are most comprehensible to the beginner.*)

General linguistics

*Fromkin, V. & Rodman, R. (1973), *An Introduction to Language*, Holt, New York.
*Gleason, H. (1961), *An Introduction to Descriptive Linguistics*, (Revised edition), Holt, New York.
*Hockett, C. (1958), *A Course in Modern Linguistics*, MacMillan, New York.
*Langacker, R. (1968), *Language and Its Structure*, Harcourt, New York.
*Sapir, E. (1921), *Language*, Harcourt, New York.

Phonology

Chomsky, N. & Halle, M. (1968), *The Sound Pattern of English*, Harper, New York.
*Halle, M. (1964a), "On the bases of phonology," In Fodor, J. A. & Katz, J. J. (1964), *The Structure of Language: Readings in the Philosophy of Language*, Prentice-Hall, Englewood Cliffs, N. J.
*Halle, M. (1964b), Phonology in a generative grammar, in Fodor, J. A. & Katz, J. J. (1964), *The Structure of Language: Readings in the Philosophy of Language*, Prentice-Hall, Englewood Cliffs, N. J.
*Harms, R. (1968), *Introduction to Phonological Theory*, Prentice-Hall, Englewood Cliffs, N. J.
*Hyman, L. (1975), *Phonology*, Holt, New York.
*Schane, S. (1972), *Generative Phonology*, Prentice-Hall, Englewood Cliffs, N. J.

Competence and Performance

Chomsky, N. (1965), *Aspects of the Theory of Syntax*, MIT Press, Cambridge, Mass.
Miller, G. A. & Chomsky, N. (1963), "Finitary models of language users," In Luce, R. D., Bush, R. R., & Galanter, E. (1963), *Handbook of Mathematical Psychology* (Vol. 2), Wiley, New York.

---

[2] See Chomsky (1965) for the original discussion of these notions in linguistics.

Semantics

Davidson, D. & Harman, G., eds. (1972), *Semantics of Natural Languages*, Reidel, Dordrecht, Holland.

Fillmore, C. & Langendoen, D. T., eds. (1971), *Studies in Linguistic Semantics*, Holt, New York.

Jackendoff, R. S. (1972), *Semantic Interpretation in Generative Grammar*, MIT Press, Cambridge, Mass.

Katz, J. J. (1972), *Semantic Theory*, Harper, New York.

Steinberg, D. & Jakobovits, L. A., eds. (1971), *Semantics: An Interdisciplinary Reader in Philosophy, Linguistics, and Psychology*, Cambridge University Press, London.

Language Acquisition

*Bar-Adon, A. & Leopold, W., eds. (1971), *Child Language: A Book of Readings*, Prentice-Hall, Englewood Cliffs, N. J.

*Brown, R. (1973), *A First Language*, Harvard University Press, Cambridge, Mass.

*Dale, P. S. (1972), *Language Development*, Dryden Press, Hinsdale, Ill.

Ferguson, C. & Slobin, D. I., eds. (1973), *Studies of Child Language Development*, Holt, New York.

*McNeill, D. (1970), *The Acquisition of Language*, Harper, New York.

Menyuk, P. (1969), *Sentences Children Use*, MIT Press, Cambridge, Mass.

Menyuk, P. (1971), *The Acquisition and Development of Language*, Prentice-Hall, Englewood Cliffs, N. J.

2

Basic Notions
and Notation

HOW TO GET STARTED

While our long-range goal is to provide a description of the native speaker's linguistic knowledge and to explain how language is acquired by the child, it is necessary to be somewhat selective in our choice of immediate goals. In the previous chapter, we agreed that our goal would be the description of the linguistic knowledge of an idealized native speaker of English. An advantage of proceeding in this way is that it permits us to answer, in a precise way, the questions of what constitutes linguistic knowledge and how such knowledge is acquired.

Any normal child will learn any language to which he or she is exposed. It is natural for us to ask why this should be. Why, for example, should there not be some languages that can be learned only by Oriental children, or by left-handed children, or by brown-eyed children?

A reasonable answer to this question is that there is something about human beings in general that permits them to learn languages, and something about human languages in general that permits them to be learned by human beings. A description of even one language, such as English, provides the basis for an answer, since whatever must be true of all human languages that permits them to be learned must be true of English.

On the other hand, it does not follow that whatever is true of English is necessarily true of all languages. In English, for example, the verb usually precedes the direct object, as in *John hit Mary* rather than *John Mary hit*. However, there are languages, such as Japanese, in which the verb in a normal sentence comes at the end of the sentence.

What we must be concerned with, in the long run, are two questions. First, what sorts of characteristics *must* a human language have that make it a human language, and second, what sorts of characteristics are *possible* characteristics of human language? A detailed answer to these questions is a **theory of grammar.** A theory of grammar, in short, is a precise specification of what kinds of grammars languages can have, and what sorts of things must be present in the grammar of every language.

In order to be able to entertain these questions seriously, we must first arrive at some understanding of the kinds of phenomena that a theory of grammar deals with. What follows, therefore, is a detailed investigation of some simple grammatical facts of English. The study of English alone will by no means tell us everything that can be known about natural language; it does provide us with a suitable point of departure.

CATEGORIES AND STRUCTURES

A possible hypothesis about a natural language (such as English) is that any sequence of words whatsoever constitutes a grammatical, or syntactically well-formed, sentence of the language. While this hypothesis is false for all languages, there are nevertheless clear cases in which the reordering of the sequence of words in a grammatical sentence yields another grammatical sentence. Take, for example, sentence (2.1) and interchange *boy* and *toy*:

(2.1)   The **boy** destroyed a **toy**.

(2.2)   The **toy** destroyed a **boy**.

Sentence (2.2) is grammatical, though it may sound peculiar at first owing to the strangeness of the phenomenon that it describes.

Interchanging the positions of *a* and *the* again yields a grammatical sentence:

(2.1)   **The** boy destroyed **a** toy.

(2.3)   **A** boy destroyed **the** toy.

The grammaticality of (2.2) and (2.3) suggests a hypothesis: Perhaps one can take any sentence of English, interchange the positions of any two words, and end up with a grammatical sentence.

This hypothesis is simply incorrect. Interchanging *the* and *boy* or *a* and *destroyed* in (2.1), for example, yields ungrammatical sequences:

(2.1)   *The **boy** destroyed a toy.*

(2.4)   *Boy the destroyed a toy.*

(2.1)   *The boy **destroyed** a toy.*

(2.5)   *The boy a destroyed toy.*

The reader will recognize that the explanation for these facts is a straight-forward one: *Boy* and *toy* are nouns, *a* and *the* are articles, and *destroyed* is a verb. **Noun** is the name of a **category** of words, of which *boy* and *toy* are members, **article** the name of another category, and so on. Categories are groups of words of a language that can substitute for one another without affecting grammaticality, as the preceding examples suggest. This leads to the following definition:

DEFINITION: A **syntactic category** is a group of words in a given language that can replace one another in any sentence of the language whatsoever without affecting grammaticality.

This definition will require further modification, but it is adequate for the present discussion. It should be noted that the name given to a category is arbitrary, in that the category can have any name that distinguishes it correctly from other categories that behave differently with respect to substitution in grammatical sentences. In this text, we will usually use the traditional grammatical terms to refer to categories.

It must be stressed, now, that categories are more than convenient groupings of words. There is no particular virtue in merely collecting all of the words of a language into groups. The real linguistic significance of categories lies in the fact that by defining certain categories we can begin to construct an elegant and revealing description of a natural language.

Let us abbreviate the categories noun, article, and verb by N, ART, and V, respectively. Observe that it is now possible to talk about categories rather than about individual words. The fact that *The boy destroyed a toy* is a grammatical sentence of English could be stated in our grammatical description of English; but this would be an extremely cumbersome and unrevealing approach to take in general, owing to the fact that we would have to list all of the other grammatical sentences of English in precisely the same way. This list would have to include sentences like *The girl destroyed the toy, A girl destroyed a toy, The man met the the woman, A horse ate the hay,* etc., all of which display the identical pattern ART, N, V, ART, N. Without having access to these categories, however, it would be impossible for us to explicitly represent the fact that sentences that display this pattern are grammatical sentences of English.

The problem is further compounded by the fact that the number of grammatical sentences of any language is infinite. This can be shown by demonstrating that there is no longest sentence. Consider, for example, *John believes that the world is flat*. A grammatical English sentence can be constructed from this sentence by adding it after *Mary believes that: Mary believes that John believes that the world is flat*. This sentence may, in turn, be added after *Sam believes that,* yielding another grammatical sentence: *Sam believes that Mary believes that John believes that the world is flat*. This process may be repeated as often as we wish, so that it will always be possible to construct a sentence that is longer than the one we are considering. Hence, the number of sentences in English is infinite. An analogous demonstration can be given for any other natural language.

It is clearly impossible to construct an exhaustive list of the grammatical sentences of a language when there are an infinite number of them. The only hope of even beginning to deal with the question of what constitutes a grammatical sentence of the language is to state the conditions under which strings of words are grammatical in terms of the categories of the words in the string. In this particular case, for example, we can state our observation about the grammaticality of the sentences under consideration in the form of such a **condition** or **rule.** For convenience, let us say that a sequence of words W_1, $W_2, \ldots$ **represents** a sequence of categories $C_1, C_2, \ldots$ if the first word W_1 is a member of the category C_1, the second word is a member of the category C_2, and so on.

CONDITION (RULE):   Any sequence of English words that represents the sequence of categories ART, N, V, ART, N is a grammatical sentence of English.

This rule has exceptions, and must therefore be qualified to a certain extent. Rather than dealing with these exceptions right away, we will introduce a notation in which such a rule can be expressed in a precise way. The symbol S represents the notion "sentence of a language." The symbol → means "may be of the form." In the grammar of English, then, the fact that a grammatical sentence may be of the form ART N V ART N is expressed as the following formula:

(2.6)   S → ART N V ART N

Such a formula is called a **phrase structure rule.** It is not a rule in the sense that it says what a grammatical sentence *must* look like, but in the sense that it says what a grammatical sentence *can* look like. There will be other rules specifying what other sentences can look like. All of these rules together specify what sentences must look like.

But what does the word *phrase* mean? Just as individual words of the language are members of categories, so are certain sequences of words. In fact, there is at least one category that may be understood as containing sequences of words, namely, the category S. A **phrase** is any sequence of words in the language that itself is a member of some category. Thus, a sentence, beside being a sentence, may also be thought of as being a phrase of the category S. The linguist's goal of distinguishing between grammatical and ungrammatical sentences of the language now becomes that of specifying which sequences of English words are members of the category S.

It is not yet clear, however, that there are any sequences of words shorter than a sentence and longer than a single word that are members of categories, that is, that are phrases. Let us pursue this question briefly.

If (2.6) were the only rule specifying the form of a grammatical sentence of English, it would follow that wherever a noun appears it is preceded by an article, and wherever an article appears it is followed by a noun. But this is false, for it is possible to have a grammatical sentence in which there is no article at all:

(2.7)   *John saw Mary.*

It is also possible to have a grammatical sentence in which the article is not followed immediately by a noun:

(2.8)   ***The** disgusting **boy** destroyed **a** fragile **toy.***

The words *John* and *Mary* are called **proper nouns** (PN). This is the name of their category. We can see that *John* and *Mary* are not nouns, since *the John saw a Mary* is not a grammatical sentence of English. That is, they are not nouns in the technical sense employed earlier in which *toy* and *boy* are nouns. An alternative terminology, which will not be used here, categorizes *toy* and *boy* as **common nouns** as opposed to the proper nouns *John, Mary,* etc.

The words *disgusting* and *fragile* are members of a category different from ART, N, and V, since it is impossible to substitute either *disgusting* or *fragile* for any words of these other categories in a grammatical sentence while preserving the grammaticality of the string. This is shown by example (2.9). The symbol * indicates that a string of words is not a grammatical sentence of the language:

(2.9)   *The disgusting boy destroyed a toy.*
              * *The disgusting boy destroyed a fragile.*
              * *The disgusting boy fragile a toy.*
              * *Fragile disgusting boy destroyed a toy.*

The category of which *fragile* and *disgusting* are members is called adjective or ADJ.

In order to accommodate sentences (2.7) and (2.8), we must now admit two new rules for expressing what sequences of categories may constitute a grammatical sentence of English. In addition to (2.6), repeated here as (2.10a), we have rules (2.10b) and (2.10c):

(2.10)   a. S → ART N V ART N
                          b. S → PN V PN
                          c. S → ART ADJ N V ART ADJ N

But it turns out that these are not the only possible sequences. In (2.11) are listed other grammatical sentences that also involve the categories ART, ADJ, N, V, and PN:

(2.11)   a. *John saw   the   disgusting boy.*
                       PN   V   ART   ADJ   N
                    b. *The disgusting boy saw John.*
                       ART   ADJ   N   V   PN
                    c. *The boy destroyed   a   fragile toy.*
                       ART   N   V   ART ADJ   N
                    d. *The disgusting boy destroyed   a   toy.*
                       ART   ADJ   N   V   ART N
                    e. *John destroyed   a   toy.*
                       PN   V   ART N
                    f. *The boy saw John.*
                       ART N   V   PN

The statement of a separate rule for each possible sequence would fail to express a rather striking fact about all of them taken together, which is that in every case PN may substitute for an entire sequence of the form ART N or ART ADJ N and vice versa, and that ART N and ART ADJ N may be substituted for one another wherever they occur without affecting grammaticality. This is true not only for the position before the verb but also for the position after the verb. In fact, replacing PN by ART N or ART ADJ N does not in general affect grammaticality, nor does replacing ART N or ART ADJ N by the other or by PN. A few examples should show that this is a reasonable assertion. In (2.12), replacement of the blank spaces bracketed by [   ] by either *John, the boy,* or *the disgusting boy* consistently yields grammatical sentences:

(2.12)   a. [   ]'s *mother's house is on fire.*
              b. *This chicken belongs to* [   ].
              c. *Next to* [   ], *I like myself best.*
              d. *I believe* [   ] *to be a discredit to his fraternity.*

The fact that PN, ART N, and ART ADJ N perform the same function in grammatical sentences indicates that they are members of the same category. Thus, the behavior of each is accounted for by more general statements about the behavior of *any* member of the category of which they are all members. This suggests that we should revise our definition of what a syntactic category is.

DEFINITION: A **syntactic category** is a group of words or sequences of words in a given language that can replace one another in any sentence of the language whatsoever without affecting grammaticality.

If a syntactic category contains single words only, it is a **lexical category.** When a syntactic category contains sequences of words, it is a **nonlexical category,** or a **phrase category.** The category containing PN, ART N, and ART ADJ N is called **noun phrase,** or simply NP. The three rules in (2.10) and the six rules suggested by the examples in (2.11) can now be replaced with the following set of rules:[1]

(2.13)	S → NP V NP
(2.14)	NP → ART ADJ N
(2.15)	NP → ART N
(2.16)	NP → PN

Let us introduce here a notational convention: When there is more than one rule that has the same symbol on the left of the arrow, all those rules will be stated as a single rule that has (i) a single instance of the symbol to the left of the arrow, (ii) a single arrow, and (iii) braces around the various sequences that appear to the right of the arrows. Thus, rules (2.14–2.16) will be expressed as (2.17):

$$(2.17) \qquad NP \rightarrow \begin{Bmatrix} ART\ ADJ\ N \\ ART\ N \\ PN \end{Bmatrix}$$

What (2.17) says is that the category NP may be formed by any one of the three sequences within the braces.

Another important notation is the **parentheses notation.** Both (2.14) and (2.15) expand the category NP. Both specify that a possible NP is one that begins with an ART and ends with an N. The only difference between the two rules, in fact, is that (2.14) states that there may be an intervening ADJ between ART and N. In other words, ADJ may appear in this position, but need not, in order for the sequence to be a possible NP. This optionality is expressed by collapsing the two rules into a single **rule schema** by the parentheses notation, as shown in (2.18):

$$(2.18) \qquad NP \rightarrow ART\ (ADJ)\ N$$

It should be emphasized that the parentheses notation is more than a convenient shorthand for stating rules. Not only does it save ink, but it expresses an important generalization: Regardless of whether a modifying adjective appears in the noun phrase or not, the first constituent of the NP is ART and the last is N. Only if such a generalization is present in the data can the

---

[1] Strictly speaking, it is possible for a single word to be a member of a phrase category; e.g., *John* is a PN, and a PN is an NP.

parentheses notation be applied. Compare rules (2.14) and (2.15) with the formally indistinguishable (2.19) and (2.20):

(2.19)   NP → N ART
(2.20)   NP → ART N ADJ

(2.14)   NP → ART ADJ N
(2.15)   NP → ART N

Each pair of rules expands NP. Each pair contains a rule that mentions N and ART, and each pair contains a rule that mentions ART, N, and ADJ. The total number of symbols in each pair is the same. Yet the pair (2.14–2.15) expresses a very general fact about the English noun phrase, while the pair (2.19–2.20) is on the whole far less general. The importance of the parentheses notation is that it will apply only when there is a general property of the language that is implicit in more than one rule.

The parentheses and braces notations may apply to a single set of rules. For example, rules (2.14–2.16) are collapsed by the braces notation, and rules (2.14) and (2.15) are at the same time collapsed by the parentheses notation. The rule schema that results is (2.21):

$$(2.21) \qquad\qquad NP \rightarrow \begin{Bmatrix} ART\ (ADJ)\ N \\ PN \end{Bmatrix}$$

This brings us back to the question of whether there are any phrases other than S. Rule (2.13) expresses a hypothesis about what a possible sentence looks like in terms of the categories NP and V; (2.21) expresses a hypothesis about what a possible NP looks like in terms of the lexical categories ART, ADJ, N, and PN. Here, then, is evidence that phrases exist that are longer than a single word but shorter than a sentence. Sequences of words of varying lengths, such as NPs, function as members of a single nonlexical category *within* the sentence. Our description of what constitutes an English sentence need only specify (i) where in the English sentence an NP may (or must) appear and (ii) what sequences are members of the category NP. In general, the problem of describing what constitutes a grammatical sentence of English can be systematically broken down into the problem of describing the various nonlexical categories that can make up a sentence.

Up to this point, what has been established is that the phrase structure of a sentence (that is, a phrase of category S) involves an NP followed by a V followed by another NP. This observation is represented in the form of rule (2.13).

Rule (2.13) is, however, inadequate, since there are grammatical sentences of English that it fails to account for. (In fact, since we are merely initiating the construction of a grammar of English at this stage, very few of our rules will be completely adequate. As we encounter sentences that cannot be accommodated, we change or add to our set of rules accordingly.)

For example, consider sentences like:

(2.22)

$$\text{The boy} \left\{ \begin{array}{l} \textit{stumbled} \\ \textit{laughed} \\ \textit{slept} \\ \textit{yawned} \end{array} \right\}.$$

Here a single verb may replace the sequence V NP. Notice that such a verb may not simply replace the verb in *The boy destroyed a toy:*

(2.23)

$$*\text{The boy} \left\{ \begin{array}{l} \textit{stumbled} \\ \textit{laughed} \\ \textit{slept} \\ \textit{yawned} \end{array} \right\} \textit{a toy.}$$

The definition of syntactic category given earlier indicates that certain verbs and sequences of the form V NP share the same category. We will call this category **verb phrase,** or VP. Some verbs may in themselves be VPs, while other verbs may appear in VPs only with NPs after them. We will call the group of verbs that appear alone V_I (for **intransitive verb**) and the others V_T (for **transitive verb**). One way of expressing these facts is as follows:

(2.24)   a. $VP \rightarrow V_I$
           b. $VP \rightarrow V_T NP$

Rule (2.13) can be revised to reflect the greater refinement of the present description: A sentence consists of an NP followed by a VP, where the structure of NP and VP must be independently specified. The rule for the category S is now (2.25):

(2.25) $S \rightarrow NP\ VP$

In summary, we have (i) established that there is evidence for lexical categories, (ii) established that there is evidence for nonlexical categories (whose members are phrases), and (iii) developed a notation for expressing what phrases look like in terms of the categories that appear in the phrases; the rules statable with this notation are called **phrase structure rules (PSR).**

We have also discussed why the words *phrase* and *rule* are used in the term *phrase structure rule,* but we have not considered why the word *structure* is used. In general, anything that is not an undifferentiated lump but has distinct elements can be said to have **structure.** A skeleton has structure in the sense that it is *made up of* individual bones. Similarly, once we recognize that a sentence contains individual words we recognize that the sentence has structure. What we have been engaged in showing thus far is that not only does the sentence have structure, but its structure can be represented in terms of phrases. Hence, "phrase structure."

It is also important to stress that not only does a phrase like S have a structure that is specified in terms of nonlexical categories; other nonlexical categories may, too. So, for example, the category VP contains any sequence of words such that the first word is a verb (e.g., *destroyed*) and the remainder of the sequence is either a single word (e.g., *John*) or a sequence of words that is a member of the category NP (e.g., *a toy*). This observation leads to a discussion of *phrase structure trees*.

PHRASE STRUCTURE TREES

The function of a grammar is to assign the category S to a sequence of words that is a grammatical sentence of the language. In particular, a grammar of English, functioning as required, should assign the category S to the sentence *The boy destroyed a toy*, just as it assigns the category NP to the sequence *a toy*.

An automatic procedure for doing this can be devised, given phrase structure rules and lexical categories of which the various words in the sequence are members. Let us take a sequence of words that constitutes a grammatical sentence of English. Above each of the words, we write the lexical category of which it is a member. The result will be a sequence of categories and the sequence of words below it, as shown in Figure 2.1a.

Next, we find a subsequence in the sequence of categories such that the subsequence appears to the right of some phrase structure rule. For example, the sequence ART N above *a toy* in Figure 2.1a appears to the right of rule (2.15). Let us say that this particular subsequence *satisfies* rule (2.15). (There is another ART N sequence that satisfies rule (2.15); we will deal with it shortly.)

For a subsequence that satisfies a rule, we write the category to the left of the arrow in the rule above the subsequence that satisfies the rule. Then we draw a line from this category to each of the categories in the subsequence below it. This is illustrated in Figure 2.1b for the rightmost sequence ART N.

Since there may be more than one subsequence in a sequence that satisfies a particular rule, we must be able to repeat this procedure as many times as necessary. However, there is no particular part of the sequence where we must begin, and there is no particular order in which subsequences must be considered. Thus, we could have begun with the subsequent ART N which begins the sequence, rather than with the subsequence ART N which ends the sequence in this example.

Observe, now, that by applying this procedure we may create sequences that satisfy rules that the original sequence did not satisfy. After introducing NP above the subsequence that represents *a toy,* we have the subsequence V_T NP, as shown in Figure 2.1b. This subsequence satisfies rule (2.24b), and application of the procedure gives the sequence ART N VP, as Figure 2.1c shows. ART N satisfies rule (2.15), as noted previously, so writing NP above ART N yields the sequence NP VP of Figure 2.1d. Finally, this sequence satisfies rule (2.25), so we write S above the entire edifice and draw lines where appropriate, as shown in Figure 2.1e. The procedure just outlined is called **bottom-up.**

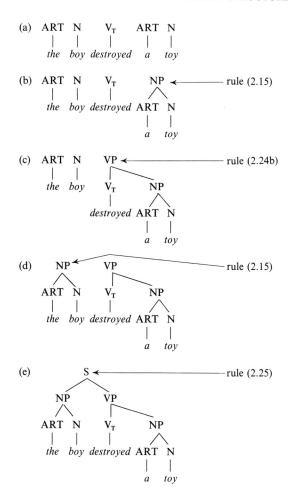

Figure 2.1. Bottom-up procedure.

Notice that at the end of the procedure the symbol S is reached. This means that the grammar has recognized that the sequence of words is a grammatical sentence.

Let us now take a closer look at Figure 2.1e. The diagram can be viewed as a tree (upside down). This tree in fact reveals in a visual way the phrase structure of the sentence: There is an NP followed by a VP; the NP contains an ART and an N; the VP contains a V and an NP; and so on. Such trees are called **phrase structure trees, phrase markers,** or **P markers**. Thus, given a sentence and a set of phrase structure rules, a phrase structure tree can be assigned to the sentence.

The problem of assigning a structure to a sentence can be viewed from an alternative point of view, however. Let us assume that the initial symbol S is given. Below each nonlexical category we write a sequence of categories that is a member of this category. To illustrate, we begin with (2.26):

(2.26)   S

Recall rule (2.25), S → NP VP, which says "S may be of the form NP VP." This can read as "write NP VP beneath an S and draw a line from S to NP and from S to VP." Doing this yields (2.27):

(2.27)

Interpreting a phrase structure rule in this way means **rewriting** the symbol to the left of the arrow as the string of symbols to the right of the arrow beneath the symbol to the left, and drawing the lines appropriately. The same may be done for the symbol VP by applying rule (2.24b) in this way:

(2.28)

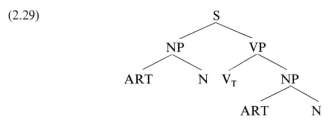

Observe that there are two NPs in (2.28) and three rules for rewriting NP. Either NP may be rewritten by any one of the three rules, yielding a total of six distinct trees. One such tree is shown in (2.29):

(2.29)

Under each instance of a lexical category, we may now insert any lexical item that is a member of that category. For example, we may insert *the* under the first ART and *a* under the second, *boy* under the first N and *toy* under the second, and *destroyed* under V_T. The resulting tree is precisely the same as that assigned to the sentence *The boy destroyed a toy* by the procedure illustrated in Figure 2.1.

This procedure, which is called **top-down,** and the *bottom-up* procedure are equivalent in that they both have the function of assigning a phrase marker to any sequence of words that is a grammatical sentence based on the rules specified in the description of the native speaker's grammatical knowledge.

Whenever a grammar assigns the symbol S to a sentence of the language, the grammar is said to **generate** the sentence. The goal of expressing what it is that a native speaker knows about his language can therefore be rephrased as follows: Construct a grammar of the language that generates *all* the grammatical sentences of the language and *only* the grammatical sentences of the language. "All" because the native speaker's ability to speak and understand is creative and unlimited; "only" because the native speaker has the ability to determine whether sequences of words are grammatical sentences of the language or not. Thus, a failure to generate all sentences would be a claim that the native speaker has a limitation that he does not in fact have, and generating nonsentences would be claiming that the native speaker lacks knowledge that he in fact possesses.

A grammar that satisfies these requirements is called a **generative grammar.** Note that a generative grammar is a **formal description** of the knowledge of an idealized native speaker of a language. As such, it is not intended to describe how we talk, how we think, how we understand, when we say what or why, and so on. It is simply a finite account of the infinite number of sentences that are in a language, the native speaker's knowledge about these sentences, and the relationships between them.

A grammar that generates all and only the grammatical sentences, and correctly accounts for the native speaker's knowledge, is said to be **descriptively adequate.**

TREE TERMS

There are a number of terms having to do with trees that should now be defined. First of all, every point in a tree where there is a branch is called a **node.**

(2.30)

$$\mid \quad \leftarrow \text{nodes} \rightarrow \quad \mid$$
$$\mid \qquad\qquad\qquad \bigwedge$$

A category name at a node is called a **node label;** the node is a **labeled node.** Example (2.31) shows a **branching** NP node with two branches, while (2.32) shows a **nonbranching** NP node:

(2.31)

$$\overset{\mid}{\underset{\bigwedge}{\text{NP}}}$$

(2.32)

$$\overset{\mid}{\underset{\mid}{\text{NP}}}$$

For a phrase structure rule of the form X → YZ, there is a corresponding tree in which there is a branching node X and the nodes Y and Z directly beneath X along the two respective branches:

(2.33)

In such a case, X **immediately** or **directly dominates** Y and also immediately or directly dominates Z. A **path** is defined as an unbroken series of branches and nodes that does not change direction with respect to the top of the tree. Thus, there is always a path from a node to any node that it immediately dominates.

Consider now the tree shown in (2.34):

(2.34)

By the preceding definition, we find that A immediately dominates B and C, B immediately dominates D and E, and C immediately dominates F. It is possible to draw an unbroken line down from A to each node in the tree; e.g., we can get to E by proceeding down from A by way of B. In general, if it is possible to find a path from one node to another, then the higher node *dominates* the lower one. Note that a node dominates all of the nodes that it immediately dominates, but it need not immediately dominate all of the nodes that it dominates. [In (2.34), A dominates D, E, and F but does not immediately dominate them.]

If A dominates B, then B is a **constituent** of A. If A immediately dominates B, then B is an **immediate constituent** of A. If B and C are immediate constituents of the same node, then B and C are **sisters.**

A node that dominates a phrase is called a **nonterminal node.** So is a node that dominates another nonterminal node. A node that has nothing beneath it but a lexical item is called a **terminal node.** The sequence of lexical items in a sentence beneath a phrase structure tree is often called a **terminal string.** Occasionally, this term may be used to refer to the sequence of terminal nodes when we are not particularly interested in the actual words of a given sentence, but in the set of all sentences that have this particular sequence of terminal nodes.

If there is a sequence A B . . . X, and if Y dominates every member of this sequence, then Y **exhaustively dominates** A B . . . X just in case Y dominates nothing else but nodes which either dominate or are dominated by members of the sequence. If there is a rule of the form A → B C, then the rule is said to **expand** A *as* B C.

Finally, there is a useful notation called the **labeled bracket** notation. It is used to represent constituent structure in a linear rather than a phrase marker format. The labeled bracketing of a phrase marker such as that in (2.35) is shown in (2.36):

(2.35)

A

B   C

(2.36) $_A$[B   C]$_A$

The general rule for going from a phrase marker to a labeled bracketing is to place a bracket on both sides of a sequence that is exhaustively dominated by a node, and to label the bracket with the label of the node. To go from a labeled bracketing to a phrase marker, simply construct a phrase marker in which every sequence that has labeled brackets around it is exhaustively dominated by a node with the label on the brackets.

By applying these rules over and over again, it is possible to reduce trees of any size to sequences that are labeled bracketings:

(2.37)

To assign a labeled bracketing to the sequence D E F G, we observe first that D E is exhaustively dominated by B and F G is exhaustively dominated by C. This gives us $_B$[D E]$_B$ $_C$[F G]$_C$. Since the entire sequence is exhaustively dominated by A, we now assign brackets labeled with A to the sequence to get $_A$[$_B$[D E]$_B$ $_C$[F G]$_C$]$_A$.

The usual convention in the use of these labeled brackets is to put the label on a left bracket only. Thus, the sequence corresponding to (2.37) would have the form $_A$[$_B$[D E] $_C$[F G]]. A particularly convenient use for labeled brackets is to represent certain aspects of a tree while other aspects are ignored. For example, if we did not wish to take note of the fact that in (2.37) B dominates D E and C dominates F G, we could write simply $_A$[D E F G]. This is permissable, since A does in fact exhaustively dominate the entire sequence.

WHAT A GRAMMAR CAN DO

Until now, the only kinds of rules that we have considered have been phrase structure rules. It is worth considering the range of linguistic phenomena that such rules can be used to account for, and the range of phenomena for which they are inadequate.

A grammar that contains only phrase structure rules is called a **phrase structure grammar.** For the sentences that we have examined so far, phrase structure rules appear to be adequate, and we set up an initial hypothesis that phrase structure grammars will be adequate to account for all sentences of all natural languages. Whether they are in fact is a question that the linguist must answer: It is an **empirical question** (that is, a question subject to verification or falsification with the use of evidence from the real world).

Thus far, we do not have much of a grammar; in fact, it has only five rules, and there are numerous facts about English that these rules are unable to describe. That is, there are numerous grammatical English sentences that will not be assigned a correct structure by our rules. One example is the sentence *The boy destroyed a toy, didn't he?*. As an exercise, you should apply the bottom-up procedure to this string to satisfy yourself that the grammar as it stands will not generate this sentence.

An important methodological question to consider, in fact the most important methodological question of this entire book, is the following: What do you do when your grammar fails to generate grammatical sentences? The obvious solution, but not necessarily the right one in every case, is to make up another phrase structure rule. A consideration that must always be kept in mind in proposing new rules, however, is whether the new rules **correctly account** for the native speaker's linguistic knowledge. Such knowledge includes not only whether a particular string of words is grammatical or not but also what the relationships are between different kinds of sentences. If it turns out that proposing a phrase structure rule satisfies this condition, well and good. If, however, we encounter a situation in which a phrase structure rule does not express a particular aspect of the native speaker's knowledge, then we have to seek further for a solution.

As a concrete problem, observe that in English the verb may often be preceded by a *modal verb*, such as *will, can, may, must, shall, should, would, could.* Observe also that in standard dialects of English at most one such verb may precede the verb:

(2.38)   a. *John owns a truck.*

               b. *John   will   own a truck*
                  John   can   own a truck.
                  John   may   own a truck.

(2.39)   **John   will can   own a truck.*
              *John   can will   own a truck.
              *John   may can   own a truck.
              *John   will may   own a truck.

The phrase structure rules already established will generate (2.38a), assigning to it the structure in (2.40):

(2.40)

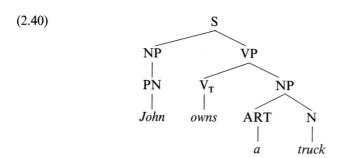

Is it possible, now, to make up a new rule that will generate (2.38) but not (2.39)? Indeed it is, and for the sake of this illustration this new rule will be formulated as (2.41) (the symbol M refers to the category of modal verbs, of which *will, can, may,* etc. are members):

(2.41)   S → NP M VP

The structure assigned by this rule is given as (2.42), assuming expansion of NP and VP and insertion of lexical items.

(2.42)

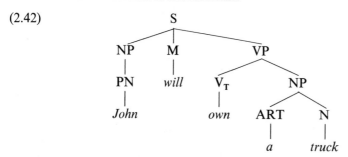

This formulation is not quite correct and will be discussed in more detail in Chapter 3. Notice, however, that it at least permits us to say correctly that in (2.38b) as well as in (2.38a) *John* is an NP and *own(s) a truck* is a VP.

The analysis that makes use of rule (2.41) is not the only one possible, however. It is worth considering in some detail an alternative to this analysis that proves to be significantly inferior. As we will show, the choice between competing descriptions is governed by the extent to which each captures the native speaker's knowledge of the language.

Consider a phrase structure grammar that treats *will own a* as a phrase.[2] Such an analysis would require the phrase structure rules in (2.43), where MX would be the name of the (pseudo-)category of which *will own a* is hypothesized

---

[2] There are other alternatives that are far more plausible than this particular one. For instance, a grammar that treated *will own* as a phrase has a certain initial plausibility. The discussion in Chapter 3 presents a number of strong arguments in favor of treating the modal as part of a constituent that is outside of the verb phrase, as in (2.41–2.42).

to be a member. Example (2.44) shows the tree assigned to *John will own a truck* by these rules:

(2.43) a. S → NP MX N
        b. MX → M V ART

(2.44)

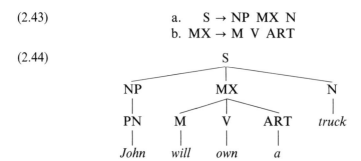

Choosing rule (2.41) instead of an analysis like (2.43) makes the claim that the introduction of a modal verb does not change the relative functions of other sequences of words in the sentence. Example (2.43), on the other hand, expresses a very counterintuitive claim to the effect that *will own a* is a constituent of the sentence *John will own a truck,* and that *a truck* does not perform the same role in this sentence as it does in *John owns a truck,* for example. Thus, (2.41) is preferable as part of a grammatical description of what constitutes the native speaker's knowledge of English.

What this shows is that a given grammatical description may be able to perform part of the task that has been set for it, but not all of it. A grammar containing (2.43) will generate the sentence *John will own a truck,* but it will not capture the structural similarities between it and *John owns a truck.* A grammar is *descriptively adequate* only when it generates all of the sentences of a language and nothing else, and also correctly describes the native speaker's implicit knowledge of the structures of these sentences and the relationships between them.

THE PROPER USE OF POWER

A theory of grammar that says that something is possible that in fact does not occur in human language is **too powerful,** in that it permits the notion of what a human language is to be wider than it has to be. If something occurs in natural language for which a theory of grammar does not permit an adequate description, then, correspondingly, that theory is **not powerful enough** to capture all there is to say about language; the theory must be revised accordingly. Naturally, our notions about whether a given theory is too powerful or not powerful enough are in constant flux as we learn more and more about what sorts of things go on in human languages.

An extremely uninformative theory of grammar would be one that said "anything is possible in human language." This would not be a particularly interesting theory, since it says nothing about what language or a language is. Furthermore, in the context of such a theory of language the absence of a particular phenomenon in every language would have to be treated as an accident and not as a potentially more interesting consequence of some property of the human mind as it is revealed through human language.

There is always the chance, of course, that the universal presence or absence of some property of human language is accidental. In principle, however, we should treat everything that looks systematic as in fact systematic, unless there is strong evidence to the contrary. For it is only by setting up the strongest and most explicit plausible hypotheses that we can eventually discover what is true.

A theory of grammar must include all of the tools necessary for adequately describing all natural languages. One such tool is phrase structure, and there are many things that can be correctly and naturally expressed in terms of phrase structure rules. We have not determined here whether the phrase structure theory of grammar is powerful enough to permit descriptions of everything about language that has to be described, however. With this in mind, let us consider the grammar that has been established thus far:

(2.21)	$S \rightarrow NP\ VP$
(2.41)	$S \rightarrow NP\ M\ VP$
(2.14)	$NP \rightarrow ART\ ADJ\ N$
(2.15)	$NP \rightarrow ART\ N$
(2.16)	$NP \rightarrow PN$
(2.24a)	$VP \rightarrow V_I$
(2.24b)	$VP \rightarrow V_T\ NP$

These rules describe, more or less correctly, the native speaker's knowledge about a large number of sentences. The number is limited, in fact, only by the number of lexical items of the categories N, ART, ADJ, M, V_I, and V_T in English.

It is possible, nevertheless, to find phenomena that cannot be accounted for by phrase structure rules alone. It was noted previously that there are certain verbs in English that take objects and that there are others that do not take objects. Thus, *John bought a truck* is a grammatical sentence while **John bought* is not, and *John was sleeping* is a grammatical sentence, while **John was sleeping a truck* is not. Many similar examples can be constructed. In the following pairs of examples, an asterisk before a sentence indicates that it is ungrammatical:

(2.45)   *John bought a truck.*
              *John bought.

> Arnold considered the problem.
> *Arnold considered.
>
> The carpenter will construct a tree house.
> *The carpenter will construct.
>
> The ocean damaged the beach.
> *The ocean damaged.

(2.46)   John was sleeping.
> *John was sleeping a truck.
>
> Mary laughs constantly.
> *Mary laughs the carpenter constantly.
>
> Several days elapsed.
> *Several days elapsed the week.
>
> The volcano erupted.
> *The volcano erupted the mountain.

The formal difference between verbs like *bought, considered,* etc. on the one hand and *sleeping, elapsed,* etc. on the other is that the former are members of the category V_T, while the latter are members of the category V_I. Phrase structure rules (2.24a) and (2.24b) specify that a V_T must be followed by a noun phrase, while a V_I must not be.

Consider now the following interrogative sentences:

(2.47)   *What kind of truck did John buy?*
> *What did Arnold consider?*
> *Which beach did the ocean damage?*

These sentences display a striking characteristic. Each of them contains a verb of the category V_T that **lacks** a following NP. As the ungrammatical examples in (2.45) show, however, verbs of this category **must** be followed by an NP.

Moreover, it is impossible to construct grammatical questions of the sort given in (2.47) in which the verb is followed by an NP. E.g.:

(2.48)   *What did John buy a truck?
> *What did Arnold consider the problem?
> *What will the carpenter construct a tree house?
> *Which beach did the ocean damage Hermosa Beach?

Let us call *what, which beach, what kind of a truck,* and so on **interrogative** NPs. Given the sentences in (2.45), (2.47), and (2.48), it appears that the only time that a V_T cannot and must not be followed by an NP is when the sentence has an interrogative NP in initial position. If this were the only fact to be accounted for, it would be sufficient to show that a phrase structure grammar could not adequately describe the full range of grammatical English questions of the sort shown in (2.47), as will be shown later.

There is a further complication, however, that makes the case against a phrase structure grammar even stronger. Observe that verbs of the category V_I, which normally do not permit an NP to follow, simply cannot appear in questions of the form illustrated in (2.48). E.g.:

(2.49)   *What was John sleeping?
                *Which carpenter does Mary laugh constantly?
                *How many weeks did several days elapse?
                *What did the mountain erupt?

In (2.47), the verbs that appear are V_T's and, as such, should be followed by NPs. The presence of the interrogative NP at the beginning of the sentence in same way satisfies the condition for the presence of a V_T. On the other hand, even though the V_I's in (2.49) are not followed by NPs, the ungrammaticality of the sentences there suggests that the sentence-initial interrogative NP acts *as though* it were after the verb.

At this stage, it might appear that a phrase structure account would be adequate. Assuming that *did*, *does*, and *will* are members of the category M, we can write the following rule for the sentences that we have been considering here:

(2.50) $S \rightarrow NP \; M \; NP \; V_T$

(This ignores the problem of guaranteeing that the first NP is interrogative.)

But there is still a further complication. It was noted earlier that an infinite number of English sentences can be produced by adding grammatical sentences to sequences of the form NP *believes that,* etc. This capacity for building members of a category from members of the same category is called **recursion,** and is an extremely important characteristic of natural language. We will discuss recursion at somewhat greater length in Chapter 8.

Recursion presents a problem for the phrase structure account of questions. Consider the grammatical (2.51):

(2.51)   *Which beach did Mary believe that the ocean damaged?*

Notice that the verb *damaged* is a member of the category V_T. In addition, rule (2.50) will not be sufficient for generating (2.51), since (2.51) has the sequence NP M NP V_T *that* NP V_T and not simply NP M NP V_T. This inadequacy suggests that we add rule (2.52) to the grammar:

(2.52) $S \rightarrow NP \; M \; NP \; V_T$ *that* NP V_T

Such a rule will represent the fact that, just as in the case of the simpler examples given earlier, the interrogative NP acts as though it were the NP following the verb.

But this is also inadequate; note the grammaticality of (2.53):

(2.53)   *Which beach did Mary believe that Sam believed that*
            the ocean damaged?

On the basis of this, we might add still another rule, e.g.:

(2.54) $S \rightarrow NP \; M \; NP \; V_T$ *that* $NP \; V_T$ *that* $NP \; V_T$

But this rule will be inadequate for sentences like (2.55):

(2.55)   *Which beach did Mary believe that Sam believed that*
                   Harold believed that the ocean damaged?

In general, for any phrase structure grammar containing a finite number of rules like (2.50), (2.52), and (2.54) it will always be possible to construct a sentence that the grammar will not generate. In fact, because of recursion there will always be an infinite number of such sentences. Hence, the phrase structure analysis will not be sufficient to generate English.

Recall, now, an observation made earlier concerning the function of the sentence-initial interrogative NP: The interrogative NP acts *as though* it immediately followed the verb. This observation would be explained if the interrogative NP were to first appear in the phrase marker in the position immediately after the verb, and then move into sentence-initial position. The distribution of grammaticality that we have noted would follow automatically from the phrase structure rules for expansion of VPs that we have already established, since rule (2.24b) states that a V_T must be followed by an NP, and rule (2.24a) states that a V_I must appear alone. Subsequent movement of the interrogative NPs to sentence-initial position would account for the state of affairs that we have observed here.

The phrase marker representing sentences such as *What did John buy?* and the other questions cited earlier cannot be assigned by phrase structure rules alone. This is very significant. Rather, the phrase marker is gotten from another phrase marker as a result of moving a constituent from one place to another in the tree. A rule that states what type of constituent is moved, where it is moved from, and where it is moved to is called a **transformation.** It is possible to imagine transformations that perform other types of operations as well, such as insertion or deletion of constituents, but the movement transformation that we have shown to be necessary here is sufficient to illustrate the most significant difference between phrase structure rules and transformations: Phrase structure rules produce trees by expanding nonterminal nodes; transformations produce trees by changing other trees.

The **derivation** of a phrase structure tree is the sequence of steps required to get the tree. If a tree can be gotten from phrase structure rules alone, then the derivation of the tree consists of the sequence of phrase structure rules that are applied in constructing the tree. If it is necessary to apply transformations to a tree in order to produce another tree, then the derivation of the latter also involves these transformations. The derivation of a particular tree depends on the form of the grammar, since in one grammar it might be possible to derive the tree by applying only phrase structure rules while in an alternative grammar the same tree might be derivable only by applying transformational rules as well.

In the theory of grammar that is developed in this book, the syntactic component has the following features: It has a set of phrase structure rules (called the **base component**), a set of transformations, and a procedure for inserting lexical items beneath terminal nodes in phrase markers. The grammar generates all and only the grammatical sentences of the language by **deriving** the phrase markers corresponding to these sentences. This is done by first constructing a phrase marker with the phrase structure rules only, then inserting the lexical items into the tree, and then applying the transformations to this tree in a precise way defined by the theory. The result of applying the transformations must be the phrase marker for some sentence of the language, and all sentences must have such a derivation.

The structure that is gotten by constructing a phrase marker with the phrase structure rules and inserting lexical items into it is called the **deep structure.** The structure that corresponds to the actual sentence, i.e., represents the actual order of constituents of the sentence, is called the **surface structure.** It is conceivable that for some sentences the derivation would involve no transformations at all. In such cases, the deep structure and the surface structure would be the same.

Let us consider an illustrative derivation. We take the sentence *What will the carpenter construct?* As has already been established, it will be possible to explain why *construct*, a V_T, appears in a grammatical sentence with no following NP if it is assumed that the surface structure of this sentence is derived from another phrase marker (i.e., the deep structure of the sentence). In the latter phrase marker, the interrogative NP *what* is a constituent of the same VP as the verb. The first part of the derivation is to construct the phrase marker according to the phrase structure rules:

(2.56)

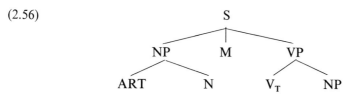

Next, we insert the appropriate lexical items in the appropriate places to get the deep structure:

(2.57)

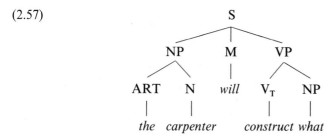

The derivation of the surface structure involves two movements: movement of *what* into initial position and movement of *will* to a position following *what*. Applying these operations to (2.57) yields the structure in (2.58), which we will assume is the surface structure for the sake of illustration:

(2.58)

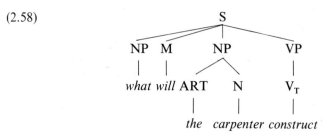

Hence, a grammar that contains the two movement operations just referred to and the phrase structure rules for deriving (2.57) will generate the sentence *What will the carpenter construct?* by providing a derivation for it.

THE POWER OF TRANSFORMATIONS

As suggested in the preceding section, there are certain facts about language (as exemplified by English) that a phrase structure grammar is insufficiently powerful to describe adequately. One solution to this problem is to hypothesize that grammatical descriptions may also include certain transformations, which relate surface structures and deep structures. Each structure captures certain facts about the language that the other does not, and the transformations capture generalizations that cannot be captured by either one of the two structures independently.

Of course, it is not immediately obvious that even transformational rules will be sufficiently powerful to describe all the facts of natural language. On the other hand, having introduced transformations into the theory of grammar, we must investigate whether these rules permit the description of phenomena that do not in fact occur in natural language. In other words, are transformations powerful enough, and are they too powerful?

It could be that the theory of grammar with transformational rules is no more powerful than the theory of grammar without them. However, it is not difficult to define a phenomenon that cannot be described by a phrase structure rule but can be described by a transformational rule. The case of questions in the preceding section is one such phenomenon. The demonstration that follows is somewhat less informal and should serve to bring the difference between phrase structure grammars and grammars with transformations into sharper focus.

First, let us consider the state of affairs in which two constituents of a sentence, call them A and B, either appear together in sequence or appear not at all. This type of phenomenon is captured by a phrase structure rule of the form

D → A B, where D is an optional constituent of some higher-level category. If D appears in the phrase marker, then A and B will, but if D does not appear, then neither will A and B.

Second, let us consider the state of affairs in which the two constituents A and B appear together or appear not at all, but do not appear as immediate constituents of the same node. Suppose that A is a constituent of D and B is a constituent of E. Furthermore, let D dominate constituents other than A, and let E dominate constituents other than B. Example (2.59) illustrates the structure when A and B are present, and (2.60) illustrates the structure when they are absent:

(2.59)

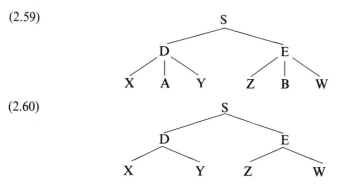

(2.60)

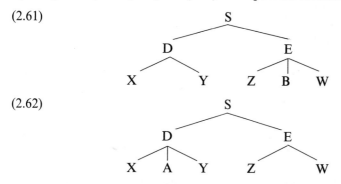

By comparison, both (2.61) and (2.62) are impossible structures in this example:

(2.61)

(2.62)

What is wrong with each of these two structures is that each violates the condition that A and B either appear together or are both absent.

Notice, now, that this phenomenon cannot be described by phrase structure rules alone. This is due to the fact that there is no way for the expansion of a particular category to be determined by the structure beneath another node in the tree. Given phrase structure rules of the type established thus far, we cannot specify that when E expands as Z B W then D must expand as X A Y, and vice versa, and when E expands as Z W then D must expand as X Y, and vice versa.

Finally, let us consider the tree in (2.63):

(2.63)

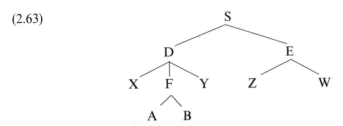

Let us suppose for the sake of illustration that F is an optional constituent of D. Then, as in the first example, A and B will either appear together in sequence or not appear at all. Let us suppose also that there is a transformation that, when presented with a tree such as (2.63), moves B to a position between Z and W, yielding (2.64):

(2.64)

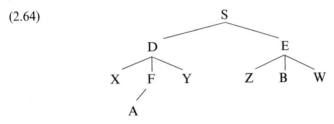

This transformation, it turns out, permits the grammar essentially to derive structure (2.59) without producing (2.61) and (2.62). Since F is optional, the grammar can also derive structure (2.60), in which neither A nor B appears. Thus, the second state of affairs we have described is one that cannot be described by phrase structure rules alone, as we have seen, but can be described by phrase structure rules and a transformation together.

The fact that grammars with transformations are, in principle, more powerful than grammars with phrase structure rules alone does not say anything about what kinds of transformations must be permitted and what kinds must be excluded in the theory of grammar. This issue is an empirical one, and requires a considerable amount of investigation of the full range of naturally occurring linguistic phenomena. At this point in our discussion, the notion of what a transformation is is still somewhat vague. What is required is a precise description of what a transformation is, analogous to the description of what a phrase structure rule looks like, and a careful examination of the linguistic phenomena that appear to be beyond the descriptive power of phrase structure grammars. The program for approaching this goal employed in this book involves the following steps:

1. Examine carefully a wide variety of sentences of a particular language.

2. Determine what transformations and phrase structure rules are necessary to provide a descriptively adequate account of the structure of the structure of the language.

3. Devise a theory of grammar that includes within it a specification of what kinds of transformational operations and phrase structure rules permit a descriptively adequate account of the language.

4. See whether it is possible to restrict the theory of grammar in such a way that certain kinds of transformational operations are forbidden in a description of any human language while making possible descriptively adequate accounts of all human languages.

The next several chapters will examine some grammatical phenomena of English in considerable detail with an eye toward carrying out the first two steps of this program. A notation will be introduced in which transformational operations can be described; this will constitute our attempt to carry out the third part of this program.

EXERCISES

1. Assign each word in the following sentences to a lexical category:

   a. *John races motorcycles.*
   b. *The old woman is walking quickly.*
   c. *Harry went to the store on Wednesday.*
   d. *I think that you should have stayed in the car.*
   e. *My dog has fleas.*
   f. *All men are mortal.*
   g. *The proof of the pudding is in the eating.*
   h. *Before John washed some dishes he put on his gloves.*
   i. *A very thin person should eat more protein for breakfast.*

If you do not know what names to give the categories, make some up.

2. Identify all of the phrases that appear in the sentences in Exercise 1 and specify the nonlexical categories of which they are members. Again, if you do not know the name of a category, make one up.

3. For each sentence in Exercise 1, give a phrase structure tree based on your answers to 1 and 2.

4. Make up a phrase structure grammar that will generate all of the sentences in Exercise 1 by using the lexical categories arrived at in 1 and the higher-level categories arrived at in 2.

5. Take each of the sentences in Exercise 1 and show how the grammar arrived at in 3 generates them by employing (i) a bottom-up procedure and (ii) a top-down procedure.

6. For each of the following strings of words, indicate (i) whether the phrase structure grammar that you developed in Exercise 4 generates the string,

(ii) whether such a grammar should, and (iii) why it should or should not generate the string:

    a. *The destroyed the barn.*
    b. *John races motorcycles with enthusiasm on Wednesdays after he has breakfast.*
    c. *My some dog has fleas.*
    d. *Harry was arrested by the police.*
    e. *A man who is mortal will certainly die at some time.*
    f. *Boy the destroyed toy a.*
    g. *Where is my dinner?*
    h. *Eating pudding is fun.*
    i. *John looked the information up.*
    j. *Is Pocatello in Idaho?*

7. (i) For each of the labeled bracketings that follow, give the corresponding phrase marker:

    a. $_A[B\,_C[DE]F]$
    b. $_{VP}[_V[sit]\,_{ADV}[down]]$
    c. $_S[_{NP}[_{ART}[the]\,_N[man]]\,_{VP}[_V[hit]\,_{NP}[_{PN}[Mary]]]]$
    d. $_A[_A[_A[B]B]B]$
    e. $_A[_A[B\,_C[DE]]F\,_A[B'\,_{C'}[DE']]]$

(ii) This chapter has a number of examples consisting of phrase markers. Give a complete labeled bracketing for (2.40), (2.44), (2.57), (2.58), (2.61), (2.62), and (2.63).

8. Apply the braces and parentheses notations wherever possible in the following sets of phrase structure rules:

    a. $S \rightarrow A\ B$
       $S \rightarrow A\ B\ C$
       $S \rightarrow B\ C$
    b. $S \rightarrow A\ B$
       $S \rightarrow B\ A\ C$
       $S \rightarrow C\ A$
    c. $S \rightarrow A\ B\ C\ D$
       $S \rightarrow A\ D$
       $S \rightarrow A\ E$
       $S \rightarrow A\ B\ C\ E$

9. For each of the following rule schemata, give the rules from which it was constructed through application of the braces and parentheses notations:

a. $S \rightarrow \left\{ \begin{matrix} A\ (B\ C) \left\{ \begin{matrix} D \\ E \end{matrix} \right\} \\ (F)\ G \end{matrix} \right\}$

b. $S \rightarrow A\ (B\ (C\ (D)\,)\,)$

c. $S \rightarrow (\,(\,(A)\ B)\ C)\ D$

PROBLEMS

1. Consider sets (a) and (b) in Exercise 8. Show that the rules in (a) express a number of general properties of sequences, while the rules in (b) are much less general by comparison. Show that this relative difference in generality is mirrored by the schemata that are gotten by applying the braces and parentheses notations in the two cases.

2. If two grammars generate the same set of sentences, they are **weakly equivalent**; if two grammars generate the same set of sentences with the same set of structures for these sentences, then the two grammars are **strongly equivalent.** Find a grammar that uses the same symbols as the following grammar that is weakly equivalent to it but not strongly equivalent to it:

$$S \rightarrow A\ B\ C$$
$$A \rightarrow D\ E\ F$$
$$B \rightarrow G\ H\ I$$
$$C \rightarrow J\ K$$

3. Sentence (a) is ambiguous (i.e., has two meanings), while sentences (b) and (c) are not:

a. *John resents visiting relatives.*
b. *Who does John resent visiting?*
c. *Who does John resent?*

First, identify what the ambiguity of (a) consists of. Second, what do sentences (a) and (b) tell you about how the grammar should represent a sentence like (a)?

4. Show that treating *will own a* as a category (cf. page 24) will make it very difficult to give a neat account of which sequences of English words can substitute for one another while preserving grammaticality.

5. In order to construct a descriptively adequate account of a language, it is first necessary to determine what the phenomena are that need to be described. For each of the following sets of examples, indicate what the phenomena are and sketch out a syntactic description of them:

a. *John looked up the information.*
   John looked the information up.
b. *A man walked in who was over seven-feet tall.*
   A man who was over seven-feet tall walked in.
c. *The child who is sleeping in the corner is my sister.*
   The child sleeping in the corner is my sister.
d. *The boss fired Mary.*
   Mary was fired by the boss.
e. *It is a real pleasure to visit Niagara Falls.*
   Niagara Falls is a real pleasure to visit.

SUGGESTED FURTHER READINGS

(*Asterisks indicate titles that are most comprehensible to the beginner.*)

Categories

*Harris, Z. (1964), "Co-occurrence and transformation in linguistic structure," in Fodor, J. A. and Katz, J. J., eds. (1964), *The Structure of Language: Readings in the Philosophy of Language*, Prentice-Hall, Englewood Cliffs, N. J.

English Syntax

*Jespersen, O. (1961), *A Modern English Grammar on Historical Principles*, Allen and Unwin, London.
*Jespersen, O. (1964), *Essentials of English Grammar*, (Reprint) University of Alabama Press, Montgomery, Alabama.
*Quirk, R., Greenbaum, S., Leech, G. & Svartvik, J. (1972), *A Grammar of Contemporary English*, Seminar Press, New York.

Fundamental Concepts of Generative Grammar

*Akmajian, A. & Heny, F. W. (1975), *Introduction to the Principles of Transformational Syntax*, MIT Press, Cambridge, Mass.
*Bach, E. (1974), *Syntactic Theory*, Holt, New York.
*Burt, M. K. (1971), *From Deep to Surface Structure*, Harper, New York.
*Chomsky, N. (1957), *Syntactic Structures*, Mouton, The Hague.
*Fromkin, V. & Rodman, R. (1973), *An Introduction to Language*, Holt, New York.
*Grinder, J. & Elgin, S. (1973), *Guide to Transformational Grammar*, Holt, New York.
*Kimball, J. (1973a), *The Formal Theory of Grammar*, Prentice-Hall, Englewood Cliffs, N. J.
*Langacker, R. (1968), *Language and Its Structure*, Harcourt, New York.
*Langendoen, D. T. (1969), *The Study of Syntax*, Holt, New York.
Ruwet, N. (1968), *Introduction à la Grammaire Générative*, Librarie Plon, Paris.

Generative Power

Chomsky, N. (1963), ":Formal properties of grammars," in Luce, R. D., Bush, R. R., & Galanter, E., eds., (1963), *Handbook of Mathematical Psychology* (Vol. 2), Wiley, New York.

Chomsky, N. & Miller, G. A. (1963), "Introduction to the formal analysis of natural languages," in Luce, R. D., Bush, R. R., & Galanter, E., eds., (1963), *Handbook of Mathematical Psychology* (Vol. 2), Wiley, New York.

*Postal, P. (1964a), *Constituent Structure: A Study of Contemporary Models of Syntactic Description,* Mouton, The Hague.

*Postal, P. (1964b), "Limitations of phrase structure grammars," in Fodor, J. A. & Katz, J. J., eds., (1964), *The Structure of Language: Readings in the Philosophy of Language,* Prentice-Hall, Englewood Cliffs, N. J.

3

A Basic Rule
of English

The grammar of English is quite complex, and satisfies very well our desire to discover a variety of grammatical phenomena that are present in human language. It is very important to realize that much of the grammar is tightly organized and interrelated, so that a description of one artificially isolated phenomenon will often suffer in generality owing to the impossibility of considering all relevant data at the same time. But we must begin somewhere. Thus, the analyses presented in these early chapters will sometimes be oversimplifications that will be revised later, when we are in a position to consider further data. In other cases, apparently arbitrary decisions will be made between alternative descriptions of the data. These decisions will be reconsidered in later chapters when further data can be brought to bear on them.

SOME DATA: VERBAL SEQUENCES

Consider the various forms of a typical English verb, such as *write*. We discover, by examining our knowledge of English as native speakers, that such a verb may appear in grammatical sentences with a variety of so-called **auxiliary verbs,** and that it is possible for there to be a number of auxiliary verbs in a single sentence. In the examples that follow, the axuiliary verbs are in italic boldface. Note that some of these verbs are modals:

(3.1)

  a. *John writes.*
  b. *John wrote.*
  c. *John **has** written.*
  d. *John **had** written.*
  e. *John **is** writing.*
  f. *John **was** writing.*
  g. *John **will write.***
  h. *John **would** write.*
  i. *John **has been** writing.*
  j. *John **had been** writing.*
  k. *John **will be** writing.*
  l. *John **would be** writing.*
  m. *John **will have** written.*
  n. *John **would have** written.*
  o. *John **will have been** writing.*
  p. *John **would have been** writing.*

It is possible to substitute certain words for the words *will* and *would* in all of the sentences of (3.1) in which they occur without creating ungrammatical sequences. These words are the following: *can, could, shall, would, may,* and *might.* None of these words may be substituted for *John, have, had, has, be, was, is, been, write, wrote,* etc. This observation (which you should satisfy yourself is correct) shows that there is a lexical category that includes *will* and *would* and the words that are substituable for them. The name of this category is **modal,** or **M.**

The term **verbal sequence** refers to any sequence in an English sentence of either a verb alone or a verb with auxiliary verbs. An account of what constitutes a grammatical sentence of English must specify what a verbal sequence looks like. This section provides such a specification and characterizes the kinds of grammatical descriptive tools necessary to do so.

First of all, there are several auxiliary verbs that may participate in a verbal sequence. As shown in (3.1), this includes *has, have,* and *had; be, is,* and *was; been;* and *will* and *would.* In addition, all the sequences in (3.1) are based on the verb *write,* and yet the actual form *write* appears only once. In fact, a verbal sequence may also involve *wrote, written, writes,* and *writing.* The superficial observation that there are differences between certain sentences [such as those in (3.1)] must be related to the intuitive knowledge that they are in some way related. A description must be formulated in which both the similarities and the differences are appropriately represented.

Such a description can be provided, given the assumption that there are in fact *two* levels at which we may simultaneously represent facts about the sentence: *deep structure* and *surface structure*. For example, *writes, wrote, written,* and *writing* are all forms of the verb *write.* Then at the deep structure level the differences between these forms is represented by associating with each form a different **marker.** The marker for *writes* is the **present tense marker,** (or Pres); the marker for *wrote* is the **past tense marker,** (or Past); the marker for *written* is the **past participle marker** (which we will indicate by *en*); and the marker for *writing* is the **progressive marker** (which we will indicate by *ing*). The deep structure representation of these forms is then (3.2), where the fact that they are all forms of the same verb is explicitly represented:

(3.2)
$$
\begin{aligned}
&writes: \quad write + \text{Pres} \\
&wrote: \quad write + \text{Past} \\
&written: write + en \\
&writing: write + ing
\end{aligned}
$$

It should be emphasized that these markers are arbitrarily named; the names they have been given have been chosen because of traditional terminology. What is crucial, however, is that where there is a difference between forms there is also a corresponding difference in the markers assigned that captures the fact that a difference in fact exists.[1]

This type of representation makes an extremely strong claim about what constitutes a grammatical sentence of English: If one form of a verb is a member of a particular category (e.g., V_I), then every form of the verb will be a member of the same category. Thus, if **John is smiling roses* is ungrammatical, then so are **John smiled roses, *John would have smiled roses,* and so on. A description of English that does not make the relationship between various forms of a verb explicit in this way will fail to make this strong and correct claim in a natural way.

In the surface structure, on the other hand, the observable differences in the forms must be represented. Thus, *write* + Pres must be represented in the corresponding surface structure as *writes* under certain circumstances (sometimes it may be *write,* as in *we write*). Similarly, *write* + Past will appear in the corresponding surface structure as *wrote,* and so on. We also say that *write* + Pres is *realized* as *writes,* or that *write* + Pres **underlies** *writes.* In general, the deep structure underlies the surface structure.

One of the characteristics of a deep structure marker is that while its name may be arbitrary, its existence must be justified. This is an important point, for while it may be necessary to assume that certain markers appear in certain deep structures, it should not be possible to assume the presence of arbitrary

---

[1] It should not be concluded from this discussion that the phonetic realization of each marker will be the same regardless of which verb it is attached to. In some cases, the marker has no phonetic effect whatsoever, e.g., *I* **hit** *the wall with my foot* (*yesterday*). In other cases, the effect is irregular and unpredictable: *write/wrote, see/saw, run/ran, think/thought, speak/spoke.* All that can be said here is that *see* + Past, *run* + Past, *think* + Past, and *speak* + Past have irregular phonetic realizations that must be specifically mentioned in the lexical entries for these particular verbs.

markers at will. Deep structures are abstract objects: They cannot be directly observed. This means that it will be difficult to justify their form on the basis of empirical evidence; it does not mean that no justification is required.

The justification of a marker consists of showing not only that the marker permits a representation of the difference between various forms but also that it permits a descriptively adequate account of the phenomenon under consideration. In returning to the question of what a possible verbal sequence of English looks like, this question of *justification* should be kept in mind so that it will be clear what role is played by the assumption that such markers exist.

Suppose that *any* sequence of verbs and verbal auxiliaries may constitute a verbal sequence of English. This hypothesis is immediately falsified by a variety of counterexamples, including the following:

(3.3)   a. *John is has wrote.*
               b. *John has will writing.*
               c. *John will written.*
               d. *John has be write.*
               e. *John would will write.*
               f. *John had writes.*
               g. *John will is writing.*

and so on.

In fact, only a certain subset of the logically possible sequences actually is found in grammatical English sentences. The sequences that do occur are just those that are illustrated in (3.1). The observations that have been made thus far concerning the internal structure of these sequences are represented schematically in Table 3.1.

Note that the form *been* in Table 3.1 is represented schematically as *be + en.* That is, it is analyzed as the past participle of the verb *to be.* This is consistent with the fact that when the verb *to be* is used as a main verb (rather than as an auxiliary verb) the form of its past participle is *been.* This is illustrated by the following examples (the main verb is in boldface italic in each case):

(3.4)   a. *Mary **is** polite.*
               *Mary **is** a nuisance.*
               b. *Mary is **being** polite.*
               *Mary is **being** a nuisance.*
               c. *Mary will **be** polite.*
               *Mary will **be** a nuisance.*
               d. *Mary has **been** polite.*
               *Mary has **been** a nuisance.*

Looking, now, at the verbal sequences in Table 3.1, we find that *has* and *had* may be substituted for one another, and that *is* and *was* may be substituted for one another. It seems, in fact, that *has* and *had* are variants of a single auxiliary verb and that *is* and *was* are variants of another. Furthermore,

Table 3.1. *Schematization of the Possible English Verbal Sequences*

Verbal sequence	Example
V + Pres	John *writes.*
V + Past	John *wrote.*
has V + *en*	John *has written.*
had V + *en*	John *had written.*
is V + *ing*	John *is writing.*
was V + *ing*	John *was writing.*
has be + *en* V + *ing*	John *has been writing.*
had be + *en* V + *ing*	John *had been writing.*
will V	John *will write*
would V	John *would write.*
will have V + *en*	John *will have written.*
would have V + *en*	John *would have written.*
will be V + *ing*	John *will be writing.*
would be V + *ing*	John *would be writing.*
will have be + *en* V + *ing*	John *will have been writing.*
would have be + *en* V + *ing*	John *would have been writing.*

Table 3.2. *Revised Schematization of Possible English Verbal Sequences*

Verbal sequence	Example
V + Pres	John *writes.*
V + Past	John *wrote.*
have + Pres V + *en*	John *has written.*
have + Past V + *en*	John *had written.*
be + Pres V + *ing*	John *is writing.*
be + Past V + *ing*	John *was writing.*
have + Pres *be* + *en* V + *ing*	John *has been writing.*
have + Past *be* + *en* V + *ing*	John *had been writing.*
will V	John *will write.*
would V	John *would write.*
will have V + *en*	John *will have written.*
would have V + *en*	John *would have written.*
will be V + *ing*	John *will be writing.*
would be V + *ing*	John *would be writing.*
will have be + *en* V + *ing*	John *will have been writing.*
would have be + *en* V + *ing*	John *would have been writing.*

examples such as those in (3.5) show that when *has/had* and *is/was* are used as main verbs, the distinction that is displayed by each pair corresponds quite exactly to the *writes/wrote* distinction:

(3.5)   a. *John has a cold.*
                                   John had a cold.
                      b. *John is a farmer.*
                                   John was a farmer.

This distinction is one that has already been captured by the Pres/Past marking of the verb; all we need do is extend it to auxiliary verbs as well. The result of doing so is illustrated in the revised schematization of the verbal sequences given in Table 3.2.

As can be seen in the table, the Pres/Past distinction is used in those sequences that begin with V, and those that begin with *has/had*, and those that begin with *is/was*. The fact that the sequences that begin with modals also form related pairs suggests that the difference between the members of each pair may be due to the same Pres/Past distinction.

There is some semantic plausibility to this suggestion. Just as *writes/wrote* in some sense represents a distinction between an activity in the present and an activity in the past, there are cases in which two members of the category M appear to display the same distinction:[2]

(3.6)   a. *When Mary was in college she wrote French well.*
            *When Mary was in college she writes French well.
      b. *When Mary was in college she could speak French well.*
            *When Mary was in college she can speak French well.

(3.7)   a. **Now that Mary is in college she wrote French well.*
            Now that Mary is in college she writes French well.
      b. **Now that Mary is in college she could speak French well.*
            Now that Mary is in college she can speak French well.

Examples (3.6a) amd (3.7a) indicate that there are contexts in which the verb must be marked Pres in order to make reference to present time and those in which it must be marked Past in order to make reference to past time. The (b) examples show that the context that requires Past on the verb requires the modal *could*. Thus, purely semantic considerations would demand that *can* be represented as *can* + Pres and that *could* be represented as *can* + Past for the purpose of achieving the most general description of this phenomenon.

---

[2] I have used the asterisk to indicate that certain of the sentences in these examples are less than perfect, following a tradition in linguistics. However, the asterisk could be used to indicate ungrammaticality only, and cases of semantic unacceptability could be indicated by some other symbol, such as ? or $ or %, reserving the asterisk for sequences that the syntax does not generate. I have not adopted another symbol here because the issue of semantic unacceptability versus syntactic ill-formedness is not raised sufficiently often in this book to justify a fuller repetoire of symbols.

Examination of further data shows, however, that Pres does not always correspond to present time and Past does not always correspond to past time. For example, sequences beginning with *will/would* do not preserve this correspondence, since it is strange to speak of present and past variants of *will* (i.e., *will* and *would*) given that *will* is an indicator of **future time.** In fact, *could* and *would*, which will be marked with the marker Past, often have nothing to do with past time at all. For example:

(3.8)   *John would never agree to letting you do that.*

(3.9)   *Could you please get off my toe?*

More generally, let us represent the time at which a sentence is uttered as t_S. The present tense may be used to describe an action taking place in the past, before t_S; in the present, at t_S; or in the future, after t_S:

(3.10)   *I come home and then John **says** to me "Where*
                   the devil have you been all day?" (takes place
                   before t_s).
(3.11)   *I **choose** Mary.* (takes place at t_s exactly)
(3.12)   *I **sail** for England next Wednesday.* (takes
                   place after t_s).

Similarly, a construction with *has* expresses an event in the past, but *has* itself is **marked** in the deep structure with Pres, a tense marker. On the other hand, *has* as a verb of possession expresses something about present time, as in *John has a cold.* Yet a description of the **form** of these words (as opposed to their semantic function in the context of the sentence as a whole) must take into account that their forms are the same: They are both *have* + Pres. Where they differ is in their interpretation, and this clearly depends on the surrounding context of the sentence:

(3.13)   *John **has** been to the bar twelve times in the*
                   last hour!
(3.14)   *John **has** a serious problem.*

In fact, *would*, while it is a realization of *will* + Past may refer to past, present, or future time:

(3.15)   *When he came home John **would** always throw his*
                   shoes into the closet. (past time)
(3.16)   *I **would** like a cup of coffee, please.* (present time)
(3.17)   *Do you think that John **would** fix the sink*
                   tomorrow? (future time)

Occasionally, a present tense does not indicate any particular time at all:

(3.18)   *Mary **races** jellyfish as a hobby.*

And finally, the so-called present progressive (*is* followed by a verb marked with *ing*) can indicate the future:

(3.19)   *Mary **is leaving** on a trip next week.*

Here, of course, *is* is marked with Pres in the deep structure.

The justification of a syntactic analysis must appeal to regularities of form, not function. In the case considered here, it turns out that the semantic facts do not support the notion that there is a one-to-one correspondence between the form of the verb (i.e., Pres or Past marking) and its function (i.e., temporal reference).

But even if there were such a correspondence, this would not justify the *can/could* distinction as being due to the Pres/Past distinction. That is, suppose that *can, will, writes, is has,* etc. always referred to the present, and suppose that *could, would, wrote, was, had,* etc. always referred to the past. It would not follow that all of the forms that referred to the present would have to be marked with Pres and all of those that referred to the past would have to be marked with Past. **Syntactic** arguments are required for the justification of syntactic structure. Semantic correspondences do not suffice as justification, even in those cases where they can be clearly established.

The syntactic justification for treating the modals as instances of the under-lying Pres/Past distinction is that we may then generalize the definition of what sequences of verbal elements in fact constitute well-formed verbal sequences. The schematization of the possible verbal sequences, given the extension of the distinction, is shown in Table 3.3.

The generalization that this schematization makes possible is that in every verbal sequence the Pres/Past distinction is marked on the *first* member of the sequence. An alternative schematization, such as that given in Table 3.2, does not explain why it is that the element that follows the modal is never marked for the Pres/Past distinction (for example):

(3.20)   a. **Mary will had written the story.*
                      *Mary would had written the story.
                      *Mary will has written the story.
                      *Mary would has written the story.
                  b. **George can is leaving by now.*
                      *George could is leaving by now.
                      *George can was leaving by then.
                      *George could was leaving by then.
                  c. **Arturo may writes the article in French.*
                      *Arturo may wrote the article in French.
                      *Arturo might writes the article in French.
                      *Arturo might wrote the article in French.

In fact, if the schematization in Table 3.2 were chosen, then the absence of the

Table 3.3   *Final Schematization of Possible English Verbal Sequences*

Verbal sequence	*Example*
{ V + Pres { V + Past	*John **writes**.* *John **wrote**.*
{ *have* + Pres V + *en* { *have* + Past V + *en*	*John **has written**.* *John **had written**.*
{ *be* + Pres V + *ing* { *be* + Past V + *ing*	*John **is writing**.* *John **was writing**.*
{ *have* + Pres *be* + *en* V + *ing* { *have* + Past *be* + *en* V + *ing*	*John **has been writing**.* *John **had been writing**.*
{ M + Pres V { M + Past V	*John **will write**.* *John **would write**.*
{ M + Pres *have* V + *en* { M + Past *have* V + *en*	*John **will have written**.* *John **would have written**.*
{ M + Pres *be* V + *en* { M + Past *be* V + *en*	*John **will be writing**.* *John **would be writing**.*
{ M + Pres *have be* + *en* V + *ing* { M + Past *have be* + *en* V + *ing*	*John **will have been writing**.* *John **would have been writing**.*

Pres/Past distinction in just the sequences that contain modals would have to be treated simply as an accident.

The schematization in Table 3.3, on the other hand, will permit us to claim that the Pres/Past distinction is marked on the first element of the verbal sequence quite generally, with no regard to what this first element happens to be in any given case. This is particularly important, since it makes the explicit prediction that if English were to acquire a new modal, then this modal would also display the Pres/Past distinction.

This prediction is a correct one. Notice that the modal *must* has lost a form for referring to past time; in order to indicate an obligation in the past, one must use *have to* :

(3.21)   *John must leave at noon.*
                John had to leave at noon.

Strikingly, the Pres form of *have to* is also a modal, and the form *has to/had to* display precisely the expected Pres/Past alternation:

(3.22)   *John has to leave at noon.*

This alternation follows immediately if one assumes the schematization in Table 3.3 and assumes that *have to* is a modal. It does not follow, however, if each modal is treated as an unanalyzed form, as in Table 3.2.

THE ANALYSIS: EXTRACTING REGULARITIES

Now, having established what the markers underlying English verbal sequences are, let us state a rule or set of rules to represent formally what in fact constitutes a possible verbal sequence. In doing so, we will treat Pres and Past as members of the category TENSE, since they substitute for one another in all contexts without affecting grammaticality.[3]

It is important to determine whether there are any properties that any sequence must have. Some of these regularities may be very trivial and obvious, such as "every sequence must have a such-and-such." Others may be more subtle.

Let us, for the moment, ignore TENSE, *en*, and *ing*. The regularities involving the distribution of these elements in the sequences will be dealt with in the next section. Here we will focus on the distributional properties of the modals and verbs alone, as they appear in the reduced schema given in Table 3.4.

Table 3.4 Schematization of Possible Verbal Sequences, Ignoring TENSE en, and ing

a.				V
b.		*have*		V
c.			*be*	V
d.		*have*	*be*	V
e.	M			V
f.	M	*have*		V
g.	M		*be*	V
h.	M	*have*	*be*	V

The first regularity to take note of is that every sequence has a V. This regularity follows automatically from the fact that every sentence contains a VP and every VP contains a V. A second regularity is that the V is always the last element in the sequence. This can be captured by assuming that the other elements in the sequence are constituents of a single node, call it AUX, that necessarily precedes VP in the deep structure. The problem of specifying the rule for deriving all and only the possible verbal sequences, thus, reduces to the problem of stating a rule for the expansion of the node AUX.

There are two striking regularities in the distribution of the verbal elements in Table 3.4. First of all, each element may or may not appear independently of whether any other appears or does not. Thus, M appears before the sequences *have* V, *be* V, and V. If M is not present, the sequences *have* V, *be* V, and V may appear anyway. When a given sequence may contain a particular element but

[3] As we have seen, the choice of Pres or Past affects the semantic interpretation of the sentence and, hence, may cause a grammatical sentence to sound peculiar.

need not, then the parentheses notation is applicable. This notation captures the generalization that the order of elements in the sequence is the same regardless of whether the optional element is present or absent. Applying the parentheses notation to the optional M gives us (3.23):

(3.23)   (M)   V
                           (M)   *be* V
                           (M) *have*   V
                           (M) *have be* V

Notice, now, that a further generalization is possible through application of the parentheses notation. The auxiliary verb *have* may appear before *be* V and V but need not. That is, just as M is an optional constituent of the verbal sequence, so is *have*. And just as M appears in a particular position with respect to the other elements in the sequence when it appears, so does *have*. The result of applying notation once again is given in (3.24):

(3.24)   (M) (*have*)   V
                           (M) (*have*) *be* V

Finally, it is clear that the parentheses notation is applicable to the sequences in (3.24). This represents the generalization that while *be* need not appear in verbal sequences, it always appears in the same position relative to the other elements when it does appear (i.e., immediately at the end of AUX and before V):

(3.25)   (M) (*have*) (*be*) V

By successive application of the parentheses notation, then, we have arrived at a general rule schema for the expansion of the node AUX:

(3.26)   AUX → (M) (*have*) (*be*)

None of the elements is obligatory; but if any element appears, then its position in the sequence relative to the others is rigidly specified by the rule. The virtue of adopting the parentheses notation in our theory of grammar is shown by the fact that it permits us to capture quite explicitly that this strict sequence holds regardless of the presence or absence of particular optional elements.

THE DESCRIPTION: AFFIX HOPPING

We return now to the distributional properties of the markers TENSE, *en*, and *ing*. The possible verbal sequences are summarized in (3.27). Note the use of the category symbol TENSE instead of Pres/Past:

(3.27)   V + TENSE
                           have + TENSE   V + *en*

		be + TENSE	V + *ing*
	have + TENSE	*be* + *en*	V + *ing*
M + TENSE			V
M + TENSE		*be*	V + *ing*
M + TENSE *have*			V + *en*
M + TENSE *have*		*be* + *en*	V + *ing*

There are several important regularities here. One of these we noted earlier: The first verbal element in the sequence has TENSE attached to it, *regardless of which element it is*. It is impossible to represent this fact in a phrase structure grammar, however, without abandoning the general rule for expansion of AUX given as (3.26). Since each of the elements in the sequence is optional, we cannot say, for all sequences, which particular verbal element will have TENSE attached to it. In some sequences, TENSE will be attached to M; in others, TENSE will be attached to *have* (when *have* is first); in others, it will be attached to *be* (when *be* is first), and in still others, it will be attached to V (when V is first).

Nor can we state a phrase structure rule that has TENSE attached to all of the verbal elements:

(3.28)   AUX → (M + TENSE) (*have* + TENSE) (*be* + TENSE)

If AUX should happen to be expanded with more than one element, e.g., M and *have*, then the sequence would contain at least two instances of TENSE. As we can see from (3.27), however, TENSE appears only once in any given sequence. By the same token, TENSE cannot be made an optional marker on each element in the sequence, since (3.27) shows that TENSE *must* appear in every sequence.

An elegant solution to this problem requires that we move beyond the phrase structure rules to consider a transformational analysis. Assume for the moment that TENSE is an obligatory constituent of the node AUX and that it appears in initial position in AUX:

(3.29)   AUX → TENSE (M) (*have*) (*be*)

By stating the rule in this way, we guarantee that every verbal sequence will have exactly one TENSE if every sentence has one AUX.

To capture the generalization that TENSE appears on the first element in the sequence, we need simply state the following transformation.

TENSE HOPPING: Attach TENSE to the first verbal element that follows it.

A more formal statement of this rule will be given shortly.

Another regularity in the sequences given in (3.27) is that the marker *en* appears just in case *have* is present in the sequence, and *have* never appears unless *en* also appears. Similarly, *be* and *ing* are either simultaneously present or simultaneously absent.

These properties of the auxiliary verbs and the markers can be represented by putting *en* between the same parentheses as *have* and *ing* between the same parentheses as *be* in the rule that expands AUX:

(3.30)   AUX → TENSE (M) (*have en*) (*be ing*)

As can be seen, the parentheses notation will capture the fact that when *have* and *en* appear they appear together (and similarly for *be* and *ing*). In fact, there is no other way of expressing this generalization within the context of phrase structure rules. However, stating the generalization in this way appears to prevent us from capturing another generalization: Whenever *en* appears, it appears on the verbal element to the right of *have*, and whenever *ing* appears, it appears on the verbal element to the right of *be*, regardless of what that element happens to be.

This makes it impossible to capture the observed generalizations in purely phrase structure terms. An elegant and revealing solution is available to us, however, given that we can also use transformational rules in a description of a natural language. The appropriate transformation in this case is the following:

EN/ING HOPPING: Attach *en* or *ing* to the first verbal element that follows it.

This rule permits us to capture the cooccurrence properties of the auxiliary verbs and the markers at the deep structure level, and also permits us to capture the generalizations concerning the surface structure distribution of the markers.

Notice, now, an important fact: The rule of *en/ing* Hopping performs exactly the same operation as Tense Hopping; the two rules simply move different markers. Thus, a further generalization of the transformational rules discovered to this point is possible.

TENSE/EN/ING HOPPING: Attach a marker TENSE, *en*, or *ing* to the first verbal element that follows it.

This rule will, in fact, capture all of the generalizations concerning the distribution of the markers that we have already noted.

Since our goal is to provide a formal grammar of English, this informal rule must be rephrased in a precise and formal way. Linguists have developed a formal notation in which transformations may be stated. This notation will now be illustrated in the precise statement of the preceding rule.

As we have already noted, the function of a transformation is to change phrase markers with certain properties into phrase markers with other properties. As an illustration of what Tense/*en/ing* Hopping must in fact do, consider the most complicated example, i.e., *John would have been writing*. We assume for the present that the constituent AUX is an immediate constituent of S.[4] The deep structure of this sentence is, then, (3.31):

(3.31)

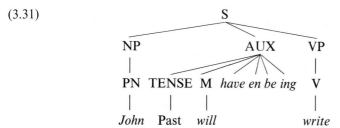

For ease of exposition, we will deal only with the terminal string (3.32):

(3.32)   *John* Past *will have en be ing write*

It is clear that the surface structure sequence has to be (3.33):

(3.33)   *John will* + Past *have be* + *en write* + *ing*

Thus, the transformation must be stated so that it formally relates deep structures, in which the markers precede the elements, to surface structures, in which the markers follow these elements.

We must ask what characteristics of the deep structure determine the applicability of this transformation. We find, for example, that the form of the verbal sequence is completely independent of the form of the NP that precedes it. This NP may be PN, ART N, or ART ADJ N, yet the markers are invariably attached to the elements in the verbal sequence in the same way. By the same token, the internal structure of the NP in the VP has no effect on the applicability of this rule, nor does it even matter whether there is such an NP in the VP. In fact, it is correct to say that the form of the verbal sequence in the surface structure depends on nothing but the particular verbal elements and the particular markers that are present in the deep structure.

While a transformation relates phrase markers to other phrase markers, it appears that all that is necessary in some cases (such as the present one) is to state a relationship between **parts** of phrase markers. In order to do this, we introduce the notion of a **variable.** A variable represents that part of the structure which is irrelevant to the transformational relationship that is being expressed. In this case, the transformation deals with the relative position in deep structure and surface structure of the markers TENSE, *en*, and *ing*, and a precise specifi-

---

[4] A plausible alternative is that AUX is a sister of VP. I know of no conclusive argument for choosing one of these analyses over the other. I have used the NP AUX VP analysis of S here primarily because it is the more traditional one.

cation of what precedes the verbal sequence is unnecessary and irrelevent for this purpose.

In fact, owing to recursion (cf. Chapter 2), it is impossible to specify precisely every sequence that may precede and follow the verbal sequence. Thus, TENSE must be hopped onto the verb *believe* in *I believed that* . . . regardless of whether "*. . .*" is *the world is flat, Mary believes that the world is flat,* and so on. The irrelevance of what follows the verbal sequence is precisely what the notion of a variable is intended to capture.

The common technical term for the markers TENSE, *en,* and *ing* is **affix.** For the purpose of stating the transformation, these markers will be treated as members of the syntactic category Affix. In addition, the symbol VE will be used here to represent the set of verbal elements, that is, the set consisting of all of the verbs, all of the modals, and the auxiliary verbs *have* and *be.*

The function of the transformation is to hop the affix over the single verbal element to the right of it and attach the affix to it. This is stated formally as the following rule, in which the symbols X and Y represent variables. This transformation is called Affix Hopping.

$$AFFIX\ HOPPING: \quad \underset{1}{\text{X}} \quad \underset{2}{\text{Affix}} \quad \underset{3}{\text{VE}} \quad \underset{4}{\text{Y}} \Rightarrow 1\ \emptyset\ \#\ 3 + 2\ \#\ 4$$

What this notation says is the following: The constituent represented by 2, i.e., the affix, is removed from its position in the original structure. This removal is shown by replacing 2 by $\emptyset$. It is moved to the right of the constituent denoted by 3, i.e., the verbal element, and attached to the right of the verbal element in precise way, which is denoted by the symbol $+$. The symbol $\#$ indicates that the resulting sequence of verbal element followed by an affix is to be considered a unit, and cannot be further analyzed by other transformations that might otherwise apply to it. (This last remark suggests that transformations might apply to the results of other transformations, and we will discuss the question of whether this is so in Chapter 5.)

The precise method of attachment denoted by $+$ is called **sister-adjunction.** One node is **sister-adjoined** to another by making the first a sister of the second. A typical case of sister-adjunction is shown in (3.34). First the rule is given, and then the two trees:

(3.34)   a. A B
                   $\underset{1}{} \quad \underset{2}{} \Rightarrow \emptyset\ 2 + 1$

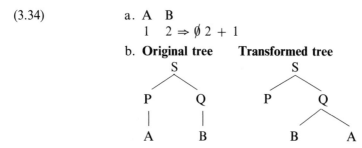

As can be seen, it is important to indicate which constituent is moved in the case of sister-adjunction in order to be precise about what the resulting structure looks like. Compare (3.34) with (3.35):

(3.35)   a. A   B
                   1   2 ⇒ 2 + 1 ∅

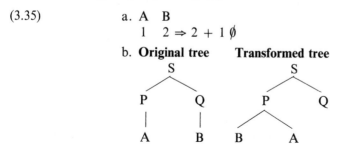

b. **Original tree   Transformed tree**

Notice that while sister-adjunction applies in such a way that A and B end up as sisters in both transformed trees, the structure of the entire tree in each case depends on which constituent is moved and which one remains in its original position.

As a final point, it should be noted that the transformed trees do not possess the symbol +. This is because + is not in fact a constituent of the sentence, but a formal notation used in the statement of the transformation to express the way in which the derived phrase marker is related to the original one.

The tree shown in (3.36) indicates the result of applying Affix Hopping to the deep structure of (3.31), *John would have been writing:*

(3.36)

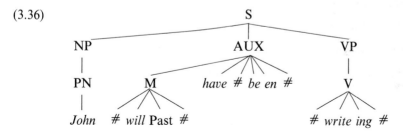

The part of a transformation that is to the left of the arrow is called the **structural condition** or **structural description**; the part that is to the right is called the **structural change.** The structural condition specifies what the structure must look like in order for the transformation to apply; the structural change specifies what the structure looks like after the transformation has applied. The phrase marker to which the transformation applies is called the **input** to the transformation; the phrase marker that results from the application of the transformation is called the **output.**

In determining whether or not a transformation may apply to a given structure, examine the structure and see if it meets the structural condition. Thus, (3.32) can in fact be analyzed as a variable followed by the sequence Affix VE, as shown in (3.37):

(3.37)   *John* Past *will have en be ing smile*
                        X   Affix VE   Y

Therefore, the transformation will apply to the sequence Past *will.*

Notice, however, that there are two other ways in which this sequence can be analyzed so that the transformation will apply. These are illustrated in (3.38):

(3.38)   a. *John* Past *will have   en   be ing smile*
                       X   Affix VE   Y

                 b. *John* Past *will have en be   ing   smile*
                       X   Affix VE Y

(Notice that in order to accommodate the analysis in (3.38b) we must allow a variable in the structural description to refer to nothing at all.)

There is no question of choosing only one of these three analyses as the correct one: In order to derive the appropriate surface structure for the sentence, all three affixes must be moved by Affix Hopping. Thus, either the transformation applies simultaneously at a number of different points in the tree, or else it applies at a single point in the tree, but several times in succession. Unfortunately, we cannot determine at this point which of these two modes of application is correct. What we can do, however, is to illustrate the potential consequences of one of the two alternatives just pointed out.

First of all, it should be clear that if all affixes are hopped at once, no problems will arise. However, if Affix Hopping may or must apply more than once in the same sentence, then there must be some way to guarantee that once an affix has been hopped, it will not hop again. For it this were not done, a situation could arise in which an affix that had been moved over a verbal element could then be moved over the next verbal element, and then over the next, until it ended up attached to the last element of the sequence. So the sequence underlying *John would have been writing* would lead to the derivation illustrated in Table 3.5.

This is clearly an unacceptable result, since it would yield a nonsentence, perhaps something like **John will have be smileding*, or something even worse. It is impossible to say precisely what we would get, since the sequence V + Past + en + ing simply does not occur in English verbal sequences.

There does not exist any clear evidence that transformations must be able to apply a number of different times to a single simple sentence. Thus, the convention that will be adopted here will be that the transformation applies simultaneously to all of those parts of the tree that meet the conditions for its application. The symbol # will not be used here as a syntactic device, but will simply represent the intuition that sequences of verbal elements and markers are in fact surface structure units and are not perceived as sequences of morphemes.

Returning, now, to the sequence given in (3.32)—*John* Past *will have en be ing write*—we apply Affix Hopping. Simultaneous application of Affix Hopping to each Affix-VE sequence yields (3.39):

Table 3.5. Result of Continuously Moving Affixes to the Right Until No Longer Possible

Stage	Sequence
0	John Past will have en be ing smile
1	John will Past have en be ing smile
2	John will have Past en be ing smile
3	John will have Past en be smile ing
4	John will have Past be en smile ing
5	John will have Past be smile en ing
6	John will have be Past smile en ing
7	John will have be smile Past en ing

(3.39)   *John # will + Past # have # be + en # # write + ing #*

This is the terminal string corresponding to the correct surface structure. (The + signs are commonly represented in such terminal strings to aid the reader. They are not actually part of the derived structure.)

MORPHOLOGY

Of course, this does not complete the derivation, because (3.39) has sequences of lexical items and markers, and not the exact form of the sentence to be derived. It is absolutely necessary in providing a derivation for a sentence that the rules produce precisely the grammatical sentence. This follows from the requirement that a grammar should generate all and only the grammatical sentences of the language.

A set of statements is needed to represent the realization of sequences such as *will + Past*, *write + ing*, and so on. In some languages, it is possible to assign a **phonological representation** to a marker (such as present tense or first person singular), so that the problem of what the sentence actually looks like can be reduced to a problem of how certain phonological representations are realized by the phonology component.

For example, the progressive marker in English may be represented as the phonological string *ing*. The progressive form of every verb is predictable from the basic form of the verb itself; it is gotten by adding *-ing*. In such a case, there is no particular need for an abstract marker like Past or Pres.

In contrast, the result of adding Past to a modal or a verb is not always predictable, although it is quite regular. The same is true of the result of adding the past participle marker to a verb. It will be necessary, therefore, to specify quite precisely the unpredictable phonological behavior of certain lexical items in the context of certain markers.

For example, it will be necessary to specify that *will* + Past is realized as *would*, that *may* + Past is realized as *might*, and so on. There must be information in the lexicon to the effect that the past participle of the verb *speak*, that is, *speak* + *en*, is realized as *spoken* and not **speaked*. Such information, along with the category of which a word is a member and the meaning of the word, is part of the **lexical entry** for the word in the lexicon of the language.

A procedure for deriving the actual form of the words in English sentences would be one that replaces a sequence such as *will* + Past by the realization specified for the past tense form of *will* in the lexical entry of *will*. This is a relatively trivial matter and need not concern us very much, but it is useful to point out that there are things about English sentences that are not predictable (and, hence, not general phenomena that may be captured by transformations) but nevertheless must be part of any complete description of the native speaker's knowledge. The phenomenon discussed here is an instance of what is often referred to as **morphology** (from the Latin *morph-* 'shape'), and the part of the lexicon that handles morphology is referred to as the **morphology component** of the grammar. Its function, in essence, is to specify what shape words take when they are modified by affixes.

Various theoretical problems arise when one entertains the possibility that there are linguistic phenomena that could be described either by the morphology component or by transformations. In such a case, we must then investigate which of the two alternatives affords us the greater degree of descriptive adequacy.

SYNTACTIC FEATURES

Thus far, we have treated transitive and intransitive verbs as two different categories. Given that they are two different categories, we would expect each to have properties that the other does not. However, there is only *one* property that the two categories do not share: that of taking a direct object in the verb phrase. Otherwise, transitive and intransitive verbs appear to be identical, as the traditional terminology **verb** suggests.

In order to represent the similarity between these two categories, we could revise our analysis of the verbs and put all verbs into the category Verb, or V. The phrase structure rule for expansion of VP would then take the following form:

$$VP \rightarrow V \ (NP)$$

Note that this is a simplification of our previous analysis of the VP, which required two phrase structure rules, i.e. :

$$VP \rightarrow V_T \ NP$$
$$VP \rightarrow V_I$$

Because of this simplification and because of the virtual identity of the two types of verb, this revision is a desirable step.

However, the proposed revision raises a new problem. There is nothing in the new analysis that prevents intransitive verbs from appearing with direct objects, or transitive verbs from appearing without direct objects:

(3.40)   a. *Seven days elapsed the week.
               b. *Mary hit.

To help solve this problem, we introduce the notation of **syntactic features.** Intuitively, a **feature** represents a property of a constituent or a lexical item. In the particular case under consideration here, we wish to establish a feature that distinguishes the verbs that have the property of taking a direct object from those that do not have this property.

Let **TRANS** mean "taking a direct object," and let + mean "has the property of." If we associate [+**TRANS**] with a lexical item, we mean that this lexical item has the property of taking a direct object. By comparison, we can indicate intransitive verbs by associating with them the feature [−**TRANS**], where − means "lacks the property of."

In order to generate only grammatical sentences, it will be necessary to formulate the lexical insertion so that it inserts verbs that are [+TRANS] when there is a direct object, and verbs that are [−TRANS] when there is not. This can be represented formally, but there is no need to do so here. A more detailed discussion of the representation of properties of verbs appears in Chapter 9.

Notice that the function of syntactic features can be viewed as that of dividing a category up into smaller categories in this case. For the transitive and intransitive verbs, we have simply given a name to the set consisting of both types of verbs and renamed the transitive verbs [+TRANS] and the intransitive verbs [−TRANS].

But there is no reason why a feature should apply only to members of a a single category. Recall that for the statement of Affix Hopping we made up the name VE for the category of elements to which affixes may attach. This category consists of all of the verbs, the auxiliary verbs, and the modals. Intuitively, each of these three categories has a common property, that of being a *verbal* category as opposed to a *nominal* category such as N. To represent this common feature, we may replace the made-up category name VE by a syntactic feature, e.g., [+V]; this feature is possessed by all lexical items in each of the categories just noted. The revised form of Affix Hopping is, then, the following:

AFFIX HOPPING: X Affix [+V] Y
$$\quad\quad\quad\quad 1 \quad\; 2 \quad\;\; 3 \quad\; 4 \Rightarrow 1\; \emptyset \; \# \; 3 + 2 \; \# \; 4$$

The term [+V] in the structural description refers to any constituent of the tree with the feature [+V].

As we will see in later chapters, the modals and the auxiliary verbs share properties that distinguish them from the true verbs. We cannot say that the modals and the auxiliary verbs are a lexical category, however, since the modals are a separate category themselves, and the auxiliary verbs are members of the category V. One solution is to establish a new feature, say [+AUX], that is associated with all of the modals and the auxiliary verbs, but not with the verbs. In the lexicon, then, there will be lexical items with various combinations of features in different categories, as illustrated by Table 3.6.

Table 3.6.   Some Features of Selected Lexical Items

Lexical item	Category	Features
hit	V	+ V, + TRANS, − AUX
sleep	V	+ V, − TRANS, − AUX
will	M	+ V, − TRANS, + AUX
have	V	+ V, + TRANS, + AUX
have en	V	+ V, − TRANS, + AUX
book	N	− V

Table 3.6 is intended to be illustrative and not definitive. Note that the *have* of *have a book* is listed separately from *have en* ; both have the property [+AUX] for reasons that will become clear in Chapter 4. *Book* has only the feature [−V]; it is not necessary to specify the values of TRANS and AUX, since these are relevant only to lexical items that are [+V].

The conventional notation for referring to a member of category A that has the feature [+F] is $\begin{bmatrix} A \\ +F \end{bmatrix}$. To refer to a constituent with two features, say, [+F] and [+G], that we wish to specify, we write $\begin{bmatrix} +F \\ +G \end{bmatrix}$. These notations can be extended to cases involving more features in the obvious way:

$$\begin{bmatrix} A \\ +F \\ -G \\ +H \\ \vdots \end{bmatrix}; \quad \begin{bmatrix} +F \\ +G \\ -H \\ \vdots \end{bmatrix}.$$

The use of syntactic features is widespread in generative grammar. It would be impossible to give here even a sketchy summary of the uses to which they have been put and the problems that they create. The reader is referred to the works mentioned at the end of this chapter for further reading on the subject.

It is important to point out, however, that features must be used prudently. If a difference between two sets of lexical items or two sets of constituents can be found, this does not automatically mean that the difference is due to a feature. It might in fact be due to the internal structure of the constituents concerned. Features should be used only when there is no apparent explanation for a well-established difference, or when it is impossible to establish natural categories (such as N, V, etc.) without missing clear generalizations.

SUMMARY

We began by looking at a collection of linguistic data of English, namely, the verbal sequences, and asked what in fact a possible verbal sequence looks like. Each verbal sequence can be assigned an analysis in terms of verbal elements and a restricted set of markers, and different markers are associated with different verbal elements in the verbal sequences.

We saw that there are regularities, and that these regularities cannot be captured (or stated) in terms of phrase structure rules alone. While a phrase structure rule can be defined to capture regularities about the relative order of the verbal elements M, *have*, *be*, and the verb, a transformation is required to capture regularities about the relative positions of the affixes, TENSE, *en*, and *ing*. A notational system was developed in which the function of transformations can be expressed, and a terminology was introduced for referring to transformations and their functions.

To conclude, the phrase structure rules and transformations that have thus far been established are listed in the following section.

SUMMARY OF RULES

Phrase Structure Rules

PSR1: S   → NP AUX VP
PSR2: AUX → TENSE (M) (*have en*) (*be ing*)
PSR3: VP   → V (NP)
PSR4: NP   → $\begin{Bmatrix} \text{ART (ADJ) N} \\ \text{PN} \end{Bmatrix}$

Transformations

AFFIX HOPPING: X Affix [+V] Y
                 1   2   3   4 ⇒ 1 $\emptyset$ # 3 + 2 # 4

EXERCISES

1. For each of the following sentences, first give the deep structure as specified by phrase structure rules PSR1–PSR4 (see the Summary of rules), and then show how the rule of Affix Hopping applies to the terminal string of each of these structures to give the surface string of thr sentence :

   a. *John likes Mary.*
   b. *John has seen Naples.*
   c. *The plumber could have fixed the faucet.*
   d. *John has been reading the newspaper.*
   e. *A fat man will be eating the pie.*
   f. *John must have been speaking French.*
   g. *John has a cold.*
   h. *Mary could have stopped the elevator.*
   i. *Sincerity admires John.*
   j. *Green ideas could bother you.*

2. For each of the following strings [corresponding to the ungrammatical examples in (3.3) in the text], show with a bottom-up procedure that the grammar containing rules PSR1–PSR4 does not generate them :

   a. **John* Pres *be* Pres *have en write.*
   b. **John* Pres *have will ing write.*
   c. **John* Pres *will* Past *write.*
   d. **John* Pres *have be write.*
   e. **John* Past *will will write.*
   f. **John* Past *have* Pres *write.*
   g. **John* Pres *will* Pres *be ing write.*

3. Consider the following phrase marker :

   a.

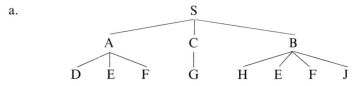

Apply each of the following transformations to this phrase marker and show the output. Each output should be a phrase marker, T1, T2, etc. are the names of the transformations, and not all of the transformations need be applicable.

   T1: X C B
      1 2 3 ⟹ 1 ∅ 3 + 2
   T2: X D E Y
      1 2 3 4 ⟹ 1 3 + 2 ∅ 4
   T3: X A F Y
      1 2 3 4 ⟹ 1 ∅ 3 + 2 4

T4: X   A   Y   F   Z
     1   2   3   4   5 $\Rightarrow$ 1 $\emptyset$ 3 4 + 2 5
T5: X   C   B
     1   2   3 $\Rightarrow$ 1 $\emptyset$ 3
T6: X   C   E   Y
     1   2   3   4 $\Rightarrow$ 1 2 $\emptyset$ 4 + 3

4. Translate each of the following transformations into the formal notation developed in this chapter:

a. Move a constituent with the feature [+F] to the front of the sentence and sister-adjoin it to a leftmost constituent A.

b. Sister-adjoin an ADJ to an N if the ADJ immediately follows the N and is itself immediately followed by nothing.

c. Sister-adjoin an NP to the right of a V that is somewhere to the right of it.

d. Delete an affix that is between two members of the category V and adjacent to both of them.

e. Insert an ADV after a V if the V is transitive but not followed by anything in the phrase marker.

f. Interchange the positions of an A and a B when the A precedes the B and the B precedes a C.

SUGGESTED FURTHER READINGS

The Verbal Sequence

Bach, E. (1967), "Have and be in English syntax," *Language* **43**, 462–485.

Burt, M. K. (1971), *From Deep to Surface Structure,* Harper, New York.

Chomsky, N. (1957), *Syntactic Structures,* Mouton, The Hague.

Edmonds, J. E. (1970), *Root and Structure Preserving Transformations,* unpublished ditto, Indiana University Linguistics Club. Bloomington, Indiana.

Labov, W. (1969), "Contraction, deletion and the inherent variability of the English copula," *Language* **45**, 715–762.

Ross, J. R. (1969c), "Auxiliaries as main verbs," in Todd, W., ed., (1969), *Studies in Philosophical Linguistics* (Series 1), Great Expectations Press, Carbondale, Ill.

Basic English Phrase Structure

Burt (1971).

Chomsky (1957).

Chomsky, N. (1964d), "A transformational approach to syntax," in Fodor, J. A. and Katz, J. J., eds., (1964), *The Structure of Language: Readings in the Philosophy of Language,* Prentice-Hall, Englewood Cliffs, N. J.

Lees, R. (1960), *The Grammar of English Nominalizations,* Mouton, The Hague.

Stockwell, R., Schachter, P. & Partee, B. (1973), *The Major Syntactic Structures of English,* Holt, New York.

Features

Chomsky, N. (1965), *Aspects of the Theory of Syntax*, MIT Press, New York.

Chomsky, N. (1970a), "Remarks on nominalizations," in Jacobs, R. & Rosenbaum, P., eds., (1970), *Readings in English Transformational Grammar*, Ginn (Blaisdell), Boston, Mass.

Lakoff, G. (1970a), *Irregularity in Syntax*, Holt, New York.

Ross, J. R. (1969d), "Adjectives as main verbs," in Reibel, D. and Schane, S. A., eds., (1969), *Modern Studies in English*, Prentice-Hall, Englewood Cliffs, N. J.

4

Questions

YES–NO QUESTIONS

Let us extend the scope of our inquiry to include English questions. One particular type of question is called a **yes–no question.** since it requires an answer of either *yes* or *no*. Some typical yes–no questions are exemplified in (4.1):

(4.1)
a. *Does John write?*
b. *Did John write?*
c. *Has John written?*
d. *Had John written?*
e. *Is John writing?*
f. *Was John writing?*
g. *Will John write?*
h. *Would John write?*
i. *Has John been writing?*
j. *Had John been writing?*
k. *Will John be writing?*
l. *Would John be writing?*
m. *Will John have written?*
n. *Would John have written?*
o. *Will John have been writing?*
p. *Would John have been writing?*

In view of the task of providing a descriptively adequate grammar of English, it is again necessary to determine whether there are any regularities present in this body of data. That is, can any sequence of English words be a yes–no question, or are there some constraints on what a yes–no question may look like?

In (4.1c–4.1p), there are several restrictions on the relative order of verbal elements in the sequence: The verb always comes last, the modal always comes first, and *have* always precedes *be*. This is an important observation, since it reveals that the relative order of verbal elements in yes–no questions is precisely that given by the expansion of the constituent AUX by PSR1 and PSR2.

PSR1: S   → NP AUX VP
PSR2: AUX → TENSE (M) (*have en*) (*be ing*)

Furthermore, the restriction on the occurrence of the markers *en* and *ing* as expressed by PSR2 is also met by all of the examples in (4.1): *en* is present if and only if *have* is present, and *ing* is present if and only if *be* is present. In fact, the actual position of these markers can be accounted for if it is assumed that Affix Hopping applies to yes–no questions. That is, in most of the examples in (4.1) *ing* appears on the element to the right of *be* and *en* appears on the element to the right of *have*. However, in (4.1c–f), (4.1i), and (4.1j) there is a noun phrase between the verbal element with which the affix is associated in PSR2 and the verbal element to which the affix is attached in the surface string. So it is clear that some work will be necessary before we can arrive at a precise and inclusive description of what constitutes a grammatical yes–no question in English.

The surface structures of the sentences in (4.1) can be represented in terms of the verbal elements and markers established in Chapter 3. This will form the basis for a formulation of the data from which an analysis of yes–no questions can be developed:

(4.2)   a. *# do +* Pres *# John write*
      b. *# do +* Past *# John write*
      c. *# have +* Pres *# John # write + en #*
      d. *# have +* Past *# John # write + en #*
      e. *# be +* Pres *# John # write + ing #*
      f. *# be +* Past *# John # write + ing #*
      g. *# will +* Pres *# John write*
      h. *# will +* Past *# John write*
      i. *# have +* Pres *# John # be + en # # write + ing #*
      j. *# have +* Past *# John # be + en # # write + ing #*
      k. *# will +* Pres *# John be # write + ing #*
      l. *# will +* Past *# John be # write + ing #*
      m. *# will +* Pres *# John have # write + en #*
      n. *# will +* Past *# John have # write + en #*

o. *# will + Pres # John have # be + en # # write + ing #*
p. *# will + Past # John have # be + en # # write + ing #*

It is quite clear that the grammar as it is now formulated will not generate the sentences of (4.1), since it will not yield the corresponding structures whose terminal strings appear in (4.2). Can a descriptively adequate account of these new data be provided in terms of phrase structure rules? It turns out that it is impossible to write a phrase structure rule that will generate just those sequences exemplified in (4.2) that does not actually list each possible sequence. Such a list, of course, does not define what form a yes–no question must take but merely mentions the possible forms that have been encountered.

It will be useful for purposes of illustration to see just what are the problems of stating a phrase structure rule for the sequences in (4.2). Assume for the sake of illustration that *do* is a member of the category M. Then, in a yes–no question the first two elements of the sequence are always M, *have*, or *be* with TENSE attached. Since TENSE is attached by the rule of Affix Hopping, it can be assumed here that the underlying structures for these sentences contain the sequence TENSE M, TENSE *have*, or TENSE *be*. Thus, a phrase structure rule for generating yes–no questions will look something like (4.3):

(4.3)
$$S \rightarrow \text{TENSE} \begin{Bmatrix} \text{M} \\ \textit{have} \\ \textit{be} \end{Bmatrix} \cdots$$

Observe that an NP follows this sequence and there is a verb at the end of the sentence. Since verbs are introduced as constituents of VP, rule (4.3) can be refined as follows:

(4.4)
$$S \rightarrow \text{TENSE} \begin{Bmatrix} \text{M} \\ \textit{have} \\ \textit{be} \end{Bmatrix} \text{NP VP}$$

At this point, some difficulties arise. In (4.2), when the sequence *be* + TENSE begins the sentence the verb has the marker *ing* attached to it, and when the sequence *have* + TENSE begins the sentence the verb has the marker *en* attached to it. Since Affix Hopping will attach an affix to the verb if it precedes the verb in the deep structure, we might hypothesize that the phrase structure rule should look like (4.5) rather than (4.4):

(4.5)
$$S \rightarrow \text{TENSE} \begin{Bmatrix} \text{M} \\ \textit{have} \\ \textit{be} \end{Bmatrix} \text{NP} \begin{Bmatrix} \textit{en} \\ \textit{ing} \end{Bmatrix} \text{VP}$$

The difficulty here is that rule (4.5) does not say which affix must appear. For example, it does not say that *en* must not appear if *be* is selected in the expansion of S by rule (4.5), and that *ing* must not appear if *have* is selected:

(4.6)   a. *Is John written?

                            b. *Has John writing?

Since *en* occurs if and only if *have* is present and *ing* occurs if and only if *be* is present, rule (4.5) makes a wrong prediction about what sequences are grammatical English yes–no questions.

Observe also that when *have* precedes the NP it is possible for *be* to follow it, as in (4.2i) and (4.2j). Similarly, when M precedes the NP it is possible for *have*, *be*, or *have* followed by *be* to follow the NP. Thus, in order for the rule to even begin to account for the grammatical sequences it will have to be revised to include sequences of verbal elements after the NP.

Recall that AUX expands as a sequence of verbal elements. However, rule (4.5) cannot be revised as (4.7) or (4.8) by the inclusion of AUX:

(4.7)
$$ S \rightarrow TENSE \begin{Bmatrix} M \\ have \\ be \end{Bmatrix} NP\ AUX\ VP $$

(4.8)
$$ S \rightarrow TENSE \begin{Bmatrix} M \\ have \\ be \end{Bmatrix} NP\ PRED $$

$$ PRED \rightarrow AUX\ VP $$

The inadequacy of either formulation is due to the fact that the expansion of AUX itself permits sequences that involve M, *have*, and *be*, and also obligatorily involves TENSE. So, for example, suppose that S is expanded as TENSE M NP AUX VP. Then AUX may be expanded as TENSE M, yielding a structure such as the one in (4.9):

(4.9)

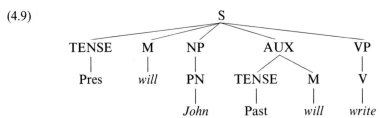

The realization of (4.9) is the ungrammatical *Will John would write?* Similar combinations of expansions of S according to (4.7) or (4.8) and the available expansions of AUX already established will yield a large number of ungrammatical examples of this type.

What actually is the problem here? To put it simply, there is a *generalization* about what constitutes a grammatical yes–no question that the hypothesized rules fail to capture. In essence, the generalization is as follows: A yes–no question looks just like a declarative sentence as far as the relative order of verbal elements and markers goes. The difference is that TENSE and the first verbal element in the sequence *precede* the subject NP in the yes–no question and follow it in the declarative. A phrase structure rule for yes–no questions must somehow guarantee that this regularity will be preserved. In addition, such a formulation must also capture the facts about the co-occurrence of *have* and *en* and of *be* and *ing*.

This generalization cannot be captured, however, unless the verbal elements are generated as constituents of a single node. This is the only way the restrictions on the relative order of the verbal elements can be maintained, and it is the only way the verbal elements can be associated with the correct markers.

These considerations demand a type of rule that is different from a phrase structure rule. In particular, a transformational analysis of yes–no questions will capture the observed regularities of yes–no questions in an elegant and revealing fashion.[1]

This analysis will make use of a transformation that applies to substantially the same deep structure that we have established for declaratives, i.e., with the order of constituents NP AUX VP. Its function is to move TENSE and the first verbal element into a position before the subject NP.

A TRANSFORMATIONAL ANALYSIS

To review, there are three generalizations that an analysis of yes–no questions should capture:

1. In yes–no questions, the sequence of elements that precedes the subject NP consists of TENSE attached to a verbal element—M, *have*, or *be*.

2. If the presence of the subject NP is ignored, the sequence before and after the NP has precisely the appearance of an expansion of AUX followed by a verb phrase.

3. The affixes in a yes–no question appear precisely where they would appear if Affix Hopping had applied everywhere in the sentence, including the sequence that precedes the subject NP.

Consider the cases in which the modal *do* does not appear, namely, (4.2c–p). The relationship between these structures and the deep structures that are provided by the phrase structure rules is that TENSE and the first verbal element in the verbal sequence appear before the subject NP. Thus, a tentative statement of the transformation, called Inversion, is the following.

---

[1] Strictly speaking, it is possible to provide a phrase structure account of the phenomena under discussion here by increasing the power of the phrase structure rules. This requires a change in phrase structure rules so that they may mention the context in which the node to be expanded is found. Such phrase structure rules are called **context-sensitive.**

In those cases in which context-sensitive phrase structure rules appear to be workable alternatives to transformations, it can be shown that the latter capture generalizations that the former do not. Thus, it is argued, context-sensitive phrase structure rules are superfluous and need not be included in the theory of grammar. A typical argument of this sort will be given in Chapter 5.

INVERSION: NP   TENSE [+V]   X

1   2   3 ⇒ 2 1 3

It can be seen that this transformation captures quite succinctly the three generalizations that we have just noted. It derives yes–no questions from essentially the same deep structure as that of the declarative, so that the relative order of verbal elements will be the same in the two types of sentences. It moves the first verbal element and TENSE to a position before the subject NP, which captures a general characteristic of yes–no questions. Finally, it does not affect the relative order of affixes in the verbal sequence and, hence, captures the generalization that the attachment of affixes will be precisely the same in yes–no questions and declaratives.

This formulation of the rule immediately leads to a counterexample. Suppose that the input to the rule had as its terminal string (4.10):

(4.10)   *John*   Past   *write*
                             NP   TENSE   [+V]   X
                             1   2   3

Since this sequence meets the structural description of Inversion, the rule should apply, yielding as its output (4.11):

(4.11)   Past   *write*   *John*
                             TENSE   [+V]   NP   X
                                 2   1   3

This would be realized, after Affix Hopping, as the ungrammatical **Wrote John?* Therefore, Inversion must be revised in some way.

As it is now stated, Inversion will derive all of the sentences listed in (4.1) with the exception of (4.1a), *Does John write?*, and (4.1b), *Did John write?*

It is important to note here that (4.1a) and (4.1b) are in fact the grammatical questions corresponding to the statements *John writes* and *John wrote*. And these examples are just the cases that constitute counterexamples to our rule of Inversion. Both of these facts will be simultaneously explained if we assume that the examples without superficial modals contain a modal *do* in their deep structures. Their derivations would have the form given in (4.12):

(4.12) $John \begin{Bmatrix} Pres \\ Past \end{Bmatrix} do\ write \Rightarrow \#\ do + \begin{Bmatrix} Pres \\ Past \end{Bmatrix} \#\ John\ write$

This proposal deserves further discussion, for it apparently destroys the parallelism between questions and declarative sentences: Declarative sentences (such as *John wrote*) are *not* required to contain a modal. A solution to this problem will be provided in a more detailed discussion of the modal *do* in the next section.

Let us assume for the present, then, that the deep structure of a yes–no question always contains *do* if it has no other modal. The rule of Inversion can now be stated in such a way that it moves TENSE followed by the first member of the verbal sequence (that is, M, *have*, or *be*) to a position preceding the subject NP. A particularly elegant statement of Inversion is achieved given the assumption that the sequence of TENSE followed by the first member of the verbal sequence is in fact a single constituent of the sentence. Inversion can then be stated so as to apply to this constituent, and there is no need to specify the internal structure of the sequence moved by the transformation. This assumption will be justified in Chapter 5 on the basis of general theoretical considerations.

This analysis requires the following phrase structure rules for the expansion of S, VP, and AUX.

> PSR1: S   → NP AUX VP
> PSR2: AUX → TENSE M
> PSR3: VP   → (*have en*) (*be ing*) V (NP).

Notice that the difference between these rules and those established in Chapter 3 is that here the elements *have en* and *be ing* are optional constituents of VP rather than of AUX. We have also revised the rule for expanding AUX (PSR2) so that now the category M is an obligatory category in the deep structure of every sentence, rather than an optional one. The modal that underlies sentences that lack a superficial modal is *do*. Justification for this assumption will be developed in the following section.

The rule of Inversion now moves the single constituent AUX, which dominates TENSE M.

INVERSION: NP AUX X
                   1   2   3 ⇒ 2 + 1 ∅ 3

This statement of Inversion raises a number of problems involving *do*, to which we now proceed.

DO DELETION AND *DO* REPLACEMENT

The assumption that *do* is present in deep structures as a member of the category M requires a specification of the crucial difference between cases in which *do* appears and cases in which it does not appear. Observe, for instance, that *do* must appear when Inversion applies, and that it does not appear when Inversion does not apply. Consider the underlying string in (4.13):

(4.13)   *John* Past *do smile*

If Inversion applies to (4.13), it yields (4.14):

(4.14)   Past *do John smile*

In (4.13), *do* must be deleted (if it is unstressed), and in (4.14) it cannot be deleted. This suggests that the crucial difference is whether or not *do* precedes a verb: *do* is deleted before a verb. The statement of *Do* Deletion is as follows.

Do DELETION: X *do* V Y
                 1 2 3 4 $\Rightarrow$ 1 $\emptyset$ 3 4
                 Condition: 2 is unstressed.

(The deletion of an element is indicated by replacing the number corresponding to it in the structural description by $\emptyset$ in the structural change.) If *Do* Deletion applies after Inversion, then *Do* Deletion will not apply in yes–no questions and will apply in declaratives as desired. This is due to the fact that prior application of Inversion removes the structural conditions for the application of *Do* Deletion.[2]

The assumption that *do* is present in deep structures as a member of the category M also requires certain other adjustments in the grammar. Most significantly, *do* never appears before *have* or *be* regardless of whether the sentence is a declarative or a question:

(4.15)   a. *Did John $\begin{Bmatrix} have\ left? \\ be\ leaving? \end{Bmatrix}$

                    b. *John did $\begin{Bmatrix} have\ left. \\ be\ leaving. \end{Bmatrix}$

This problem interacts with the statement of Inversion in the following way. Since Inversion precedes *Do* Deletion, Inversion will always yield sequences like (4.15a) and *Do* Deletion then will not apply. Hence, it is impossible to express the fact that *do* never precedes *have* or *be* by applying *Do* Deletion.

On the other hand, when Inversion applies to sentences containing *have* or *be* it treats these elements as though they were members of the category M:

(4.16)   *Will John leave?*
                            Has John left?
                            Is John leaving?

It is clear, however, that *have* and *be* are not modals, since no sentence can have

---

[2] A more detailed discussion of rule ordering appears in Chapter 5. As can be seen, the question of how rules may or must be ordered is an important one, since a grammar containing certain rules can be descriptively adequate given one method of ordering the rules and not descriptively adequate given an alternative method. To preview our later discussion somewhat, we will find that while there are some rules that need not be ordered with respect to one another, there are some pairs of rules whose relative order of application must be specified in the grammar.

more than one modal, and *have* and *be* can follow modals (e.g., *John will have left*).

Both of these problems can be solved by stating a transformation that replaces *do* by the first instance of *have* or *be* that follows it. Since *do* is a constituent of AUX, replacement of *do* by *have* or *be* will have the result that *have* or *be* will then be treated as a constituent of AUX and will undergo Inversion. This rule of *Do* Replacement is stated as follows, and its application is illustrated in (4.17).[3]

Do REPLACEMENT:

$$X \; do \; \begin{Bmatrix} have \\ be \end{Bmatrix} \; Y$$

$$1 \quad 2 \qquad 3 \qquad 4 \Rightarrow 1 \; 3 \; \emptyset \; 4$$

(4.17)   a.

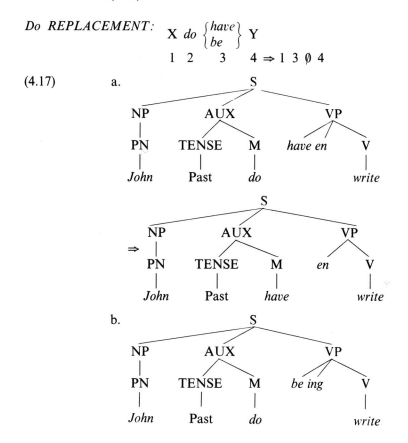

---

[3] The analysis of the auxiliary that involves *Do* Replacement was first discussed in Emonds (1970), following a suggestion by Klima. Emonds also pointed out a number of advantages of the rule as compared with previously proposed analyses. See the discussion in Chapter 5 for a comparison of *Do* Replacement and the more traditional *Do* Support analysis.

Notice also that in some dialects of English the rule does not apply to *have* when *have* functions as a main verb. If the rule applied to all *have*s all of the time, it would be impossible to derive sentences like *Does John have a cold?* (see Problem 2).

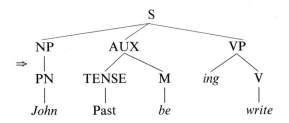

Wh QUESTIONS

A discussion of yes–no questions could lead quite naturally into a variety of other topics. For the sake of completeness, we continue by considering another type of question, called the **wh question.** Some examples of *wh* questions are given in (4.18):

(4.18)
    a. *What did John see?*
    b. *Who did John meet?*
    c. *Where did John buy the yogurt?*
    d. *When did John meet Mary?*
    e. *Why did John slam the door?*
    f. *How does John spell his name?*
    g. *Which books did John buy?*
    h. *What books did John buy?*
    i. *Which does John like?*

A characteristic of *wh* questions is that they are introduced by *what, who, where, when, why, how,* and *which.* It is also apparent that the rule of Inversion applies in *wh* questions. In addition, the presence of the *wh* word (namely, *what, who, where,* etc.) at the beginning of the sentence and the application of Inversion are intimately connected: The sentences are ungrammatical if Inversion does not apply:

(4.19)
    a. **What John saw?*
    b. **Who John met?*
    c. **Where John bought the yogurt?*
    d. **Where John met Mary?*
    e. **Why John slammed the door?*
    f. **How John spells his name?*
    g. **Which books John bought?*
    h. **What books John bought?*
    i. **Which John likes?*

On the other hand, if Inversion applies and the *wh* word is not at the beginning of the sentence, the resulting sequence is ungrammatical:

(4.20)   a. *Did John see what?

                                    b. *Did John meet who?

                                    c. *Did John buy the yogurt where?

                                    d. *Did John meet Mary where?

                                    e. *Did John slam the door why?

                                    f. *Does John spell his name how?

                                    g. *Did John buy which books?

                                    h. *Did John buy what books?

                                    i. *Does John like which?

These examples show quite clearly that there is an interaction in *wh* questions between Inversion and the presence of the *wh* word in sentence-initial position. In Chapter 2 it was established that a descriptively adequate account of *wh* questions involving *what* requires a transformation that moves *what* into sentence-initial position. We will call this transformation *Wh* Fronting. It is possible in light of these two observations to guarantee that Inversion will apply in *wh* questions.[4] Inversion applies when there is a sentence-initial *wh* word.

---

[4] It is possible to make the ungrammatical sentences in (4.20) acceptable by radically changing the intonation. Let us indicate a rising intonation by ↑. There are contexts in which a sentence like (i) is appropriate:

    a. *Did John see what ↑?*

In general, if the hearer does not quite catch all of a speaker's utterance, the hearer may "echo" the speaker's utterance, replacing the unclear portion(s) with an interrogative. Thus, (i) might be a response to *Did John see (unclear)?*

Questions of this sort are called **echo questions.** Echo questions are far less restricted syntactically than normal questions. We have noted that it is not necessary to apply *Wh* Fronting in an echo question. Nor is it necessary to apply Inversion unless there is a fronted *wh* word:

    b. *John saw what ↑?*

    c. **What ↑ John saw?*

    d. *What ↑ did John see?*

In fact, in an echo question it is possible to use *what* as a replacement for an unclear verb phrase. (v) is an appropriate response to *John (unclear)*:

    e. *John what ↑?*

The relative unrestrictedness of echo questions makes it unprofitable to attempt to integrate them into the analysis of the more usual type of questions considered here. Furthermore, while normal questions can be discussed without making substantial reference to the contextual factors that may or must be involved in their use, the analysis of echo questions is much more closely tied to considerations of language use and human social interaction. Such considerations take the study of echo questions outside the scope of this text.

A first approximation to the statement of *Wh* Fronting is as follows:

Wh FRONTING:

$$X \left\{ \begin{array}{l} \textit{what} \\ \textit{who} \\ \textit{when} \\ \textit{where} \\ \textit{why} \\ \textit{how} \\ \textit{which} \end{array} \right\} Y$$

$$1 \qquad 2 \qquad 3 \Rightarrow 2 + 1 \; \emptyset \; 3$$

This rule will have the function of moving all the *wh* words to the front of any sentences that contain them.[5] However, there are a number of things wrong with it as stated. For one thing, if the underlying string is as given in (4.21a), it will derive (together with Inversion) the ungrammatical (4.21b) instead of (4.21c):

(4.21) a. *John* Past *do buy which books?*
  b. **Which did John buy books?*
  c. *Which books did John buy?*

That is, this rule of *Wh* Fronting simply states that the *wh* word is moved to the front, and says nothing about moving the entire noun phrase *which books* in (4.21a). Clearly, then, some revision is required.

In addition, since the rule is stated in terms of a list of elements, it provides no understanding of what it is about these elements that makes them all subject to the rule. The rule does not distinguish whether the list mentioned is somehow systematic, or whether it is simply an accident that all seven of these words happen to behave in the same way with respect to *Wh* Fronting. This, too, should lead to a revision of the rule.

It is reasonable to make the assumption that all of the *wh* words share some deep structure marker in common. If this assumption can be justified, then it will permit the *Wh* Fronting transformation to be revised in such a way that it makes reference only to the element that the *wh* words have in common, and not the entire list of words themselves. Assume, therefore, that the marker *Wh* is a constituent of NP, and that it is introduced by the following phrase structure rule.

$$\text{PSR5}': \text{NP} \rightarrow \textit{Wh} + \cdots$$

[5] A commonly held assumption in transformational grammar is that both the *wh* questions and the yes–no questions contain an underlying abstract marker Q. This marker appears in sentence-initial position in deep structures, serves as a condition for Inversion and *Wh* Fronting, and participates in the semantic interpretation of the sentence. In particular, it indicates to the semantic component that the deep structure in which it appears is in fact that of an interrogative.

There does not appear to be any compelling purely syntactic evidence in favor of assuming the existence of this abstract marker, however. For further discussion of Q, see the "Suggested Further Readings" at the end of this chapter.

It can also be established that the marker *Wh* is attached to NPs that contain *some*. Thus, for example, the underlying representation of *what* is *Wh* + *something*, the underlying representation of *who* is *Wh* + *someone*, the underlying representation of *where* is *Wh* + *someplace*, and so on. Similarly, the underlying representation of *which* book as *Wh* + *some book*. By a variety of arguments, it can be established that the expansion of NP that yields underlying representations of *wh* words is the following:

$$\text{PSR5}': \text{NP} \rightarrow Wh + some \ (\text{ADJ}) \ \text{N}$$

This analysis will be assumed for the remainder of this discussion. A revision of it, as well as arguments that support it, are given in the next Section.

It is now possible to state *Wh* Fronting in terms of the marker *Wh*.

Wh FRONTING: X NP Y
                 1   2   3 $\Rightarrow$ 2 + 1 $\emptyset$ 3
                 Condition: 2 dominates *Wh*.

In general, whenever we state a rule we must determine that it does not generate ungrammatical sentences, and that it generates all of the sentences that we intend it to generate. The rule of *Wh* Fronting provides a nice illustration of the interaction between the rule and the data.

It is possible to construct English NPs that dominate NP. Some examples follow:

(4.22)   a. $_{\text{NP}}$[*the brother of* $_{\text{NP}}$[*Susan*]]
              b. $_{\text{NP}}$[*the height of* $_{\text{NP}}$[*the building*]]
              c. $_{\text{NP}}$[*the cover of* $_{\text{NP}}$[*the book*]]
              d. $_{\text{NP}}$[*the solution to* $_{\text{NP}}$[*the problem*]]

Suppose that we replace *Susan, the building, the book*, and *the problem* in the preceding examples by *wh* words. We will then have *two* NPs to which *Wh* Fronting could apply equally well, according to the statement of the rule given earlier:

(4.23)

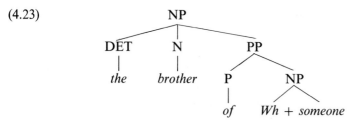

In fact, this prediction is correct, as shown by the following examples:

(4.24)   a. **John met the brother of whom?*
              b. *Who did John meet the brother of?*
              c. *The brother of whom did John meet?*

(4.25)   a. *They measured the height of what.
                b. What did they measure the height of?
                c. The height of what did they measure?

and so on. In this respect, then, the evidence provides confirmation that our statement of the rule is fundamentally correct.

There are, however, examples that *Wh* Fronting cannot account for:

(4.26)   a. Who did you give the books to?
                b. To whom did you give the books?

The rule as stated will generate (4.26a), but it fails to generate the equally grammatical (4.26b).

The sequence *to whom* is in fact a constituent of the sentence. However, even though it appears to have been moved by *Wh* Fronting in (4.26b), it is not an NP but a **prepositional phrase,** or PP. The structure of PP is given by PSR6.

$$\text{PSR6: PP} \rightarrow \text{P NP}$$

(P signifies the category **preposition,** which includes elements such as *to, in, for, at, on,* etc.)

Thus, a revised version of *Wh* Fronting must permit the movement of either an NP that dominates *Wh* or a PP that contains such an NP.

Wh FRONTING: $X \begin{Bmatrix} PP \\ NP \end{Bmatrix} Y$
$$1 \quad 2 \quad 3 \Rightarrow 2 + 1 \ \emptyset \ 3$$

Condition: 2 dominates *Wh*.

THE DEEP STRUCTURE OF *Wh* WORDS

Notice first of all that there is a paraphrase for each of the *wh* words of the form *what person, at what place,* and so on. Thus, for example, the first six sentences of (4.19) correspond to those in (4.27):

(4.27)   a. What thing did John see?
                b. What person did John meet?
                c. (At) what place did John buy the yogurt?
                d. At what time did John meet Mary?
                e. For what reason did John slam the door?
                f. In what way does John spell his name?

The paraphrases given in (4.27) make it clear that the *wh* words function as phrases under certain circumstances. One case of single words that function as noun phases is that of proper nouns. There is another set of words that also function as noun phrases, namely, the **pronouns**—*he, she, it,* etc. Pronouns are not nouns, since it is impossible to replace nouns by pronouns while maintaining the grammaticality of the sequence:

(4.28)
$$The \ (fat) \begin{Bmatrix} man \\ *he \end{Bmatrix} spoke \ to \ me \ about \ Mary.$$

(Hence, pronouns are not really pro-"nouns" but pro-"noun phrases.")

By the same token, *what* and *who* may be viewed as pronouns in that they function as noun phrases and, like pronouns, do not refer to the same person or thing in every sentence in which they appear. The difference between *what* and *who*, on the one hand, and *it* and *him*, on the other (for example), is that the *wh* words, since they are used in questions, not only have no fixed reference but cannot have reference established by prior context; in fact, they presuppose that the reference has not been established. This is their function in *wh* questions. The *wh* words are therefore **interrogative pronouns.**

We have assumed that there is a marker *Wh* that serves to distinguish between interrogative pronouns, on the one hand, and referential pronouns, on the other. The difference between interrogative pronouns and other kinds of pronouns will be that the former class have this marker in their underlying representation in deep structures.

The similarity between the *wh* words may be represented in terms of the marker *Wh*. Thus, the underlying representations of *what* and *who* are of the form *Wh* + PRO, where PRO represents a pronoun of some form that is different for the two *wh* words *what* and *who*. A question to deal with now is what the form of this pronoun might be.

This pronoun is *something* in the case of *what* and is *someone* in the case of *who*. The argument to support this rests on three observations concerning the similarity in behavior between the *wh* words, on the one hand, and the pronouns beginning with *some-*, on the other.

One observation concerns the fact that the word *else* may appear after a noun phrase only when (i) that noun phrase is of the type *someone, something,* etc. or (ii) that noun phrase is a *wh* word. To see this, consider the following examples:

(4.29)
　　　a.　*John was looking for* $\begin{Bmatrix} someone \\ something \end{Bmatrix}$ *else.*

　　　b.　$\begin{Bmatrix} Who \\ What \end{Bmatrix}$ *else was John looking for?*

　　　c.　**John was looking for the* $\begin{Bmatrix} man \\ book \end{Bmatrix}$ *else.*

　　　　　*John was looking for a $\begin{Bmatrix} man \\ book \end{Bmatrix}$ *else.*

　　　　　*John was looking for some $\begin{Bmatrix} man \\ book \end{Bmatrix}$ *else.*

If this restriction on the occurrence of *else* after noun phrases is noted for *someone, something,* etc., then it will automatically apply to *who* and *what* as well if they are analyzed as underlying *Wh + someone* and *Wh + something,* respectively.

The second observation concerns the fact that the word *some* may be used in two ways: The phrase *some books* may refer to a random set of books, as in *Give me some books, please,* or it may refer to a particular set of books that the speaker has in mind, as in *Some books make me very angry.* The distinction may be noted in actual speech, in which the first use of *some* may be indicated by reduced stress on *some* (as in *Give me s'm books, please*) while the second use may not be so indicated (e.g., **S'm books make me very angry*). The un-reduced *some* may also indicate a random set, so that there are two uses of the unreduced *some* but only one use of the reduced *some.*

Now, this difference corresponds precisely to the difference between *What did you see?* and *Which did you see?* or to the difference between *What books did you buy?* and *Which books did you buy?* When *what* is used the speaker either may or may not have a particular set from which the answer is to be selected, while when *which* is used the speaker certainly must have a particular set in mind. If the unreduced version of *some* is called *some₁* and the second version *some₂*, then the difference between *what* and *which* can be expressed in terms of underlying *Wh + some₁* and *Wh + some₂*, respectively.

The last observation has to do with sentences with existential *there.* As the following examples show, only indefinite noun phrases may appear after *there is/there are.*[6]

(4.30)   *There is a man in the room.*
                There are some men in the room.
                There are three tall women on the team.
                There is some ketchup on your tie.

(4.31)   **There is the man in the room.*
                *There are those men in the room.
                *There are the three tall women on the team.
                *There is the old ketchup on your tie.

A more extensive discussion of *there* sentences appears in Chapter 9. Here it is sufficient to note that *wh* words may also appear in *there* sentences, showing that they are indefinites:

(4.32)   *Who is there in the room?*
                How many tall women are there on the team?
                What kind of ketchup is there on my tie?

This follows automatically if *wh* words are derived from underlying *some.*

[6] Sentences such as these should be contrasted with enumeration *there* sentences, which do permit definite noun phrases:

a. *"Name all of the great emperors."* *"Well, **there's** Julius Caesar, Augustus, the one who burned down Rome . . . ."*

A preliminary hypothesis, then, is that there are rules that realize *Wh +
someone* as *who* and *Wh + something* as *what* or *which*. This hypothesis fails
to account for those cases in which *what* and *which* immediately precede a
noun, as in (4.33):

(4.33)   *What books did John buy?*
                       Which books did John buy?

The failure of the hypothesis is due in this case to the fact that it is impossible
to have a pronoun of the form *something* immediately before a noun in examples
parallel to (4.33). Thus, there is no source from which (4.33) could have been
derived:

(4.34)   **John bought something books.*

We can show, however, that the occurrence of *what* and *which* both as independent pronouns and as constituents of noun phrases [as in (4.33)] is predictable from more general facts about noun phrases that contain *some*. The
internal structure of the noun phrase is considered in detail in Chapter 8; here
we will consider only those characteristics that are directly relevant to the *wh*
words.

The word *some* is a member of the category **quantifier.** Other members of
this category are *all, each, every, any, few,* and *many*. Because of the fact that
the syntactic properties of some quantifiers are not shared by all of the others,
it may very well be the case that quantifier is not a true syntactic category, but
simply a traditional informal one. The variations among quantifiers are illustrated by the following examples:

(4.35)   a.   *all of the books*
                            some of the books
                            each of the books
                            *every of the books
                            few of the books

                       b.   **all one(s) of the books*
                            *some one(s) of the books
                            each one of the books
                            every one of the books
                            *few ones of the books

                       c.   *all the books*
                            *some the books
                            *each the books
                            *every the books
                            *few the books

d. *the all books
    *the some books
    *the each books
    *the every books
    the few books

Thus, quite possibly there are several syntactic categories containing several of the quantifiers each, and no category that contains all of them.

Since we are concerned particularly with *some*, let us assume for the sake of the analysis that there is a category QUAN that contains at least *some*. The examples in (4.35c) and (4.35d) show that *some* and the definite article *the* cannot cooccur in the sequence at the beginning of the NP. Hence, either QUAN and ART are in fact the same category, or there is a nonlexical category DET that expands either as QUAN or as ART but not as a sequence of the two. The latter alternative is the one that is traditionally adopted, and we will adopt it here, again for the sake of the analysis and not because we have demonstrated that it is necessarily correct.

The expansion of NP will, thus, be given by the following rules.

$$\text{PSR4: NP} \rightarrow \left\{ \begin{array}{l} \text{DET (ADJ) N} \\ \text{PN} \end{array} \right\}$$

$$\text{PSR5: DET} \rightarrow \left\{ \begin{array}{l} (Wh) \text{ QUAN} \\ \text{ART} \end{array} \right\}$$

From this point, the analysis becomes somewhat complicated. To summarize in advance, it will be shown that there are two different *ones* in English that are used pronominally. The instances of *which* and *what* with no following noun are derived by deletion of the general pronominal *one* by a transformation that is motivated on independent grounds. The other *one* is not deleted, and is incorporated into *someone*, *everyone*, etc.

Consider first (4.36):

(4.36)   *Mary has a cat and I have a cat also.*

In this example, the phrase *a cat* appears twice. Notice that it does not refer to the same cat in both instances, but to different cats. Under such circumstances, it is possible to paraphrase the second instance of the phrase by *one*:

(4.37)   *Mary has a cat and I have one also.*

This phenomenon will be described in detail in Chapter 8. The transformation that will be established there, and will be assumed here, is called *One* **Substitution.**

Examples such as (4.38) show that One Substitution replaces a noun with *one* when it is identical to another noun in the sentence. That is, the rule does not apply to noun phrases:

(4.38)

$$Mary\ has\ a\ gray\ cat\ and\ I\ have\ a\ red \begin{Bmatrix} cat. \\ one. \end{Bmatrix}$$

Examples such as (4.39) show that *one* cannot appear immediately after a number or after the quantifier *some*:

(4.39)

$$Mary\ has\ a\ gray\ cat \begin{cases} and\ I\ have\ some\ cats. \\ *and\ I\ have\ some\ ones. \\ and\ I\ have\ two\ cats. \\ *and\ I\ have\ two\ ones. \\ and\ I\ have\ some. \\ and\ I\ have\ two. \end{cases}$$

The essential point to be noted here is that nothing appears where we would expect *one* when *some* or a number precedes the noun position.

This suggests that we can explain the distributional properties of *what* and *which* by deriving them from *Wh* + *some one(s)*. However, notice that while *one(s)* can never appear after *some*, it may appear after *which*, as in *which one(s)*.

Another problem with this suggestion is that it does not permit forms such as *someone*, given that there is a rule that prevents *one(s)* from immediately following *some*. But obviously, forms such as *someone* cannot be ruled out by the grammar, since they exist in the language.

The way out of these difficulties to be proposed here is to differentiate between a number of different *ones*. Notice, along these lines, that *someone* must be used to indicate a person, while in those expressions where *some* and *one* appear separately, e.g., *some red ones*, this restriction does not hold. Let us assume, therefore, that one *one* means "person" and the other is a general pronoun. We will distinguish the two with the feature **GEN**, for "general," where the person *one* has the feature [−GEN] and the pronominal *one* has the feature [+GEN]. It is the latter that is deleted after quantifiers and the former that is incorporated with *some* to form *someone*.

This type of distinction can be extended to account for other cases that we have not yet considered. For example, notice that there is a difference between the *body* that can be used in *somebody* and the *body* that means the physical substance of an organism:

(4.40) a. *The body of a cow was hanging in the butcher shop.*
Somebody of a cow was hanging in the butcher shop.

b. *Some bodies of cattle were hanging in the butcher shop.*
Somebodies of cattle were hanging in the butcher shop.

c. *We encountered somebody strange in the castle.*
We encountered some body strange in the castle.
We encountered some strange body in the castle.

Similar distinctions can be drawn between the various uses of nouns like *place*, *thing*, and *time*:

(4.41)   a.   *We went to someplace cold.*
                                 **We went to some place cold.*
                                 **We went to a place cold.*
                                 We went to a cold place.
                                 We went to some cold place.

                          b.   *John said something stupid.*
                                 **John said some thing stupid.*
                                 **John said a thing stupid.*
                                 John said a stupid thing.
                                 John said some stupid thing.

                          c.   **We have sometime extra.*
                                 **We have some time extra.*
                                 **We have time extra.*
                                 We have extra time.
                                 We have some extra time.

The evidence shows that each of these words has two functions.

However, the situation with *body*, *time*, *place*, and *thing* is somewhat different from the situation with *one*. We saw that *one* functions either as a general pronoun or as a more specific class name. On the other hand, a word such as *body* functions either as a specific class name (as in *somebody*) or as a common noun (as in *some bodies*). The latter distinction will be indicated by another feature, that of PRO, for "pronoun." The feature GEN will be applicable only to items that are [+PRO]. The features of the various items considered here are given in Figure 4.1.

By categorizing these words with the features PRO and GEN, we are able to account for a number of shared properties of the words in each sub-class. First, words marked $\begin{bmatrix} +\text{PRO} \\ -\text{GEN} \end{bmatrix}$ combine with *some*, as noted. Second, they combine with *no*, *any*, and *every* to form *no one*, *anyone*, *everyone*; *nothing*, *anything*, *everything*; etc. Third, they are the only words in the language that permit single adjectives to appear to the right of them, e.g.:

(4.42)   a.   *something interesting*
                                 **a thing interesting*
                                 **the thing interesting*

                          b.   *someplace nice*
                                 **a place nice*
                                 **the place nice*

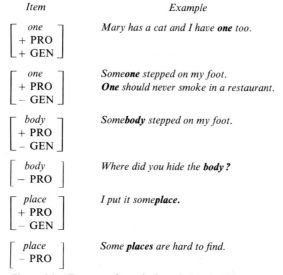

Item	Example

$\begin{bmatrix} one \\ + \text{PRO} \\ + \text{GEN} \end{bmatrix}$ *Mary has a cat and I have* **one** *too.*

$\begin{bmatrix} one \\ + \text{PRO} \\ - \text{GEN} \end{bmatrix}$ *Some***one** *stepped on my foot.*
One *should never smoke in a restaurant.*

$\begin{bmatrix} body \\ + \text{PRO} \\ - \text{GEN} \end{bmatrix}$ *Some***body** *stepped on my foot.*

$\begin{bmatrix} body \\ - \text{PRO} \end{bmatrix}$ *Where did you hide the* **body** *?*

$\begin{bmatrix} place \\ + \text{PRO} \\ - \text{GEN} \end{bmatrix}$ *I put it some***place.**

$\begin{bmatrix} place \\ - \text{PRO} \end{bmatrix}$ *Some* **places** *are hard to find.*

Figure 4.1. Features of *one*, *body* and *place* in different uses.

c. *someone happy*
*a person happy
*the one happy

d. *sometime soon*
*a time soon
*the time soon

Sequences such as *something interesting* are derived from sequences such as *some interesting thing* by a transformation that moves adjectives over nouns that are $\begin{bmatrix} + \text{PRO} \\ - \text{GEN} \end{bmatrix}$.

Fourth, as noted earlier, only the nouns that are $\begin{bmatrix} + \text{PRO} \\ - \text{GEN} \end{bmatrix}$ permit *else* to the right of them. This applies as well to most combinations with *no*, *any*, or *every*:

(4.43)
a. *someone else*
someplace else
somebody else
something else
?sometime else

b. *no one else*
noplace else

> *nobody else*
> *nothing else*
> *no time else
> *never else

c. *anyone else*
   anyplace else
   anybody else
   anything else
   ?*anytime else*

d. *everyone else*
   everywhere else
   everybody else
   everything else
   *everytime else

A plausible way to account for this is to derive *else* obligatorily from *other* when *other* appears in final position in the noun phrase. Notice that the only time *other* can appear after the noun is when it is followed by something:

(4.44)   a. *I was talking to someone other **than Mary.***
              **I was talking to someone other.*

          b. *We want to go to someplace other than New York.*
              **We want to go to someplace other.*

The movement of *other* to the right of the noun is due to the transformation that moves adjectives to the right of nouns that are $\begin{bmatrix} +\text{PRO} \\ -\text{GEN} \end{bmatrix}$, discussed in connection with the examples in (4.42). Then another, minor transformation changes *other* to *else* just in case it is the rightmost constituent in the noun phrase.

   Let us proceed now to the derivation of the *wh* words. As we have seen, each of the words *one, thing, place,* and *time* has two distinct feature representations. Since *Wh* is a constituent of NP, it may appear in NPs that contain either of the two forms of each word. For *one,* then, we will have both of the following NPs, depending on which form of *one* appears:

(4.45)

a. *Wh some* $\begin{bmatrix} one \\ +\text{PRO} \\ +\text{GEN} \end{bmatrix}$

b. *Wh some* $\begin{bmatrix} one \\ +\text{PRO} \\ -\text{GEN} \end{bmatrix}$

We have shown that there is a transformation that incorporates *some* and a word that is $\begin{bmatrix} +\text{PRO} \\ -\text{GEN} \end{bmatrix}$. This transformation will apply only to the sequence in (4.45b), yielding the following:

(4.46)
$$Wh \;\#\; some \;+\; \begin{bmatrix} one \\ +\text{PRO} \\ -\text{GEN} \end{bmatrix} \#$$

The intuition that *someone* is a single word is represented here by placing $\#$ in the appropriate places in the sequence.

Notice, now, that the difference between (4.46) and (4.45a) is that *some* is an independent constituent in the latter but not in the former. This difference can be used to determine the precise realization of the various sequences as *wh* words. We let *Wh some* be realized as *which* or *what;* this is applicable only to sequences in which *some* has not been incorporated. The same realization will apply to sequences like *Wh some book* to derive *which book/what book*.

For those cases in which *some* has been incorporated, there will be other realization rules that will yield the other *wh* words. Thus, *Wh # someone #* will be realized as *who*, *Wh # something #* as *what*, *Wh # sometime #* as *when*, and so on. The situation is complicated slightly by the fact that there must be realizations not simply for *wh* words but for prepositional phrases that contain *wh* words, e.g.:

(4.47) a. *John is leaving* **at some time.**
        b. *When is John leaving?*
        c. **When is John leaving at?*

(4.48) a. *Mary left* **for some reason.**
        b. *For what reason did Mary leave?*
          Why did Mary leave?
        c. *?What reason did Mary leave for?*
          *Why did Mary leave for?

Thus, it will be necessary to specify that *at Wh some time* is realized as *when*, *for Wh some reason* is realized as *why*, and so on.

SUMMARY

There are four transformations that, taken together, serve to characterize the set of grammatical yes–no and *wh* question in English: Inversion, *Wh* Fronting, *Do* Replacement, and *Do* Deletion. The first captures the generalization that the sequence of verbal elements in questions is identical to that in declarative sentences, the only difference being that in the former case part of the verbal sequence appears before the subject NP. The second captures the generalization that the *wh* word appears in sentence-initial position regardless of its syntactic function in the sentence. The last two transformations are required to account for the distribution of *do* in questions and in declaratives. In addition, a number of morphological rules are required in order to achieve the correct surface realization of the *wh* words.

There are a number of important theoretical issues that we did not consider in this chapter, and they are discussed at length in Chapter 5. Of particular importance is the question of rule ordering, which plays a central role in syntactic description. A number of other issues can be most effectively discussed in the context of a comparison between the analyses established here and possible alternatives to them; this is also taken up in Chapter 5. One aspect of the analysis in this chapter that has theoretical significance beyond the actual syntactic description is the decision to separate the verbal sequence into two parts, one appearing in the constituent AUX and the other appearing in the constituent VP. Another is the decision to treat the nonappearance of *do* in certain contexts as a case of deletion rather than as a case of insertion in complementary contexts. A third is the relationship between syntactic and semantic representation.

The next section consists of a list of the phrase structure rules and transformations established thus far. It should be pointed out that since the question of rule ordering has not yet been considered, several of the transformations do not appear in their final form at this point.

SUMMARY OF RULES

Phrase Structure Rules

PSR1: S   → NP AUX VP
PSR2: AUX → TENSE M
PSR3: VP   → (*have en*) (*be ing*) V (NP)
PSR4: NP   → $\left\{ \begin{array}{l} \text{DET (ADJ) N} \\ \text{PN} \end{array} \right\}$
PSR5: DET → $\left\{ \begin{array}{l} (Wh) \text{ QUAN} \\ \text{ART} \end{array} \right\}$
PSR6: PP   → P NP

Transformations

Affix Hopping: X Affix [+V] Y
                  1   2   3   4 $\Rightarrow$ 1 $\emptyset$ # 3 + 2 # 4

Inversion: NP AUX X
                  1   2   3 $\Rightarrow$ 2 + 1 $\emptyset$ 3

Do Deletion: X *do* V Y

1 2 3 4 $\Rightarrow$ 1 $\emptyset$ 3 4

Condition: 2 is unstressed

Do Replacement: X *do* $\left\{ \begin{array}{c} have \\ be \end{array} \right\}$ Y

1 2   3   4 $\Rightarrow$ 1 3 $\emptyset$ 4

Wh Fronting: X $\left\{ \begin{array}{c} PP \\ NP \end{array} \right\}$ Y

1   2   3 $\Rightarrow$ 2 + 1 $\emptyset$ 3

Condition: 2 dominates *Wh*

EXERCISES

1. Derive each of the following sentences in terms of the rules given in the Summary of Rules. First indicate the deep structure, and then give the output of each transformation that must apply. Assume that the order of transformations is as follows:

> *Do* Replacement
> Inversion
> *Do* Deletion
> Affix Hopping

  a. *Is John smiling?*
  b. *Would the police have caught Mary?*
  c. *Have the swallows destroyed Capistrano?*
  d. *Did Mary find the peanut butter?*

2. Show the derivation of the following sentences as in Exercise 1 (assume that *Wh* Fronting precedes Inversion and that Inversion applies to the output of *Wh* Fronting):

  a. *What did John see?*
  b. *Which books did John buy?*
  c. *Why did John slam the door?*
  d. *When did John meet Mary?*

For these examples, assume that the deep structure representation of *why* is PP[*for Wh some reason*] and that of *when* is PP[*at Wh some time*].

PROBLEMS

*1. Try to find some other instances where *Do* Deletion does not apply but Inversion is not involved. Are such cases consistent with the current analysis? Why?

2. Consider the rule of *Do* Replacement. Observe that it makes no particular reference to the fact that the *have* involved is the one that governs the affix *en* or that the *be* involved is the one that governs the affix *ing*. Therefore, if *Do* Replacement is a correct transformation, it makes the prediction that it will also apply to any instances of *have* or *be* that do not govern these affixes. (i) Find cases of *have* and *be* that do not govern affixes. (ii) Does *Do* Replacement apply in any or all of these? Give illustrations to support your answers.

3. Notice that the sequence (*Wh*) QUAN may appear in any noun phrase independently of whether it appears in any other in the same sentence. What prediction does this aspect of the analysis make? Does this analysis appear to be correct or incorrect? Why?

4. In the discussion of the deep structure of *Wh* words (pp. 76–85), three transformations are stated informally. One combines *some, no, any,* and *every* with certain nouns; one permutes adjectives to the right of these nouns, and one rewrites *other* as *else* in NP-final position. (i) Provide a formal statement for each of these transformations. (ii) Determine the order in which these transformations must apply so as to derive all of the relevant sequences, and give the linguistic data that support your answer.

SUGGESTED FURTHER READINGS

Questions

Bach, E. (1971), "Questions," *LI,* **2,** 153–166.

Baker, C. L. (1970), "Notes on the desctiption of English questions: The role of an abstract question morpheme," *FL,* **6,** 197–219.

Bresnan, J. (1972), *Theory of Complementation in English Syntax,* Unpublished doctoral dissertation, MIT, Cambridge, Mass.

Katz, J. J. & Postal, P. (1964), An integrated Theory of Linguistic Description, MIT Press, Cambridge, Mass.

Klima, E. S. (1964), "Negation in English," in Fodor, J. A. & Katz, J. J., eds., (1964), *The Structure of Language: Readings in the Philosophy of Language,* Prentice-Hall, Englewood Cliffs, N. J.

Kuno, S. & Robinson, J. (1972), "Multiple wh questions," *LI,* **3,** 463–488.

Pope, E. (1971), "Answers to yes-no questions," *LI,* **2,** 69–82.

Do Deletion and Do Replacement

Emonds, J. E. (1970), *Root and Structure Preserving Transformations,* unpublished ditto, Indiana University Linguistics Club, Bloomington, Indiana.

Do Support

Klima (1964).

Q

Baker (1970).

Bresnan (1972).

Langacker, R. (1974), "The question of Q," *FL,* **11,** 1–37.

5

Aspects of
a Theory of Grammar

INTRODUCTION

The process of devising rules for describing natural language often raises more questions than it answers. The kinds of questions that arise out of the attempt to provide a detailed description of linguistic phenomena are often of considerable theoretical importance. Given the kinds of transformations permitted by the theory of grammar, on what basis is one account of a linguistic phenomenon to be chosen over another? How are transformations to be constrained so that they will be able to perform only the kinds of operations required by natural languages? Given that languages have transformations, how should the ordering of transformations in general be dealt with in the theory of grammar?

In the preceding chapters, we have been engaged in constructing a precise description of certain aspects of English syntax. In doing so, we have had to make a number of general decisions concerning the types of operations that are possible transformational operations, the conditions under which such operations may apply, and the order in which such operations may apply. In principle, it is possible that these decisions are peculiar to English and that for other languages different answers will have to be provided to the questions dealing with possible transformations, possible orderings, and so on. It is important to note that linguists have hypothesized that these answers will *not* differ significantly from language to language. Rather, it is claimed that it is possible to construct a universal theory of grammar that will specify quite precisely what a grammar of a natural language may consist of.

This chapter is concerned with a number of theoretical questions that arise from the description given in the preceding chapters. First we examine the notion of rule ordering in detail, and present an ordering and restatement of some of the transformations established in Chapter 4. Then we compare two alternative analysis of *do* and arrive at a constraint on the statement of transformations such that the more preferable of the two alternatives is automatically selected by the theory of grammar.

SOME NOTIONS OF RULE ORDERING

Consider a phrase marker and a transformation. To review briefly, the structural description of the transformation specifies a particular set of conditions that the phrase marker must meet. If the phrase marker satisfies these conditions, then it is said to meet the structural description of the transformation. Under such circumstances, the transformation either may or must apply to the phrase marker, depending on whether the transformation is **optional** or **obligatory.** (Until now, all of the transformations that we have considered have been obligatory. Some optional transformations are discussed in Chapters 6–10.)

Given a deep structure and a sentence, the grammar provides a **derivation** of that sentence if there are rules in the grammar that, when applied in some precise way to this structure, yield as a consequence the surface structure that corresponds to the sentence. Thus, to say that the grammar **generates** the sentence is to say that the grammar **provides a derivation** of the sentence.

It is logically possible that all the transformations involved in the derivation of a sentence apply simultaneously to the deep structure. Alternatively, it is possible that some transformations apply to the output of other transformations. In the former case, the derivation can be expressed as a pair of phrase markers such that the first is the deep structure and the second is the surface structure. In the latter case, the derivation must be expressed as a **sequence** of phrase markers such that the first member of the sequence is the deep structure, the last is the surface structure, and each intermediate member of the sequence is related to the one that precedes it by a transformation. Call such phrase markers **intermediate phrase markers.**

If a theory of grammar is formulated so that a particular method of applying transformations is employed, this will define the notion of a *possible human language* differently than another procedure for applying transformations. Since a theory of grammar must provide a precise formulation of what a human language can be, this question of rule ordering must be seriously examined.

It turns out that it makes a difference how the transformations are applied. Several abstract examples will serve to illustrate this point before actual linguistic data are once again considered. Assume the following set of rules, some of which are phrase structure rules and some of which are transformations. The phrase structure rules provide a characterization of what structures the transformations may apply to; the transformations characterize the relationships between deep and surface structures.

$$\text{PSR:} \quad S \rightarrow M\ A\ (B)\ C$$

$$\text{T1:} \quad \underset{1 \quad 2 \quad 3}{M\ A\ \underbrace{(B)\ C}} \Rightarrow 2\ 1\ 3$$

$$\text{T2:} \quad \underset{1 \qquad 2 \quad 3}{X\ \underbrace{A}\ \begin{Bmatrix} M \\ B \end{Bmatrix}\ C} \Rightarrow 1\ 2\ \emptyset$$

Rule T1 says that A and M are permuted when A precedes either C or B C. Rule T2 says that C is deleted if it follows X A M or X A B. There are a number of logically possible ways in which these transformations can be applied to the possible structures given by PSR. Part a of Table 5.1 shows the derivations when T1 must apply before T2; part b shows the derivations when T2 must apply before T1; part c illustrates what happens when both transformations apply simultaneously but only once in a derivation; and part d illustrates what happens when both transformations apply simultaneously but as many times as possible.

If this set of rules is a grammar of a "language" and each of the nodes M, A, B, and C is a terminal node with a lexical item attached to it, then in each case a different set of sentences is generated by the same grammar depending on the order in which the rules are applied. This can be seen in Table 5.1, where the resulting strings are different in each of the four cases.

Observe, now, that it is possible to construct an example that gives the *illusion* of rule ordering without actually requiring that any ordering of the rules be explicitly specified. Consider the following sample grammar.

$$\text{PSR:} \quad S \rightarrow (M)\ A\ B$$

$$\text{T1:} \quad \underset{1 \quad 2 \quad 3}{X\ A\ B} \Rightarrow 1\ 2\ \emptyset$$

$$\text{T2:} \quad \underset{1 \quad 2 \quad 3}{M\ A\ X} \Rightarrow 2\ 1\ 3$$

Part a of Table 5.2 shows what happens when the transformations are applied in the order T1, T2. Part b shows what happens when the transformations are applied simultaneously and only once each.

Certain set of rules will generate precisely the same language with the rules whether they are applied in order or simultaneously once. This does not mean

Table 5.1.   Results of Applying Transformations (a) in the Order T1, T2,
(b) in the Order T2, T1, (c) Simultaneously Once, and (d) Simultaneously
More Than Once

a.	Possible underlying sequence:	M A B C	M A C
	Apply T1:	A M B C	A M C
	Apply T2:	—	A M
	Resulting string:	A M B C	A M
b.	Possible underlying sequence:	M A B C	M A C
	Apply T2:	M A B	—
	Apply T1:	—	A M C
	Resulting string:	M A B	A M C
c.	Possible underlying sequence:	M A B C	M A C
	Apply T1 and T2 simultaneously:	A M B	A M C
		(both	(T1
		apply)	applies)
	Resulting string:	A M B	A M C
d.	Possible underlying sequence:	M A B C	M A C
	Apply T1 and T2 simultaneously:	A M B	A M C
		(both	(T1
		apply)	applies)
	Apply T1 and T2 simultaneously:	—	A M
			(T2
			applies)
	Resulting string:	A M B	A M

Table 5.2.   Result of (a) Applying Rules in a Certain Order and (b)
Applying the Same Rules Simultaneously Only Once

a.	Possible underlying sequence:	M A B	A B
	Apply T1:	M A	A
	Apply T2:	A M	—
	Resulting string:	A M	A
b.	Possible underlying sequence:	M A B	A B
	Apply T1 and T2 simultaneously:	A M	A

that every set of rules, that is, every grammar, has this feature, but simply that one must consider the fact that what appears to be rule ordering in a certain domain of the language may in fact be expressible in terms of a single simultaneous application of all the rules. It is logically possible that what looks like ordering between, say, three transformations may be expressible by a series of simultaneous applications of all of the rules at once. Consider, for example, the following grammar.

$$\text{PSR:} \quad S \rightarrow M\ A \begin{Bmatrix} B \\ C \end{Bmatrix}$$

T1:   M A B
       1 2 3 $\Rightarrow$ 2 1 3

T2:   M A C
       1 2 3 $\Rightarrow$ 1 3 2

T3:   M C X
       1 2 3 $\Rightarrow$ $\emptyset$ 2 3

Part a of Table 5.3 illustrates the results of applying these rules in the order given, while part b illustrates the result of applying these rules simultaneously as many times as they can apply. Notice that the reason for the identical results is that at any given time only one rule can apply; that is, each output structure meets the structural description of only one rule at a time. Thus, it makes no difference whether the rules are explicitly ordered or not.

Table 5.3. Result of (a) Applying Three Rules in Order and (b) Applying All Simultaneously Until None Can Apply

a.	Possible underlying sequence:	M A B	M A C
	Apply T1:	A M B	—
	Apply T2:	—	M C A
	Resulting string:	A M B	C A
b.	Possible underlying sequence:	M A B	M A C
	Apply all rules at once:	A M B (T1 applies)	—
	Apply all rules at once:	—	M C A (T2 applies)
	Apply all rules at once:	—	C A (T3 applies)

The case in which the ordering of the transformations must be explicitly specified is called **extrinsic ordering,** and the case in which the ordering is a consequence of the way in which the rules are stated is called **intrinsic ordering.**[1] Table 5.1 illustrates several instances of extrinsic ordering, while the example given in part b of Table 5.3 shows an instance of intrinsic ordering. To summarize briefly, intrinsic ordering results when the rules are stated in such a way that only one can apply at a time even when we attempt to apply all simultaneously. Extrinsic ordering requires an explicit statement about how

---

[1] The question of whether rules have to be explicitly (i.e., extrinsically) ordered was originally raised with respect to phonological rules in the work of Koutsoudas and others at Indiana University. The question has been investigated significantly less in syntax to date. See Ringen (1972) and Koutsoudas (1973).

the rules are to be applied. In principle, the task of a linguist is to determine what the method of applying transformations is for natural language. In practice, the question is a rather complex one, and not all of the logical alternatives will be pursued in this book.

The problem of rule ordering would not be as difficult as it actually is if we were given the rules and the sentences of a language simultaneously and asked to determine the ordering of the rules. But the linguist (or the child) is given the sentences only,[2] and the task is made more complex by the need to hypothesize the rules *and* their ordering simultaneously. As we will see, different orderings will lead to different statements of the rules; some formulations of the rules may be more revealing than others, and will suggest that the rule ordering that led us to them is to be preferred over orderings that require more complex and less revealing formulations.

A PRELIMINARY RULE ORDERING

Consider, now, the relative ordering of two of the transformations established thus far. *Do* Deletion must apply before the rule of Affix Hopping, given the current statement of both rules.

$$\begin{array}{llll} Do\ DELETION: & \text{X} \quad do \quad \text{V} \quad \text{Y} \\ & 1 \quad 2 \quad 3 \quad 4 \Rightarrow 1 \ \emptyset \ 3 \ 4 \\ & \text{Condition: 2 is unstressed} \end{array}$$

$$\begin{array}{llll} AFFIX\ HOPPING: & \text{X} \quad \text{Affix} \quad [+\text{V}] \quad \text{Y} \\ & 1 \quad 2 \quad 3 \quad 4 \Rightarrow 1 \ \emptyset \ \# \ 3 + 2 \ \# \ 4 \end{array}$$

We can show that Affix Hopping must not apply before *Do* Deletion. Taking a typical underlying sequence, we find that if Affix Hopping precedes *Do* Deletion, there are grammatical sentences that cannot be generated.

Consider the string in (5.1):

(5.1)   *John* Past *do smile*

The structural description of *Do* Deletion specifies that unstressed *do* is deleted when *do* immediately precedes a verb. If Affix Hopping applied *before Do* Deletion, then the structural description of *Do* Deletion would never be met. Thus, we would never be able to generate *John smiled* and would generate only **John did smile* with unstressed *do*.

Suppose, on the other hand, that *Do* Deletion precedes Affix Hopping. If *do* is unstressed, (indicated by *dŏ*) then *Do* Deletion applies, giving in the end the derivation illustrated in (5.2a). If *do* is stressed, (indicated by *dó*) then *Do*

---

[2] The child has an advantage over the linguist, actually. The child has a theory of grammar built in. The linguist, not knowing what the theory of grammar looks like, is obliged to consider logically possible alternatives that the child's innate theory automatically rules out.

Deletion cannot apply, and the derivation that results is shown in (5.2b). By comparison, the single derivation possible with Affix Hopping ordered before *Do* Deletion is (5.2c):

(5.2) a. Input   *John* Past *dŏ smile*
      Do Deletion *John* Past ∅ *smile*
      Affix Hopping *John # smile + Past #*
           "John smiled."
    b. Input   *John* Past *dó smile*
      Do Deletion — (cannot apply)
      Affix Hopping *John # dó + Past # smile*
           *"John **did** smile."*
    c. Input   *John* Past *dŏ smile*
      Affix Hopping *John # dŏ + Past # smile*
      Do Deletion — (cannot apply)
           *"*John dĭd smile."*

Notice with respect to (5.2c) that we could preserve this ordering and prevent the grammar from generating the ungrammatical sentence that contains unstressed *do* before the verb (i.e., **John dĭd smile*) by stating a rule to stress *do* before a verb if it is not already stressed. As can be seen, this rule is not particularly convincing, because its function is not to capture a generalization but to save a weak analysis. Furthermore, even this addition will not permit the grammar to derive the grammatical *John smiled* with the ordering shown in (5.2c).

Given that the statements of the two rules are correct, then, it is clear that one ordering is greatly preferred over the other on grounds of descriptive adequacy.

There are, however, additional alternatives that must be considered. As noted earlier, in most cases it is not only necessary to investigate which of two possible orderings of two rules is more descriptively adequate; it is also necessary to determine whether there is an alternative formulation of the rules that is consistent with the less preferred ordering and is also more elegant than the original formulation of the rules. In addition, it is also possible that rules may apply simultaneously. To illustrate what is involved, let us first consider what changes will be required if we try to maintain the hypothesis that *Do* Deletion is strictly ordered *after* Affix Hopping.

Clearly, what is required is that when Affix Hopping applies it does not automatically block *Do* Deletion. Thus, we must restate *Do* Deletion so that it can apply to the output of Affix Hopping. As the derivation given in (5.2c) shows, the output of Affix Hopping is *John # do + Past # smile*. What we must end up with is *John # smile + Past #*. This suggests the following three options:

1. *Do* Deletion moves *smile* into the position occupied by *do*, as illustrated in Figure 5.1a.

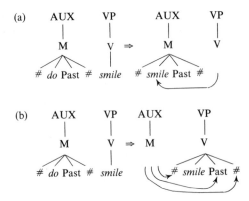

Figure 5.1. Alternative reformulations of *Do* Deletion.

2. *Do* Deletion deletes *do* and at the same time hops the affix onto the verb *smile*, as illustrated in Figure 5.1b.
3. *Do* Deletion deletes *do* and there is a second application of Affix Hopping that moves the affix onto the verb.

Each of these three options has different consequences that must be weighed carefully. The first option employs the following statement of *Do* Deletion.

Do DELETION (i):   X # *do* TENSE # V Y
  1 2 3   4   5 6 7 ⟹ 1 2 6 4 5 ∅ 7

Notice that this rule is intrinsically ordered after Affix Hopping: Even if we tried to apply both rules simultaneously, Affix Hopping would have to apply before the structural description of *Do* Deletion (i) can be met. This follows simply from the fact that the structural description of *Do* Deletion mentions the output of Affix Hopping.

We must now consider whether this formulation of *Do* Deletion in fact captures any generalizations that our original formulation does not. This is important, because the original formulation requires extrinsic ordering, while this formulation does not require extrinsic ordering. Thus, if extrinsic ordering is to be ruled out of the theory of grammar, it should be possible to show that the alternative formulation involving intrinsic ordering leads to a simpler statement of the rules and captures greater generalizations.

Interestingly, the formulation of *Do* Deletion (i) fails to capture a generalization that our original formulation captures. As can be seen, *Do* Deletion (i) moves the verb in such a way that it becomes a constituent of AUX. In sentences in which *Do* Deletion (i) does not apply, such as sentences with modals other than *do* (e.g., *John will smile*), the verb remains a constituent of the verb phrase. The claim of *Do* Deletion (i) is that the derived structure of *John smiled* and *John will smile* is radically different. There is no evidence that this claim is a correct one.

The second option does not suffer from this difficulty. In this case, *Do* Deletion takes the following form.

Do DELETION (ii):   X   #   *do*   TENSE   #   V   Y
               1   2   3   4   5   6   7 $\Rightarrow$ 1 $\emptyset$ $\emptyset$ $\emptyset$ $\emptyset$ $\emptyset$ 2 6 + 4 5 7

The argument against this formulation of *Do* Deletion is that of the two operations it performs, one, the movement of the affix onto the verb, is the same operation that is performed by Affix Hopping. This is an undesirable redundancy in the grammar, which can easily be removed if the ordering is *Do* Deletion, Affix Hopping. *Do* Deletion (ii) has to hop the affix only because of the particular rule ordering Affix Hopping, *Do* Deletion.

It should also be pointed out that in this case, as in the case of the first option, the rules as stated are intrinsically ordered. Again, this suggests that at least in certain cases the requirement that rules apply in order and that the ordering be intrinsic does not lead to the most elegant characterization of the data.

The third option is considerably different from the first two. Here we suppose that once a transformation has applied it may apply later to the same sentence if its structural description is met again. This is quite a radical departure from a theory that specifies that a rule may apply only once to any given sentence, although in a number of places at one time. So far as is known, there are no indications that such a departure is necessary, with the exception of the present case. Since there already exists a satisfactory formulation of *Do* Deletion and Affix Hopping such that the two rules apply in order, and only once to any given sentence, there does not appear to be any reason to adopt the alternative demanded by the third option.

To summarize to this point, we have shown that requiring transformations to apply in order and, furthermore, requiring that they be intrinsically ordered will not lead to more revealing descriptions in every case. The original formulation of *Do* Deletion and Affix Hopping in which the ordering is extrinsic is the one that appears to achieve the greatest level of generalization.

As noted in the preceding section, there is also the possibility that transformations apply simultaneously. It was shown that it is possible to construct sets of transformations that are intrinsically ordered when all transformations are applied simultaneously, and only once each. It is also possible to construct sets of transformations that are intrinsically ordered when all applications are done simultaneously until no transformation can apply.

Given the original statements of *Do* Deletion and Affix Hopping, it is not possible to apply the transformations simultaneously and once each. When the structural description of one is met, so is the structural description of the other, so that no ordering will automatically emerge if rules are applied more than once. It is not possible to actually perform both operations simultaneously because *Do* Deletion deletes the element that the affix is to be attached to by Affix Hopping. The notion of simultaneous application is somewhat ill-defined under such a circumstance, and so this case does not fall within the scope of the simpler states of affairs discussed in the preceding section. To deal with it adequately would require a more extensive digression than is possible here.

It should be clear from the preceding discussion that the question of what kinds of rule ordering should be permitted is an empirical one. Certain methods of the rule application may lead to complications in the statement of the transformations, while other methods may permit significantly simpler characterizations of the data. In each instance, the form taken by the linguistic data determines which rules and which orderings will in fact achieve the greatest degree of generalization.

Our discussion has also led us to consider a number of cases in which the question of relative complexity of grammars could be effectively raised. As we have seen, certain assumptions permit a more elegant, less redundant, and simpler formulation of rules to account for a body of data than other competing assumptions. For example, by permitting extrinsic ordering we were able to preserve the straightforward statements of *Do* Deletion and Affix Hopping as originally arrived at. This notion of **simplicity** is an important one in linguistics. A grammar is said to be **simpler** than another if it captures more generalizations than the other while generating the same set of sentences. The construction of an adequate theory of grammar may then be viewed as the establishment of a group of notations and conventions and a formal measure of complexity so that the grammar that actually captures the greater degree of generalization will be formally less complex in terms of the notations, conventions, and measure of complexity in the theory. A theory that correctly chooses the preferred grammar over less satisfactory alternatives in every case is said to be **explanatorily adequate.** It is difficult, if not impossible, to discuss the notion of explanatory adequacy successfully without first having developed an intuition about what constitutes a satisfactory syntactic description. In view of the priority of the latter goal in this book, the reader is merely directed to the "Suggested Further Readings" at the end of this chapter.

The issue of rule ordering is also too complex to be pursued further with any profit here. In subsequent discussion, it will be assumed that rules are extrinsically ordered, with no presumption that this has been well established in every case. This means that we will assume that rules can be ordered in a sequence, each rule appears once in the sequence, each rule applied to the output of the previous rule that has applied (except, of course, for the first rule), and the sequence is applied once from beginning to end.[3] This is the principle of **linear ordering.** Each rule may apply at a number of locations in the phrase

---

[3] In Chapter 8. an important revision of this last assumption will be introduced. This is the notion of the **transformational cycle,** according to which the rules are applied in sequence at each level of the phrase marker, starting from the lowest S in the tree and proceeding upward in the tree through each S node until the topmost S node is reached. The cycle is introduced to preserve the principle of linear ordering.

marker if its structural description is met at a number of locations at once. These assumptions are the conventional ones in generative grammar.[4]

Finally, it is important to note the distinction between the **ordering** of rules and the **order of application** of rules. The claim that rule X is **ordered after** rule Y is not equivalent to the claim that rule X **applies after** rule Y in every derivation. Rather, the claim is that for every derivation in which the two rules apply, the rule that is ordered first will apply before the other in the derivation.

Given, for example, that *Do* Deletion is ordered before Affix Hopping, it does not follow that *Do* Deletion will apply before Affix Hopping in the derivation of every grammatical sentence. One simply *attempts* to apply *Do* Deletion to the phrase marker in every derivation: If the structural description is met, then the rule applies; if the structural description is not met, then it does not apply. In either case, we then move on to the next transformation in the sequence.

MORE RULE ORDERINGS

Consider Inversion. In terms of the way in which the transformations are now stated, it can be seen that Inversion must precede *Do* Deletion in any derivation.

INVERSION: NP AUX X
$$1 \quad 2 \quad 3 \Rightarrow 2 + 1 \ \emptyset \ 3$$

To see this, we test both possible orderings against a typical example:

(5.3)   *John* Past *do smile*

If *Do* Deletion preceded Inversion, the following derivation would result:

(5.4)   Input   *John* Past *do smile*
                 Do Deletion   *John* Past $\emptyset$ *smile*
                 Inversion   Past *John* $\emptyset$ *smile*

The resulting string in (5.4) is not one that corresponds to a grammatical sentence in English.

Hence, the ordering is Inversion, *Do* Deletion (and then Affix Hopping). The derivation of *Did John smile?* will be as given in (5.5):

(5.5)   Input   *John* Past *do smile*
                 Inversion   Past *do John smile*
                 Do Deletion   —(blocked)
                 Affix Hopping # *do* + Past # *John smile*

---

[4] Occasionally, it has been suggested that there are rules that may apply at any point in any derivation. Such rules, known as **anywhere rules,** are postulated in Ross (1967).

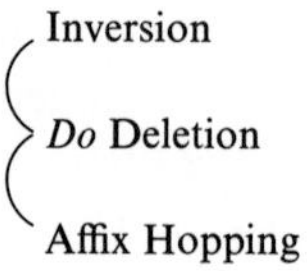

$$\left.\begin{array}{l} \text{Inversion} \\ \\ Do \text{ Deletion} \\ \\ \text{Affix Hopping} \end{array}\right\}$$

Figure 5.2.   Extrinsic ordering of three rules.

The ordering between Inversion and *Do* Deletion is extrinsic. There is nothing about the sequence in the first line of (5.5) that would prevent *Do* Deletion from applying rather than Inversion. But, as can be seen, it is necessary to apply Inversion before *Do* Deletion. The grammar has to wait and see whether Inversion is going to occur before it knows whether it should go ahead and delete *do*. *Do* is required if there is inversion, but otherwise is not. Until Inversion has occurred, the grammar cannot determine whether or not to apply *Do* Deletion. More formally, the application of Inversion creates the conditions for the application of *Do* Deletion.

Let us consider next the rules of *Do* Replacement and *Wh* Fronting. The ordering of the three transformations considered to this point is given in Figure 5.2, where the lines connecting the transformations indicate their extrinsic ordering.

$$DO \ REPLACEMENT: \quad \text{X } do \left\{\begin{array}{l} have \\ be \end{array}\right\} \text{Y}$$
$$1 \quad 2 \quad\quad 3 \quad\quad 4 \Rightarrow 1\ 3\ \emptyset\ 4$$

$$WH \ FRONTING: \quad\quad\quad \text{X} \left\{\begin{array}{l} \text{PP} \\ \text{NP} \end{array}\right\} \text{Y}$$
$$1 \quad\quad 2 \quad\quad 3 \Rightarrow 2 + 1\ \emptyset\ 3$$
Condition: 2 dominates *Wh*

Do Replacement must apply before Inversion to derive sentences like *Is John smiling?* To see this, consider the following derivations:

(5.6)   Input   *John* Pres *do be ing smile*
        Do Replacement   *John* Pres *be* ∅ *ing smile*
        Inversion   Pres *be John* ∅ *ing smile*
        Affix Hopping   # *be* + Pres # *John* # *smile* + *ing* #

(5.7)   Input   *John* Pres *do be ing smile*
        Inversion   Pres *do John be ing smile*
        Do Replacement   —(blocked)
        Affix Hopping   # *do* + Pres # *John be* # *smile* + *ing* #

In (5.7), Inversion applies first and, hence, blocks *Do* Replacement. Since the ungrammatical sequence **Does John be smiling?* is derived with this ordering, the ordering must be that illustrated in (5.6).

56640

Finally, let us consider *Wh* Fronting. The only transformation with which *Wh* Fronting interacts crucially is Inversion. This case turns out to be particularly significant. Let us take the case in which the *Wh* word is the subject NP of the sentence. A typical sequence in which this holds is (5.8):

(5.8)   *Wh + someone* Past *do see Mary*

The superficial string corresponding to this underlying sequence is (5.9):

(5.9)   *Who saw Mary?*

It appears on the face of it that there is no inversion of subject and AUX in (5.9). Yet the rule of Inversion, as we have formulated it, will apply to (5.8) to give (5.10).

INVERSION: NP AUX X
               1   2   3 ⇒ 2 + 1 ∅ 3

(5.10)   Past *do Wh + someone see Mary*

Sentence (5.9) can now be derived by applying *Wh* Fronting to (5.10). This suggests that *Wh* Fronting is ordered after Inversion. This analysis is appealing, since it apparently explains why sentences with *wh* words in the subject do not seem to undergo Inversion.

Further investigation into the relationship between Inversion and *Wh* Fronting shows that this advantage of ordering Inversion before *Wh* Fronting is illusory. First of all, as noted in Chapter 4, sentences with *wh* words cannot have Inversion unless they also have *Wh* Fronting. This is illustrated by ungrammatical examples such as those in (5.11):

(5.11)   a. *Did Mary see who?*
                b. *Will Sam go where?*
                c. *Can Mary sing which songs?*

From this, it is natural to conclude that *Wh* Fronting is a transformation that is **obligatory**—it must always apply when its structural description is met.

By comparison, it appears that Inversion is an optional transformation. If Inversion were obligatory, we would never be able to derive declarative sentences. From this, it follows that there should be sentences with derivations in which Inversion does not apply and *Wh* Fronting does. It is easy to see that such derivations would lead to ungrammatical sentences:

(5.12)   a. *Who Mary saw?*
                b. *Where Sam will go?*
                c. *Which songs Mary can sing?*

We cannot solve this problem by making the application of *Wh* Fronting dependent on some aspect of the output of Inversion. There are two reasons for this. First, if Inversion is optional, then if it does not apply we will be unable to apply *Wh* Fronting. This will predict, incorrectly, that the examples in (5.13) are grammatical:

(5.13)
    a. *Mary saw who?*
    b. *Sam will go where?*
    c. *Mary can sing which songs?*

Second, there are constructions in which *Wh* Fronting applies and Inversion does not apply. The most obvious is the indirect question:

(5.14)
    a. *I asked Bill who Mary saw.*
       I asked Bill who did Mary see.
    b. *Mary wonders where Sam will go.*
       Mary wonders where will Sam go.
    c. *I forget which songs Mary can sing.*
       I forget which songs can Mary sing.

What this means, clearly, is that we cannot derive all and only the grammatical sentences if the ordering is Inversion, *Wh* Fronting.

There are problems with the alternative ordering, however. One, which we have already encountered, is that Inversion cannot apply if the subject is a *Wh* word. But if *Wh* Fronting precedes Inversion, what is to prevent Inversion from applying in such sentences? A mechanical solution would be to state explicitly that the Inversion transformation cannot apply if the subject is a *wh* word, but this would not be an explanation for why this is so. Such mechanical solutions, insofar as they fail to capture generalizations, are not really solutions at all.

A more satisfactory account would be one in which the output of *Wh* Fronting created the condition for the application of Inversion. Note that there is a significant difference between sentences in which the *wh* word is the subject and those in which the *wh* word plays some other role: After *Wh* Fronting applies to the former, the sequence corresponding to the intermediate phrase marker is *Wh* + $\cdots$ NP AUX. That is, there is a *wh* word to the left of the subject. When the *wh* word *is* the subject, however, the sequence both before and after *Wh* Fronting is *Wh* + $\cdots$ AUX. There is no subject NP between the *wh* word and AUX. This difference can be used to account for the failure of Inversion to apply in the latter case, by stating Inversion in roughly the following form.

INVERSION: *Wh* + $\cdots$ NP AUX X
            1   2   3   4 $\Rightarrow$ 1 3 + 2 $\emptyset$ 4

When the *wh* word is the subject, the structure will fail to meet the structural description of Inversion as stated. This analysis, of course, requires that *Wh* Fronting precede Inversion.

This creates yet another problem. If the presence of a *wh* word before the subject is taken to be the condition for application of Inversion, why is it that

Inversion can apply in yes–no questions? In yes–no questions, there is no *wh* word in surface structure and, hence, no obvious way to explain the application of Inversion.

Perhaps yes–no questions are really *wh* questions in disguise. While yes–no questions do not contain *wh* words, sentences used to report yes–no questions, like *I asked whether it was Tuesday, I wonder whether it's all right to have another beer*, and so on, do contain a *wh* word. In other respects, these *whether* clauses are related to direct yes–no questions just as indirect *who, which,* and *what* questions are related to direct *who, which* and *what* questions, in that there is no Inversion in the indirect questions. [cf. (5.14)]. This suggests that we take the indirect question to be indicative of the deep structure of the direct yes–no question. What is required for this analysis is that (i) *whether* is present in the deep structure of every yes–no question and (ii) there is a transformation that deletes *whether* in direct yes–no questions after the application of Inversion.

To support this analysis, we observe an interesting similarity between indirect *whether* clauses and the direct yes–no questions. It is possible to use the phrase *or not* in connection with *whether*, as illustrated by the following examples:

(5.15)   a. *I wonder whether or not John will buy the yogurt.*
            b. *I wonder whether John will buy the yogurt or not.*

It is also the case that *or not* cannot be used generally with *wh* questions or declaratives, but it can be used with yes–no questions:

(5.16)   a. *I wonder what John did (*or not).*
            b. *I bought the yogurt (*or not).*
            c. *Did John buy the yogurt (or not)?*

However, there is a special class of declaratives that can have *or not*, namely, those that contain *either*, as illustrated by the following:

(5.17)   *Either John bought the yogurt or* $\begin{Bmatrix} not. \\ he\ didn't. \end{Bmatrix}$

These facts are accounted for nicely if we treat *whether* as being derived from underlying *Wh either* and yes–no questions as being derived by Inversion in the context of *Wh either*. *Whether* must be deleted subsequent to Inversion in the case of yes–no questions, of course.

This analysis also permits us to generalize significantly the rules for deriving questions. In particular, we may now restate Inversion so that it applies in both yes–no and *wh* questions under identically stated conditions, and obligatorily in both types of question. Furthermore, the rule of *Wh* Fronting applies to certain constituents that dominate *Wh*. Not only does *Wh* Fronting apply to PP, NP, and *whether*, but it also applies to constituents whose main elements are adjectives or adverbs:

(5.18)   *How intelligent is John?*

(5.19)   *How fast can John run?*

(5.20)   *How often do you read the "Times?"*

The phrase *how intelligent* is a member of the category **adjective phrase,**
while the phrases *how fast* and *how often* are members of the category **adverbial
phrase.** Not every category that dominates *Wh* may undergo *Wh* Fronting,
however. Notice, for example, that a verb phrase dominates *Wh* if it dominates
an NP that dominates *Wh*, but the verb phrase is not moved to the front by
Wh Fronting:

(5.21)   a.   *John* Past *do* $_{VP}$[*see Wh + some movie*]
                b.   *What movie did John see?*
                c.   *$_{VP}$[*see what movie*] *did John?*

The most adequate account of *Wh* Fronting must include a general specification of which categories can undergo the rule. While there is a generalization
that covers the categories to which *Wh* Fronting applies and excludes those to
which it does not, we are not in a position to discuss it here. As a purely abbrevi-
atory step, we adopt the symbol A to indicate the set of categories to which
Wh Fronting applies. A is introduced here solely for the purpose of stating the
rule, and in no way should be viewed as a well-motivated syntactic category.

The statements of *Wh* Fronting and Inversion now take the following form.

Wh FRONTING: X A Y
                 1 2 3 $\Rightarrow$ 2 + 1 $\emptyset$ 3

                 Condition: 2 dominates *Wh*

INVERSION: A NP AUX X
               1   2   3   4 $\Rightarrow$ 1 3 + 2 $\emptyset$ 4

               Condition: 1 dominates *Wh*

A RESTRICTION ON TRANSFORMATIONAL POWER

Let us consider now the question of how the theory of grammar is to choose
between competing descriptions of the same linguistic phenomena. In principle,
if one of the competing descriptions requires a certain type of transformation
that the other does not require, then a theory of grammar that rules out this
kind of transformation will automatically choose the description that does not
require it. If it can be independently shown that the description that does not
require this kind of transformation is in fact preferable to the one that does,

then this constitutes evidence that this kind of transformation should not be permitted by the theory of grammar.

Do: Two Analyses

The theoretical restriction of the statement of transformations to be formulated here rests on a comparison of two alternative analyses of the distribution of *do* in English. Under one analysis, the assumption is made that *do* is not present in the deep structure of any sentence; rather, it is inserted in the appropriate contexts by a transformation of *Do* Support. Under the other analysis, which is the one established in Chapter 4, the assumption is made that the constituent M is obligatory, rather than optional in deep structures, and that there is a transformation called *Do* Deletion that deletes the modal *do* in certain contexts. Since the *Do* Deletion analysis was discussed in detail in Chapter 4, only the *Do* Support analysis will be described here.

Let us assume that the expansion of AUX is given as the original PSR2 of Chapter 3.

PSR2:   AUX → TENSE (M) (*have en*) (*be ing*)

This entails that there will be certain deep structures that lack a modal. Let us consider the terminal string of one such deep structure:

(5.22)   *John* Past *smile*

It is not possible to simply insert *do* into this structure; It must also be specified that if *do* is inserted here it must be stressed. Otherwise, we will generate the ungrammatical (5.23) with unstressed *do*:

(5.23)   **John did smile.*

In the case of a yes–no question, on the other hand, *do* must be inserted if there is no modal, and there is no requirement that *do* has to be stressed in such a case:

(5.24)   *Did John smile?*

This contrasts with the sequence that would be gotten if Inversion applied to the verb in case there was no modal, e.g.:

(5.25)   **Smiled John?*

This shows that there is something about the application of Inversion that establishes the context in which *Do* Support will apply. The specification of this context relies on the observation that in the yes–no question the element marked with TENSE does not immediately precede the verb.

For example, when *do* is present it is marked with the same TENSE as the corresponding declarative. TENSE is not marked on the verb in yes–no questions, as shown by (5.26):

(5.26)

$$*Do\ John \begin{Bmatrix} smiles? \\ smiled? \end{Bmatrix}$$

Since it is possible for a yes–no question to lack an underlying modal, Inversion must be revised so that it moves only TENSE when there is no modal. A first approximation is the following.

INVERSION: A NP $\underbrace{\text{TENSE (M)}}$ X

1   2   3   4 ⇒ 1 3 + 2 ∅ 4

Condition: 1 dominates *Wh*

After the application of Inversion in the case in which there is no modal, TENSE will appear alone before the NP; hence, it will not precede a verb, and *Do* Support will apply. However, this reformulation of Inversion is not correct.

What this rule says is that Inversion may move either TENSE alone or TENSE followed by M. However, Inversion cannot move TENSE alone unless TENSE actually precedes a verb in the underlying structure. If TENSE was moved when a member of the category M was present, the following ungrammatical strings would be generated:

(5.27)

$$*\begin{Bmatrix} Does \\ Did \end{Bmatrix} John \begin{Bmatrix} will \\ can \\ shall \\ must \\ \vdots \end{Bmatrix} smile?$$

This problem can be avoided by adopting the convention that if a transformation that contains parentheses can apply either to the sequence with the material in the parentheses included or to the sequence without the material in parentheses, then the longer of the two sequences is chosen. This convention has somewhat greater support from phonology than from syntax. The present analysis, if it is correct, constitutes evidence that the convention should be applied to transformations.

Next, let us consider the fact that *have* and *be* also undergo Inversion. In order to represent this, we may establish a new category that contains just those elements that may be moved along with TENSE, namely, M, *have*, and *be*. Call this category [+AUX]. (Cf. pages 56–59 for a discussion of the use of syntactic features to designate subcategories.)

The next restatement of Inversion will now be the following.

INVERSION: A NP $\underbrace{\text{TENSE ([+AUX])}}$ X

1   2   3   4 ⇒ 1 3 + 2 ∅ 4

Condition: 1 dominates *Wh*

Essentially, there are now two rules of Inversion, one of which applies when there is a modal, *have*, or *be* in the deep structure, and the other of which applies when there is not.

If the longer version of this rule applies, it yields a string of the form illustrated in (5.28a), and if the shorter version applies, it yields a string like (5.28b):

(5.28)   a. Past *John smile*
                             b. Past *will John smile*

The rule of *Do* support must apply to (5.28a) and cannot apply to (5.28b). The crucial difference between the two structures is that in the first case TENSE does not precede a verbal element. Observe that when this is the case Affix Hopping cannot apply, because the statement of Affix Hopping requires that there be a verbal element immediately following the affix. Thus, *Do* Support can be ordered after Affix Hopping, and it can be stated to apply just in case Affix Hopping fails to apply.

Do SUPPORT: X TENSE Y
                1   2   3 $\Rightarrow$ 1 # *do* + 2 # 3

This formulation of the rule rests on the assumption that after Affix Hopping applies to an affix that affix is no longer subject to any later transformation (cf. the discussion in Chapter 3). Thus, *do* is not inserted before an affix that has already been hopped.

The derivations of the two examples in (5.28) will take the following form.

Deep Structure:	*John* Past *smile*	*John* Past *will smile*
Inversion:	Past *John smile*	Past *will John smile*
Affix Hopping:	(does not apply)	# *will* + Past # *John smile*
Do Support:	# *do* + Past # *John smile*	(does not apply)

Comparison of the Analyses

In general, when we are in a position of having two analyses to choose between we must consider a variety of factors. We must determine what predictions each makes about other sentences in the language. We must compare them in complexity and determine whether one captures a greater degree of generalization than the other. Finally, they must be compared with respect to the theory of grammar they each permit: We wish to select the analysis that allows the stronger constraints to be placed on the notion of possible transformation consistent with the data.

In terms of the data considered already, it can be shown that the *Do* Deletion analysis is preferable. The crucial difference between the two analyses is that the *Do* Deletion analysis explicitly treats *do* as an underlying modal, and predicts that in any area of the language in which modals are involved *do* will function in precisely the same way as any other modal. No particular conditions are required for the case in which the modal happens to be *do*. *Do* Support, on the other hand, treats the insertion of *do* into environments that normally contain modals as an accidental phenomenon. The interesting fact about *Do* Support is that it does insert *do* into precisely the position occupiable by a modal in yes–no questions. In contrast to the *Do* Deletion analysis, it does not provide any explanation as to why *do* should appear precisely in this position and not in any other position in the sentence, such as after the subject NP. It is possible to imagine a rule like (5.29a), which inserts *do* after the subject NP, or a rule like (5.29b), which inserts *do* at the end of the sentence:

(5.29)   a. X TENSE NP Y

                       1   2   3 ⇒ 1 2 *do* 3
                    b. X TENSE Y
                       1   2   3 ⇒ 1 2 3 *do*

It should be noted that the real difference between the two analyses is not that one inserts *do* and the other deletes it but that the *Do* Support analysis as outlined here does not presuppose an underlying modal for every sentence. Given an underlying modal, it follows automatically that anything that replaces it will possess all of the distributional properties of modals. If there is not always an underlying modal, then the fact that the inserted modal possesses all of these distributional properties is not explained by the analysis.

It is not sufficient to argue that *Do* Support is an equally adequate formulation because it inserts *do* into the correct position. The *Do* Deletion analysis provides an explanation, in terms of the language and its structure, as to why it is that *do* appears in precisely this position. The assumption that *do* is a modal in the *Do* Deletion analysis does provide such an explanation: *Do* acts like a modal precisely because it *is* a modal in underlying structure. The *Do* Support analysis does not provide an explanation of this sort. As we will see in the next section, it is possible to construct a formulation in which *do* is inserted that captures some of the same generalizations as the *Do* Deletion analysis.

Arbitrary and Nonarbitrary Sequences

Given that the *Do* Deletion analysis is preferable to the *Do* Support analysis, the question arises as to how to formulate the theory of grammar so that it will identify the preferable analysis. Consider once again the part of the Inversion transformation in the *Do* Support case that applies when there is a modal *have* or *be* present.

INVERSION: A NP TENSE [+AUX] X

              1 2   3   4 ⇒ 1 3 + 2 ∅ 4

              Condition: 1 dominates *Wh*

Notice that this transformation moves a sequence of two constituents, TENSE and [+AUX], from one part of the phrase marker to another. (This is to be contrasted with the more restricted type of transformation that moves a single constituent.) If the statement of Inversion just given were correct, then we would have to construct the theory of grammar so that it would allow transformations that move sequences of constituents at once. This type of transformation is a very powerful one, and may be too powerful for the description of natural language.

As an example, consider a sentence like (5.30):

(5.30)   *The man who married Mary's sister used to
                be an encyclopedia salesman.*

It is possible to envision a transformation that applies to a certain sequence of elements in this sentence. So, for example, it is possible to formulate a transformation in the notation already established that moves the sequence *sister used to* to the front of the entire sentence. This transformation will yield a string like (5.31):

(5.31)   ***Sister used to** the man who married Mary's
                ∅ be an encyclopedia salesman.*

(The symbol ∅ here indicates the original position of the sequence that has been moved.) This hypothetical transformation is not, of course, a transformation of English, nor does it appear that it or anything like it is a transformation of any human language. If, however, a transformation like Inversion can be stated as we have just stated it, then machinery must be incorporated into the theory of grammar for stating transformations that in general apply to sequences of elements in the structure. If transformations cannot move arbitrary sequences, then some means must be developed to constrain the operation of transformations that move sequences, such as Inversion. The question, therefore, is whether there is any way to distinguish in principle between the notions "arbitrary sequence" and "nonarbitrary sequence." If a definition of these terms can be found, then the following constraint on transformations can be incorporated into the theory of grammar: **No transformation may move an arbitrary sequence of elements.** This constraint is a restriction on the kinds of grammars that can be formulated within the theory; hence, the definition of what constitutes a natural language will have been made more precise.

Consider once again the rule of Inversion. The sequence TENSE [+AUX] is not an arbitrary sequence, and there is a way of distinguishing between it and the sequence *sister used to*, which is an arbitrary sequence. The distinction is simply that both TENSE and [+AUX] are immediately dominated by the node AUX.

On the other hand, an analysis of sentences like (5.30) would show that the constituents *sister*, *used*, and *to* are not all immediately dominated by the same node. Hence, a first approximation of a nonarbitrary sequence is to say that it is a sequence whose elements all are immediately dominated by the same node.

However, this definition of what constitutes a nonarbitrary sequence will not be an adequate one. Consider, for example, a typical sentential structure, such as (5.32):

(5.32)

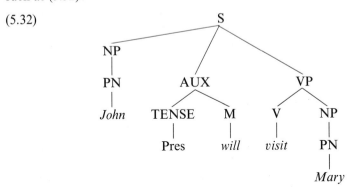

The structure in (5.32) underlies the sentence *John will visit Mary*. There are transformations whose functions involve the movement of an entire sentential structure in the context of a larger structure; such transformations will be discussed in detail in later chapters. One case is illustrated by the two sentences in (5.33), which are related by a movement transformation that moves the structure corresponding to the sequence in bold face:

(5.33)   a. *It is very surprising* **that John will visit Mary.**
          b. **That John will visit Mary** *is very surprising*

As can be seen, the sequence *that John will visit Mary*, which is analyzed as an S, is not a sequence all of whose elements are immediately dominated by the same node. Hence, by definition, this sequence is an arbitrary sequence. If this is so, then the constraint to the effect that transformations cannot move arbitrary sequences will not permit the statement of the transformation that relates (5.33a) and (5.33b). This means that the definition of what constitutes nonarbitrary sequence is incorrect.

Let us, therefore, redefine what a nonarbitrary sequence is: A nonarbitrary sequence is a sequence all of whose elements are dominated (*not* immediately dominated) by the same node. Given such a reformulation, the sequence *that John will visit Mary* will then be defined as a nonarbitrary sequence, and the constraint that transformations may move only nonarbitrary sequences can be maintained. However, the transformation that moves the arbitrary sequence *sister used to* now moves a nonarbitrary sequence under this reformulation, since *every* element of the sentence *The man who married Mary's sister used to be an encyclopedia salesman* is in fact dominated by a single node, namely S. In fact, it will always be the case that in every structure there will be one node that dominates everything, and this node will be the highest S node in the tree.

Hence, this reformulation of the notion of nonarbitrary sequence is also incorrect.

Let us now define a nonarbitrary sequence as a sequence all of whose elements are dominated by the same node **such that that node dominates nothing else but this sequence.** So, for example, in (5.32) the sequence Pres *will* will be a nonarbitrary sequence, since there is a node AUX that dominates all elements of the sequence, and nothing else but this sequence. Similarly, *visit Mary*, *Pres will visit Mary* and *John Pres will visit Mary* are all nonarbitrary sequences. On the other hand, *Pres will visit* under this definition is an arbitrary sequence, since the node that dominates every element in the sequence, namely S, also dominates an element that is not in the sequence, namely *Mary*. When a node dominates every element in a sequence and only the elements of the sequence, then that node **exhaustively dominates** the sequence. This definition of a non-arbitrary sequence does in fact distinguish between the sequence *John Pres will visit Mary* and the sequence *sister used to* correctly, as required. Hence, the constraint to the effect that transformations may move only nonarbitrary sequences can be maintained if nonarbitrary sequences are only those that are exhaustively dominated by a node. We can impose this constraint formally by requiring that in the structural description of a movement transformation the term that is to be moved consists of a single node, i.e., the node that dominates the nonarbitrary sequence.[5]

To see this last point clearly, consider again the status of the argument here. First, Inversion was stated in terms of a sequence of elements in the sentence. If transformations are formulated in this way in general, this would permit the statement of transformations that are impossible in any human language. Thus, it was necessary to redefine what kinds of things a transformation can apply to in order to make impossible transformations impossible to state in the theory. In practical terms, this means that transformations cannot be stated that move arbitrary sequences of elements; this will follow automatically if any transformation that moves a sequence must be stated in terms of the single node that exhaustively dominates the sequence.

The constraint on the movement of arbitrary sequences, along with the definition of what constitutes a nonarbitrary sequence, clearly points to the selection of the *Do* Deletion analysis as preferable. The underlying structure of the verbal sequence is given by the following phrase structure rule in the *Do* Support analysis.

PSR: AUX → TENSE (M) (*have en*) (*be ing*)

[5] A somewhat weaker constraint is that a transformation may move a sequence of constituents mentioned in its structural description, but the sequence of these constituents must itself be a constituent of the sentence. This weaker constraint might be necessary because of the difficulty of stating transformations such as Tag Formation (Chapter 6) adequately in the context of the stronger constraint given in the text.

Assume an underlying string of the form given in (5.34):

(5.34)   *John* Past *will have en be ing walk*

In order to maintain the hypothesis that transformations can apply only to nonarbitrary sequences, the rule of Inversion must move a nonarbitrary sequence when it applies to (5.34). However, since Past *will* is the sequence that is moved by Inversion here, it must be the case that it is exhaustively dominated by some node. This is impossible, since the node that immediately dominates Past *will* in this structure is AUX, and AUX dominates other elements as well.

It can be seen that the *Do* Deletion analysis satisfies the constraint against the movement of nonarbitrary sequences by moving AUX, which always contains the sequence TENSE [+AUX] that is to be moved. This is achieved by the rule of *Do* Replacement, which moves *have* and *be* into AUX so that they may be moved by Inversion.

This suggests that we could formulate an analysis in which *do* was inserted, but that did not violate the constraint. The crucial property of any alternative would be that it divided the verbal sequence into two parts, and moved the auxiliary verbs *have* and *be* under a constituent that would later undergo Inversion.

Let us suppose, for example, that instead of having an obligatory modal *do* in AUX when no other modal was generated, there would be an obligatory dummy modal in AUX under the same circumstances. That is, one possible modal would be the dummy symbol Δ. There would then be a transformation that replaced this dummy symbol by *have* or *be* (a transformation like *Do* Replacement) and another transformation that realized Δ as *do* in the surface if it was not otherwise eliminated during the derivation (a rule like *Do* Support).

This alternative would then claim to be an analysis in which *do* was inserted, but that would capture the generalizations of the *Do* Deletion/*Do* Replacement analysis. It can be shown that this alternative is more complicated than the *Do* Deletion/*Do* Replacement analysis and does not capture any further generalizations.

Let us consider the sequence in (5.35):

(5.35)   ... TENSE $_M[\Delta]$ V ...

Suppose that this sequence appears in a declarative sentence, so that *do* should not appear in the surface structure. We do not wish to realize Δ as *do* here, and we wish to attach TENSE to the verb. Since there is a dummy modal between TENSE and the verb, Affix Hopping must either apply twice, which is not permitted by the theory, or must be complicated so that just in case there is a dummy modal it will ignore it. This complication is not compensated for by a simplification of the grammar (as compared with the *Do* Deletion/*Do* Replacement analysis) and appears to be motivated purely by the need to save the dummy modal analysis. A comparison of the two analyses in terms of the rules that each requires is as follows.

Do REPLACEMENT/Do DELETION

1. *Do* Replacement
2. *Do* Deletion
3. Affix Hopping

DUMMY MODAL ANALYSIS

1. Δ Replacement
3. Realization of Δ as *do* unless before V
3. More complex version of Affix Hopping

It would not simplify the dummy modal analysis to delete the dummy modal immediately before a V. The analysis would then be a combination of the *Do* Support analysis and the *Do* Replacement/*Do* Deletion analysis and would, hence, be more complex than either of the two taken alone.

REVISED DUMMY MODAL ANALYSIS

1. Δ Deletion
2. Δ Replacement
3. Affix Hopping
4. Realization of Δ as *do*

The fourth rule of this analysis, the realization of Δ as *do*, could apply auto-automatically. All cases in which it should be blocked would be eliminated by the prior application of Δ Deletion, a rule that is identical to *Do* Deletion except for the form of what is deleted. Hence, nothing is gained by calling the dummy modal Δ rather than *do* as originally proposed.

An alternative proposal that bears less resemblance to the *Do* Replacement/*Do* Deletion analysis is one that has the following rule for the expansion of AUX.

$$\text{PSR:} \quad \text{AUX} \rightarrow \text{TENSE (M)}$$

This analysis would be like the *Do* Replacement/*Do* Deletion analysis in dividing the verbal sequence into two parts, but it would be like the *Do* Support analysis in actually inserting *do* into a position not already designated by some symbol. This analysis would require a rule similar to *Do* Replacement, i.e.:

(5.36)   . . . AUX   VP . . .   . . . AUX   VP . . .

TENSE $\left\{ \begin{array}{c} have \\ be \end{array} \right\}$ . . . ⇒ TENSE $\left\{ \begin{array}{c} have \\ be \end{array} \right\}$ . . .

The argument against this alternative is the same as that against the original *Do* support analysis. It does not explain why it is that the modal *do* behaves just like a modal after it has been inserted. Rather, it treats this generalization as accidental. In favor of this alternative, on the other hand, is the fact that it does not violate the constraint against movement of nonarbitrary sequences.

It can be seen, then, that there are two independent considerations that must go into our choice of analysis. On the one hand, we must divide the verbal sequence into two parts such that the sequence that undergoes Inversion will be a constituent; this motivates an underlying AUX and a rule of *Do* Replacement (or its equivalent). On the other hand, we must assume that there is an underlying modal in all sentences in order to explain the modal-like behavior of *do*. Consequently, the analysis that we settle on is the *Do* Replacement/*Do* Deletion analysis originally proposed.

THE RELATIONSHIP BETWEEN THE SYNTACTIC AND SEMANTIC COMPONENTS

As mentioned in Chapter 1, the major concern of this book is with the syntactic component. Since the structures generated by the syntactic component are generally assumed to provide at least part of the input to the semantic component, it is worthwhile to discuss the formal relationship between the two at this point.

Early linguistic theory, based on Chomsky (1957), essentially ignored the question of how semantic and syntactic information were related, and was concerned primarily with the question of what kinds of descriptions would be adequate to account for the syntactic phenomena of natural language. The theory arrived at in Chomsky (1957) differs from the one assumed in this book, which is based on Chomsky (1965). In the original theory, the notions of deep structure and surface structure were not made use of.

It was assumed in Chomsky (1957) that there was a set of phrase structure rules that specified an infinite set of *phrase markers* for a language, and two types of transformations: (i) **singulary transformations,** which applied to a single sentence, and (ii) **generalized transformations,** which formed new sentences out of two or more sentences. An example of a singulary transformation is Affix Hopping, while an example of a generalized transformation would be one that derived (5.38) from (5.37a) and (5.37b):

(5.37)   a. *John met the man.*
              b. *The man is eating pizza.*

(5.38)   *John met the man who is eating pizza.*

On the other hand, it is possible to apply this generalized transformation in a different way and arrive at a sentence that is different from (5.38):

(5.39)   *The man who John met is eating pizza.*

Katz and Postal (1964) argued that no singulary transformations affect the interpretation of the sentence. (Several singulary transformations proposed in Chomsky (1957) did appear to affect the meaning of the sentences. Katz and Postal gave independent arguments that these transformations were incorrectly formulated and that the correct formulations were transformations that did not change meaning.) However, given examples like (5.38) and (5.39), they observed that there are generalized transformations that do affect the meaning of the sentence, depending on which way the generalized transformations combine simple sentences.

Katz and Postal also argued that a linguistic theory must provide an account of the way in which the meaning of a sentence is composed from the meanings of its parts. Since generalized transformations affect the meaning of the sentences that they apply to, the obvious conclusion would be that the interpretation of a sentence must be a function of (i) the interpretation of its parts and (ii) the transformation that apply to derive it.

Katz and Postal, thus, observed that it would be necessary within this framework to have two kinds of semantic interpretation rules: (i) those that operate on simple phrase markers and (ii) those that operate on the sequence of generalized transformations. They noted that within this framework there was a peculiar lack of symmetry between singulary and generalized transformations, in that the former did not appear to affect the interpretation of the sentence while the latter did. In view of this, they investigated the question of whether or not it would be possible to eliminate generalized transformations completely, thus making it possible to require that no transformations affect the meaning of the sentence, and also making it possible to eliminate those semantic interpretation rules that operate on the sequence of generalized transformations.

One consequence of this investigation was the observation that there was no evidence that any singulary transformation had to be ordered before any generalized transformation.[6] However, since it was therefore possible to apply all generalized transformations before all singulary transformations, it was seen to be possible to replace the notion of generalized transformation by the notion of *generalized phrase marker*, in which the relationship between the simple sentences that form a complex sentence are already made explicit through the use of the recursive symbol S. The recursiveness of the language is captured directly in the phrase structure component, and not in the transformational component. Hence, the contribution previously made by the generalized transformations to the interpretation of the sentence would now be taken over by the relative position of the parts of the sentence within the generalized phrase marker. Katz and Postal could then make the following claim: Transformations do not contribute to the interpretation of a phrase marker; all of the information necessary for the interpretation of a sentence is present in the underlying generalized phrase marker. This claim is referred to occasionally as the **Katz–Postal Hypothesis** (cf. Jackendoff, 1972).

As a further consequence of their investigation, Katz and Postal observed that since transformations do not appear to affect the interpretation of sen-

---

[6] This observation is originally due to Fillmore (1963).

tences, a worthwhile working principle for linguists would be something like
the following:

> Given a sentence for which a syntactic derivation is needed; look for simple paraphrases
> of the sentence which are not paraphrases by virtue of synonymous expressions; on finding
> them, construct grammatical rules that relate the original sentence and its paraphrases in
> such a way that each of these sentences has the same sequence of underlying P-markers.
> Of course, having constructed such rules, it is still necessary to find *independent syntactic
> justification* for them [1964: 157].

In commenting on this principle, they observed that while it would necessarily
be the case that transformationally related sentences would be paraphrases
of one another, the converse would not be the case. That is, not all synonymous
sentences would have to have the same underlying structures.

Katz and Postal did not overlook the importance of requiring independent
syntactic justification for syntactic analyses. Unfortunately, there has been a
tendency in linguistics to use the hypothesis as justification for analyses, rather
than as merely a device for finding analyses to investigate.[7] The consequence
of this is that correct analyses are more weakly justified than they can be, and
incorrect analyses are judged to be correct simply because they are consistent
with the Katz–Postal Hypothesis. In order to avoid these consequences, we
will not employ the Katz–Postal Hypothesis as a working principle in this book,
but will attempt to use syntactic considerations both to motivate and to justify
analyses.

It should also be noted that the Katz–Postal Hypothesis is too strong in
restricting semantic interpretation to the level of deep structure. Recent work
shows that certain aspects of the interpretation of a sentence can more adequately be represented in terms of the surface structure. The issue is an involved
and controversial one, and to pursue it would take us far beyond the scope of
this text. We will take the position that there are certain aspects of semantic
interpretation that can be adequately specified in the deep structure.

SUMMARY OF RULES

The current versions of all of the rules considered thus far are given here.
In addition, the ordering of the transformations is indicated by a line drawn
from each transformation to the transformation(s) that can be shown to
follow it.

---

[7] Jackendoff (1972) notes the use of a stronger form of the Katz–Postal hypothesis in some of the
literature. The strong form considers paraphrase due to synonymous expressions sufficient to
motivate an analysis, and to justify one in certain cases. See Jackendoff (1972) and Chomsky
(1970b; 1972) for further discussion.

Phrase Structure Rules

PSR1: S   → NP AUX VP
PSR2: AUX → TENSE M
PSR3: VP   → (*have en*) (*be ing*) V (NP)
PSR4: NP   → $\begin{Bmatrix} \text{DET (ADJ) N} \\ \text{PN} \end{Bmatrix}$
PSR5: DET → $\begin{Bmatrix} (Wh)\ \text{QUAN} \\ \text{ART} \end{Bmatrix}$
PSR6: PP   → P NP

Transformations

Do REPLACEMENT: X *do* $\begin{Bmatrix} have \\ be \end{Bmatrix}$ Y
                   1 2   3   4 ⇒ 1 3 $\emptyset$ 4

Wh FRONTING: X A Y
                   1 2 3 ⇒ 2 + 1 $\emptyset$ 3

                   Condition: 2 dominates *Wh*

INVERSION: A NP AUX X
                   1 2   3   4 ⇒ 1 3 + 2 $\emptyset$ 4

                   Condition: 1 dominates *Wh*

Do DELETION: X *do* V Y
                   1 2 3 4 ⇒ 1 $\emptyset$ 3 4

                   Condition: 2 is unstressed

AFFIX HOPPING: X Affix [+V] Y
                   1   2   3   4 ⇒ 1 $\emptyset$ # 3 + 2 # 4

Ordering of Transformations

Do Replacement
Wh Fronting
Inversion
Do Deletion
Affix Hopping

EXERCISES

1. Assume that instead of the rules of *Do* Replacement and *Do* Deletion we use the rule of *Do* Support to account for the distribution of the modal *do*. What must the rule ordering be between *Do* Support, Inversion, and Affix Hopping?

2. Derive the following sentences by using the *Do* Support analysis instead of the *Do* Replacement *Do* Deletion analysis.

   a. *Is John smiling?*
   b. *Would the police have caught John?*
   c. *Have the swallows destroyed Capistrano?*
   d. *Did Mary find the peanut butter?*

3. How does the *Do* Support analysis explain why it is that *do* does not appear before *have en* or *be ing* in either declaratives or questions?

PROBLEMS

1. How would you express the difference between a dialect in which the sentences in (a) are grammatical and a dialect in which the sentences in (b) are grammatical?

   a. *I asked Mary what she did.*
      Bill wonders whether the world is flat.
      Sam inquired as to why you left.
      I wonder who Fortune will smile upon today.
      Mary asked who wanted to leave.
   b. *I asked Mary what did she do.*
      Bill wonders is the world flat.
      Sam inquired as to why did you leave.
      I wonder who will Fortune smile upon today.
      Mary asked who wanted to leave.

*2. We have analyzed *wh* questions as being derived by application of two separate transformations, *Wh* Fronting and Inversion. A superficially plausible alternative involves the following two transformations.

   T1: Move the *wh* word to the front and put the AUX after it.
   T2: Move the *wh* word to the front.

The first would apply to derive sentences such as:

   a. *What did John see?*

and the second would derive sentences such as:

b. *I wonder what John saw.*

(i) Why is this alternative less preferable than the *Wh* Fronting/Inversion analysis proposed in the text? (ii) Suggest a constraint on the power of transformations that will rule out the superficially plausible but less preferable analysis. If properly formulated, the constraint asked for should automatically cover those cases handled by the constraint against movement of nonarbitrary sequences, and you should be able to demonstrate that it does.

*3. Observe that there is a rule of English that relates sentences like (a) and (b):

a. *John looked ŭp the informátion.*
b. *John looked the information úp.*

Notice that in the first sentence there is weak stress on *up*, while in the second sentence the stress on *up* is heavier.

In a sentence like (c), it is impossible to have weak stress on *up*:

c. *What books did John look up?*

What does this tell you about the relative ordering between the rule that assigns stress and *Wh* Fronting? Justify your answer.

*4. Consider indirect questions such as:

a. *John wonders what Bill is mowing the lawn with.*
b. *I forgot where I put the caterpillar.*
c. *Do you remember who told you about the party?*

Propose an analysis of indirect questions. Assume a phrase structure rule of the following form:

d. VP → V S

*5. There is a reason to argue that the phrase structure rule suggested in Problem 4 generalizes to a variety of constructions besides indirect questions. Give examples of sentences that show that this is the case.

6

Negation

INTRODUCTION

In the preceding chapter, we considered a rule of English, Inversion, that captures a number of significant generalizations about the distribution and cooccurrence of auxiliary verbs in English sentences. This chapter deals with another construction that fits in quite nicely with the analysis of *wh* and yes–no questions, in that the generalizations to be captured here are substantially the same as those for questions and the analysis that emerges has many of the characteristics of the analysis of questions. This construction involves **negation,** as illustrated in (6.1):

(6.1) $\qquad John \begin{Bmatrix} did\,not \\ didn't \end{Bmatrix} buy\ the\ yogurt.$

In addition, we will investigate the interaction between negation and questions in terms of the rules required and their ordering. For example, there are some restrictions on whether a negative element may immediately follow the modal in a question, as shown by the following examples:

(6.2) $\qquad \begin{Bmatrix} *Did\,not \\ Didn't \end{Bmatrix} John\ buy\ the\ yogurt?$

(6.3)
$$Did\ John \begin{Bmatrix} not \\ *n't \end{Bmatrix} buy\ the\ yogurt?$$

Finally, we will look at a construction of English that is strikingly similar to questions containing negation, namely, the so-called **tag question,** illustrated in the following examples:

(6.4)   *John didn't buy the yogurt, did he?*

(6.5)   *John bought the yogurt, didn't he?*

SENTENTIAL NEGATION

First, consider the kind of negation in which the negative element is either *not* or *n't.* This involves cases in which these negative elements are used in connection with the auxiliary verbs, as the following sentences show:

(6.6)

a. *John* $\begin{Bmatrix} did\ \textbf{not} \\ did\textbf{n't} \end{Bmatrix}$ *buy the yogurt.*

b. *John* $\begin{Bmatrix} will\ \textbf{not} \\ wo\textbf{n't} \end{Bmatrix}$ *open the door.*

c. *John* $\begin{Bmatrix} has\ \textbf{not} \\ has\textbf{n't} \end{Bmatrix}$ *seen Naples yet.*

d. *John* $\begin{Bmatrix} is\ \textbf{not} \\ is\textbf{n't} \end{Bmatrix}$ *driving very carefully.*

The full range of sentences like those in (6.6) reveals a restriction on the distribution of negation among the elements of the verbal sequence. Part of the task of providing a description of the syntax of English is to arrive at a precise, formal characterization of this restriction.

Observe that it is impossible for *not* to precede the verbal sequence entirely:

(6.7)

$$John\ (*not) \begin{Bmatrix} will\ smile. \\ has\ smiled. \\ would\ have\ smiled. \\ is\ smiling. \\ smiles. \end{Bmatrix}$$

and so on. By comparison, *not* or *n't* after the first member of the verbal sequence is perfectly acceptable; the following examples show this for cases in which the verbal sequence contains more than one auxiliary verb:

(6.8)

a. *John would* $\begin{Bmatrix} not \\ n't \end{Bmatrix}$ *have bought the yogurt.*

b. *John would* $\begin{Bmatrix} not \\ n't \end{Bmatrix}$ *be standing here now.*

c. *Mary would* $\left\{ \begin{matrix} not \\ n't \end{matrix} \right\}$ *have been standing there.*

d. *John has* $\left\{ \begin{matrix} not \\ n't \end{matrix} \right\}$ *been standing there very long.*

Examples such as (6.8a–d) with other modals and auxiliaries are similarly unobjectionable. Furthermore, the examples in (6.6) show that if there is only one member of the verbal sequence other than the verb, then negation follows this member.

Consider, now, the question of whether it is possible to account for the distribution of *not* and *n't* in English sentences in terms of phrase structure rules only or whether a transformational analysis will be required. The argument for the transformational analysis of sentential negation parallels the argument for the transformational analysis of questions very closely.

There is a problem with proposing that the distribution of negation in the verbal sequence can be handled adequately by a phrase structure analysis. This has to do with the question of what the phrase structure rule or rules should look like.

Consider a phrase structure rule or set of phrase structure rules to generate all of the verbal sequences that contain negation, and only those sequences. Those verbal sequences that contain negation are summarized in Table 6.1.

Table 6.1.   Possible Verbal Sequences Containing Sentential Negation

	Verbal sequence	Example
a.	TENSE M *not* V	*John will not smile.*
b.	TENSE *have en not* V	*John has not smiled.*
c.	TENSE *be ing not* V	*John is not smiling.*
d.	TENSE *have en not be ing* V	*John has not been smiling.*
e.	TENSE M *not have en*	*John will not have smiled.*
f.	TENSE M *not be ing* V	*John will not be smiling.*
g.	TENSE M *not have en be ing* V	*John will not have been smiling.*

There are two significant observations to be made about the verbal sequences illustrated in this table. First, the order of elements is precisely the same as that in the verbal sequences without negation, and second, negation follows the first element in the sequence after TENSE. It is possible, therefore, to recapitulate here the argument in Chapter 5 to the effect that a comprehensive phrase structure analysis of the verbal sequence would inevitably fail to capture generalizations in the case of the negated verbal sequence.

The structure of the argument is as follows: The syntax of the language appears to require reference to two distinct parts of the verbal sequence. These two parts are TENSE, followed by the first verbal element, and the rest of the sequence. The first part of the sequence is relevant for questions because it is the part that appears before the subject noun phrase; for negative sentences, the first part is relevant because it is the part that precedes *not* or *n't*. However, it is not adequate in both cases to state simply that the first part of the verbal sequence is a constituent and that the second part of the verbal sequence is a constituent, and to specify the form of both constituents. It must also be noted that the form of the second part of the verbal sequence depends on the form of the first part.

For example, suppose we try to express the fact that negation follows TENSE $\left\{ \begin{matrix} M \\ have \\ be \end{matrix} \right\}$ with a phrase structure rule of the following form.

$$\text{PSR: } AUX_1 \rightarrow \text{TENSE} \left\{ \begin{matrix} M \\ have\ en \\ be\ ing \end{matrix} \right\} (not)$$

It will then be necessary to state a rule for the rest of the verbal sequence such that (i) when M appears in AUX_1 the rest of the verbal sequence may contain only *be ing* or *have en be ing*, (ii) when *have en* appears in AUX_1 the rest of the verbal sequence may contain only *be ing*, and (iii) when *be ing* appears in AUX_1 the rest of the verbal sequence must be null, with the exception of the verb. Hence, the rule for the expansion of the rest of the verbal sequence cannot be expressed simply as a phrase structure rule of the familiar sort introduced in this book, since it depends on the expansion of AUX_1.

There is a technical device available that will permit us to state the possible verbal sequences that internally contain *not*. This type of device is called a **context-sensitive phrase structure rule.** It can be shown that while the context-sensitive phrase structure rule, or **CS rule,** takes account of all of the relevant data, it does not capture the generalizations that a transformational account captures.

The CS rule account of this data would be a formalization of the observations just listed. Suppose that the verbal sequence is viewed as being composed of two parts, the first being AUX_1 and the second being AUX_2. The expansion of AUX_1 will be given as in the PSR; the expansion of AUX_2 will be stated as follows.

$$\text{CS: } AUX_2 \rightarrow \left\{ \begin{matrix} (have\ en)\ (be\ ing) & [\text{if } AUX_1 \text{ dominates M}] \\ (be\ ing) & [\text{if } AUX_1 \text{ dominates } have\ en] \\ \emptyset & [\text{if } AUX_1 \text{ dominates } be\ ing] \end{matrix} \right\}$$

While this rule accounts for the data, it completely obscures the elegant generalization that the order of elements in the verbal sequence is strictly M, *have*, *be*. While the later generalization can be preserved for affirmative declarative sentences, the rules required for negation (and for questions as well) suffer under the additional complications that result from the attempt to capture all of the data in terms of phrase structure rules.

A transformational analysis, on the other hand, permits us to capture the generalizations that a phrase structure account, even a CS rule account, fails to capture. In this case, there are three approaches of comparable plausibility:

1. The expansion of S that we have arrived at thus far is given as PSR1.

PSR1: S → NP AUX VP

To capture the generalization that *not* always appears after TENSE and the first verbal element, we may simply revise this rule so that it permits *not* to appear after AUX in the deep structure.

PSR1′: S → NP AUX (*not*) VP

Given that *not* may intervene between AUX and VP, it will be necessary in this approach to revise *Do* Replacement slightly so that it will apply even when *not* is present.

2. The second plausible alternative is virtually identical with the first, with the difference that in this case *not* is treated as an underlying constituent of VP rather than of S. The phrase structure rules would then be as follows.

PSR1: S → NP AUX VP
PSR2′: VP → (*not*) V (NP)

Here the same revision of *Do* Replacement is required as in the first alternative.

3. The third alternative treats *not* as a constituent of the sentence that is generated in a position outside of the verbal sequence and is moved after AUX by a transformation. The traditional treatment involves PSR1″ and the transformation of Neg Placement.

PSR1″: S → (*not*) NP AUX VP

NEG PLACEMENT: X *not* Y AUX Z
1   2   3   4   5 ⇒ 1 ∅ 3 4 + 2 5

For purposes of comparison, the complete derivation of *Mary is not leaving* is given in Figure 6.1 using each of the three alternatives presented here.

Note that alternative 3 does not require complication of *Do* Replacement if Neg Placement is ordered after it, as shown in Figure 6.1c. When *Do* Replacement applies, in this analysis, *not* has not yet been moved into the verbal sequence. In the other two analyses, however, *not* originates in the middle of the verbal sequence, and therefore the possibility of its presence must be taken into account in the statement of *Do* Replacement. It would be difficult to argue, however, that this slight simplification of *Do* Replacement justifies postulating a completely new transformation of Neg Placement. There is evidence to suggest that the rule of *Do* Replacement must be complicated anyway, in order to apply when the AUX is followed by adverbs such as *just, ever* and *so*.

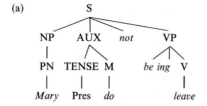

(a)

Do Replacement: *Mary* Pres *be not ∅ ing leave*
Affix Hopping: *Mary # be +* Pres *# not ∅ # leave + ing #*

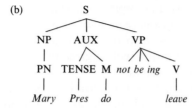

(b)

Do Replacement: *Mary* Pres *be not ∅ ing leave*
Affix Hopping: *Mary # be +* Pres *# not # leave + ing #*

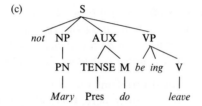

(c)

Do Replacement: *not Mary* Pres *be ∅ ing leave*
Neg Placement: *∅ Mary* Pres *be not ∅ ing leave*
Affix Hopping: *∅ Mary # be +* Pres *# not # leave + ing #*

Figure 6.1. Alternative derivations of *Mary is not leaving.*

(6.9)   a.   *John has just left the room.*
                    No one has ever said that before.
                    Mary will so win the prize.
               b.   **Just, John has left the room.*
                    *Ever, no one has said that before.
                    *So, Mary will win the prize.
               c.   **John has left the room, just.*
                    *No one has said that before, ever.
                    *Mary will win the prize, so.

These adverbs can only appear in the position after AUX, and there is no evidence that they must be moved into this position from elsewhere in the sentence by a transformation.

Interestingly, there is some evidence that suggests that **both** (1) and (2) are correct analyses. Notice, first of all, that it is possible to have **two** instances of negation in the verbal sequence. Such cases are awkward, but appear to be grammatical nevertheless:

(6.10) a. *John has **not** deliberately **not** paid his taxes for*
      at least two years.
    b. *You simply **can't not** take advantage of this offer.*
    c. *Charley would**n't** have **not** seen the money if he*
      had been looking for it.

Without permitting *not* to be generated in more than one place in the sentence, it will be impossible to derive examples such as these.

In the absence of strong evidence in favor of Neg Placement, we will restrict the remainder of the discussion to the first two alternatives outlined earlier. Further support for this decision will be given in Chapter 9 in relation to the analysis of infinitival complements.[1]

Second, there is a construction in English that serves as a diagnostic for the presence of a VP. We can use this diagnostic to show that in some sentences negation is on the VP and in other sentences it is not. This construction, called **pseudo-cleft**, is exemplified in (6.11):

(6.11) a. ***What John did** was **(to) leave the door open**.*
    b. ***What Mary will do** will be **(to) read a book**.*
    c. ***What John wants to do** is **(to) sleep all day**.*
    d. ***What Mary is doing** is **feeding the pigeons**.*

The descriptive and theoretical problems raised by this construction are considerable, and we will not pursue them here. It is sufficient for our present purposes to observe that the pseudo-cleft is composed of three parts: (i) the left-hand part, which takes the form of a *wh* question that lacks Inversion, (ii) an AUX consisting of some form of the verb *be*, and (iii) the right-hand part, which appears to provide the answer to the question "asked" by the left-hand part.

To illustrate, in the preceding example; *leave the door open* answers the question *What did John do?*, *read a book* answers the question *What will Mary do?*, and so on. When the left-hand part of the pseudo-cleft seeks the nature of the action performed, the right-hand side provides the answer in the form of a verb phrase.

It is important to note that the answer to the question can take the form of *not* followed by a verb phrase:

---

[1] While the Neg Placement analysis is the traditional one, there are many linguists who do not accept it. Analyses of the syntax of negation that do not employ Neg Placement can be found in Jackendoff (1972) and Emonds (1970). Analyses that do postulate the transformation appear in Klima (1964) and Stockwell *et al.* (1973). The issue is complicated by the fact that certain generalizations that appear to fit in with a syntactic analysis involving Neg Placement are not necessarily syntactic generalizations, but may plausibly be viewed as semantic. Capturing these generalizations in the semantic component removes much of the original motivation for the rule. Compare the analyses in Klima (1964) and Jackendoff (1972, chap. 8).

(6.12)   a. *What John did was (to) not leave the door open,*
                (but (to) close it).
            b. *What Mary will do will be (to) not read a book*
                (but (to) write one).
            c. *What John wants to do is (to) not sleep all day.*
            d. *What Mary will be doing will be not feeding the*
                pigeons.

Again, while some of these examples are somewhat awkward, they appear to
be grammatical nevertheless.

A general characterization of these pseudo-cleft sentences can be achieved
if *not* is treated as a constituent of VP. How this is to be accomplished is a complicated question, but it is clear that the analysis of sentences such as those in
(6.12) will be simplified if *not* is a constituent of VP rather than a sister of VP.
In the latter framework, it will be necessary to explain why *not* can appear
after *will be* in the pseudo-cleft before a VP but not before other constituents.
As can be seen in the following examples, the position after *will be* is not one
in which *not* can normally appear, even in pseudo-clefts:

(6.13)   a. **What John buys will be not a toy.*
            b. **What Mary fixes next will be not the sink.*
            c. **Where John goes will be not to Chicago.*

Of course, the examples in (6.13) can be improved by introducing a *but*
clause in each case, e.g.:

(6.14)   a. *What John buys will be not a toy, but a gun.*
            b. *What Mary fixes next will be not the sink, but the*
                garbage disposer.
            c. *Where John goes will be not to Chicago, but to New York.*

However, in these cases the *not* is part of the constituent that contains the two
phrases and *but*. This can be seen from the fact that the *not–but* construction
can be used independently of those contexts in which sentential negation could
be operating:

(6.15)   a. *Not a toy, but a gun, arrived in the mail.*
            b. *Mary fixed not the sink, but the garbage disposer.*
            c. *Not in Chicago, but in New York, there is a certain*
                excitement in the air.

In summary, the *not* can most simply and revealingly be located after *will be*
if it is treated as a constituent of the constituent that follows *will be*. This means
that *not* must be a constituent of VP in certain cases. Given that this is the case,
it then becomes possible to generate sentences with two instances of negation,
one in the VP and the other attached to S and preceding VP.

Before continuing with our discussion of negation, it is worth pointing out
that the diagnostic power of the pseudo-cleft construction can be applied

further to our analysis of the verb phrase. Note that our phrase structure rule for the expansion of VP does not assign any substructure to the VP beyond the individual constituents.

PSR3: VP → (*not*) (*have en*) (*be ing*) V (NP)

The sequence V (NP) is not treated as a constituent by this analysis. The following examples show that this is incorrect:

(6.16)   a. *What John has done has been (to) **open the door.***
        b. *What Mary is doing is **feeding the pigeons.***
        c. *What Mary has been doing is **feeding the pigeons.***
        d. *What Mary should have done was **feed the pigeons.***
        e. *What Mary should have been doing was **feeding the pigeons.***

In each of these examples, the sequence to the right of *be* is of the form V NP. By contrast, verb phrases with *have en* or *be ing* cannot appear in this position:

(6.17)   a. **What John does is **have left the area.***
        b. **What John will do will be **have left the area.***
        c. **What Mary has done has been **be leaving the area.***
        d. **What Mary does is **be leaving the area.***

etc.

This suggests that the phrase structure expansion of VP involves a non-lexical constituent that itself expands as V NP. Since this constituent is the one that appears to the right of *be* in the pseudo-cleft, and since negation is a constituent of this constituent, the phrase structure rules must be the following.

PSR3a: VP → (*have en*) (*be ing*) VP′
PSR3b: VP′ → (*not*) V (NP)

Such a formulation will require that all rules that intuitively appear to involve VP (= V NP) will in fact apply to VP′. While one would prefer arguments somewhat stronger than those presented here, the analysis given as PSR3a and PSR3b appears to be fundamentally correct and will be assumed from this point on.

NEGATIVE QUESTIONS AND CONTRACTION

When negation appears in the form *n't*, it is called **contracted negation,** and the process by which *n't* is derived from *not* is called **contraction.** The analysis of contraction will show why *not* is generated after AUX, rather than in AUX as might be supposed. This has to do with negative questions like the following:

(6.18)   a. *Won't John buy the yogurt?*
        b. *Didn't Mary fix the faucet?*

c. *Wouldn't they have returned home before dinner?*
d. *Haven't you seen Naples?*
e. *Aren't you running for President next year?*

As suggested at the beginning of this chapter, there are certain restrictions on the distribution of negation in negative questions. To summarize, the only form of negation that may be moved with the modal in Inversion is contracted negation, and the only form of negation that may be left behind when Inversion moves the modal is uncontracted negation. E.g.:

(6.19)

a. $\left\{\begin{array}{l}*Will\ not\\ Won't\end{array}\right\}$ *John buy the yogurt?*

b. $\left\{\begin{array}{l}*Did\ not\\ Didn't\end{array}\right\}$ *Mary fix the faucet?*

c. $\left\{\begin{array}{l}*Would\ not\\ Wouldn't\end{array}\right\}$ *they have returned home before dinner?*

d. $\left\{\begin{array}{l}*Have\ not\\ Haven't\end{array}\right\}$ *you seen Naples?*

e. $\left\{\begin{array}{l}*Are\ not\\ Aren't\end{array}\right\}$ *you running for President next year?*

It appears, then, that when negation is moved by Inversion the form of negation must be the contracted form, and when negation is not moved by Inversion it cannot be the contracted form.

This distribution of contracted negation can be easily accounted for if it is assumed that the rule of contraction, which is called Neg Contraction, not only replaces *not* by *n't* but also attaches it to AUX before Inversion applies. Similarly, it must also be assumed that if Neg Contraction does not apply, then negation is not attached to AUX, since otherwise Inversion would move the uncontracted form of negation to the front, as in the starred examples in (6.19).

An additional consideration to be taken into account in our formulation of Neg Contraction is that the rule applies only when negation immediately follows AUX. That is, it is not sufficient for negation to follow an auxiliary verb, as shown by the ungrammatical examples in (6.20):

(6.20)   a. **Charley would not haven't seen the money.*
b. **Charley wouldn't haven't seen the money.*
c. *Charley wouldn't have not seen the money.*
d. *Charley would have not seen the money.*
e. **Charley would haven't seen the money.*

In view of these facts, we state Neg Contraction as follows.

NEG CONTRACTION: X AUX *not* Y
                       1   2   3   4 $\Rightarrow$ 1 2 > *n't* $\emptyset$ 4

(The symbol > is used here to indicate that *n't* is attached to the right of AUX in such a way that AUX ends up dominating it.) The effect of this transformation is illustrated by (6.21):

(6.21)

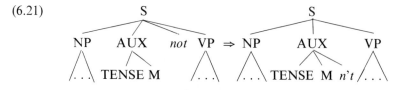

It should be pointed out that the rule does not distinguish between a *not* that is immediately dominated by S and a *not* that is immediately dominated by VP′, just in case the latter immediately follows AUX.

The ordering of the rules will now be as follows:

> *Do* Replacement
> Neg Contraction
> Inversion

Neg Contraction precedes Inversion for reasons that we have already dealt with in detail. *Do* Replacement is ordered before Neg Contraction so that *Do* Replacement will not be required to mention the possibility that contracted negation might be present. If Neg Contraction applied before *Do* Replacement, we would have to apply *Do* Replacement to the sequences *do have* and *do be*, *do not have* and *do not be*, and *don't have* and *don't be*. This slight complication can be avoided by the ordering suggested here.

Furthermore, if Neg Contraction is reformulated so that it actually attaches *n't* to the modal and forms a single item from the two, then Neg Contraction must follow *Do* Replacement for this reason as well. The linguistic evidence in fact suggests that combinations of modal and *n't* are single units. Note, for example, that while it is possible to apply heavy stress to *not*, it is impossible to apply heavy stress to *n't*:

(6.22)   a. *John did not leave on time.*
           b. **John didn't leave on time.*

Another piece of evidence that shows that a modal plus *n't* is to be treated as a unit involves a transformation that deletes a modal when there is an identical modal preceding it somewhere in the phrase marker. This rule will not be given a formal statement here; its effect can be seen in the following examples:[2]

(6.23)   a. *John will leave and Mary will stay.*
             John will leave, and Mary, stay.
         b. *Mary should call the doctor and John should feed the baby.*
             Mary should call the doctor, and John, feed the baby.
         c. *Harry could fail and Larry could succeed.*
             Harry could fail, and Larry, succeed.

---

[2] The rule appears to be a special case of the rule of Gapping discussed in Ross (1971).

When *not* is present, it cannot be deleted when the modal is deleted by this transformation. On the other hand, when *n't* appears it cannot be left behind by this deletion transformation and must be deleted along with the modal:

(6.24) a. *John will not leave and Mary will not stay.*
            John will not leave and Mary, not stay.
            *John will not leave and Mary, stay.
        b. *Mary should not call the doctor and John should not feed the baby.*
            Mary should not call the doctor and John, not feed the baby.
            *Mary should not call the doctor and John, feed the baby.
        c. *Harry could not fail and Larry could not succeed.*
            Harry could not fail and Larry, not succeed.
            *Harry could not fail, and Larry, succeed.

(6.25) a. *John won't leave and Mary won't stay.*
            John won't leave and Mary, stay.
            *John won't leave and Mary, n't stay.
        b. *Mary shouldn't call the doctor and John shouldn't feed the baby.*
            Mary shouldn't call the doctor and John, feed the baby.
            *Mary shouldn't call the doctor and John, n't the baby.
        c. *Harry couldn't fail and Larry couldn't succeed.*
            Harry couldn't fail and Larry, succeed.
            *Harry couldn't fail and Larry, n't succeed.

These judgments, while subtle, are fairly firm. Note that they are predicted from an analysis in which *n't* is incorporated into the modal just as the affixes are incorporated into the verbal element.

This concludes our discussion of negation per se. The next section deals with the important tag question construction, which bears many similarities to negative and positive questions.

TAG QUESTIONS

The tag question construction is illustrated in (6.26) and (6.27):

(6.26)   *John didn't buy the yogurt, did he?*

(6.27)   *John bought the yogurt, did he not?*
                John bought the yogurt, didn't he?

A tag question has two identifiable parts: the part to the right of the comma, called the **tag,** and the part to the left of the comma, which is referred to here as the **main clause.** There are a number of characteristics that relate the tag and the main clause, and an adequate description of tag questions requires a revealing characterization of what these are.

It is necessary to ask, therefore, what restrictions there are on the form of the tag, what the relationship between the tag and the rest of the sentence might be, and whether there are any other characteristics that serve to identify tag questions. An observation of particular interest is that while it is possible for there to be negation in either the tag or the main clause, it does not appear to be possible for there to be negation in the tag and the main clause at the same time.

So, for example, the following distribution of judgments of acceptability holds for most speakers of English:

(6.28)   a. *Mary won't read the book, will she?*
          b. *Mary will read the book, won't she?*
          c. *Mary will read the book, will she?*
          d. **Mary won't read the book, won't she?*

Examples with one or with no occurrence of negation are acceptable, but the one with two instances of negation is not acceptable. Of course, there is also a difference in the meanings of these sentences, there are differences in intonation when the tag is uttered, and there are differences in the length of the pause before the tag as well. The present discussion ignores these facts.

A second observation about tag questions is that the form of the tag is related to the form of the main clause. There is a modal in the tag just in case there is a modal in the main clause, and the two modals must be the same. This is true for *have* and *be* as well when they initiate the verbal sequence in the rest of the sentence. For example:

(6.29)

a. *Mary won't read the book,* $\left\{ \begin{array}{l} will \\ *can \\ *may \\ *shall \\ *would \\ *is \\ *has \\ *should \\ *must \\ etc. \end{array} \right\}$ *she?*

b. *Mary has read the book,* $\left\{ \begin{array}{l} hasn't \\ *isn't \\ *won't \\ *can't \\ *couldn't \\ *mustn't \\ etc. \end{array} \right\}$ *she?*

A third observation is that generally there must be a definite pronoun in the tag, and this pronoun must agree with the subject of the main clause.

"Agree" means that both the pronoun and the subject of the sentence must have the same **gender** (masculine, feminine, or neuter), **number** (singular or plural), and **person** (first person, second person, or third person). For example:

(6.30)

$$John\ isn't\ smiling,\ is \left\{ \begin{array}{l} he? \\ *she? \\ *John? \end{array} \right\}$$

(6.31)

$$You\ haven't\ read\ my\ book,\ have \left\{ \begin{array}{l} you? \\ *they? \\ *we? \\ *I? \end{array} \right\}$$

(6.32)   The woman who John met yesterday was a gypsy,

$$wasn't \left\{ \begin{array}{l} she? \\ *he? \\ *the\ woman\ who\ \ldots? \end{array} \right\}$$

To summarize, then, there are three significant characteristics of tag questions that have been identified thus far:

1. There can be at most one instance of negation shared between the tag and the main clause.
2. The verbal element in the tag is identical to the one in the main clause. (We will not consider what happens when there is a more complex verbal sequence in the rest of the sentence.)
3. There must be a pronoun in the tag that agrees with the subject of the rest of the sentence in gender, number, and person.

Clearly, these are regularities that an adequate account of tag questions must express.

The analysis of tag questions to be presented here is a comparatively simple one, and one that attempts to account for only the most salient aspects of the construction, i.e., those just given. Our characterization of what constitutes a grammatical tag question in English will take the form of a transformation of Tag Formation. In fact, most if not all accounts of tag questions in the literature postulate a transformational analysis. There are, however, considerable problems with the tag question that suggest that a transformational analysis may not be correct. These have to do with the relationship between the syntactic representation of the tag question and its semantic interpretation, and therefore they will not be discussed here.

Let us proceed with the formulation of the rule. A characteristic of tag questions that is of considerable importance is that there are no tag questions that have overt *wh* words in the tag. This is demonstrated by the examples in (6.33):

(6.33)   a. *John saw someone, who did he?
           b. *You are going somewhere, where are you?
           c. *Someone is smiling, who is?

In spite of the absence of an overt *wh* word in the tag, however, the form that a tag may take is that which we would expect if Inversion applied in the derivation of the tag question. As we have already shown, the application of Inversion in yes–no questions is due to the underlying presence of the *wh* word *whether*, which is later deleted.

The notion that Inversion applies in tags is further substantiated by the fact that the distribution of negation in the tags is precisely that which is accounted for by applying Inversion to the output of Neg Contraction in the derivation of negative questions. E.g.:

(6.34) a. *Isn't John smiling?*
           Is John not smiling?
           *Is not John smiling?
           *Is John n't smiling?
       b. *John is smiling, isn't he?*
           John is smiling, is he not?
           *John is smiling, is not he?
           *John is smiling, is he n't?

This is a generalization that the grammar must capture. We formulate the analysis of the tag question so that Inversion will apply in the tag just as it applies in yes–no and negative questions. This means that at some point in the derivation of the tag question the *wh* word *whether* must appear in the tag, since this is the only *wh* word that will be deleted after causing Inversion to apply.

Given that the tag is not present in the deep structure, *whether* must be introduced into the tag by the application of Tag Formation. Logically, either *whether* is simply created by Tag Formation or it appears in the input to Tag Formation and is put into the tag by the structural change of the rule. The second alternative permits a somewhat simpler formulation than the first.

To see this, consider the two alternative formulations of Tag Formation that are involved. In the first case, *whether* is introduced by the transformation; hence, a typical derivation would be roughly as illustrated in (6.35).

(6.35)

Input	*John* Pres *will leave*
Tag Formation	*John* Pres *will leave, whether he* Pres *will*
Inversion	*John* Pres *will leave, whether* Pres *will he*
Affix Hopping	*John* # *will* + Pres # *leave, whether* # *will* + Pres # *he*

After deletion of *whether*, this derivation yields the grammatical *John will leave, will he?*

Suppose, now, that the input structure contains a *wh* word. By carrying out an analogous derivation, we find that an ungrammatical sequence is generated in this case:

(6.36)

Input	*John* Pres *will leave who*
Tag Formation	*John* Pres *will leave who, whether he* Pres *will*
Wh Fronting	*who John* Pres *will leave, whether he* Pres *will*
Inversion	*who* Pres *will John leave, whether* Pres *will he*
Affix Hopping	*who* # *will* + Pres # *John leave, whether* # *will* + Pres # *he*

After deletion of *whether*, this derivation yields **Who will John leave, will he?* In general, it is impossible to apply Tag Formation to a structure that underlies either a *wh* question or a yes–no question, as the derivation in (6.36) and the additional examples given in (6.37) indicate:

(6.37)   a. **Who left early, did he?*
            b. **Where are you going, are you?*
            c. **When did Bill get here, did he?*
            d. **Are you leaving for New York, are you?*
            e. **Did Mary like the movie, did she?*

In order to make this formulation of Tag Formation work, then, we must organize the grammar in such a way that Tag Formation will be blocked when the phrase marker takes the form of a *wh* question. Notice that to do this it will not be sufficient simply to specify that the phrase marker to which Tag Formation applies cannot contain a *Wh*, since there are phrase markers that do contain *Wh* to which Tag Formation may apply, e.g.:

(6.38)   a. *John forgot what Mary said, didn't he?*
            b. *Mary questioned whether the world was flat, didn't she?*

In fact, what is required is that Tag Formation cannot apply when *Wh* Fronting has moved the *wh* constituent to the front of the main clause.

This is also a difficult condition to specify in terms of a structural description. It is impossible to differentiate between *wh* questions and declaratives in terms of a very simple structural condition, because there are *wh* questions that look just like declaratives; e.g., *who saw John?* has the basic structure NP AUX VP, just as the declarative *Mary saw John* does. Nevertheless, Tag Formation cannot apply even to this *wh* question [cf. (6.37a)].

In view of these facts, the formulation of the Tag Formation transformation would have to be as follows. It will have to apply after *Wh* Fronting, so that it will apply when there is an indirect *wh* question but not when there is a direct *wh* question. It will have to take as input a structure of the form NP AUX X, and yield as output a structure of the form NP AUX X, *whether* $\left[\begin{matrix} \text{NP} \\ +\text{PRO} \end{matrix} \right]$ AUX. Finally, it cannot apply to NP AUX X if the NP is a *wh* word. A more formal statement of the rule follows; note that the question of where *not* may appear in the structure is ignored for the present.

TAG FORMATION (i):   NP AUX X

$$1 \quad 2 \quad 3 \Rightarrow 1\ 2\ 3, \textit{whether} \begin{bmatrix} 1 \\ +\text{PRO} \end{bmatrix} 2$$

Condition: 1 is not a *wh* word

Notice that by stating the structural description in terms of the initial sequence NP AUX we automatically prevent this rule from applying to the output of *Wh* Fronting, which yields a sentence-initial sequence of the form A NP AUX. The complication of the transformation has to do with the fact that this device does not work for cases in which the *wh* word is in subject position; hence, the additional condition is required.

Consider, now, the alternative formulation of Tag Formation. Here we place a condition on the rule to the effect that it can apply only if *whether* appears in initial position. The following is a formal statement of this version of Tag Formation. (We again ignore the question of where *not* appears.)

TAG FORMATION (ii):   *whether* NP AUX X

$$1 \quad 2 \quad 3 \quad 4 \Rightarrow \emptyset\ 2\ 3\ 4,\ 1 \begin{bmatrix} 2 \\ +\text{PRO} \end{bmatrix} 3$$

This formulation of Tag Formation blocks the derivation of a tag question from a structure that underlies a *wh* question. The movement of *whether* out of the main clause into the tag ensures the correct application of Inversion in the tag and blocks application of Inversion to the main clause.

Let us now consider the distribution of negation in tag questions. As we have seen, negation appears either in the main clause or in the tag, but not in both:

(6.39)   a.   *Mary won't read the book, will she?*
               b.   *Mary will read the book, won't she?*
               d.   **Mary won't read the book, won't she?*

This can be accounted for very naturally in terms of the analysis of negation given in this chapter, in which *not* is an immediate constituent either of S or of VP′.

When Tag Formation applies, it must either move *not* into the tag or leave it in the main clause. It **cannot** copy negation, since this would result in two instances of negation in the sentence, which is ungrammatical [cf. (6.28d)]. We can account for this by stating Tag Formation so that it moves *not* when it is an immediate constituent of S, and ignores *not* when it is in VP′. This is done in the following restatement of Tag Formation.

TAG FORMATION: *whether* NP AUX (*not*) VP

$$1 \quad 2 \quad 3 \quad 4 \quad 5 \Rightarrow \emptyset\ 2\ 3\ \emptyset\ 5,\ 1 \begin{bmatrix} 2 \\ +\text{PRO} \end{bmatrix} 3\ 4$$

By convention (cf. page 106), the longest sequence that satisfies the structural description determines the sequence to which the rule applies. Thus, if *not* appears **between** AUX and VP, Tag Formation will move this *not* into the tag along with AUX. This will derive sentences such as (6.39b). On the other hand, if *not* is present but is not an immediate constituent of S, only AUX will be moved into the tag, deriving sentences such as (6.39a). The two derivations are illustrated in Table 6.2.

This last version of Tag Formation is the one that we will adopt here. There are a number of problems that still remain, which we will not go into in detail but should be taken note of. First of all, the rule of Neg Placement suggested in the preceding section provides an elegant solution to the problem of the distribution of negation in tag questions. In this analysis, we would assume that *not* originates completely outside of the main clause, and would first apply Tag Formation. This transformation yields a structure in which there are two instances of AUX, the one of the main clause and the one of the tag. The structural description of Neg Placement may be satisfied in two ways by the output of Tag Formation, and the rule may move *not* into the AUX of the main clause or into the AUX of the tag. It is impossible in this analysis to get *not* in both the tag and the main clause at the same time. This analysis is discussed in considerable detail in Culicover (1971); it is not adopted here primarily because of the lack of strong independent evidence in favor of the Neg Placement transformation.

A second problem concerns the application of Tag Formation to verb phrases that contain negation. Our analysis of the verb phrase currently positions *not* after *have* or *be* if they appear, as the following shows.

PSR3a: VP → (*have en*) (*be ing*) VP′
PSR3b: VP′ → (*not*) V (NP)

We have formulated Tag Formation in such a way that a *not* that appears in the main clause will be a constituent of VP, and not an immediate constituent of S. Since *not* in the VP follows *have*, in a sentence in which *not* appears between a modal and *have* this *not* cannot be in the VP, but must be on the Ṡ, E.g.:

(6.40)   *John could not have said that.*

The reason why this is a problem is that tag questions can be formed from sentences like (6.40) in which negation appears in the main clause. We have already established that *not* in (6.40) is an immediate constituent of S, and we have established that such instances of negation will always end up in the tag. This contradiction is shown by (6.41):

(6.41)   *John couldn't have said that, could he?*

This problem can be avoided if we reanalyze the verb phrase so that (i) each auxiliary verb is the main verb of a separate verb phrase and (ii) *not* can be a constituent of any verb phrase. The phrase structure rules for expansion of VP

Table 6.2. Derivation of Two Tag Questions with Negation

a.

Input	whether	Mary Pres will not	∅	vp[read the book]
Tag Formation	whether	Mary Pres will ∅		read the book, whether she Pres will not
Neg Contraction	whether	Mary Pres will ∅		read the book, whether she Pres will + n't
Inversion	whether	Mary Pres will ∅		read the book, whether Pres will + n't she
Affix Hopping	∅	Mary # will + Pres # ∅		read the book, whether # will + n't + Pres # she
Delete whether	∅	Mary # will + Pres # ∅		read the book, ∅ # will + n't + Pres # she
		Mary will		read the book, won't she?

b.

Input	whether	Mary Pres will	∅	vp[not read the book]
Tag Formation	whether	Mary Pres will	∅	not read the book, whether she Pres will
Neg Contraction	whether	Mary Pres will + n't	∅	read the book, whether she Pres will
Inversion	whether	Mary Pres will + n't	∅	read the book, whether Pres will she
Affix Hopping	∅	Mary # will + n't + Pres #		read the book, whether # will + Pres # she
Delete whether	∅	Mary # will + n't + Pres #		read the book, ∅ # will + Pres # she
		Mary won't		read the book, will she?

138

would then look something like PSR3′, and a typical structure generated by these rules would be (6.42).

$$\text{PSR3}': \text{VP} \rightarrow (not)\ \text{V} \begin{Bmatrix} \text{NP} \\ \text{VP} \end{Bmatrix}$$

(6.42)

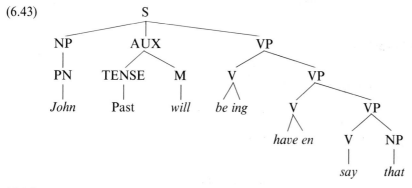

The major problem with this alternative is that there is now no natural syntactic formulation for the strict order of the auxiliary verbs *have* and *be*. Since each of these verbs is the main verb of a separate VP, this analysis will generate structures in which *be* is to the left of *have*, e.g.:

(6.43)

(6.44)   *John would be having said that.*

Such an analysis could be maintained, however, if it could be shown that all of the incorrect orders are derived from deep structures that will independently receive unacceptable semantic interpretations. Sentences such as (6.44) would then be syntactically acceptable but semantically unacceptable.

Further discussion of this analysis can be found in Emonds (1970) where it was originally proposed and where a number of arguments can be found in favor of its adoption. Discussion of the problems involved in treating auxiliaries as main verbs appears in Ross (1969c) and McCawley (1971). Since we cannot go into these problems further here, the analysis to be adopted in this book will be the one originally proposed in this chapter, i.e., that of PSR3a and PSR3b. The virtues of the alternative analysis, involving PSR3′, should not be overlooked, however.

SUMMARY OF RULES

This is the last point in the book at which all of the transformations previously considered are stated in full. In later chapters, only those transformations will be stated that have been introduced in those chapters themselves: rules previously introduced will be indicated by name only.

Phrase Structure Rules

$$
\begin{aligned}
&\text{PSR1:} \quad \text{S} \quad\;\; \rightarrow \text{NP AUX (\textit{not}) VP} \\
&\text{PSR2:} \quad \text{AUX} \rightarrow \text{TENSE M} \\
&\text{PSR3a:} \quad \text{VP} \quad\;\; \rightarrow \text{(\textit{have en}) (\textit{be ing}) VP}' \\
&\text{PSR3b:} \quad \text{VP}' \;\;\; \rightarrow \text{(\textit{not}) V (NP)} \\
&\text{PSR4:} \quad \text{NP} \quad\;\; \rightarrow \left\{ \begin{array}{l} \text{DET (ADJ) N} \\ \text{PN} \end{array} \right\} \\
&\text{PSR5:} \quad \text{DET} \rightarrow \left\{ \begin{array}{l} \text{(\textit{Wh}) QUAN} \\ \text{ART} \end{array} \right\} \\
&\text{PSR6:} \quad \text{PP} \quad\;\; \rightarrow \text{P NP}
\end{aligned}
$$

Transformations

Do REPLACEMENT: $\quad$ X do $\left\{ \begin{array}{l} have \\ be \end{array} \right\}$ Y

$\qquad\qquad\qquad\quad$ 1 $\;$ 2 $\quad$ 3 $\quad\;$ 4 $\Rightarrow 1\ 3\ \emptyset\ 4$

Wh FRONTING: $\qquad$ X A Y

$\qquad\qquad\qquad\;$ 1 2 3 $\Rightarrow 2 + 1\ \emptyset\ 3$

$\qquad\qquad\qquad\;$ Condition: 2 dominates *Wh*

TAG FORMATION: $\qquad$ *whether* NP AUX (*not*) VP

$\qquad\qquad\qquad\qquad\quad$ 1 $\quad\;$ 2 $\quad\;$ 3 $\quad\;$ 4 $\quad$ 5 $\Rightarrow$

$\qquad\qquad\qquad\;$ $\emptyset\ 2\ 3\ \emptyset\ 5, 1 \left[\begin{array}{c} 2 \\ +\text{PRO} \end{array} \right] 3\ 4$

NEG CONTRACTION: $\;$ X AUX *not* Y

$\qquad\qquad\qquad\qquad$ 1 $\quad$ 2 $\quad\;$ 3 $\quad$ 4 $\Rightarrow 1\ 2 > n't\ \emptyset\ 4$

INVERSION: $\qquad\qquad$ A NP AUX X

$\qquad\qquad\qquad\qquad$ 1 $\;$ 2 $\quad$ 3 $\quad$ 4 $\Rightarrow 1\ 3 + 2\ \emptyset\ 4$

$\qquad\qquad\qquad\;$ Condition: 1 dominates *Wh*

Do DELETION:	X *do* V Y 1 2 3 4 $\Rightarrow$ 1 $\emptyset$ 3 4

Condition: 2 is unstressed

AFFIX HOPPING:	X Affix [+V] Y 1 2 3 4 $\Rightarrow$ 1 $\emptyset$ # 3 + 2 # 4

Ordering of Transformations

Do Replacement
Wh Fronting
Tag Formation
Neg Contraction
Inversion
Do Deletion
Affix Hopping

EXERCISES

1. Derive each of the following sentences:

a. *John doesn't like yogurt.*
b. *Mary doesn't like John, does she?*
c. *Doesn't Mary like John?*
d. *John likes yogurt, doesn't he?*
e. *Isn't John sick of yogurt?*
f. *Has Mary not washed the dishes?*

PROBLEMS

1. Justify the rule ordering given in the summary of rules for each of the following pairs of rules:

a. *Do* Replacement and Tag Formation
b. *Wh* Fronting and Tag Formation
c. Neg Placement and Tag Formation
d. *Do* Deletion and Tag Formation
e. Neg Placement and *Do* Deletion

2. Show that it would be possible to remove the condition on *Do* Deletion that *do* must be unstressed by assuming that stress is carried by an element E whose syntactic behavior is identical to *not*, and whose semantic function is to indicate emphasis. Consider sentences such as the following:

a. *Jean does not speak French.*
   Jean does too speak French.

Jean does só speak French.
Jean dóes speak French.
b. *Mary is not a genius.*
Mary is tóo a genius.
Mary is só a genius.
Mary iś a genius.
c. *Sam has not left.*
Sam has tóo left.
Sam has só left.
Sam hás left.

3. Give arguments to support the assumption that there is a transformation of Neg Contraction, as contrasted with having both *not* and *n't* in the deep structure.

4. A plausible alternative to Tag Formation is to derive the tag question by deleting part of a question that is attached in deep structure to a declarative. For example, *John left, didn't he?* would be derived from something like (a) or (b):

a. *John* Past *do leave, whether John* Past *do not leave*
b. *John* Past *do leave, or whether John* Past *do not leave*

The only difference between (a) and (b) is that (b) assumes that there is an underlying conjunction *or*, while (a) does not. Hence, the rule would have to be obligatory if (a) was the underlying structure; otherwise, a sentence like (c) would be generated:

c. **John left, didn't John leave?*

On the other hand, failure of the deletion rule to apply to (b) would result in the grammatical (d):

d. *John left, or didn't John leave?*

Give a formal statement of each of the two versions of the deletion rule proposed here.

*5. Using CS rules, work out a purely phrase structure account of *wh* questions and yes–no questions. Compare this analysis with the transformational analysis and show why the transformational analysis is preferable.

SUGGESTED FURTHER READINGS

Negation

Jackendoff, R. S. (1969), "An interpretive theory of negation," *FL*, **4**, 422–442.
Jackendoff, R. S. (1972), *Semantic Interpretation in Generative Grammar*, MIT Press, Cambridge, Mass.

Klima, E. S. (1964), "Negation in English," in Fodor, J. A. & Katz, J. J., eds., (1964), *The Structure of Language: Readings in the Philosophy of Language*, Prentice-Hall, Englewood Cliffs, New Jersey.

Lakoff, G. (1970b), "Global rules," *Lg*, **46**, 627–639.

Lakoff, G. (1971), "On generative semantics," in Steinberg, D. & Jakobovits, L. A., eds., (1971), *Semantics: An Interdisciplinary Reader in Philosophy, Linguistics, and Psychology*, Cambridge University Press, London.

Tag Questions

Arbini, R. (1969), "Tag-questions and tag-imperatives in English," *JL*, **5**, 205–214.

Culicover, P. W. (1973), "On the coherence of syntactic descriptions," *JL*, **9**, 35–51.

Huddleston, R. (1970), "Two approaches to the analysis of tags," *JL*, **6**, 215–222.

Klima (1964).

7

More Transformations

INTRODUCTION

This chapter surveys a number of grammatical phenomena that are central to the grammar of English: **reflexives,** the **imperative,** the **dative,** and **passives.** The major characteristics of each construction are outlined and some central problems are pointed out; possible solutions and lines of arguments are suggested as well, but the primary goal here is to provide an introduction to the phenomena as something to be dealt with, and not to provide grammatical descriptions in great detail. Thus, many of the more technical points and tangential questions appear in the problems at the end of the chapter, and not in the body of the text.

REFLEXIVE PRONOUNS

In English, the reflexive pronouns share the characteristic of ending in -*self* or -*selves: myself, yourself, itself, himself, herself, ourselves, your-selves, themselves, oneself.* While reflexive pronouns share numerous properties with noun phrases in general, their distribution is somewhat limited. That is, there are positions within the sentence where the reflexive pronouns cannot appear without making the sentence unacceptable:

(7.1) a. *John saw himself.*
b. **Himself saw John.*

It is generally the case that a reflexive pronoun may not function as the subject of a simple sentence.[1]

Another important characteristic of reflexive pronouns is that they must refer to the same individual as some other noun phrase in the sentence. The situation in which two noun phrases refer to the same individual is called **coreferentiality.** Examples like the following show that there are limitations on which noun phrase in the sentence the reflexive pronoun can be coreferential with:

(7.2) a. *John shot himself.*
b. *John talked to Bill about himself.*
c. *John wants Bill to shave himself.*
d. *Mary talked to Bill about herself.*

In order for a noun phrase and a reflexive pronoun to be coreferential, they must agree in person, number, and gender. In the case of the personal pronouns *I, you,* and *he,* for example, the corresponding reflexives are *myself, yourself* or *yourselves,* and *himself,* respectively.

In (7.2a), *John* and *himself* must refer to the same individual: The sentence cannot mean, for example, that John Smith shot John Jones. In (7.2b), either *John* and *himself* may be coreferential or *Bill* and *himself* may be coreferential: however, either one or the other must be the case. In (7.2c), on the other hand, *himself* must be coreferential with *Bill* and cannot be coreferential with John. Finally, in (7.2d) *herself* must be coreferential with *Mary.*

Consider, now, the relationship between the reflexive and another NP in the sentence in terms of their positions in the syntactic structure. A comparison of (7.2b) and (7.3) makes it clear that structural considerations are relevant:

(7.3) *John talked about himself to Bill.*

As we have already observed, in (7.2b) *himself* may be coreferential with either *John* or *Bill.* In (7.3), on the other hand, *himself* cannot be coreferential with *Bill* and must be coreferential with *John.* It appears, therefore, that a reflexive pronoun must be coreferential with a noun phrase to the left of it.[2]

Example (7.2c) shows that not just any noun phrase to the left of the reflexive pronoun will do. While *John* and *Bill* are both to the left of *himself* in this sentence, *himself* must be coreferential with *Bill.* Notice, however, that this example

---

[1] However, when the sentence itself is functioning as the object of a verb like *believe,* then the subject of the object sentence may be a reflexive, e.g., *John believes himself to have seen Mary.* See the discussion in Chapter 9 for details.

[2] There are some exceptions to this generalization. When the reflexive pronoun appears in a phrase such as *this picture of herself,* it may be coreferential with a noun phrase to the right of it. E.g., *This picture of herself is certain to terrify Susan.* See Problem 8 in Chapter 10 and the following discussion.

contains two verbs, *wants* and *shave*. As the analysis in Chapter 9 will show, the underlying representation of sentences like (7.2c) contains two S nodes such that each verb that appears in the surface string is the main verb of one of the S's:

(7.4)

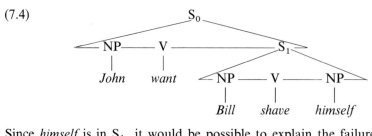

Since *himself* is in S_1, it would be possible to explain the failure of *himself* to be coreferential with *John* by restricting the coreference possibilities of reflexives to noun phrases within the same S.

Our preliminary hypothesis is that a reflexive pronoun must be coreferential with a noun phrase that (i) agrees with it, (ii) is to the left of it, and (iii) is in the same S as it. Any reflexive pronoun that immediately follows the verb, then, must be coreferential with the subject, since the only noun phrase that is both to the left of the pronoun and in the same sentence is the subject.

Let $\begin{bmatrix} NP \\ +PRO \\ +REFL \end{bmatrix}$ denote the set of reflexive pronouns. The statement of the reflexive rule is, then, the following.

REFLEXIVE: X NP Y NP Z

$$1 \quad 2 \quad 3 \quad 4 \quad 5 \Rightarrow 1\,2\,3 \begin{bmatrix} 4 \\ +PRO \\ +REFL \end{bmatrix} 5$$

Conditions: (i) 2 and 4 are coreferential
(ii) 2 and 4 are in the same simple S.

There are a number of observations to make about this transformation. First, there are apparent counterexamples to the claim made by this transformation that the reflexive appears to the right of the noun phrase with which it is coreferential, and in the same simple S as it:

(7.5)   a. *Shooting himself made John angry.*
b. *The picture of herself in the post office frightened Mary.*

Some linguists have argued that (7.5a) is derived from *John's shooting John made John angry* as follows:

(7.6) $_S$[*John's shooting John*] *made John angry.*
⇒ $_S$[*John's shooting himself*] *made John angry.*
⇒ $_S$[∅   *shooting himself*] *made John angry.*

The two crucial features of this account are that *John's shooting John* is an underlying S and that there is a transformation that deletes the subject of this S under identity with another noun phrase in the sentence. While not the only account possible for (7.5a), this explanation permits us to maintain the general formulation of Reflexive given earlier.

The case of (7.5b) presents a different problem. Here it appears that there must be a rule of reflexivization that applies from right to left. It is well known that this rule operates in the context of the so-called **picture nouns** like *picture*, *story*, *movie*, *book*, but the structural conditions on its applications are extremely complex and will not be dealt with here. See Harris (1974) and Jackendoff (1972) for discussion of this special type of reflexivization.

The second point to make about the Reflexive transformation is that certain lingusts have argued that it is not a transformation at all but a rule of semantic interpretation. In particular, Jackendoff (1972) has proposed that the reflexive pronouns are lexical items that are introduced into deep structure by lexical insertion. There are, he argues, rules of semantic interpretation that determine for each pair of NP and reflexive pronoun whether the two may be coreferential. One condition for coreferentiality is that the two agree in number, gender, and person; other conditions involve the location of the NP and the reflexive pronoun relative to one another in the syntactic structure. The reader is referred to Jackendoff (1972) for the details of the interpretive analysis and a comparison between it and the more traditional transformational account outlined here.

Finally, Reflexive as stated here cannot account for reflexivization in sentences such as (7.7), given that there is independent motivation for the deep structure indicated by the labeled bracketing.

(7.7)   Mary expects $_S$[*herself to succeed at everything*].

How this counterexample is to be accounted for will be taken up in detail in Chapter 9.

THE IMPERATIVE

Typical imperative sentences are the following:

(7.8)   a. *Give me the apple juice, please.*
          b. *Take me to your leader.*
          c. *Don't step on the grass.*
          d. *Do not smoke when the red light is lit.*

An **imperative sentence** generally is one that is used to make a request or to give an order. There are, however, a large number of real-world contexts in which an imperative sentence that does not make a request or give an order is appropriate. Similarly, there are numerous ways of expressing requests or orders that are not, strictly speaking, imperatives, if the term **imperative** is restricted to a certain syntactic characteristic.

It is not difficult to imagine that these examples could be used as orders, requests, suggestions, hints, advice, wishes, etc. For each of these uses, however, one could construct a sentence that does not look like the examples in (7.8):

(7.9)   a. *I order you to take me to your leader.*
         b. *I request that you take me to your leader.*
         c. *I suggest that you take me to your leader.*
         d. *How about taking me to your leader.*
         c. *Why don't you take me to your leader.*
         f. *I would advise you to take me to your leader.*
         g. *I wish you would take me to your leader.*

etc.

The syntactic characteristic that distinguishes the sentences in (7.8) from those in (7.9) is that the former lack a superficial subject. The central point of this section will be to present the classical argument that the imperatives in (7.8) have underlying subjects, and that the subjects are demonstrably *you* in each case. This can be shown by appealing to the linguistic evidence.

The Reflexive transformation provides a way of testing the nature of the native speaker's knowledge of imperatives. Recall that in a simple sentence a reflexive pronoun must be coreferential with the subject. For this reason, the distribution of reflexives in imperatives shows that there must be a subject in the imperative, and that that subject must be *you:*

(7.10)

$$
\text{Please shave}
\begin{cases}
*myself. \\
yourself. \\
*himself. \\
*herself. \\
*ourselves. \\
yourselves. \\
*themselves.
\end{cases}
$$

The pattern of asterisks in (7.10) is precisely what we would get if the subject were *you.* Any description of English that failed to explain this fact would be deficient, since it would implicitly be claiming that the identical patterns were accidental. They are not accidental, since there are a variety of other tests that show the same distribution in the case of the imperative as in sentences where there is an overt subject *you:*

(7.11)   a. **Don't lose my way home.*
                     Don't lose your way home.
                     *Don't lose her way home.
                  b. *I lost my way home.*
                     *I lost your way home.

*I lost her way home.
c. *You lost my way home.
    You lost your way home.
    *You lost her way home.
d. *She lost my way home.
    *She lost your way home.
    She lost her way home.

On the basis of these observations, we establish that the underlying subject of subjectless S's is *you*. Thus, there must be a transformation of *You* Deletion. The grammatical sentence *Shave yourself*, for example, is derived by applying first Reflexive and then *You* Deletion, as illustrated in (7.12):

(7.12)   Input   *you* VP[*shave you*]
                Reflexive   *you* VP[*shave yourself*]
                You Deletion: ∅   VP[*shave yourself*]

Problem 1d takes up the question of whether these two transformations must be extrinsically ordered.

Notice, now, that *You* Deletion can apply only in main clauses, and that it cannot apply when either there is tense marked on the verb or there is a modal present:

(7.13)

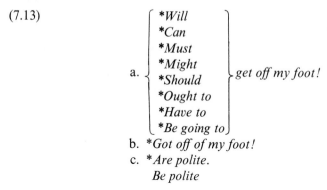

b. *Got off of my foot!
c. *Are polite.
    Be polite

Example (7.13c) is particularly important, because it is the only case in English of a verb whose present tense form with subject *you* is different from the form that it takes in the infinitive, the **bare** form. In this case, the present tense is not possible, but the bare form of the verb is required. This shows that there is no TENSE at all in imperatives.

This makes possible a significant generalization. The discussion of the verbal sequence in Chapter 5 concluded that there is a node AUX that dominates only TENSE and M. *You* Deletion cannot apply when either TENSE or M (or both, of course) is present, as the preceding examples show. This is elegantly accounted for if (i) imperative sentences lack AUX and (ii) *You* deletion applies only when AUX is absent.

Furthermore, note that in imperatives the location of *not* is precisely what we would expect if *Do* Replacement had not applied:

(7.14)

a. $\begin{Bmatrix} Do \\ Don't \\ Do\ not \end{Bmatrix}$ *have a piece of pizza with your beer.*

b. $\begin{Bmatrix} Do \\ Don't \\ Do\ not \end{Bmatrix}$ *be here when the band begins to play.*

(7.15)

a. *Have a piece of pizza with your beer.*
  **Haven't a piece of pizza with your beer.*
  **Have not a piece of pizza with your beer.*

b. *Be here when the band begins to play.*
  **Ben't here when the band begins to play.*
  **Be not here when the band begins to play.*

One way to represent this would be to place an ad hoc constraint on *Do* Replacement that would prevent it from applying in imperative sentences. The analysis proposed earlier makes available a more compelling explanation, however: *Do* Replacement does not apply in imperatives because imperatives lack AUX; hence, they lack *do*.

The situation is complicated by the fact that *do* actually appears in imperatives, as the examples in (7.14) show. The assumption that imperatives lack AUX would require us to state a special transformation to insert *do* in examples such as these. There are two arguments that suggest that this is correct, but these are not very strong and should not be viewed as conclusive.

First, by treating imperatives as lacking AUX it is possible to accommodate imperatives in which the subject is not *you*. In the following examples, the asterisks indicate that the examples so marked are unacceptable as imperatives.

(7.16)

a. *Everybody stand up.*
  **Everybody stands up.*

b. *Somebody answer the phone.*
  **Somebody answers the phone.*

c. *Don't anybody burn himself.*
  **Doesn't anybody burn himself.*

The last example shows that the subject of these sentences is in fact a noun phrase other than *you*. Otherwise, one might argue that (7.16a), for instance, is derived from *Everybody, you stand up.*

Compare, now, the following examples:

(7.17)

a. *Do sit down.*
  **Do you sit down.*

b. *Don't sit down.*
    Don't you sit down.
c. *Do not sit down.*
    **Do you not sit down.*

These examples suggest two conclusions: (i) Some type of inversion transformation applies in imperatives; (ii) *you* is deleted after *do* (as contrasted with *don't*).

The first conclusion is supported by (7.16c), in which inversion applies in the case of a non-*you* subject. Just in case the emphatic *do* is present, however, inversion cannot occur:

(7.18)   a. **Do everybody sit down.*
                    **Do somebody answer the telephone.*
                b. *Everybody do sit down.*
                    Somebody do answer the telephone.

It turns out, therefore, that we cannot account for the distribution of grammaticality in (7.17) by first applying inversion and then deleting *you*. While this works adequately when the subject is *you*, there are difficulties when it is a noun phrase other than *you*. Hence, the fact that *do* appears to undergo inversion in imperatives is not an argument that it must be underlying.

The best that can be accomplished here seems to be the following: In case of an emphatic imperative, insert *do* before the verb phrase unless the subject is *you*. If *not* follows the subject, insertion of *do* will yield *do not*. In case the imperative expresses a negative attitude toward an action, insert *don't* in initial position. If there happens to be an overt subject, this will give the illusion of inversion.

A second argument against assuming that the *do* of imperatives is present in underlying structure has to do with the subjunctives illustrated in (7.19):

(7.19) a. *It is important that Bill be polite.*
            It is important that Bill not be polite.
            **It is important that Bill do be polite.*
            **It is important that Bill do not be polite.*
        b. *It is mandatory that Mary have seen you before noon.*
            It is mandatory that Mary not have seen you before noon.
            **It is mandatory that Mary do have seen you before noon.*
            **It is mandatory that Mary do not have seen you before noon.*

One indicator of the subjunctive is the lack of tense and modal. As the examples show, we get grammatical *Bill be* . . . and *Mary have seen* . . . in the preceding examples. Furthermore, *Do* Replacement does not apply in subjunctives, as shown by the location of *not* before *be* and *have*. These facts can be captured by treating the subjunctive as an AUX-less construction similar to the imperative.

To summarize, we can achieve considerable generalization in the grammar if we derive both the imperative and the subjunctive from an AUX-less structure. The resulting description will account for the absence of tense marking, the absence of modals, the peculiar location of *not* in these constructions, and the apparent failure of *Do* Replacement.

As far as the presence of *do* in imperatives is concerned, the imperative is an idiosyncratic construction in most languages, and the introduction of an ad hoc *Do* Insertion transformation for the English imperative is not particularly unsatisfactory from the point of view of the general theory. No attempt will be made to state the rule here because of its ad hoc nature and lack of theoretical interest in the present context.

One final point should be noted. Traditional treatments of the imperative in general grammar assume the existence of an **abstract imperative morpheme,** called IMP, that is generated in S-initial position.[3] The morpheme IMP has two functions: (i) It indicates that the structure is that associated with an imperative sentence for the purpose of the semantic interpretation rules, and (ii) it functions as the trigger for rules such as *You* Deletion, the rules having to do with *do* in the imperative, and so on. More generally, IMP indicates to the grammar that it is dealing with an imperative.

It can be readily shown that if there is such a morpheme, it cannot have a particular meaning or small set of meanings, but must be a purely syntactic device. Sentences such as those given in (7.20) are imperative in their syntax but lack the interpretation normally associated with imperatives:

(7.20)   a. *Close the door and the hinge will fall off.*
         b. *Don't call up your mother and she'll think your phone is busted.*
         c. *Take one more step and I'll shoot.*
         d. *Be polite and people walk all over you.*

These sentences are not requests, wishes, orders, suggestions, etc. They express the consequence of a particular course of action. While it can easily be shown that these sentences have *you* subjects, in (7.20d) at least the *you* subject does not refer to the addressee but is the impersonal *you* meaning *one*.

In order to justify the use of IMP in the various transformations that apply to imperatives, it would have to be demonstrated that sufficient syntactic simplification results from assuming that it exists. At present, there does not appear to be strong evidence to support this position. Consequently, our statement of *You* Deletion will be given in terms of the more salient feature of imperatives, namely, the absence of AUX in them.

You DELETION: *you* **VP X**
                   1   2   3 $\Rightarrow \emptyset$ 2 3

Condition: main clauses only

---

[3] See Katz and Postal (1964) for the original argument in support of IMP in terms of its presumed semantic and syntactic properties.

The condition blocks generation of the ungrammatical examples in (7.21):

(7.21)　　　　　a.　*It is important that you leave immediately.*
　　　　　　　　　　*It is important that ∅ leave immediately.
　　　　　　　　b.　*Bill ordered that you fix the tent.*
　　　　　　　　　　*Bill ordered that ∅ fix the tent.

THE DATIVE

Consider the following sentences:

(7.22)　　　　　a.　*John gave a book to Mary.*
　　　　　　　　b.　*John gave Mary a book.*

(7.23)　　　　　a.　*Mary sent her tax return to the govenment.*
　　　　　　　　b.　*Mary sent the government her tax return.*

(7.24)　　　　　a.　*Bill showed the pictures to his agent.*
　　　　　　　　b.　*Bill showed his agent the pictures.*

(7.25)　　　　　a.　*John built a cabin for his children.*
　　　　　　　　b.　*John built his children a cabin.*

(7.26)　　　　　a.　*Mary bought a dress for Susan.*
　　　　　　　　b.　*Mary bought Susan a dress.*

(7.27)　　　　　a.　*Bill found a present for Sam.*
　　　　　　　　b.　*Bill found Sam a present.*

The examples in (7.22–7.24) are called *To* **datives,** while those in (7.25–7.27) are called *For* **datives.** The difference, of course, is the preposition that appears in the (a) examples.

The argument that there is a Dative transformation that derives the (b) sentences from the (a) sentences in the preceding examples is a straightforward one. Observe that there are certain verbs that permit both orders of constituents in the verb phrases following them, such as *give, send, show, build, buy, find,* and so on.

There are, therefore, three logical alternatives. First, it might be the case that both variants of the dative construction are underlying deep structures. In such a case, the lexical entries for these verbs would have to specify that they could appear in either construction. Second, it might be the case that the (a) sentences are derived from deep structures that have the order of constituents illustrated by the (b) sentences. In this case, the transformation would have to specify which preposition should appear in the (a) sentences, since some of the verbs govern *to* and some govern *for.* Third, it might be the case that there is a transformation that derives the (b) sentences from the (a) sentences. In this last case, the transformation would have to delete the preposition.[4]

It can be shown that the correct alternative is the third one. The logic of the argument is as follows. There is a transformation called **Complex NP Shift.** This transformation applies generally in verb phrases. However, it cannot apply to sentences of the (b) form in (7.22–7.27). This can be accounted for if Complex NP Shift is stated in such a way that it blocks the derivation of the (b) form from the (a) form. But if the first or second alternative is chosen, there is no explanation for why Complex NP Shift applies only to the (a) form and not the (b) form.

Complex NP Shift relates sentences of the following form:

(7.28)   a. *John found **a book with lots of pretty pictures in**
                 it in the garden.*
            b. *John found in the garden **a book with lots of pretty**
                 pictures in it.*

Complex NP Shift takes the NP *a book with lots of pretty pictures in it* in (7.28a) and moves it to the end of the VP, yielding (7.28b). The formal statement of the rule is given as follows.

COMPLEX NP SHIFT: X V NP Y
                      1 2 3   4 $\Rightarrow$ 1 2 $\emptyset$ 4 + 3

Condition: 3 is "complex"[5]

It is important to distinguish between the dative construction and the output of the rule of Complex NP Shift. The latter is very general, and moves a complex NP to the right regardless of what follows. The following examples show that complex NP can be moved over an adverb, a pair of prepositional phrases, and an adjective.

---

[4] A fourth possibility also exists, i.e., that the deep structure of these two constructions is not like either of the surface structures. This is always a possibility when two constructions have a common deep structure source. There does not appear to be any compelling reason for proposing this as a serious alternative, given the available data.

[5] The notion "complex" is not an easy one to define. However, it may not be necessary to restrict the operation of Complex NP Shift to complex NPs. There is some evidence that there are restrictions on the surface structure ordering of constituents in the verb phrase such that the more complex constituents appear toward the end of the sentence and the less complex constituents appear toward the beginning.

Such a restriction would be a *surface structure constraint.* (Perlmutter, 1971). Given such a constraint, transformations could apply freely to constituents in the sentence. Then, at the end of the derivation, if the surface structure constraints were violated, the sentence would be judged ungrammatical. This does not solve the problem of what constitutes a complex NP, but it does make it unnecessary to mention the complexity of the NP in the structural conditions of Complex NP Shift, and of any other transformation that moves constituents around. [Cf. Ross (1967: Chapter 3) for a discussion of the restrictions on surface structure constituent order in the verb phrase.]

(7.29)   a. *Mary destroyed **the car which she had bought** completely.*
          *Mary destroyed completely **the car which she had bought.***
       b. *John sent **the letter which he had written** from New York to L.A.*
          *John sent from New York to L.A. **the letter which he had written.***
       c. *Mary made **the people she had met** very agitated.*
          *Mary made very agitated **the people she had met.***

The most general formulation of this rule involves movement of the NP to the right rather than movement of the various other constituents to the left. In the argument that follows, we will show how Complex NP Shift applies to the dative construction; the preceding examples should make it clear that Complex NP Shift is a rule whose application goes far beyond the dative construction.

The three alternative analyses of datives make different predictions about the effects of Complex NP Shift. The first alternative and the second both treat the order V NP NP as an underlying order, while the third alternative treats this order as derived. If V NP NP were underlying, we would expect Complex NP Shift to apply when the first NP is complex. On the other hand, if this order is derived, it is not necessarily the case that Complex NP Shift must apply to it.

To show this, let us suppose for the sake of argument that V NP NP is derived from underlying V NP *to* NP or V NP *for* NP. The transformation involved is called Dative.

DATIVE: $\text{X V NP} \begin{Bmatrix} to \\ for \end{Bmatrix} \text{NP Y}$
          $1\ 2\ \ 3\quad\ \ 4\quad\ \ 5\ \ 6 \Rightarrow 1\ 2\ 5\ 3\ \emptyset\ \emptyset\ 6$

Since transformations apply in some linear order, Dative either precedes or follows Complex NP Shift. The following examples show that Dative must follow Complex NP Shift:

(7.30)   a. *John gave **a book about roses** to the man in the garden.*
       b. *John gave to the man in the garden **a book about roses.***

(7.31)   a. *John gave **the man in the garden** a book about roses.*
       b. **John gave a book about roses **the man in the garden.***

Example (7.30b) illustrates the result of applying Complex NP Shift to the assumed underlying dative structure, (7.30a). Example (7.31b) illustrates the result of applying Complex NP Shift to the supposed **derived** structure, (7.31a). As can be seen, Complex NP Shift cannot apply to the derived structure, which can be accounted for if Complex NP Shift is ordered before Dative.

Notice that it would not be possible to block (7.31b) by specifying that Complex NP Shift cannot move an NP over another NP. There are certain constructions for which V NP NP appears to be underlying, and not derived by Dative, e.g.:

(7.32)   a. *Mary called Mathew an elephant.*
              b. *The people elected Harry President.*
              c. *We named Charley chief berry picker.*

In these cases Complex NP Shift may apply:

(7.33)
      a. *Mary called an elephant the man who had stepped on her foot.*
      b. *The people elected President the man who had never won anything before.*
      c. *We named chief berry picker the man who asked for the job.*

Hence, a simple restriction against moving a complex NP over an NP will not suffice.

The ordering of Dative after Complex NP Shift accounts for the ungrammaticality of (7.31b). Without such a transformational derivation of V NP NP, we would not be able to explain the failure of Complex NP Shift to apply to this structure, except perhaps by claiming that (7.31b) is not in fact ungrammatical, but unacceptable for some other reason. Short of that, the evidence argues strongly for a transformational derivation of the V NP NP order.

Similar arguments can be made with respect to the ordering of other transformations and Dative. In each case, it can be shown that in order to account for the distribution of grammaticality we must order Dative after these transformations, thus preventing them from applying to the V NP NP structure.

There are two transformations in English that extrapose constituents of NPs to the right. One rule is called **Extraposition of PP** and the other **Extraposition from NP**. The first is illustrated in (7.34) and the second in (7.35):

(7.34)   a. *A woman **from Pittsburgh** walked into the room.*
          *A woman walked into the room **from Pittsburgh**.*
      b. *A story **about spaceships** appeared in the papers last week.*
          *A story appeared in the papers last week **about spaceships**.*
      c. *We elected a man **with a low IQ** President.*
          *We elected a man President **with a low IQ**.*

(7.35)   a. *A woman **who was six feet tall** walked into the room.*
          *A woman walked into the room **who was six feet tall**.*
      b. *A story **which made me angry** appeared in the papers.*
          *A story appeared in the papers **which made me angry**.*
      c. *The hypothesis **that the transformation is made of
          spaghetti** is completely invalid.*
          *The hypothesis is completely invalid **that the
          transformation is made of spaghetti**.*

I will not attempt to motivate these transformations here or to discuss the main difficulties that arise in formulating them. Intuitively, the motivation for them is based on the fact that a grammar in which the extraposed clauses are not contiguous with the NPs that they modify in deep structure would be considerably more complicated than one in which they are contiguous. See Ross (1967) for a detailed discussion of both of these transformations, and Akmajian (1975) for discussion of Extraposition of PP.

An interesting fact about these two transformations is that they cannot apply to V NP NP just in case this order is a dative. We would expect that the following examples would be grammatical if V NP NP was underlying, but they are not:

(7.36)   a. *We gave **a woman** a big smile **from Philadelphia.**
            *We gave **a woman** a big smile **who was six feet tall.**
         b. *We bought **a man** a gift **with a low IQ.**
            *We bought **a man** a gift **who tells funny stories.**
         c. *John sold **the library** his collection **on the corner.**
            *John sold **the library** his collection **which couldn't afford it.**

By comparison, extraposition is possible when the V NP NP construction is not a dative, and is presumably underlying:

(7.37)   a. We elected **a woman** President **from Philadelphia.**
            We elected **a woman** President **who was six feet tall.**
         b. We call **people** smart **with a high IQ.**
            We call **people** smart **who tell funny** stories.
         c. Pablo named **a painting** "Vision" **about apparently nothing.**
            Pablo named **a painting** "Vision" **which is completely green.**

Finally, extraposition is possible when the order is V NP *to* NP or V NP *for* NP. The examples will not be given here; the reader should ascertain that this is correct. The conclusion of all this is, again, that there are transformations that cannot apply to the V NP NP construction just when it is dative, which can be explained if there is a Dative transformation ordered after they apply. If V NP NP is underlying, these facts have no apparent explanation.

There are some minor problems with the Dative transformation that should be noted here. First, the transformation does not apply whenever the prepositions *to* or *for* are present, but only when *to* and *for* are used in such a way that a change of possession takes place. So, for example, we cannot say *John drove New York a truck* (from *John drove a truck to New York*) or *The people sent Congress Mary* (from *The people sent Mary to Congress*).

By the same token, *Harry mowed Sam the lawn* must not be derived from *Harry mowed the lawn for Sam*, and *Susan watched Mary the car* must not be derived from *Susan watched the car for Mary.* Apparently, Dative must be restricted so that it will be blocked just in case the verb and the preposition do not combine to reflect change of possession.

One solution to this problem is to postulate several lexical items with the phonological form of *to* and several with the phonological form of *for*. Dative could then be restricted so that it would apply only when the appropriate lexical items were present. For example, let us call *for*ₙ the *for* that indicates that an event is done in behalf of someone else, and for_g the *for* that indicates that an object is to be given to someone. The use of these *for*s is illustrated in the following examples:

(7.38)   a. *Mary mowed the lawn for$_b$ Susan.*
              **Mary mowed the lawn for$_g$ Susan.*
          b. *John made a phone call for$_b$ the President.*
              **John made a phone call for$_g$ the President.*
          c. *We watched the car for$_b$ Susan.*
              **We watched the car for$_g$ Susan.*

(7.39)   a. *John's friends bought a new stove for$_g$ him.*
              John's friends bought him a new stove.
          b. *We built a house for$_g$ our family.*
              We built our family a house.
          c. *Jim found a present for$_g$ Mary.*
              Jim found Mary a present.

That this is more than a mechanical solution is shown by the fact that in some contexts both *for*s are possible, with different meanings:

(7.40)   a. *John bought a watch for$_b$ Mary.* (She didn't have time to go shopping for the watch, and gave him the money so that he could buy it.)
          b. *John bought a watch for$_g$ Mary.* (She didn't have a watch, and he thought that he would give her one for her birthday.)
          c. *John bought Mary a watch.* [same as (b)]

Notice that Dative can apply only when for_g is present.

Similarly, we can restrict the application of Dative to true *to* datives. Let to_d be the *to* of direction and to_g the *to* of change of possession. We can find ambiguities depending on which *to* is present when the verb **could** involve change of possession and where the object of *to* **could** be understood as being capable of possessing something:

(7.41)   a. *Mary sent a painting to$_d$ the White House.* (The White House is the destination.)
          b. *Mary sent a painting to$_g$ the White House.* (The painting is to become the property of the government and to hang in the White House.)
          c. *Mary sent the White House a painting.* [same as (b)]

When the destination cannot be a possessor, only the to_d preposition is appropriate, and Dative is inapplicable:

(7.42)   a. *Mary sent a letter to Europe.*
              **Mary sent Europe a letter.*
          b. *Susan tossed the package to the floor.*
              **Susan tossed the floor the package.*

Compare (7.42b) with (7.43), in which the destination may be understood as a potential possessor:

(7.43)   *Susan tossed the package to John.*
              Susan tossed John the package.

On the basis of these observations, we revise Dative as follows.

$$DATIVE: \quad X \ V \ NP \begin{Bmatrix} to_g \\ for_g \end{Bmatrix} NP \ Y$$
$$\qquad\qquad 1 \quad 2 \quad 3 \qquad 4 \qquad 5 \quad 6 \Rightarrow 1\ 2\ 5\ 3\ \emptyset\ \emptyset\ 6$$

In order to generate the deep structure of datives in the first place, we hypothesize the following phrase structure rule.

PSR3c: VP → VP PP

This rule is a departure from the more traditional analysis of the indirect object as a sister to the direct object and the verb. The two are equivalent in many respects; however, the rule given here is consistent with a number of general theoretical constraints that the other is not. Since the arguments are fairly complex and require a variety of assumptions that require extensive justification in themselves, for the purposes of this book PSR3c will be adopted without empirical justification.

Finally, let us consider the interaction between Dative and Reflexive:

(7.44)   Input   *John* Past *do buy a book for$_g$ John*
              Reflexive   *John* Past *do buy a book for$_g$ himself*
              Other rules   *John bought a book for himself*

The derivation sketched in (7.44) shows that Reflexive may apply to the indirect object in a dative construction if Dative does not apply. Reflexive and Dative may apply in the same derivation also, as the following shows:

(7.45)   Input   *John* Past *do buy a book for$_g$ John*
              Dative   *John* Past *do buy John a book*
              Reflexive   *John* Past *do buy himself a book*
              Other rules   *John bought himself a book*

In this example, it does not appear to matter whether Dative applies before or after Reflexive; the other order would yield the same structure.

The ordering must be as given in (7.45), however. Consider a case in which both of the coreferential NPs are objects of a verb to which Dative may apply. Dative must precede Reflexive in order for both of the following derivations to be possible:

(7.46)   a. Input   *John* Past *do show Bill to Bill*
              Reflexive   *John* Past *do show Bill to himself*
              Other rules   *John showed Bill to himself.*
              b. Input   *John* Past *do show Bill to Bill*

Dative   *John* Past *do show Bill Bill*
Reflexive   *John* Past *do show Bill himself*
Other rules *John showed Bill himself.*

The second derivation would be impossible if Dative followed Reflexive. Furthermore, the order Reflexive, Dative would yield the sentence *John showed himself Bill,* which does not express the coreferentiality between *himself* and *Bill* that we would expect. To illustrate:

(7.47)   Input   *John* Past *do show Bill to Bill*
            Reflexive   *John* Past *do show Bill to himself*
            Dative   *John* Past *do show himself Bill*
            Other rules *John showed himself Bill.*

This concludes our analysis of the dative for the moment. It will be taken up again briefly in our discussion of the passive construction in the following section.

THE PASSIVE

A transformation that has been studied extensively in modern linguistics is the Passive transformation. The function of Passive is to relate pairs of sentences such as the following:

(7.48)   a. *John saw Mary.*
            b. *Mary was seen by John.*

(7.49)   a. *The directors considered his proposal.*
            b. *His proposal was considered by the directors.*

(7.50)   a. *John should have fed the baby.*
            b. *The baby should have been fed by John.*

(7.51)   a. *John frightened the horse.*
            b. *The horse was frightened by John.*

It is first necessary to demonstrate that there is in fact a transformational relationship here, i.e., that there are significant generalizations that cannot be captured by phrase structure rules alone. Having established this, one may then determine what the precise statement of the transformation is. In the following discussion, it will be shown that the passive sentences, that is, the (b) sentences in the preceding examples, are derived from a deep structure that is identical in most respects to the deep structure of the active sentences. Notice that this is not the only conceivable state of affairs. Both could be derived from a deep structure that resembles neither, or the active could be derived from the passive. There is no particular reason to suppose that the first of these two alternatives is correct. However, it is necessary to provide arguments against the second.

The analysis to be presented here has the following features.[6] The passive is derived from the active (in essence) by three distinct transformational operations: (i) movement of the underlying subject into a *by* phrase to the right of the verb phrase, (ii) insertion of *be en*, and (iii) movement of the underlying direct object into subject position. While the theory as it stands does not prevent us from performing all of these operations in one transformation, we will group these operations into two transformations for reasons that will be made clear in the following discussion.

One of these two transformations, Agent Postposing, obligatorily moves the subject into a dummy position in the *by* phrase, leaving behind a dummy noun phrase Δ in subject position. A statement of Agent Postposing and an illustration of how it applies follow.

AGENT POSTPOSING: X NP Y VP′ *by* Δ Z
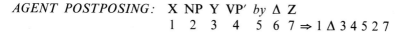
$$1 \quad 2 \quad 3 \quad 4 \quad 5 \; 6 \; 7 \Rightarrow 1 \, \Delta \, 3 \, 4 \, 5 \, 2 \, 7$$

(7.52)

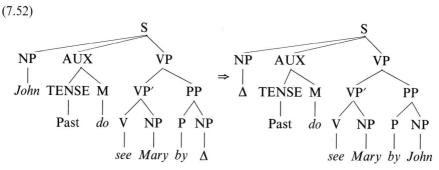

As can be seen, this formulation treats the *by* phrase of the passive as present in deep structure. An alternative that is often found in the literature is to create the *by* phrase through the application of the transformation. Justification for stating the rule in the way we have here will be provided later.

The other transformation, NP Preposing, moves the direct object into the position occupied by Δ and simultaneously inserts *be en* before V.[7]

NP PREPOSING: X Δ Y V NP Z
$$1 \quad 2 \quad 3 \quad 4 \quad 5 \quad 6 \Rightarrow 1 \; 5 \; 3 \; be \; en \; 4 \; \emptyset \; 6$$

---

[6] Our analysis of the passive relies heavily on the analysis put forth in Chomsky (1970a).

[7] The insertion of *be en* captures the generalization that the form of the verb in the passive construction is always the same as the form of the past participle, which is formed by attachment of *en*. This aspect of the analysis will not be discussed in detail here.

(7.53)

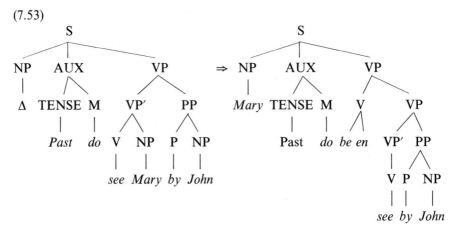

For the sake of convenience, the two rules together may occasionally be referred to as Passive.

The remainder of this section is divided into three parts. In the first part, we present some arguments that the passive is transformationally derived as we have just outlined. In the second part, we provide justification for the assumption that the *by* phrase is not created by Agent Postposing but is present in deep structure. In the third part, we show why Agent Postposing leaves behind a dummy NP, and why the transformational analysis of the passive construction should be broken up into two transformations.

Why the Passive is Transformationally Derived

The position that the passive is transformationally derived is one that has become more and more controversial since Chomsky's original analysis in 1957. If the relationship between active and passive is a transformational one, then the general outlines of the transformation are not difficult to establish, and the details, while they may be open to dispute, are not completely implausible. We will indicate here what the source of the controversy is, and then proceed with an analysis of the consequences of treating the relationship between active and passive as transformational.

In the case of other syntactic phenomena, it has not been difficult to demonstrate that significant syntactic generalizations are lost if a transformational account is not adopted. As the work of Emonds (1970, forthcoming) has shown, the passive construction is notable in that the surface structure of a passive possesses many properties that are characteristic of deep structure. More simply, the phrase structure rules that will generate structures other than the passive will also generate the passive with little or no revision. Hence, the argument for a transformational treatment of the passive must go beyond consideration of the obvious syntactic characteristics of the construction.[8]

To see this point, consider the following sentences:

(7.54)   a. *Mary was seen by Bill.*
                   b. *Mary was angry at Bill.*

The phrase *angry at Bill* is an **adjective phrase,** or AP. Adjectival phrases are generated by phrase structure rule PSR7.

PSR7: AP → ADJ (PP)

The similarity between the passive construction and the adjectival phrase is obvious. Both cooccur with the verb *be,* and both permit a prepositional phrase. Furthermore, *be* appears in the passive sentence precisely where we would expect it to appear if the phrase *seen by Bill,* for example, was actually an adjectival phrase. A similar observation can be made about the location of the prepositional phrase relative to the rest of the construction in the two cases.

The traditional term for *seen* in the passive [(7.54a)] is **passive participle.** The passive participle functions as an adjective in certain noun phrases, as the following examples show:

(7.55)

$$
\text{Larry is the most} \left\{ \begin{array}{l} \textit{amazed} \\ \textit{surprised} \\ \textit{applauded} \\ \textit{praised} \\ \textit{sought after} \\ \textit{stepped on} \\ \textit{respected} \end{array} \right\} \textit{member of the club.}
$$

Such examples suggest that the passive participle is in fact a member of the category ADJ, and that the passive construction is based on an adjectival phrase as just outlined. However, unless it can be shown that all passive participles may be treated as adjectives, it cannot be concluded that there are no passive participles that are derived independently by a Passive transformation.

The attempt to generate the passive participle as an adjective in an adjectival phrase raises a number of problems. The most obvious is that this analysis does not in itself capture the fact that the logical subject of the passive sentence, that is, the NP that refers to the performer of the action, is the NP in the *by* phrase and not the subject in the surface structure. This fact does not present a problem if the passive is transformationally derived from the active, because

---

[8] It is for this reason that Emonds calls Passive *structure preserving :* The output of the transformation (if there is one) is a structure that could have been generated by the phrase structure rules themselves.

the interpretation of the sentence is established in terms of the deep structure before the transformation moving the underlying subject has applied.

Another problem involves the dative construction and other constructions in which the verb phrase contains more than one NP. In general, if a verb takes a direct object followed by at least one prepositional phrase, then the passivized verb phrase corresponding to this verb will be identical *except that the NP that immediately follows the active verb cannot appear*. E.g.:

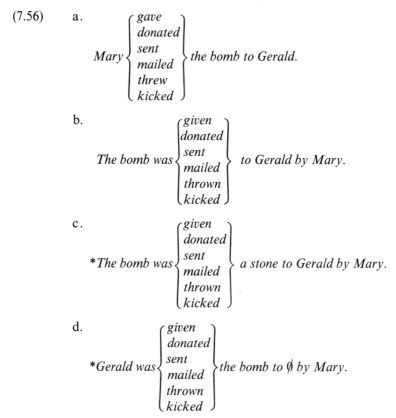

(7.56) a.

Mary $\left\{ \begin{array}{l} gave \\ donated \\ sent \\ mailed \\ threw \\ kicked \end{array} \right\}$ the bomb to Gerald.

b.

The bomb was $\left\{ \begin{array}{l} given \\ donated \\ sent \\ mailed \\ thrown \\ kicked \end{array} \right\}$ to Gerald by Mary.

c.

*The bomb was $\left\{ \begin{array}{l} given \\ donated \\ sent \\ mailed \\ thrown \\ kicked \end{array} \right\}$ a stone to Gerald by Mary.

d.

*Gerald was $\left\{ \begin{array}{l} given \\ donated \\ sent \\ mailed \\ thrown \\ kicked \end{array} \right\}$ the bomb to ∅ by Mary.

As (7.56c) shows, verbs that normally take two objects cannot when they are in the passive. Example (7.56b) shows that the noun phrase that is absent in the passive is the one immediately following the verb in the active; (7.56d) shows that no other noun phrase may be omitted from the passive verb phrase and put into superficial subject position.

This generalization applies even when the noun phrase that immediately follows the verb in the active is moved into that position transformationally. Earlier in this chapter we argued for a Dative transformation that has this effect. As the following examples show, the passive corresponding to the V NP NP construction is precisely what we would expect if the noun phrase immediately following the verb in the active were moved into superficial subject position by a transformation (the examples indicated by asterisks are just those to which Dative does not apply):

(7.57)

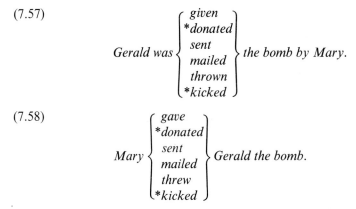

$$Gerald\ was \left\{ \begin{array}{l} given \\ *donated \\ sent \\ mailed \\ thrown \\ *kicked \end{array} \right\} the\ bomb\ by\ Mary.$$

(7.58)

$$Mary \left\{ \begin{array}{l} gave \\ *donated \\ sent \\ mailed \\ threw \\ *kicked \end{array} \right\} Gerald\ the\ bomb.$$

If the V NP NP structure is derived only by a transformation and is not underlying, as we have argued, then there must be a transformation of Passive that will derive the grammatical examples in (7.57). A typical derivation is illustrated in (7.59):

(7.59) Input   *Mary* Past *do send a bomb to Gerald by* Δ
        Dative   *Mary* Past *do send Gerald a bomb by* Δ
        Agent Postposing   Δ Past *do send Gerald a bomb by Mary*
        NP Preposing   *Gerald* Past *do be en send a bomb* ∅ *by Mary*
        Do Replacement   *Gerald* Past *be* ∅ *en send a bomb by Mary*
        Affix Hopping   *Gerald* # *be* + Past # # *send* + *en* #
                           a bomb by Mary
                           Gerald was sent a bomb by Mary.

This demonstrates a more general point, and one that is of considerable importance. If a particular structure must be transformationally derived, then any syntactic regularities that must be defined in terms of this structure must be accounted for by transformations also. Thus, in spite of the similarity between the passive construction and the adjectival phrase, the transformational approach captures generalizations that the purely phrase structure approach does not capture.[9] On this basis, we must conclude that the passive is transformationally derived.

[9] It is possible to envision a semantic framework in which the synonymy of active and passive would be captured not by a transformation but by the application of different rules of semantic interpretation that yield the same semantic representations. I have not discussed this alternative in detail here because of the relative lack of understanding of what kinds of semantic rules there are and what a semantic representation for natural language looks like. A study in linguistics that deals with this question is Jackendoff (1972); the logician's approach is exemplified by Montague (1973).

A second argument for deriving the passive transformationally is that it does not function like an adjectival phrase in all respects, contrary to what we would predict if the passive verb phrase was actually an adjectival phrase. There are a number of transformations that apply to adjectives but not to passive participles.

Let us consider first the case of **To Be Deletion.** This transformation is one that has been hypothesized often in the literature, but it is not completely without problems.[10] Its function is to relate pairs of sentences like those given in (7.59):

(7.59)   a. *John considers Mary to be very intelligent.*
                   John considers Mary very intelligent.
               b. *John seems to be very angry.*
                   John seems very angry.
               c. *Susan finds Edgar to be amusing.*
                   Susan finds Edgar amusing.

To Be Deletion applies just before adjectival phrases. It does not apply before passive participial phrases in general:

(7.60)   a. *John considered Mary to be offended by everything.*
                   *John considered Mary offended by everything.
               b. *Mary doesn't seem to be* $\begin{cases} \textit{desired by the king.} \\ \textit{attended to by the press.} \end{cases}$
                   *Mary doesn't seem $\begin{cases} \textit{desired by the king.} \\ \textit{attended to by the press.} \end{cases}$

If these passive participial phrases were underlying adjectival phrases, then the fact that they do not behave like adjectives with respect to *To Be* Deletion would be a puzzling one. This fact is explained if the passive is transformationally derived from an underlying verb phrase, since then there would be no reason why *To Be* Deletion should apply in the passive cases.

A second transformation that applies to adjectival phrases and not to passive participles is the one that moves an adjective to the front of a *though* phrase. This transformation, which will be called **Though Attraction,** derives the second member of each pair in (7.61) from the first:

(7.61)   a. *Though Mary is polite, nobody will admit it.*
                   Polite though Mary is, nobody will admit it.
               b. *Though John is angry at Bill, nobody believes it.*
                   Angry though John is at Bill, nobody believes it.

---

[10] I would like to thank Tom Wasow for reminding me of the interaction between *To Be* Deletion and the passive. For discussion of the myriad problems involved in the formulation of *To Be* Deletion, see Borkin (1973). It is not at all clear that *To Be* Deletion is a transformation. Regardless of whether it is or not, the observations made here are valid, since they do not depend on the prior demonstration that a transformation of *To Be* Deletion exists.

   c. *Though Susan is eager to leave, no one will let her.*
      Eager though Susan is to leave, no one will let her.
   d. *Though Sam is afraid that you'll go, he won't admit it.*
      Afraid though Sam is that you'll go, he won't admit it.

If passive participial phrases were adjectival phrases, then we would expect them to be subject to *Though* Attraction. The following examples show that they are not:

(7.62) a. *Though Jill was arrested by the police, she wasn't upset.*
        *Arrested though Jill was by the police, she wasn't upset.
     b. *Though Harry was ignored by the press, he called a meeting.*
        *Ignored though Harry was by the press, he called a meeting.
     c. *Though the king was laughed at by the peasants, he*
          continued to rule.
        *Laughed at though the king was by the peasants, he
          continued to rule.

Along with the argument given previously, this constitutes support for the position that the passive participle is not an adjective. The Dative argument shows that a transformational derivation of the passive captures a significant generalization. The last two arguments for a transformational analysis of passive that will be given here have to do with idioms.

An **idiom,** roughly speaking, is a phrase whose meaning is not completely predictable from the meaning of its parts. By this definition, a single word is an idiom, since its meaning must be specified in the lexicon and cannot be predicted from other facts. More complex idioms are those that contain a number of lexical items, such as *kick the bucket, look askance at, make eyes at, take off* (as an airplane), *flash in the pan, red herring,* and so on.

Certain idioms contain elements that are not usable independently in non-idiomatic contexts. For example, the words *advantage, tabs, note,* and *homage* may appear in idioms, but cannot appear without a determiner in positions that normally permit NPs:

(7.63)   a. *John took **advantage** of Bill's exhaustion.*
           b. *The directors kept **tabs** on Mary's progress.*
           c. *Susan took **note** of the arguments.*
           d. *The warriors paid **homage** to their chief.*

(7.64)

$$\text{a. } John\ was\ interested\ in \left\{ \begin{array}{l} *advantage. \\ *tabs. \\ *note. \\ *homage. \end{array} \right\}$$

$$\text{b. } Frankly, \left\{ \begin{array}{l} *advantage \\ *tabs \\ *note \\ *homage \end{array} \right\} make(s)\ me\ sick.$$

$$\text{c. } \textit{Have you heard the latest story about} \begin{cases} \textit{*advantage?} \\ \textit{*tabs?} \\ \textit{*note?} \\ \textit{*homage?} \end{cases}$$

$$\text{d. } \textit{I plan to make an in-depth study of} \begin{cases} \textit{*advantage} \\ \textit{*tabs} \\ \textit{*note} \\ \textit{*homage} \end{cases} \textit{next year.}$$

It is especially important to note that *advantage, tabs, note*, and *homage* cannot function as subject under normal circumstances. The only exception is in passive variants of the idioms given in (7.63):

(7.65)   a. ***Advantage*** *was taken by John of Bill's exhaustion.*
          b. ***Tabs*** *were kept by the directors on Mary' progress.*
          c. ***Note*** *was taken by Susan of the arguments.*
          d. ***Homage*** *was paid by the warriers to their chief.*

If the argument was made that the passive should be generated as an underlying structure, then it would be necessary to treat the noun phrases *advantage, tabs, note*, and *homage* as underlying subjects. However, these noun phrases appear for the most part only in the idioms, and do not function freely in sentences as noun phrases are expected to function.

Thus, treating passives as underlying structures completely obscures the idiomatic nature of these noun phrases and fails to explain why they appear only in examples like (7.65) in the passive. The transformational account of the passive, on the other hand, explains these distributions nicely.

The second idiom argument is the following. There are certain idioms that take the superficial form of a verb phrase, e.g., *break the ice, bury the hatchet, draw the line*. These idioms are idioms because they have a nonliteral interpretation: Idiomatically, *break the ice* has nothing to do with ice, *bury the hatchet* has nothing to do with a hatchet, and *draw the line* has nothing to do with a line. It will be necessary to specify in the lexicon of English, then, that these phrases are idioms and that they have specific nonliteral interpretations.

Notice, now, that these idioms may be passivized, and that when they are passived they preserve their nonliteral interpretation:

(7.66)   a. *The ice was broken suddenly when John laughed.*
          b. *The hatchet was buried by the Good Guys and the Bad Guys.*
          c. *The line was drawn at transformations which paint the sentence green.*

If the passive were derived not transformationally but from a structure generated in the base, then it would be necessary to specify that each of the passives in (7.66) had an idiomatic interpretation. Thus, a separate lexical entry would have to be made for the active and the passive variant of the idiom. On the

other hand, this duplication would not be required if the passive were transformationally derived, since the nonliteral interpretation of both the active
and the passive idiom would be represented identically at the deep structure
level in terms of the single lexical entry for the idiom. The interpretation would
not be affected if the passive derivation applied.

There are a number of other arguments that show that passive sentences are
transformationally derived; these are taken up in Chapters 9 and 10. It should
be emphasized that the essence of the arguments is not that the surface structure
of the passive cannot be generated in the base by phrase structure rules; rather,
it is that there are generalizations that can be captured by a transformational
analysis alone.

We have established that the active/passive relation is a transformational
one. We have also shown that a significant generalization can be captured if
the active order of constituents is taken to be underlying and the passive is
transformationally derived.

Why the By Phase Is Underlying

There are two major reasons (at least) for treating the *by* phrase as underlying.

1. There is no evidence that the *by* phrase in the passive functions any differently than a prepositional phrase in any normal active verb phrase. This fact
can be represented by transformationally inserting the *by* phrase in the appropriate position in the structure, but only the assumption that the *by* phrase is
underlying can explain this fact.[11]

2. If the *by* phrase were not generated in deep structure, then we would require
a transformation with the power to *create* structure. A theory that permits
such transformations is clearly less restrictive than one that does not. Given
that such transformations can be excluded by the theory, we can limit types of
transformations to the following restrictive class: (i) copying transformations,
where the new structure is identical to some structure already present in the
tree, (ii) movement transformations, where something that originally appeared
in a phrase marker appears elsewhere in a derived phrase marker, (iii) deletion
transformations, which delete material under identity with a part of the tree
that is preserved in the derived structure, or delete members of a set of designated elements, such as *do*. With the exception of this alternative formulation
of a passive transformation that creates a *by* phrase, there is little evidence that
any more power is required by the theory; therefore, such a transformation
should be excluded by the theory of grammar.

---

[11] This claim is somewhat too strong, actually. Certain types of transformations might be
allowed to insert constituents into positions where they could be generated in deep structures. Such
a formulation would not require that there actually be a prepositional phrase in the verb phrase
underlying the passive. We would have to show that Passive is a transformation of the appropriate
type; this is not difficult to do.

Why There Are Two Transformations for the Passive

Agent Postposing and NP Preposing move only one constituent each. By comparison, the alternative formulation that involves a single transformation requires this transformation to move two constituents. From the point of view of restricting the notion of possible transformation, it is preferable to allow transformations to move only one constituent each. However, it must be demonstrated that there are significant generalizations to be gained from restricting the notion of possible transformation in this way.

The traditional one-rule analysis of the passive construction makes use of the following transformation.

PASSIVE: X NP AUX V NP Y
               1   2   3   4   5   6 $\Rightarrow$ 1 5 3 *be en* 4 $\emptyset$ 6

A problem with this analysis is that it does not account for the so-called *truncated passives* illustrated in (7.67):

(7.67)   *Mary was arrested.*
                       Sam was praised.
                       Susan was simply ignored.
                       Larry was viciously attacked.
                       Manfred was laughed at.
                       Igor has never been catered to.

The traditional solution to this problem is not particularly satisfying. It is assumed that the examples in (7.67) are derived from the examples in (7.68) by deletion of the *by* phrase:

(7.68)   *Mary was arrested by someone.*
                       Sam was praised by someone.
                       Susan was simply ignored by someone.
                       Larry was viciously attacked by someone.
                       Manfred was laughed at by someone.
                       Igor has never been catered to by anyone.

However, this analysis treats *Mary was ignored by someone* as synonymous with *Mary was ignored*, which is simply wrong. The latter means *Mary was ignored by everyone*. Hence, this transformation of *By* Phrase Deletion would not capture any significant generalization, and merely saves the Passive analysis rather than supporting it.

The existence of truncated passives is elegantly accounted for in a framework that treats the derivation of the passive as a two-step process. We recall, first, that the *by* phrase, being an optional constituent of VP, does not have to appear in every S. When it does appear, however, the Agent Postposing transformation applies obligatorily.

AGENT POSTPOSING: X NP Y VP′ *by* Δ Z
                      1 2 3 4   5 6 7 ⇒ 1 Δ 3 4 5 2 7

The dummy left behind by Agent Postposing is filled by the direct object through the application of NP Preposing.

NP PREPOSING: X Δ Y V NP Z
                  1 2 3 4 5 6 ⇒ 1 5 3 *be en* 4 ∅ 6

The truncated passive may be derived by extending the notion of dummy NPs so that they can appear in deep structures. If a dummy NP happens to appear as the subject of a verb that may undergo the passive derivation, then NP Preposing will obligatorily apply. A typical derivation illustrating this is shown in (7.69):

(7.69)   Input   NP[Δ] Past *do arrest Mary*
         Agent Postposing   (does not apply)
         NP Preposing   NP[*Mary*] Past *do be en arrest* ∅
         Do Replacement   *Mary* Past *be* ∅ *en arrest* ∅
         Affix Hopping   *Mary # be +* Past *# # arrest + en #*
                             Mary was arrested.

This approach requires, of course, that we construct a complete and coherent theory of dummies, so that we may handle those cases that are not directly connected with the passive construction as well. For example, we must specify how a dummy is to be treated by the grammar when it appears as the direct object of a verb:

(7.70)   *John saw* Δ.
                            John hit Δ.
                            John bought Δ.
                            John introduced Δ.
                            John built Δ.

The difference between the examples in (7.70) and the truncated passive is illuminating. In the latter case, the dummy NP appeared in deep structure but was replaced transformationally. In the ungrammatical examples in (7.70), the dummy NP appears in the surface structure as well. A plausible way of treating dummies, then, and one that is argued for explicitly by Emonds (1970, 1975), is that any derivation that results in a surface structure that contains a dummy is ruled out as ill-formed and not leading to a grammatical sentence.

This convention is important for the analysis of the passive. If the subject is a dummy NP and there is a *by* phrase in the VP, the resulting derivation will be (7.71):

(7.71)   Input $_{NP}[\Delta]$ Past *do arrest Mary by* Δ
         Agent Postposing $_{NP}[\Delta]$ Past *do arrest Mary by* $_{NP}[\Delta]$
         NP Preposing $_{NP}[$ *Mary* $]$ Past *do be en arrest by* $_{NP}[\Delta]$
         Other rules $_{NP}[$ *Mary* $]$ # *be* + Past # # *arrest* + *en* # *by*$_{NP}[\Delta]$
                            *Mary was arrested by Δ.

The problem here is that Agent Postposing moves the subject dummy NP into the position occupied by Δ, leaving behind another dummy NP in subject position. The one in subject position is filled by NP Preposing, but the one in the *by* phrase remains unfilled. This problem can be eliminated by the general convention noted earlier.

SUMMARY

In this chapter, we considered the major aspects of four fundamental constructions of English: the reflexive, the imperative, the dative, and the passive. The points mentioned here are central ones and must be taken into account in any description of English that attempts to approach completeness. To summarize:

1. There is a systematic structural relationship between a reflexive pronoun and the noun phrase in the sentence with which it is coreferential.
2. There is clear evidence that there is a rule of *You* Deletion that applies in imperatives.
3. There is a Dative transformation in English that relates the positions of the direct object and the indirect object in the verb phrase.
4. There is a two-part Passive transformation that expresses the systematic relationship between active and passive sentences in English.

SUMMARY OF RULES

Phrase Structure Rules

PSR1:   S   → NP AUX (*not*) VP
PSR2:   AUX → TENSE M
PSR3a: VP   → (*have en*) (*be ing*) VP′
PSR3b: VP′ → (*not*) V (NP)
PSR3c: VP   → VP PP

PSR4:   NP   → $\left\{ \begin{matrix} \text{DET (ADJ) N} \\ \text{PN} \end{matrix} \right\}$

PSR5:   DET   → $\left\{ \begin{matrix} (Wh)\ \text{Quan} \\ \text{ART} \end{matrix} \right\}$

PSR6:   PP   → P NP

PSR7:   AP   → ADJ (PP)

Transformations (*Introduced or revised in Chapter 7*)

COMPLEX NP SHIFT: X V NP Y
$$1\ \ 2\ \ \ 3\ \ \ 4 \Rightarrow 1\ 2\ \emptyset\ 4 + 3$$

Condition: 3 is complex

DATIVE: X V NP $\left\{ \begin{matrix} for_g \\ to_g \end{matrix} \right\}$ NP Y
$$1\ \ 2\ \ \ 3\ \ \ \ \ \ 4\ \ \ \ \ \ 5\ \ \ \ 6 \Rightarrow 1\ 2\ 5\ 3\ \emptyset\ \emptyset\ 6$$

AGENT POSTPOSING: X NP Y VP *by* Δ Z
$$1\ \ 2\ \ 3\ \ 4\ \ \ 5\ \ 6\ 7 \Rightarrow 1\ \Delta\ 3\ 4\ 5\ 2\ 7$$

NP PREPOSING: X Δ Y V NP Z
$$1\ \ 2\ \ 3\ \ 4\ \ 5\ \ \ \ 6 \Rightarrow 1\ 5\ 3\ be\ en\ 4\ \emptyset\ 6$$

REFLEXIVE: X NP Y NP Z
$$1\ \ \ 2\ \ \ 3\ \ \ 4\ \ \ 5 \Rightarrow 1\ 2\ 3\ \begin{bmatrix} 4 \\ +\text{PRO} \\ +\text{REFL} \end{bmatrix} 5$$

Conditions: (i) 2 and 4 are coreferential
(ii) 2 and 4 are in the same simple S

You DELETION: *you* VP X
$$1\ \ \ \ 2\ \ \ 3 \Rightarrow \emptyset\ 2\ 3$$

Condition: main clauses only

Ordering of Transformations (*Not all of the ordering relationships are given   cf.*
Problem 1.)

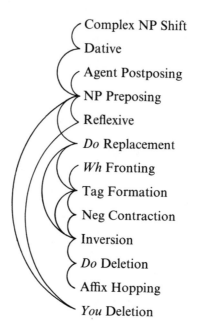

Complex NP Shift
Dative
Agent Postposing
NP Preposing
Reflexive
Do Replacement
Wh Fronting
Tag Formation
Neg Contraction
Inversion
Do Deletion
Affix Hopping
You Deletion

EXERCISES

1. Derive the following sentences (give the deep structure and the terminal
sequences corresponding to the intermediate phrase markers, along with the
rules that derive each intermediate phrase marker from the preceding one):

a. *Be seen at the movies, and everyone applauds you.*
b. *Give Mary the cake.*
c. *Give yourself a present.*
d. *Who was this book written by?*
e. *What was Mary given by John?*
f. *Mary saw herself.*
g. *Mary was seen by herself in the mirror.*
h. *John showed to Mary a book about spiders, didn't he?*

2. Explain why each of the following examples is unacceptable:

a. **John shaved herself.*
b. **John talked about herself to Mary.*
c. **John said that Mary hit himself.*
d. **John and Mary shaved herself.*

3. Show that the assumption that there is a Passive transformation leads to the conclusion that there is a Tag Formation transformation. (Hint: If the two parts of the tag question are generated independently in the base, what happens if Passive applies to one part and not to the other?)

4. What general constraint on transformations will prevent us from stating Passive as a single rule? Cite evidence that shows that your constraint has general application beyond the Passive case.

PROBLEMS

1. Determine what the ordering is for each of the following pairs of transformations (give relevant examples to support the ordering that you argue for in each case):

   a. Dative and NP Preposing
   b. Dative and Complex NP Shift
   c. Complex NP Shift and NP Preposing
   d. Reflexive and *You* Deletion
   e. Reflexive and NP Preposing
   f. NP Preposing and *You* Deletion
   g. Complex NP Shift and Agent Postposing

2. Show that there is no unique ordering of Dative, *Wh* Fronting, and Passive that will generate all and only the grammatical examples in the following sequences:

   a. *John gave a book to Mary.*
   b. *John gave Mary a book.*
   c. *What did John give to Mary?*
   d. **Who did John give a book?*
   e. *Who did John give a book to?*
   f. *What did John give Mary?*
   g. *Mary was given a book by John.*
   h. *A book was given to Mary by John.*
   i. **A book was given Mary by John.*
   j. *Who was Mary given a book by?*

Some of these judgments may be open to dialectal variation. You should take this distribution of grammaticality judgments as something to be accounted for, whether or not you happen to share them.

One explanation for this unusual situation, in which no unique linear ordering of the rules can be found, is suggested in Jackendoff and Culicover (1971). Another proposal is outlined in Chapter 11.

3. What constraint would have to be placed on Dative to account for the following distribution of grammaticality:

a.   *I gave the book to Mary.*
     I gave it to Mary.
     I gave the book to her.
     I gave it to her.
b.   *I gave Mary the book.*
     **I gave Mary it.*
     I gave her it.
     I gave her the book.

*4. The active/passive relationship appears to hold between noun phrases as well as sentences:

a. *John destroyed the toy.*
   John's destruction of the toy . . .
b. *The toy was destroyed by John.*
   The toy's destruction by John . . .
   The destruction of the toy by John . . .

This suggests either that the noun phrases are derived from sentences after the passive construction has been derived, or that the same transformations apply to sentences and noun phrases in certain cases. (i) The following examples, and others like them, can be used to argue against the derivation of the passive noun phrases from passive sentences. Construct the argument, and provide similar examples to support it.

c.   *John laughed.*
     John's laughter.
d.   *John laughed at Bill.*
     John's laughter at Bill . . .
e.   *Bill was laughed at by John.*
     **Bill's laughter at by John . . .*

(ii) Examples like the following also argue against deriving the passive noun phrases from passive sentences. Construct the argument, giving other examples where necessary.

f. *The failure by the government to solve our problems . . .*
   The fall by Harry from the top of the roof . . .
   The attempt by Mary to stop the car . . .

(iii) Show that NP Preposing would have to be revised considerably to apply in noun phrases because of examples (c–e) and because of the following examples:

g. *The destruction of the toy by John . . .*
   The decision by John to leave . . .
   The discovery of the answer by Mary . . .
   The reference by Susan to the article . . .

SUGGESTED FURTHER READINGS

Reflexives

Jackendoff, R. S. (1972), *Semantic Interpretation in Generative Grammar*, MIT Press, Cambridge, Mass.

Lees, R. & Klima, E. S. (1969), "Rules for English pronominalization," in Reibel, D. & Schane, S. A., eds., (1969), *Modern Studies in English*, Prentice-Hall, Englewood Cliffs, N. J.

Imperatives

Bolinger, D. (1967), "The imperative in English," in *Festschrift for Roman Jakobson*, Mouton, The Hague.

Lakoff, R. (1968a), *Abstract Syntax and Latin Complementation*, MIT Press, Cambridge, Mass.

Thorne, J. P. (1966), "English imperative sentences," *JL.* **2**, 69–78.

Datives

Emonds, J. E. (1972), "Evidence that indirect object movement is a structure-preserving rule," *FL*, **8**, 546–561.

Fillmore, C. (1965), *Indirect Object Construction in English and the Ordering of Transformations*, Monographs in Linguistic Analysis 1, Mouton, The Hague.

Jackendoff, R. S. and Culicover, P. W. (1971), "A reconsideration of dative movement," *FL*, **7**, 397–412.

Passive

Chomsky, N. (1957), *Syntactic Structures*, Mouton, The Hague.

Chomsky, N. (1970a), "Remarks on nominalizations," in Jacobs, R. & Rosenbaum, P. S., eds., (1970), *Readings in English Transformational Grammar*, Ginn (Blaisdell), Boston, Mass.

Emonds, J. E. (1970), *Root and Structure Preserving Transformations*, Unpublished ditto, Indiana University Linguistics Club, Bloomington, Indiana.

Freidin, R. (1975), "The analysis of passives," *Lg*, **51**, 384–405.

Hasegawa, K. (1968), "The passive construction in English," *Lg*, **44**, 230–243.

8

Relative Clauses

INTRODUCTION

Chapters 2–7 had two major goals: (i) to establish some of the basic principles for formulating linguistic descriptions and (ii) to apply these principles to a number of grammatical phenomena in English. For the most part, these phenomena have been **local** in that transformations that account for them all deal with constituents of a single S node. There are also grammatical sentences whose underlying phrase markers contain more than one S node. These are called **complex sentences.**

RECURSION

A suitable point from which to commence an investigation into complex constructions is the **relative clause.** The relative clause bears a large number of similarities to the *wh* question; hence, it will be possible to rely on a number of conclusions about *wh* questions without an excessive amount of repetition in the analysis of relative clauses. Some typical relative clauses are in boldface in the following examples.

(8.1)   a. *This is the house **that Jack built**.*
        b. *John is a man **who likes to go fishing**.*
        c. *Mary lives in a city **where everyone goes into
            hiding in winter**.*
        d. *I found three children **whose shoes were untied**.*
        e. *This is a book **which I always enjoy reading**.*

It is apparent that in its function a relative clause, like an adjective, is a modifier of the noun. In many instances, it is possible to paraphrase an expression that has an adjective with one that has a relative clause.

(8.2)   a. *John is a **very bald** man.*
        b. *John is a man **who is very bald**.*

It is also apparent that the relative clause itself is an S: It contains a subject, a predicate, and AUX, and all of the other characteristics that identify S's. In fact, the phrase structure rules as now stated would assign a structure to many relative clauses that is identical to that of a simple sentence. The rules do not yet represent the fact that the relative clause is itself a constituent of a noun phrase.

What is required is a phrase structure rule of the following general form.

(8.3)   NP → . . . S . . .

That is, NP is expanded as a constituent that contains at least an S, and possibly material to the right or to the left of it. Example (8.3) is a rule that explicitly states that an S may be a constituent of a noun phrase.

Such a rule makes a number of important predictions. It is already known that an NP may be a constituent of an S: This is true of subject NPs, direct object NPs, indirect object NPs, and so on. Rule (8.3) states that an S may be a constituent of an NP. The unavoidable conclusion is, therefore, that it is not possible to construct a longest grammatical English sentence.

The reason for this is not difficult to see. Suppose someone claims that some sentence, call it S, is the longest English sentence. S must contain a subject, so that it contains at least one NP. To make this sentence longer, one can simply attach a relative clause to the NP. Therefore, S is not the longest sentence, since the same sentence with a relative clause on it is longer.

Let us call this new, longer sentence S'. Suppose, now, that it was claimed that S' is the longest sentence of English. By appropriate selection of the relative clause that gave S', it will be possible to add a relative clause onto S', yielding a longer S". This shows that there is no longest sentence, since for virtually any sentence a longer one can always be constructed. This also means that there are an infinite number of English sentences.

The following concrete example will illustrate this point. Suppose that S is the sentence *The man has false teeth*. To get the longer sentence, we attach a relative clause to *the man*, e.g., *who stole my umbrella*. This yields *The man who stole my umbrella has false teeth*. We can attach a relative clause onto *umbrella* to get a still longer sentence, e.g., *The man who stole my umbrella which was on the clothes tree has false teeth*. Similarly, we can attach a relative clause onto *clothes tree*. This procedure can be applied indefinitely, just as long as there is an NP in the last relative clause to which a new relative clause can be attached.

As noted briefly somewhat earlier in the book, this phenomenon is called **recursion.** Recursion occurs when one rule produces a node to which a second rule can apply, and the second rule produces a node to which the first rule can apply. There is no point at which these rules may not be applied; hence, they can be reapplied indefinitely to produce indefinitely long sentences.

It is possible for a single rule to be recursive if the symbol to the left of the arrow appears to the right of the arrow as well. For example, consider the minigrammar in (8.4).

(8.4)   P1:   S → A S B
                                 P2:   S → C

Starting from the initial symbol S, we apply P1 to get (8.5):

(8.5)   S
                                    ⟋ | ⟍
                                  A   S   B

If we had chosen P2 first, then the resulting tree would have been (8.6):

(8.6)   S
                                        |
                                        C

As can be seen, the result of applying P2 terminates the derivation, since it produces a structure whose lowest nodes are not subject to further expansion. On the other hand, application of P1 always yields another S. Since there are two rules that can expand S, either may apply. As long as P1 keeps applying to the S at the bottom of the tree, the derivation will not be terminated:

(8.7)
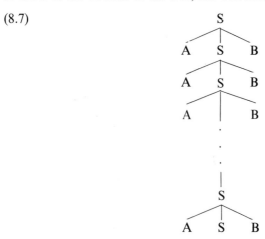

There is no limit to the number of times that P1 can be applied.

A more complex situation is the relative clause type illustrated earlier, in which a set of two rules causes recursion. Neither, however, is recursive in itself. An illustration is the set of rules given in (8.8).

(8.8)
$$P1: S \rightarrow A \; X \; B$$
$$P2: X \rightarrow C \; S \; D$$
$$P3: X \rightarrow C \; E \; D$$

In this case, there is no rule such that the symbol to the left of the arrow is also to the right of the arrow. However, P1 introduces X, and P2, which expands X, introduces S. This sort of derivation can be extended indefinitely, until X is expanded by P3:

(8.9)

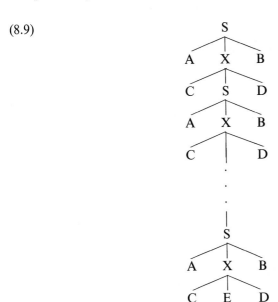

It is possible, in principle, to construct a set of rules of any size whatsoever such that no one of the rules is recursive and no subset causes recursion, but the entire set causes recursion. Consider the example in (8.10).

(8.10)
$$P1: S \rightarrow A \; X \; B$$
$$P2: X \rightarrow C \; Y$$
$$P3: Y \rightarrow Z \; D$$
$$P4: Z \rightarrow E \; S \; F$$
$$P5: Z \rightarrow E \; G \; F$$

This grammar produces trees of the form given in (8.11):

(8.11)

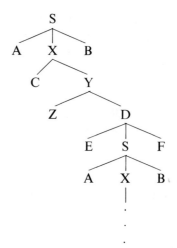

This more complicated type of case is typical of natural languages and is an essential property of grammars of natural languages, as will be seen clearly in the following chapters.

Another concrete example of recursion in English is the following. A noun phrase may be used to refer to the possessor of the object referred to by another noun phrase, e.g., *John's dog, the man's vegetables,* and so on. This structure arises from a special case of the rule for expanding NP, given as (8.12).

(8.12)   NP → NPs N

The phrase marker generated by (8.12) is:

$$\text{NP}$$
$$\diagup\diagdown$$
$$\text{NPs}\quad\text{N}$$

Notice, now, that the lower NP may also be subject to (8.12), so that we will get:

This can be repeated again and again; the only limit on the length of the expression will be the ability of the speaker and the hearer to remember what has been said. In principle, however, there is no longest sequence of this form:

(8.13)   a. *John's dog*
              b. *John's dog's vegetables*

    c. *John's dog's vegetables' vitamins*
    d. *John's dog's vegetables' vitamins' analyst*
    e. *John's dog's vegetables' vitamins' analyst's wife*

Examples of this sort can be constructed without limit. For example, each instance of *John* in (8.13a–e) can be replaced by the entire expression in (8.13e). Doing this for (8.13e) would yield *John's dog's vegetables' vitamins' analyst's wife's dog's vegetables' vitamins' analyst's wife,* and so on.

It should be emphasized that this process of recursion is not restricted to English. While all of the examples here are English examples, comparable demonstrations of recursion can be constructed with comparable examples from any natural language. The function of recursion is to build up large structures from smaller ones. *By using recursive sets of rules, it is possible to generate an infinite number of grammatical sentences with a finite number of rules.*

In the next few sections, we will concentrate on relative clauses. In Chapters 9 and 10, we will turn to other structures that also permit recursion.

THE STRUCTURE OF THE NOUN PHRASE

In order to discuss relative clauses profitably, it is first necessary to be somewhat more specific about the structure of the noun phrase. The rules for the expansion of NP are at present the following.

$$\text{PSR4: NP} \rightarrow \begin{Bmatrix} \text{DET (ADJ) N} \\ \text{PN} \end{Bmatrix}$$

$$\text{PSR5: DET} \rightarrow \begin{Bmatrix} (Wh) \text{ QUAN} \\ \text{ART} \end{Bmatrix}$$

One characteristic of noun phrases that we have not previously discussed is that between the article and the noun there may be any number of adjectives. E.g.:

(8.14)   *John is a (pleasant) (friendly) (intelligent) (helpful) . . . (boring) person.*

One might try to represent this fact in a number of ways. The one that will be argued for here is based on the following phrase structure rule.

$$\text{PSR8: N} \rightarrow \text{ADJ N}$$

In generating a deep structure in which the symbol N appears at the bottom of the tree, we may either expand this N as ADJ N or terminate the expansion by inserting a lexical item of the category N beneath this N. This will generate structures of the following form:

(8.15)

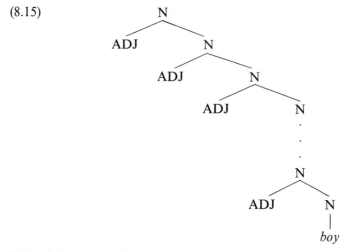

This rule is recursive in that the symbol on the left of the arrow is also mentioned in the same rule to the right of the arrow.

There are other constituents that may begin the noun phrase: **quantifiers (QUAN)** like *every* and *some* and **demonstratives (DEM)** like *this*. Also, ART, QUAN, and DEM cannot cooccur at the beginning of the noun phrase:

(8.16)   a. *the every man*
          b. *every the man*
          c. *this the man*
          d. *the this man*
          e. *this every man*
          f. *every this man*

and so on. To accommodate these facts, we must revise the phrase structure rule that expands DET as follows.

$$\text{PSR5: DET} \rightarrow \left\{ \begin{array}{l} (Wh) \text{ QUAN} \\ \text{ART} \\ \text{DEM} \end{array} \right\}$$

It is possible to demonstrate that the structure suggested in (8.15) is the correct one. The way to do this is to establish the existence of a rule that refers to the constituent N, and then show that this rule will apply to any subtree in a tree of the form (8.15). In fact, there is such a rule, and its function is to replace an N by *one*. This rule is illustrated by the examples in (8.17):

(8.17)   *John owns this Maserati, and Susan owns the other* $\left\{ \begin{array}{l} \textit{Maserati.} \\ \textit{one.} \end{array} \right\}$

This rule, called *One* Substitution, substitutes *one* for an identical N elsewhere in the sentence. Basically, the statement of the rule is as follows.

ONE SUBSTITUTION: X N Y N Z

1 2 3 4 5 ⇒ 1 2 3 *one* 5

Condition: 2 = 4

As can be seen, this rule will operate to derive the example in (8.17) that contains *one*.

A slight complication of *One* Substitution arises from the fact that when the N for which *one* substitutes is immediately preceded by *a* it does not yield *a one*, but simply *one*. E.g.:

(8.18)

John owns a Maserati, and Susan owns $\begin{Bmatrix} a\ Maserati, \\ *a\ one, \\ one, \end{Bmatrix}$ too.

Also, if there is a numeral preceding the noun to be replaced, as in *two Maseratis*, or if the noun is plural, as in *those Maseratis, One* Substitution does not give *ones:*

(8.19)

a. John owns three Maseratis, and Susan owns $\begin{Bmatrix} two\ Maseratis. \\ *two\ ones. \\ two. \end{Bmatrix}$

b. John owns these Maseratis, and Susan owns $\begin{Bmatrix} those\ Maseratis. \\ *those\ ones. \\ those. \end{Bmatrix}$

c. John owns one Maserati, and Susan owns $\begin{Bmatrix} one\ Maserati, \\ *one\ one, \\ one, \end{Bmatrix}$ too.

These facts can be handled by postulating several low-level transformations or by adding a number of special statements to the rule of *One* Substitution. This is left as an exercise for the reader.

Consider, now, what happens when *One* Substitution applies to a noun phrase that contains a number of adjectives:

(8.20)   John owns a sleek green metallic speedy Maserati,
          and Susan owns a sleek green metallic speedy Maserati, too.

If the analysis is correct, the noun phrase that appears in this sentence will have the following structure:

(8.21)

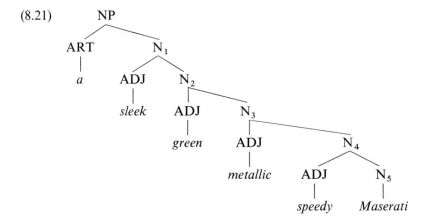

Since *One* Substitution is stated in terms of identical Ns, it should be possible to replace any of the Ns in this tree by *one*. Notice that what this means is that the entire subtree dominated by a given N will be replaced by *one*. This is in fact what happens:

(8.22)   *John owns a sleek green metallic speedy Maserati,*
      N_5: *. . . and Susan owns a sleek green metallic speedy one, too.*
      N_4: *. . . and Susan owns a sleek green metallic one, too.*
      N_3: *. . . and Susan owns a sleek green one, too.*
      N_2: *. . . and Susan owns a sleek one, too.*
      N_1: *. . . and Susan owns (*a) one, too.*

Thus, the analysis of the noun phrase here accurately predicts what the consequence of applying *One* Substitution will be.

To summarize, then, the rules for the noun phrase are the following:

$$\text{PSR4: NP} \rightarrow \text{DET N}$$
$$\text{PSR5: DET} \rightarrow \left\{ \begin{array}{l} \text{(\textit{Wh}) QUAN} \\ \text{ART} \\ \text{DEM} \end{array} \right\}$$
$$\text{PSR8: N} \rightarrow \text{ADJ N}$$

Having established *One* Substitution as a transformation, we can use it as a diagnostic device for determining the internal structure NPs. The next section illustrates the application of *One* Substitution to the relative clause. What we will show is that *One* Substitution may ignore the relative clause, but need not. Hence, the relationship between the relative clause and the noun will be very much like the relationship between the adjective and the noun. Just as we found that we must treat ADJ N as a member of the category N, so we must treat N S as a member of the category S.

LOCATING THE RELATIVE CLAUSE

Consider the following examples:

(8.23) a. *John has a green Maserati that has flow-through ventilation and Mary has a green Maserati that has flow-through ventilation, too.*

b. *John has a green Maserati that has flow-through ventilation but Mary has a green Maserati that doesn't.*

In both examples, the rule of *One* Substitution may apply to the noun *Maserati* alone, since it appears in both clauses of both examples. This yields the following:

(8.24)   a. *John has a green **Maserati** that has flow-through ventilation and Mary has a green **one** that has flow-through ventilation, too.*

b. *John has a green **Maserati** that has flow-through ventilation but Mary has a green **one** that doesn't.*

Notice, now, that (8.23a) can be paraphrased by replacing *Maserati that has flow-through ventilation* by *one*:

(8.25)   *John has a green **Maserati that has flow-through ventilation** and Mary has a green **one** too.*

In order for *One* Substitution to derive (8.24) from (8.23a), it must be the case that the sequence *Maserati that has flow-through ventilation* is an N. Thus, the rule that introduces relative clauses in the NP must be the following.

$$\text{PSR9: } N \rightarrow N \; S$$

The structure of the NP in the clause that undergoes *One* Substitution in this example is shown in (8.26):

(8.26)

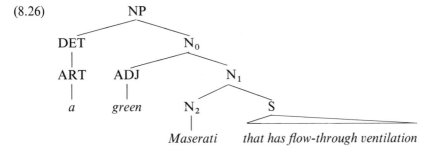

One Substitution applies to N_1 to derive (8.25). Since the entire NP shown in (8.26) is identical to a preceding NP for the example (8.23a), it also follows that *One* Substitution may apply to N_0 to derive the grammatical (8.27):

(8.27)   *John has a **green Maserati that has flow-through***
                 ***ventilation** and Mary has **one**, too.*

Given the rules N → N S and N → ADJ N, there is an alternative phrase structure representation of the sequence ADJ N S. According to the two phrase structure rules, it should be possible for a relative clause to be a sister to the N that branches into ADJ N. This is illustrated in (8.28):

(8.28)

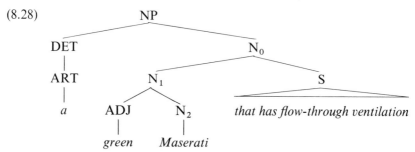

Such a formulation predicts that *One* Substitution should be applicable to the sequence *green Maserati* while ignoring the relative clause. The following example shows that in fact *One* Substitution need not include the relative clause when one is present:

(8.29)   *John has a **green Maserati** that has flow-through*
                 *ventilation and Mary has **one** that has flow-through*
                 ventilation, too.

Here *one* clearly means *green Maserati*, as the rules predict.

Furthermore, *One* Substitution is applicable when the relative clause in the right-hand clause is not identical to the relative clause to the left. From (8.23b), for example, it is possible to derive (8.30).

(8.23b)   *John has a **green Maserati** that has flow-through*
                 *ventilation but Mary has a **green Maserati** that*
                 doesn't.
(8.30)   *John has a **green Maserati** that has flow-through*
                 *ventilation but Mary has **one** that doesn't.*

This substantiates the correctness of the structure in (8.28).

SOME REMARKS ON SEMANTIC INTERPRETATION

Before continuing with the syntactic analysis of the relative clause, let us take note of some of the consequences that this analysis has for the semantic component. While the major concern of this book is to investigate the purely syntactic considerations that contribute to the construction of grammatical descriptions, the present case permits a relatively uncomplicated digression into matters concerning the relationship between syntactic representation and semantic interpretation.

All linguists agree that there must be a relationship of some kind between the two. Clearly, what a sentence means depends on the words that are in it and their location with respect to one another.

What is open to investigation and dispute is the extent to which the various levels of syntactic representation are relevant to semantic interpretation. The derivation of a sentence is composed of a sequence of phrase markers; in principle, any or all of them could have some property that determines some aspect of the interpretation of the sentence.

The earliest position taken on this question in linguistics was that the only level of syntactic representation relevant to semantic interpretation is the deep structure. This principle is one of the cornerstones of the "standard theory" presented in Chomsky (1965) and employed by Katz and Postal (1964). It will be assumed in the discussion that follows.[1]

If deep structure is the sole determiner of semantic interpretation, then two things follow. First, if two sentences have the same deep structure, then they have the same semantic interpretation. Second, if two sentences have different semantic interpretations, then they *may* have different deep structures. We say "may" because it is logically possible that different rules of semantic interpretation can apply to a single deep structure to produce different interpretations. Whether such situations should be ruled out in principle is an empirical question that we cannot go into here.

The analysis of relative clauses given in the previous section is relevant to the principle of deep structure determination of semantic interpretation. Note that this principle is a hypothesis that must be supported by empirical evidence. With this in mind, consider the following sentence:

(8.31)   *Mary is a former mayor who wanted to become President.*

Sentence (8.31) is ambiguous: It can mean either that Mary is no longer a mayor and also wanted to become President or that Mary is a mayor who formerly wanted to become President but no longer does. The first interpretation would correspond to the structure in (8.32a) and the second to the structure in (8.32b):

---

[1] As noted in Chapter 5, there is evidence that certain aspects of semantic interpretation are most revealingly accounted for in terms of surface structure. In assuming the principle of deep structure determination, we are actually assuming that it will be possible to distinguish effectively between those aspects of interpretation that are determined at the deep structure level and those that are determined in surface structure. It is also assumed that the semantic phenomena that are discussed here are determined by deep structure. None of these assumptions are necessarily correct, of course, and they would require considerable additional support before we would adopt them without question.

(8.32)   a.

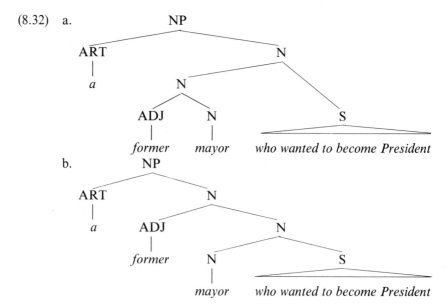

b.

A similar example is (8.33):

(8.33)   *John is an alleged thief who sells highchairs on the black market.*

Under one interpretation, John is alleged to be a thief and also sells high-chairs; under the other, John is alleged to be a thief who sells highchairs for his sinister purposes.

What these examples show is that there is in fact a difference in meaning corresponding to the difference in deep structure made possible by our analysis. While the difference in deep structure does not *predict* that there will be a dif-ference in interpretation, the difference in interpretation cannot be accounted for in our framework unless there exists a deep structure difference to correlate it with.[2]

The ambiguity here depends on the presence of adjectives like *former* and *alleged*. In the case of *alleged*, for example, the difference depends on whether what is in the relative clause is part of what was alleged. While this type of dif-ference is in principle possible with any adjective, adjectives of purely descrip-tive content, such as *green*, are neutral with respect to this structural difference. Thus, an expression like *a green Maserati that has flow-through ventilation*, while it has two deep structure representations, has only one interpretation.

An explanation of why *green* is neutral would entail an involved digression. An indication is the following: *Greenness* is something that is independent of the things to which it can be attributed, and it is independent of the person doing the attributing and the time of attribution. To illustrate, given a Maserati,

---

[2] Ruling out the logical possibility noted earlier that a single deep structure may yield more than one interpretation though the action of different rules of interpretation.

the sentence *This Maserati is green* is true or false when uttered about the Maserati in question regardless of when it is uttered or who utters it.

By comparison, whether someone is a former mayor depends in part on when we claim that she is. Mary becomes a former mayor at the point in time that she ceases to be a mayor. More generally, someone is a former X when one ceases to be an X. When a noun phrase contains a relative clause following the noun, then the ambiguity corresponds to whether X is understood to be the reference of the noun alone or of the noun combined with the relative clause.

The factor that permits this type of ambiguity to occur may be the meaning of the noun to which the adjective applies, in some cases. For example, an adjective such as *large* in a construction of the form *large X* may be interpreted either as " large in an absolute sense" or as "large for an X." Thus, *Dumbo is a large elephant* could mean that Dumbo is a large object or that Dumbo is large for an elephant. When a relative clause is introduced, the "large for an X" interpretation yields an ambiguity, the meaning depending again on whether X is taken to be the noun or the noun plus relative clause. E.g.:

(8.34)   *Dumbo is a large elephant that wears earrings.*

Sentence (8.34) can mean either that Dumbo is large for an elephant and wears earrings or that Dumbo is large for an elephant that wears earrings. By comparison, if *large* is taken to mean "large in an absolute sense," (8.34) is not ambiguous. Like *green*, this interpretation of *large* is neutral to the context.

INSIDE THE RELATIVE CLAUSE

Now that we have some idea of where the relative clause goes in the noun phrase, we may attempt to develop some notion of what the interval structure of the relative clause is. Let us define, first, the **relative pronouns,** which are the elements that appear at the beginning of relative clauses. These are *who, that, which,* and, less obviously, *where, when,* and *why.* The examples in (8.35) show the position occupied by the relative pronouns:

(8.35)

    a. *a man* **who** $\begin{Bmatrix} you\ know \\ likes\ you \end{Bmatrix}$ [3]

    b. *the man* **that** *you saw*

    c. *the books* **which** *I bought*

    d. *the place* **where** *Mary lives*

    e. *the hour* **when** *the clock chimed twice*

    f. *the reason* **why** *I came*

---

[3] For some speakers of English *whom* must be used here, and for others it is optional. This is a dialectal difference that is not crucial to the present account of relative clauses.

Consider first the relative pronouns *who, that*, and *which*. It might appear at first that there would be a significant generalization to be gained by treating relative clauses as types of *wh* questions, since the relative pronouns, with the exception of *that*, appear to be the same as the interrogative pronouns. It is quite clear, for one thing, that much the same type of fronting is going on in relative clauses as applies in *wh* questions. The derivation of the relative clause clearly involves a rule that fronts a noun phrase. Consider the following sentence:

(8.36)   *I met a man who you know.*

Note that there is no noun following *know*. *Know* normally occurs with a noun phrase, but it cannot be followed by an NP in a relative clause:

(8.37)   **I met a man who you know a woman.*

More generally, relative clauses systematically lack exactly one noun phrase in those positions where we would normally expect such a noun phrase to appear on the basis of the verb:

(8.38)   **I met the man who you gave the book to the woman.*
           **We discussed the library that Bill intends to visit New York.*
           **Mary saw the man who John lost his wallet.*

These examples demonstrate that relative clauses are not to be analyzed simply as relative pronoun followed by S. The hypothesis that there is a movement transformation that operates in relative clauses is further supported by the observation that it is impossible to have relative clauses that have the relative marker in a position other than initial position in the clause:

(8.39)   **I met the man you gave a book to who.*
           **We discussed the library Bill intends to visit which.*
           **Mary saw the man Bill sold the book to whom for a nickel.*

These data show the striking similarity between relative clauses and *wh* questions. As was shown in Chapter 4, *wh* questions clearly involve a fronting transformation: The *wh* word always appears in initial position, and there is always an NP missing elsewhere in the sentence (except when the *wh* word is the subject of the sentence).

Furthermore, the relative pronouns, with the exception of *that*, are a subset of the set of interrogative pronouns. The only interrogative pronoun that does not appear to function as a relative pronoun as well is *what*. Thus, it appears that a generalization can be achieved by (i) treating *wh* questions and relative clauses as identical in deep structure and (ii) applying *Wh* Fronting in the derivation of both.

There are a number of obstacles to generalizing between *wh* questions and relative clauses, however. The most important ones are the following:

1. While a *wh* question may have more than one *wh* word, a relative clause may not:

(8.40)   a. *Who said what?*
              What did Mary do when?
              Who gave what to whom?
          b. **I met the man who said what.*
              *John told me all of the things and times that Mary did when.
              *I met the man who gave what to whom.

The implication of this is that while the interrogative pronoun is derived from an NP that contains a *Wh* marker, the relative pronoun must be derived by the attachment of a single relative marker to some element of the relative clause. This will be elaborated on later.

2. While an interrogative pronoun is derived from an underlying indefinite pronoun, there is evidence that the relative pronoun is derived from an underlying **definite** pronoun.

Let us consider the second problem first. As can be seen in the statement of *Wh* Fronting, no mention is made of the fact that the constituent that is moved must be an indefinite.

Wh FRONTING: X A Y
                 1 2 3 $\Rightarrow 2 + 1 \emptyset 3$

In fact, *Wh* Fronting will apply to any constituent of the appropriate category that dominates *Wh*. We would not have to complicate *Wh* Fronting at all to accommodate evidence that *Wh* Fronting applied to other than indefinites. Rather, we could reformulate the phrase structure rules so that all of the constituents to which *Wh* Fronting applied could dominate *Wh*.

The evidence that the relative pronouns are not derived from underlying indefinites emerges when we attempt to apply to the relative pronouns the arguments that showed that indefinites underlie interrogative pronouns. For example, we find that it is impossible to have *else* after the relative pronoun:

(8.41)   a. *Who else did you see?*
               b. **I met the woman who else you saw.*

Similarly, while it is possible to have a *there* sentence with an interrogative pronoun, it is impossible to have one in a relative clause in parallel contexts:

(8.42)   a. *Who was there to meet at the party?*
          b. **I knew all of the people who there were to meet at the party.*

Not all of the arguments that show that the interrogatives are indefinite can be applied to the relative pronouns; however, the applicable tests we have cited show clearly that the relative pronoun cannot be indefinite.

The obvious move to make here would be to generalize the phrase structure account of the NP so that *Wh* could appear as a marker on definite pronouns as well as indefinite pronouns. The rules that expand NP do not accommodate such an extension in an obvious way, however.

$$\text{PSR4: NP} \rightarrow \text{DET N}$$

$$\text{PSR5: DET} \rightarrow \left\{ \begin{array}{l} (Wh) \text{ QUAN} \\ \text{ART} \\ \text{DEM} \end{array} \right\}$$

While PSR5 requires a noun phrase to have a constituent DET in order to have a constituent *Wh*, no other constituents of DET may appear with definite pronouns:

(8.43)   a. **some I's*
                    **some you's*
                    **those them*
                    **several we*

                b. **each me*
                    **every you*
                    **this her*
                    **the it*
                    **that him*

This generalization is captured by treating pronouns as expansions of NP.[4]

There is another source for definiteness besides pronouns, however. The article *the* is clearly definite; furthermore, it is a constituent of DET and can cooccur with *Wh* if we change PSR5 slightly.

$$\text{PSR5}': \text{DET} \rightarrow \left\{ \begin{array}{l} (Wh) \left\{ \begin{array}{l} \text{QUAN} \\ \text{ART} \end{array} \right\} \\ \text{DEM} \end{array} \right\}$$

Through this revision of PSR5, it is possible to generate *Wh* on both definite and indefinite noun phrases. The derivation of the relative pronouns will be like that of the interrogative pronouns given in chapter 4; the basic difference

is that while *Wh some* $\left[\begin{array}{c} \text{N} \\ +\text{PRO} \\ -\text{GEN} \end{array} \right]$ underlies the interrogative pronouns, *Wh the*

---

[4] There is also some evidence that definite pronouns function like nouns—they may take relative clauses, and relative clauses are sisters of nouns:

> *We who are about to die salute you.*
> *He who laughs last laughs longest.*
> *You who failed the exam stand up.*

If these pronouns are in fact members of the category N, then the ungrammatical sequences in (8.43) will have to be accounted for in the semantic component rather than in the syntactic component.

$$\begin{bmatrix} N \\ +PRO \\ -GEN \end{bmatrix}$$ underlies the relative pronouns.

Let us consider, now, the first problem we mentioned in regard to the proposal to generalize *Wh* Fronting to relative clauses. We noted that a relative clause can contain only one *wh* word. The relevant examples are repeated here:

(8.44)   *I met the man who said what.*
           John told me all of the things and times that Mary did when.
           I met the man who gave what to whom.

It will be useful in this discussion to be able to refer to the **head noun** of a relative clause. The head noun is the noun that is the sister of the relative clause, i.e., the N circled in (8.45):

(8.45)

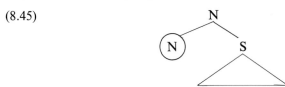

An additional fact about relative clauses is that the *Wh* Fronting transformation will not apply at all unless there is some *Wh*-marked NP in the relative clause. If *Wh* Fronting is not applicable in a nonrelative clause, the result will be a normal declarative sentence. If *Wh* Fronting is not applicable in a relative clause, however, the result will be ungrammatical:

(8.46)   *This is the man* s[*John found Mary a present*].
           The house s[*Mary took her dog for a walk*] *was sold.*
           The woman s[*Bill saw her*] *is my sister.*
           The place s[*I lost the book here*] *is eerie.*

These examples are characterized by their lack of a relative pronoun to which *Wh* Fronting must apply.

This constitutes a serious problem for the grammar. To see why, let us take a typical obligatory transformation like Affix Hopping.

AFFIX HOPPING: X Affix [+V] Y
                    1   2   3   4 $\Rightarrow$ 1 $\emptyset$ # 3 + 2 # 4

An obligatory transformation is one that applies when its structural description is met. If the structural description is not met by a part of the tree, then there is no question of applying the transformation. So, for example, Affix Hopping plays no role in the derivation of the noun phrase *a green Maserati with red stripes*, since the noun phrase does not dominate any affixes or verbal elements. Affix Hopping is irrelevant to the derivation of the noun phrase.

Similarly, if an S does not contain a *Wh*-marked NP, then *Wh* Fronting is irrelevant to the derivation of this S. *Wh* Fronting is obligatory when a *wh* constituent is present, but inapplicable when there is no such constituent in the phrase marker.

However, we have found that failure of *Wh* Fronting to apply in relative clauses leads to ungrammaticality. This means that in certain cases the structure *must* be such that it will satisfy the structural description of a transformation. In this case, for example, the relative clause S *must* contain a relative pronoun so that *Wh* Fronting will apply.

How is the presence of a relative pronoun to be guaranteed? If the phrase structure rules are context free, then the presence of a relative pronoun cannot be guaranteed by the phrase structure rules themselves. This is simply because in the expansion of the relative clause it would be necessary to expand at least one NP into the structure in (8.47):

(8.47)

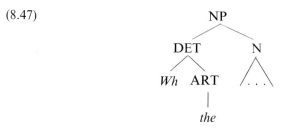

But this requirement is in effect only if the S is a relative clause. In order to *know* whether the S is a relative clause, the phrase structure rules for expanding NP would have to *know* whether or not the S that dominated them was a sister of an N. This requirement cannot be stated in terms of context free phrase structure rules.[5]

This discussion shows that what is required is a device that will check all potential relative clause structures and throw out those that will be unable to undergo *Wh* Fronting. A device that has this function is called a **filter.** It is important to recognize that filters are extremely powerful. since they permit us to construct the wrong grammar and then undo our error by throwing out

---

[5] It would not be a trivial matter to state this requirement for a context-sensitive phrase structure analysis, either. The problem is that the NP that is to become the relative pronoun can be anywhere within a relative clause:

> *This is the man who John believes that Mary said . . .*
> *that Harold claimed ∅ was eating the cake.*

Because of the infinite number of such clauses (due to recursion), the rules cannot pick out a particular NP (say, the first one) and require it to be the relative pronoun. No single NP *must* be the relative pronoun, but there must be *one* relative pronoun in the S. One can get around this problem by introducing a special device that looks at the relative clause to find out whether there is a relative pronoun and throws out all those structures that lack one; this is necessary for any analysis of relative clauses, however, and does not make a context-sensitive approach more desirable than the alternative context-free-plus-transformation approach.

those structures to which the rules of the grammar misapply. Hence, they should be approached with caution.

The problem that we have encountered with relative clauses is one of **overgeneration;** that is, the grammar will generate all the grammatical sentences, but it will also generate ungrammatical ones. If the overgenerating grammar that we have established is complex and unrevealing in itself, then there can be little justification for setting up a filter to eliminate the overgeneration. However, if the grammar is elegant and revealing and appears to capture linguistically significant generalizations, then it *is* worth establishing a filter to eliminate the overgeneration. The filter should take the form of a general condition, since it is intended to capture a generalization itself. A filter composed of a long list of unrelated structures is suspect and should not be easily incorporated into the grammatical description.

The general condition in the case of relative clauses is that the relative clause must contain exactly one relative pronoun, that is, exactly one constituent of the form shown in (8.47). Notice that this filter will not only solve the problem that arises when the relative clause contains no relative pronouns but will also solve the problem of having too many relative pronouns in the relative clause. The following is an informal statement of the filter.

RELATIVE CLAUSE FILTER: Every relative clause must contain exactly one relative pronoun in deep structure.

Finally, it should be emphasized that while the analysis proposed here requires the introduction of filters into the theory of grammar, any alternative analysis of relative clauses will also require such a filter if it generates the head noun and the relative clause independently. A more traditional analysis of relative clauses that also requires a filter is presented in Problem 6. In addition, Problem 7 deals with an analysis of relative clauses that does not require a filter but does not permit semantic interpretation to be defined on deep structure alone.

To summarize, we have attempted to capture the generalization between *wh* questions and the relative clause by treating the two constructions as essentially the same in deep structure and derivation. This results in a slight generalization of the rules for expanding the NP, and requires that we introduce a filter to handle problems of overgeneration.[6]

---

[6] It is conceivable that the Relative Clause Filter is simply a syntactic formulation of what is essentially a semantic condition. If this were so, then we could maintain that there is no justification for filters at all; every time there appears to be a need for a filter, the solution to the problem that the filter is intended to solve can be found by considering the well-formedness conditions on the semantic interpretations that are associated with the structures in question.

In this particular case, for example, we might be able to rule out *the man* $_S$[*John saw Mary*] by ruling out all semantic interpretations of the form *the x* $(f(y, z, \ldots))$ and permitting only semantic interpretations of this structure that have the form *the x* $(f(\ldots x \ldots))$. For a solution along these lines, see Rodman (1972).

To conclude our examination of relative clauses, we turn to the rule that specifies the conditions under which *that* may appear.

THAT IN RELATIVE CLAUSES

There is a crucial difference between the relative clause marker *that* and the relative pronouns that we considered in the preceding section. The relative pronoun must agree with the head noun on the dimension of *humanness: Who* is used with nouns that refer to human beings and *which* is used with all other nouns:

(8.48)   a. *Mary is the only person who John likes.*
              **Mary is the only person which John likes.*

          b. **This book is the only thing who was on the table.*
              This book is the only thing which was on the table.

          c. *I met the children who you had told me about.*
              **I met the children which you had told me about.*

          d. **I bought the dog who you had told me about.*
              I bought the dog which you had told me about.

In some dialects, *which* may be used with nouns that refer to humans as well as those that refer to nonhumans. However, in all dialects *who* can be used only with nouns that refer to humans.

The distribution of *that* is similar to the distribution of *which* in dialects that do not restrict *which* to nonhumans:

(8.49)   a. *Mary is the only person that John likes.*
          b. *This is the only book that was on the table.*
          c. *I met the children that you had told me about.*
          d. *I bought a dog that you had told me about.*

There are many cases, however, where *that* cannot be used in a position that permits a relative pronoun. This suggests that *that* is more than a simple alternative spelling of *which*, in spite of the similarities between the two in certain dialects:

(8.50)   a. *This is the book whose cover is missing.*
              **This is the book that's cover is missing.*

          b. *New York is the place to which Mary is heading.*
              **New York is the place to that Mary is heading.*

          c. *The person to whom I gave the book was very thankful.*
              **The person to that I gave the book was very thankful.*

    d.   *I called up the philosopher about whom I was writing.*
      *I called up the philosopher about that I was writing.

A comparison of the examples in (8.50) with those in (8.49) shows that *that* is prohibited unless the relative pronoun is the phrase that has been fronted by *Wh* Fronting, rather than a phrase that is a constituent of the phrase that has been fronted.

This condition can be formulated only with difficulty in the framework of the present phrase structure rules for S. Our present analysis of the output of *Wh* Fronting when the *wh* constituent is not the subject is that of (8.51a); if the *wh* constituent is the subject, then *Wh* Fronting does not apply and the resulting structure is that of (8.51b):

(8.51)   a.

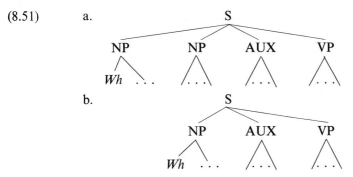

In order to specify where *that* may appear, we would like to identify those fronted noun phrases that are entirely *wh* constituents. That is, we wish to rule out *whose* from becoming *that's*; while the *wh* constituent *whose* is a noun phrase, there is more to the fronted NP than the *wh* word alone.

A comparison of (8.51a) and (8.51b) shows, however, that there is no straightforward way of identifying the NPs that will become *that* in terms of their surrounding context. When the NP is subject, it is followed by AUX; when it is not a subject, it is followed by NP.

The solution to this problem previews an analysis that will be given further support in Chapter 9. We revise the rules for expanding S in such a way that there is a single constituent of the sentence that is a sister of the node that dominates everything else in the sentence. This single constituent is called COMP, and is introduced by PSR1a. PSR1b introduces the rest of the phrase marker.

        PSR1a: S → COMP S′
        PSR1b: S′ → NP AUX VP

The primary function of COMP is to designate a node in sentence-initial position to which constituents of the sentence can be attached by fronting transformations.

Given COMP, we can revise *Wh* Fronting so that it will function as shown in (8.52):

(8.52)

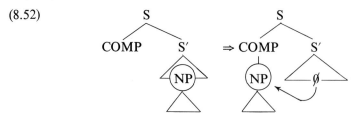

By reformulating *Wh* Fronting in this way, we achieve an analysis in which the condition for changing a relative pronoun into *that* can be easily stated. Just in those cases where *that* is permitted, COMP exhaustively dominates the noun phrase marked with *Wh*. If the noun phrase is a constituent of PP, this condition is not met, and as we have seen, that is not in fact permitted in PPs. Similarly, if the *Wh*-marked NP is a possessive in a larger NP, it cannot be realized as *that*.

The rule for realizing *that* in relative clauses is given as *That* Formation.

THAT FORMATION: X $_{\text{COMP}}[_{\text{NP}}[Wh \ Y]] \ Z$

1   2   3 ⇒ 1 *that* 3

There is an argument that shows that *That* Formation must be a transformation and cannot be treated as an alternative spelling of certain NPs in certain contexts. We assume, first of all, that all spelling rules apply to surface structure after all transformations have applied. The argument to be presented is that *That* Formation must *precede* another transformation in order to capture a linguistically significant generalization and, hence, cannot be a surface structure spelling rule.

Consider the following examples. These show that under certain circumstances it is possible to delete the relative marker:

(8.53)   a. *Mary is the only person ∅ John likes.*
               b. **This is the only book ∅ was on the table.*
               c. *I met the children ∅ you had told me about.*

The ∅ in these examples indicates the position that the relative marker would occupy if it was present. Note that a relative marker cannot be omitted when the relativized constituent is the subject of the relative clause, as in (8.53b).

Next, we observe that when the relative marker is itself a constituent of a PP or an NP, then it cannot be deleted:

(8.54)   a. *This is the book* $\begin{Bmatrix} *∅ \\ whose \end{Bmatrix}$ *cover is missing.*

b. *New York is the place to* $\begin{Bmatrix} *\emptyset \\ which \end{Bmatrix}$ *Mary is heading.*

c. *The person to* $\begin{Bmatrix} *\emptyset \\ whom \end{Bmatrix}$ *I gave the book was very thankful*

d. *I called up the philosopher about* $\begin{Bmatrix} *\emptyset \\ whom \end{Bmatrix}$ *I was writing.*

A comparison of these examples with those in (8.49) and (8.50) reveals a striking generalization: The relative marker can be deleted from just those positions in which *that* may appear. This generalization must be captured by stating the rule that deletes the relative marker in such a way that it applies only when the relative marker is *that*. Otherwise, the grammar would be considerably complicated by the need to state the same set of conditions for both the transformational deletion of the relative marker and the realization of the relative marker as *that* by a late spelling rule. If these conditions are incorporated in a *That* Formation transformation as we have done here, then the rule that deletes *that* for relative clauses may be simply stated as follows.

THAT DELETION (REL):   X N *that* NP Y
                           1   2   3   4   5 $\Rightarrow$ 1 2 $\emptyset$ 4 5

Condition: 3 is relative *that*

It is necessary to specify that an NP must follow *that* for the rule to apply. This prevents the rule from applying to *that* corresponding to the subject of the relative clause.

The condition that the rule may apply to *that* in relative clauses only will prevent it from applying to the *that* that appears in expressions like *John admitted that he saw Mary* and *Edward ridiculed Bill's claim that the world was an oyster*. While the latter *that* also deletes, the conditions that govern its deletion are different from those that govern the deletion of *that* in relative clauses, and the two must be distinguished. This is discussed further in Chapter 10.

Finally, *that* can only be deleted if the relative clause immediately follows the head noun:

(8.55)   a.   *John looked up the information that Mary had requested.*
            John looked up the information $\emptyset$ Mary had requested.
     b.   *John looked the information up that Mary had requested.*
            *John looked the information up $\emptyset$ Mary had requested.

RELATED CONSTRUCTIONS

There are a number of constructions in English that bear a striking similarity to the relative clause but do not share all of the characteristics that we have found relative clauses to have. A careful consideration of the syntax of each of these constructions would further illustrate the kinds of evidence and arguments that one brings to bear in formulating linguistic analyses. Because the problems that arise are quite intricate, however, it would be more useful at this stage simply to survey the syntax without presenting the arguments in great detail.

For each of the following constructions, we will present some relevant data, one or more plausible solutions, and a summary of the more important arguments. These problems are taken up in the problems at the end of the chapter, and are dealt with extensively in the literature cited in the "Suggested Further Readings."

Extraposed Relatives

Under certain circumstances, it is possible to move a relative clause to the right, away from its head noun. This usually takes place in cases where the verb is either intransitive or passivized, since the presence of another noun phrase in the verb phrase might create an ambiguity:

(8.56)   a. *The man who was from Philadelphia tripped.*
          b. *The man tripped who was from Philadelphia.*

(8.57)   a. *The test which we have developed will be used later.*
          b. *The test will be used later which we have developed.*

(8.58)   a. *The plant which was on the pedestal fell off.*
          b. *The plant fell off which was on the pedestal.*

(8.59)   a. *The man who was from Philadelphia went to the theater.*
          b. ?*The man went to the theater who was from Philadelphia.*

The major problem that arises in the formulation of the transformation is that it cannot apply when its application would lead to a surface structure that has a natural interpretation different from the one assigned to the sentence on the basis of the deep structure. For example, it appears that the transformation should be inapplicable in a case like (8.60):

(8.60)   a. *The man who was from Philadelphia hit the woman.*
          b. *The man hit the woman who was from Philadelphia.*

One way to avoid this problem would be to somehow prevent this transformation from applying just in case the output of the rule would be subject to another interpretation. In the present theory, however, it is not possible for a transformation to have access to information about the semantic interpretation of various structures to which it may apply. Hence, in the context of the present theory this phenomenon must be treated as **extragrammatical**, that is, not something to be accounted for by the grammar itself. The solution will be that relative clauses may be freely extraposed; the fact that there are instances in which the extraposed relative clause cannot be interpreted as applying to its original head is due to a processing strategy. This strategy leads the listener to interpret the relative clause as applying to the closest noun phrase to the left of it unless such an interpretation is impossible. This would explain, for example, why it is easier to associate the relative clause in (8.61a) with *the man* than the relative clause in (8.61b):

(8.61)   a. *The man was pushed off of the train who was from Philadelphia.*
         b. *The man was pushed off of the train that was from Philadelphia.*

Free Relatives

Free relatives are relative clauses that lack head nouns. Some examples are the following:

(8.62)   a. *What you have in that box smells awful.*
             b. *New York is very near to where I was born.*

Notice that free relatives cannot begin with *that*, *who*, or *which;* on the other hand, relative clauses cannot begin with *what*. Compare the following with (8.62a):

(8.63)   a. **Which you have in that box smells awful.*
             b. **That you have in that box smells awful.*
             c. **The cake what you have in that box smells awful.*
             d. **Who you introduced to me is in the next room.*

Furthermore, free relatives look just like indirect questions. A difference between the two is that free relatives do not permit *else*, while indirect questions do.

FREE RELATIVES

(8.64)   a. *I sold what (*else) you had in that basket.*
             b. *I met the mayor of where (*else) John owns property.*
             c. *Mary never introduced me to who (*else) she was dating.*

INDIRECT QUESTIONS

(8.65)   a. *I told them what (else) you had in that basket.*
             b. *I asked the mayor where (else) John owns property.*
             c. *Mary never informed me of who (else) she was dating.*

In certain cases, we can discover an ambiguity between the free relative and the indirect question:

(8.66)   *John discovered what Mary had brought home.*

Under the free relative interpretation, Mary had brought home an object that John discovered. That is, he discovered the physical object itself. Under the indirect question interpretation, John found out what the thing was; that is, he found out the answer to the question "What had Mary brought home?"

Both constructions have the property of being NPs, since they both undergo Passive. E.g.:

(8.67)   a. *What you had in that basket was sold yesterday.*
                  (free relative)
              b. *What (else) you had in that basket was told to*
                  everyone who asked. (indirect question)

The independently motivated rule of Extraposition that applies to S when it is exhaustively dominated by NP (cf. Chapter 10 for discussion) shows that the indirect question is such an S, while the free relative is not:

(8.68)   a. *What Mary brought home was discovered by John.*
                  (ambiguous)
              b. *What else Mary brought home was discovered by John.*
                  (indirect question)

(8.69)   a. *It was discovered by John what Mary had brought home.*
                  (indirect question)
              b. *It was discovered by John what else Mary had brought*
                  home. (indirect question)

The examples in (8.69) are derived from the examples in (8.68) by moving the subject clause to the end of the sentence and leaving an *it* behind. Note that while (8.68a) is ambiguous between the free relative and the indirect question interpretation, only the latter is possible when Extraposition has applied. Thus, the indirect question is an S exhaustively dominated by NP, while the free relative is not.

Two plausible alternatives for representing free relatives are (i) that they are constituents of NPs with dummy heads and (ii) that they are constituents of NPs whose heads are *thing, person, place, time,* etc., which are deleted. These two alternatives are illustrated in (8.70):

(8.70)   a.

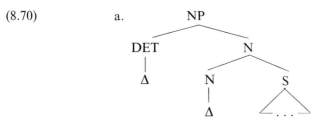

b.

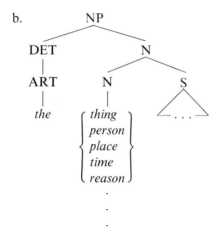

The second alternative is more satisfactory, because it accommodates a wider range of data. In the structure shown in (8.70a), it is necessary either to require that there be nothing in DET as well as in N or to filter out structures that have an article, demonstrative, or quantifier in DET. In the case of (8.70b), however, the transformation that deletes the head noun can be stated so that it will be delete *the* if it is present and will not apply otherwise. Hence, all free relatives will be derived as in (8.71a), while structures such as that in (8.71b) will not be affected:

(8.71)   a. *the thing which John bought*
                ⇒ ∅ *what John bought*
                b. *every thing which John bought*

Furthermore, structures such as (8.70b) are required in any case for the derivation of sentences like (8.72):

(8.72)   *Whatever John does results in success.*

It seems quite likely that the derivation of this type of sentence and the derivation of the free relative can be accomplished by a single rule, with slightly different conditions for the two cases. Problem 1 deals with the problem of formalizing an account of the free relative.

Pseudo-Clefts

The following are called **pseudo-cleft** sentences:

(8.73)   a. *What Bill brought home was a skunk.*
                b. *Where Bill lives is near Chicago.*
                c. *What I believe is that the world is flat.*
                d. *What surprised Bill was your answer.*
                e. *What Mary did was answer the question.*

The first four examples here are superficially identical with sentences containing free relatives: *what Bill brought home, where Bill lives, what I believe, what surprised Bill.* Notice, for example, that in just those cases where free relatives are ungrammatical, so are pseudo-clefts:

(8.74)   a. *Which Bill brought home was a skunk.* [cf. (8.63a)]
          b. *That you have in that basket is an apple.* [cf. (8.73b)]
          c. *Who just called me up is Harold.*

It appears, therefore, that a pseudo-cleft is simply a sentence whose subject NP is a free relative and whose main verb is *be.*

   The situation is complicated by two facts. First of all, a verb phrase without *ing* may follow *be* in pseudo-clefts but is not normally a complement of *be*:

(8.75)   a.   *What John did was close the door.*
                        **John's action was close the door.*
                  b.   *What Mary did was turn off the light.*
                        **Harold's opinion was turn off the light.*
                  c.   *What Bill wants to do is leave.*
                        **Bill's desire is leave.*

   Second, certain pseudo-clefts are ambiguous, which would not be predicted if their deep structure source was only the one mentioned previously. E.g.:

(8.76)   a. *What Mary brought home was a tadpole.*
                  b. *What John became was irritable.*

The ambiguity of the first example depends on whether Mary actually brought home a tadpole or whether she brought home something that had been a tadpole previously, i.e., a frog. In the second case, either John became irritable or John became something (e.g., a frog) that was irritable.

   A natural solution to these problems is the following: The pseudo-cleft construction is derived by a transformation, and it is also derived from a deep structure in which the subject NP is a free relative and the main verb is *be.* The traditional transformational approach to the pseudo-cleft construction involves a rule that applies as illustrated in (8.77):

(8.77)

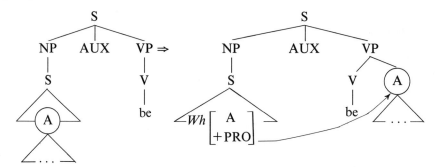

Roughly speaking, the rule extracts a constituent from the subject S, moves it around to the right of *be*, and leaves behind a pronoun that will be realized as a *wh* form. Such a formulation explains how a VP can appear to the right of of *be* without *ing* attached to it.

Given this transformation, it follows that there will be ambiguities just in case a particular type of constituent can appear in deep structure as the complement of *be* and can also be moved to that position by the transformation. Complements of *be* are the *-ing* verb phrase, PP, AP, and NP. The ambiguity with NP and AP is illustrated in (8.76); the other predicted ambiguities are shown in the following examples:

(8.78)   a. *What John was doing was annoying the children.* (VP)
           b. *Where John was born was in Chicago.* (PP)

In the first case, either John was annoying the children or he was doing something that was annoying the children. In the second case, either John was born in Chicago or he was born in a place that was in Chicago. The latter ambiguity is a subtle one because anything that happens in a place in Chicago also happens in Chicago.

Ambiguities will not arise just in case the constituent to the right of *be* could not have been generated as a complement of *be* in deep structure. This includes the nonprogressive verb phrase and S:

(8.79)   a. *What John said was that the world was an oyster.*
           b. *What Mary did was leave.*

It appears, then, that a promising approach to the pseudo-cleft construction is to derive it both by transformation and from any underlying free relative. This approach is not without problems, of course, and the topic is a lively one.

Cleft Sentences

Examples of **cleft** sentences include the following:

(8.80)   a. *It was a skunk that John brought home.*
           b. *It is near Chicago that John lives.*
           c. *It is that the world is flat that I believe.*
           d. *It was your answer that surprised Bill.*
           e. **It was answer the question that Mary did.*

The part of each sentence beginning with *that* has the superficial appearance of a relative clause. Note also that each cleft sentence can be paraphrased by a pseudo-cleft sentence, for example, *It was a skunk that John brought home* and *What John brought home was a skunk*. It is therefore worth entertaining the notion that there is a rule similar to the rule that extraposes relative clauses that operates in deriving cleft sentences from the structures that underlie pseudo-cleft sentences. Such a derivation would have the following general features:

(8.81)   (*The thing*) REL *John brought it home was a skunk* ⇒
        (*The thing*) *was a skunk* REL *John brought it home* ⇒
        It was a skunk that John brought home.

For a full discussion of this possibility, see Akmajian (1970).

SUMMARY

This chapter considered a particular complex structure of English, namely, the relative clause. The structure of the noun phrase is such that an adjective–noun sequence may be considered to be a member of the category N, as may a sequence of the form N S, where S is a relative clause. The transformation of *One* Substitution is used as a test for what the constituent structure of the noun phrase looks like.

The surface structure of the relative clause is accounted for by the independently motivated rules that derive *wh* questions. These rules have a natural extension to the definite *Wh*-marked constituents that underlie the relative pronouns. In particular, the rule of *Wh* Fronting captures the generalizations that precisely the same fronting takes place in both *wh* questions and relative clauses.

There is evidence that the relative marker *that* in relative clauses is transformationally derived and is not an alternative spelling of the constituents underlying the relative pronouns. The evidence rests on the demonstration that the grammar is considerably simplified if the relative clauses that lack all relative markers whatsoever are derived by deletion of *that*. This shows that *that* must be formed by a transformation because it must be ordered before the transformation of *That* Deletion (Rel).

Finally, it was shown that there are a number of constructions that bear a strong resemblance to relative clauses. It appears that free relatives are a transformationally derived variant of relative clauses, and that some pseudo-clefts contain deep structure free relatives, while some are transformationally derived.

SUMMARY OF RULES

Phrase Structure Rules

PSR1a: S → COMP S′
PSR1b: S′ → NP AUX VP
PSR2:   AUX → TENSE M
PSR3a: VP → (*have en*) (*be ing*) VP′

$$\text{PSR3b: } VP' \rightarrow (not)\ V \begin{Bmatrix} AP \\ NP \\ PP \end{Bmatrix}$$

$$\text{PSR4: } NP \rightarrow \begin{Bmatrix} DET\ N \\ PN \end{Bmatrix}$$

$$\text{PSR5: } DET \rightarrow \begin{Bmatrix} (Wh) \begin{Bmatrix} QUAN \\ ART \end{Bmatrix} \\ DEM \end{Bmatrix}$$

PSR6: PP → P NP
PSR7: AP → ADJ (PP)
PSR8: N → ADJ N
PSR9: N → N S

Transformations

ONE SUBSTITUTION: X N Y N Z
1 2 3 4 5 ⇒ 1 2 3 *one* 5
Condition: 2 = 4

THAT FORMATION: $X\ _{\text{COMP}}[_{\text{NP}}[\underline{Wh}\ Y]]\ Z$
1   2   3 ⇒ 1 *that* 3

THAT DELETION: X N *that* NP Y
1 2 3   4 5 ⇒ 1 2 ∅ 4 5
Condition: 3 is relative *that*

The ordering of transformations is left as an exercise (cf. Exercise 1).

EXERCISES

1. Determine the ordering between *One* Substitution, *That* Formation, *That* Deletion, and the transformations discussed in previous chapters.

2. Derive the following sentences (give the deep structure and intermediate terminal strings, and indicate each transformation that applies):

a. *I met the policeman who John was arrested by.*
b. *Is this the book which John gave Mary?*
c. *Show me the restaurant where you ate lunch.*
d. *Who are the people Mary likes?*

PROBLEMS

1. On the basis of the following sentences and examples similar to them, formulate the rules for deriving free relatives based on the discussion of relative clauses in this chapter:

a. *John sat down on* $\left\{\begin{array}{l} \text{the thing which} \\ \textbf{what} \\ \text{*which} \\ \text{*that} \end{array}\right\}$ ***Bill had brought home.***

b. *John sat down* $\left\{\begin{array}{l} \text{at the time when} \\ \textbf{when} \\ \text{*at which} \\ \text{*that} \\ \text{*at that} \\ \text{at the time at which} \end{array}\right\}$ ***Mary came home.***

c. *I was amazed at* $\left\{\begin{array}{l} \text{the reason why} \\ \textbf{why} \\ \text{the reason for which} \\ \text{*for which} \end{array}\right\}$ ***Mary came home.***

d. *This is a book* $\left\{\begin{array}{l} \text{which} \\ \text{that} \\ \text{*what} \end{array}\right\}$ *I like very much.*

Assume that the acceptable free relatives (in boldface in these examples) are derived from underlying relative clauses whose head nouns are of the form *thing*, *person* (or *one*), *place*, *time*, *manner*, and *reason*. Take special note of the fact that a free relative cannot be introduced by *which* or *that;* also observe that *how* may not introduce a relative clause, but may introduce a free relative:

e. **The* $\left\{\begin{array}{l} manner \\ way \end{array}\right\}$ *how John did that is a mystery.*

f. *I was amazed at how John did that.*

2. The following sentences are examples of pseudo-clefts:

a. *Where John lives is in Philadelphia.*
b. *What John bought was a camel.*
c. *When John came home was after four o'clock.*
d. *Why John left was because he was unhappy.*
e. **How John did that was by climbing the wall.*
f. *?Who Susan saw is Mary.*
g. *What Mary did was buy a camel.*

While (a–f) can be generated by independently needed phrase structure rules,

(g) cannot. Show that this is the case. Next, notice that there is a restriction on what part of the sentence may appear to the right of *be* in a pseudo-cleft:

   h.   *John saw a man who came from New Jersey.*
      *Where John saw a man who came from was New Jersey.
   i.   *John should have visited the hospital.*
      *What John should do is have visited the hospital.

Determine what the limits on "pseudo-clefting" are and state a precise transformation that will generate these pseudo-cleft sentences. Assume that the underlying structure is the one indicated in the text, i.e.:

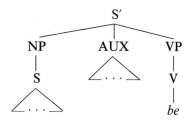

3. The following sentences are examples of cleft sentences:

   a.   *It is in Philadelphia* $\left\{\begin{matrix} where \\ that \end{matrix}\right\}$ *John lives.*

   b.   *It was a camel* $\left\{\begin{matrix} *what \\ that \end{matrix}\right\}$ *John bought.*

   c.   *It was after four o'clock* $\left\{\begin{matrix} when \\ that \end{matrix}\right\}$ *John came home.*

   d.   *It was because he was unhappy* $\left\{\begin{matrix} *why \\ that \end{matrix}\right\}$ *John left.*

   e.   *It was by climbing the wall* $\left\{\begin{matrix} *how \\ that \end{matrix}\right\}$ *John did that.*

   f.   *It is Mary* $\left\{\begin{matrix} who \\ that \end{matrix}\right\}$ *Susan saw.*

   g.   **It was buy a camel* $\left\{\begin{matrix} what \\ that \end{matrix}\right\}$ *Mary did.*

Suggest a set of rules that will derive these sentences. Try to integrate these examples into the examples of pseudo-clefts. Notice that it is impossible to delete *that* from some cleft sentences (Akmajian, 1970).

   4. State a transformation that relates the two forms of the following sentences:

   a. *John met a woman (who was) able to leap tall buildings at a single bound.*
   b. *Mary was the only person (who was) arrested by the police.*

c. *All the people (who are) sitting in the back of the room should move to the front.*

d. *John is a man* $\left\{\begin{array}{l} who\ is \\ *\emptyset \end{array}\right\}$ *a doctor.*

e. *Mary is a woman* $\left\{\begin{array}{l} who\ is \\ *\emptyset \end{array}\right\}$ *pleasant.*

What do examples like the following suggest in this context:

f. *All people (*who are) possessing rabbits should leave them outside.*

g. *Any person (*who is) knowing the answer will certainly pass the exam.*

5. Formalize a rule generating *whose* in questions and relative clauses that takes into consideration the difference illustrated in the following examples:

a. **Whose cover is red?*

b. *Whose face is red?*

c. *I have a book whose cover is red.*

d. *I met a man whose face is red.*

6. The analysis of relative clauses given in this chapter differs somewhat from the traditional one. In the traditional approach, the relative pronoun is transformationally derived from a full noun phrase that is identical to the head:

$$\textbf{the man}\ [Mary\ saw\ \textbf{the man}] \Rightarrow the\ man\ [Mary\ saw\ who]$$

This approach prevents the introduction of too many relative pronouns into the relative clause, since the transformation applies to one and only one noun phrase. (i) Show that there will nevertheless be overgeneration in this approach. (ii) State informally the filter that will eliminate the overgeneration.

7. A nonstandard analysis of relative clauses that avoids the problem of overgeneration is the following: The phrase structure rule that introduces the relative clause is not N → N S but NP → S. That is, the relative clause is generated without a head in deep structure:

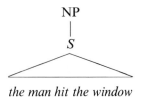

the man hit the window

The relative clause construction is formed by moving one of the NPs dominated by S to the left and attaching it as an immediate constituent of the NP that dominates S. At the same time, a relative pronoun is left in the position vacated by the moved NP:

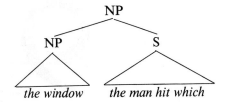

(i) Show that this approach avoids the overgeneration problem. (ii) Show that it is impossible to assign a semantic interpretation on the basis of the deep structure with this approach if the sentence contains a relative clause (iii) Show that this analysis makes incorrect predictions with respect to the transformation of *One* Substitution.

SUGGESTED FURTHER READINGS

Relative Clauses

Bresnan, J. (1972), *Theory of Complementation in English syntax,* Unpublished doctoral dissertation, MIT, Cambridge, Mass.

Kuroda, S.-Y. (1969), "English relativization and certain related problems," in Reibel, D. & Schane, S. A., eds., (1969), *Modern Studies in English,* Prentice-Hall, Englewood Cliffs, N. J.

Smith, C. S. (1969), "Determiners and relative clauses in a generative grammar of English," in Reibel, D. & Schane, S. A., eds., (1969), *Modern Studies in English,* Prentice-Hall, Englewood Cliffs, N. J.

NP Structure

Carden, G. (1970), "On post-determiner quantifiers," *LI,* **1,** 415–428.

Chomsky, N. (1970a), "Remarks on nominalizations," in Jacobs, R. & Rosenbaum, P. S., eds., (1970), *Readings in English Transformational Grammar,* Ginn (Blaisdell), Boston, Mass.

Jackendoff, R. S. (1971), "Gapping and related rules," *LI,* **2,** 21–35.

Extraposed Relatives

Ross, J. R. (1967), *Constraints on Variables in Syntax,* Unpublished doctoral dissertation, MIT, Cambridge, Mass. Available from Indiana University Linguistics Club, Bloomington, Indiana.

Pseudo-cleft and Cleft Sentences

Akmajian, A. (1970), "On deriving cleft sentences from pseudo-cleft sentences," *LI,* **1,** 149–168.

Ross, J. R. (1972), "Act," in Davidson, D. & Harman, G., eds., (1972), *Semantics of Natural Languages,* Reidel, Dordrecht, Holland.

9

Verb Complements I: Infinitival Complements

THE VARIETIES OF VERB COMPLEMENTS

Informally, a **verb complement** is a constituent that appears in the verb phrase following the verb. It turns out that verbs can be classified according to what kinds of complements they occur with. For transitive verbs, such as *hit*, the complement is the direct object NP. A formal representation of the range of complements that may appear with a particular verb is part of the lexical entry for the verb. The lexical entry specifies those characteristics of the verb that are part of the native speaker's knowledge of the language.

Part of a typical lexical entry is the following:[1]

(9.1)   *hit:* +[——— NP]

The + indicates that the item to the left of the colon has the property represented between the brackets. This property is that the item to the left of the colon can appear to the left of an NP. That is, replacing the underscore by the item to the left of the colon is an acceptable sequence.

---

[1] This representation is a translation of the feature [+ TRANS] associated with transitive verbs introduced in Chapter 3. While [+ TRANS] is an arbitrary feature, [+ ———NP] is not arbitrary, since it is defined in terms of the independently motivated syntactic structure.

The lexical entry must represent the semantic and phonological properties of a lexical item in addition to its syntactic properties. Only the syntactic properties will be indicated here, and for the sake of exposition the term **lexical entry** will be used even though only syntactic properties are at issue.

There are verbs that do not take a complement. Such verbs are **intransitive,** e.g., *sleep*, and have the following kind of lexical entry:

(9.2) $\qquad\qquad\qquad$ *sleep:* $-[\text{——— NP}]$

The minus sign indicates that the item to the left of the colon does not have the property represented between the brackets.

Finally, there are verbs like *eat* that may take direct objects but need not:

(9.3) $\qquad\qquad\qquad$ *John was eating (strawberries).*

The lexical entry of such a verb contains the following information:

(9.4) $\qquad\qquad\qquad$ *eat:* $\pm[\text{——— NP}]$

The representation of verb complements becomes more interesting when cases like *expect, try, force, believe,* and *wish* are considered. Some verbs take complements that appear to be full sentences introduced by *that*; others take complements that involve **infinitives,** as in *try to leave*, where the sequence *to leave* is the **infinitive phrase.** Furthermore, some verbs take more than one kind of complement.

The range of possible complements is indicated by the following examples:

(9.5) $\qquad$ a. $\quad$ *John expects a victory.*
$\qquad\qquad\qquad$ *John expects that Mary will leave.*
$\qquad\qquad\qquad$ *John expects Mary to leave.*
$\qquad\qquad\qquad$ *John expects to leave.*

$\qquad\qquad$ b. $\quad$ *John tried a new procedure.*
$\qquad\qquad\qquad$ **John tried that Mary would leave.*
$\qquad\qquad\qquad$ **John tried for Mary to leave.*
$\qquad\qquad\qquad$ **John tried Mary to leave.*
$\qquad\qquad\qquad$ *John tried to leave.*

$\qquad\qquad$ c. $\quad$ *John forced the door.*
$\qquad\qquad\qquad$ **John forced that Mary would leave.*
$\qquad\qquad\qquad$ **John forced for Mary to leave.*
$\qquad\qquad\qquad$ **John forced to leave.*
$\qquad\qquad\qquad$ *John forced Mary to leave.*

$\qquad\qquad$ d. $\quad$ *John believed the data.*
$\qquad\qquad\qquad$ *John believed that Mary would leave.*
$\qquad\qquad\qquad$ **John believed for Mary to have left.*
$\qquad\qquad\qquad$ **John believed to leave.*
$\qquad\qquad\qquad$ *John believed Mary to have left.*

e. *John wished for a miracle.*
*John wished for that Mary would leave.
John wished for Mary to leave.
John wished Mary to leave.
John wished to leave.
*John wished for to leave.

Ignoring the complements that consist simply of a direct object NP, there are five classes of verbs definable in terms of the range of complements they can take. These classes are represented schematically as follows. The infinitive phrase is represented here as INFP.

Class A: + [——— $\begin{Bmatrix} \textit{that S} \\ \text{(NP) INFP} \end{Bmatrix}$] (example: *expect*)

Class B: + [——— INFP] (example: *try*)

Class C: + [——— NP INFP] (example: *force*)

Class D: + [——— $\begin{Bmatrix} \textit{that S} \\ \text{NP INFP} \end{Bmatrix}$] (example: *believe*)

Class E: + [——— $\begin{Bmatrix} \textit{that S} \\ (\textit{for} \ \text{NP)} \ \text{INFP} \end{Bmatrix}$] (example: *wish*)

Let us assume for the moment that Class E is in fact a special case of Class A, in which the verb is not *wish* but actually *wish for*. This assumption will require a transformation that will delete *for* before *that* and before the infinitive, in order to rule out the ungrammatical examples in (9.5e). Given this assumption, the five classes of verbs can be collapsed into four; furthermore, the range of possible complements can be expressed by the following phrase structure rule.

$$\text{PSR4}': \ \text{VP} \rightarrow \text{V} \begin{Bmatrix} \textit{that S} \\ \text{(NP) (INFP)} \end{Bmatrix}$$

It is important not to confuse the functions of phrase structure rules and lexical entries. The phrase structure rules specify the range of possible complements of verbs, for example, by providing those structures into which verbs may be inserted. Lexical entries, on the other hand, specify which structures particular lexical items may be inserted into.

If the only facts about complements that had to be considered were those having to do with the order of constituents and the possible sequence of constituents in the verb phrase, then the analysis would be complete in the form of PSR4'. However, there are two phenomena that have played a significant role in the analysis of complements, particularly of infinitives, that must be attended to as well. The first has to do with the fact that it is generally clear to the native speaker who the understood subject of the verb in the infinitive is, and the second has to do with the fact that verbs that take infinitive complements generally may undergo Passive. A grammatical description that takes into account these two phenomena involves a number of rather interesting and complex grammatical devices, as will be shown in the following discussion.

THE UNDERSTOOD SUBJECT OF THE INFINITIVE

Consider the following examples:

(9.6)   a. *John expected Mary to leave.*
       b. *John expected to leave.*

(9.7)   a. **John tried Mary to leave.*
       b. *John tried to leave.*

(9.8)   a. *John forced Mary to leave.*
       b. **John forced to leave.*

(9.9)   a. *John believed Mary to have left.*
       b. **John believed to have left.*

In (9.6a), (9.8a), and (9.9a), it is clear that the person whose leaving is being talked about is not John but Mary. So, for example, if (9.6a) is true, it follows that what John expected was that Mary would leave, not that he himself would leave; if (9.8a) is true, it follows that Mary left, and not John; if (9.9a) is true, it follows that John's belief is about Mary's leaving and not his own leaving. By contrast, when there is only one noun phrase present, then this noun phrase, which is the subject of the main verb (i.e., the verb that is not in the infinitive) is also the understood subject of the infinitive. This can be seen in the case of examples (9.6b) and (9.7b).

On intuitive semantic grounds, then, it appears that the underlying representations of sentences that contain verbs like *force, expect, try,* and *believe* with infinitives must also contain noun phrases that are the subjects of the infinitives. So, for example, the intuition that the subject of *leave* in *John expects to leave* is *John* could be expressed by representing it in the deep structure as follows (for the moment we ignore the presence of COMP):

(9.10)

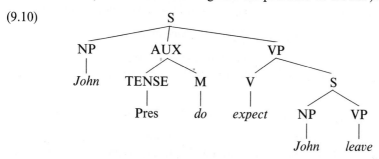

We will assume, without justification, that there is a late transformation that inserts *to* to form the infinitive from structures such as (9.10). For discussion of how this rule may be formulated, see Emonds (forthcoming).

Notice that the embedded S lacks AUX. In fact, there is no justification for assuming that infinitives contain AUX's, since the infinitive lacks modals and tense marking. (You should satisfy yourself that this is the case.) This provides some justification for our decision in Chapter 6 not to insert *not* into the appropriate position in the sequence transformationally, but to generate it in that position in the deep structure. Recall that the rule of Neg Placement that we discussed in Chapter 6 moved *not* to a position after AUX. Since infinitives lack AUX, this would block derivation of the following grammatical sentences:

(9.11)   *I convinced John not to leave.*
              We decided not to try on the shoes.
              I expected Mary not to say anything to Bill.

Generating *not* immediately before VP in the deep structure eliminates this problem.

Let us return now to the more important characteristics of the infinitival complement. The understood subject intuition, being a semantic intuition, is not a sufficient justification for syntactic structures and syntactic rules. To maintain (9.10) as the underlying structure of *John expects to leave*, it will be necessary to provide a syntactic justification for this structure. In addition, the transformation that derives *John expects to leave* from this structure must be justified on syntactic grounds. Such a transformation will involve the deletion of the subject NP in the lower S in (9.10). This transformation is usually called Equi-NP Deletion.

The question of whether the infinitival complement of *expect* must be derived from an underlying S is a controversial one. The problem, in essence, is the following: There are numerous properties of NP INFP complements that are also properties of S. Logically, there are two avenues one might take to account for this similarity between the two. First, one might derive infinitive complements from S, so that the properties of the infinitive complement will follow automatically. Second, one might try to show that a precise formulation of the rules that apply to S will apply to infinitive complements as well, even if they are not members of the syntactic category S.

To illustrate a typical property, let us consider the following sentence:

(9.12)   *Mary expected John to shave himself.*

The reflexive *himself* is coreferential with the noun phrase *John*. A reflexive object of *shave* could not be coreferential with *Mary* even if it was the appropriate pronoun:

(9.13)   **Mary expected John to shave herself.*

The Reflexive transformation specifies that in order for a noun phrase to become reflexive, it must be coreferential with another noun phrase *in the same simple S*. By the first line of reasoning just outlined, it would follow that *John* is the subject of the simple S of which *shave himself* is the VP:

(9.14)

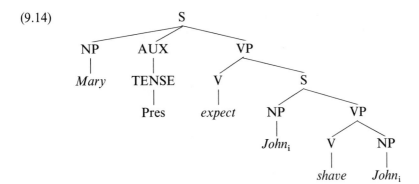

On the other hand, suppose that the structure of (9.12) was the following:

(9.15)

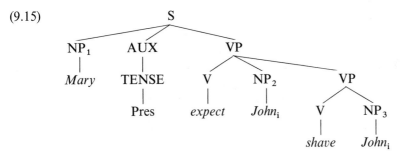

Since there is only one S node, it turns out there that both instances of *John* are again in the same simple S. Hence, Reflexive would automatically apply to this structure; in fact, the rule would have to be considerably complicated to prevent Reflexive from applying here. This would be consistent with the second position outlined earlier.

This is somewhat surprising, since our formulation of Reflexive predicts that (9.13) should be grammatical; by structure (9.15), all of the NPs are in the same simple S. Compare this with (9.16):

(9.16)   *Mary told Susan about herself.*

In this example, all of the NPs are clearly in the same simple S, and the reflexive may be coreferential with either *Susan* or *Mary*. Hence, the Reflexive rule will have to be complicated in order to rule out (9.13) but permit (9.16) as long as the sequence NP INFP is not dominated by S.

A second example concerns a rule that derives (9.17b) from (9.17a):

(9.17)   a. ***All** the men refused to serve.*
                         b. *The men **all** refused to serve.*

This rule of Quantifier Shift,[2] which we will not state formally here, moves the quantifiers *all* and *both* from their noun phrases to the right. An important fact is that this rule operates only on subjects when the NP is not a pronoun:

(9.18)   a.   *We gave the books to **all** the men.*
               b.   **We gave the books to the men **all**.*
               c.   *We gave the books to them **all**.*

Quantifier Shift operates on the NP in the complement of *expect*, however:

(9.19)   a.   *I expected **all** the men to refuse to serve.*
               b.   *I expected the men **all** to refuse to serve.*

This is predicted if the complement of *expect* is an S. If the complement of expect is assumed to be NP INFP, then Quantifier Shift can of course be revised to generate the grammatical (9.19b), but it must also be complicated so that it will not generate the ungrammatical (9.18b). The reason for the complication in this case is that the NPs *the men* in both (9.18) and (9.19) is a syntactic direct object. Hence, the rule of Quantifier Shift would have to take note of some other aspect of the phrase marker to distinguish between the two cases.

However, the failure of Quantifier Shift in (9.18b) is not due simply to the fact that there is no verb phrase following the NP that contains the quantifier. In the examples in (9.20), the presence of a following verb phrase does not improve the situation:

(9.20)   a.   **I persuaded the men all to refuse to serve.*
               b.   **We gave the books to the men **all** to entertain them.*

It is not at all clear what difference can be used to explain the application of Quantifier Shift in (9.19) and its failure in these examples. The subject/object distinction (assuming that the complement of *expect* is an S) accounts satisfactorily for the difference. Furthermore, it is consistent with the fact (to be demonstrated shortly) that the NP *the men* in (9.20a) is a direct object.

The final argument to be given here for treating the complement of *expect* as an underlying S has to do with the kinds of NPs that can appear immediately after it in the sentence. This argument can be made very elaborate and detailed, but it is sufficient to simply point out what is going on in essence. Recall that we noted in Chapter 7 that the noun phrases *homage, tabs, headway*, etc. could appear without determiners only in idioms like the following:

(9.21)   a.   *The people paid **homage** to the king.*
               b.   *The police keep **tabs** on protestors.*
               c.   *We made **headway** against the problem.*

On this basis, it was argued that if there is a Passive transformation, then the grammar will not have to contain an extensive list of the contexts in which these NPs may appear. All the grammar needs is a list of the idioms, and the

---

[2] Postal (1974) calls this rule Q-Pro Attachment.

transformations will derive all non-deep structure configurations involving these idiomatic NPs.

A similar argument shows that the complement of *expect* must be an S. Note that *homage, tabs,* and *headway* cannot appear as direct objects of *expect* when *expect* does not take an infinitive complement:

(9.22)   *I expect an explosion.*
                                I expect many presents.
                                *I expect homage.
                                *I expect tabs.
                                *I expect headway.

A striking exception to this occurs just in case the verb *expect* takes an complement of the form NP INFP. The complement, furthermore, is in the passive, and expresses one of these idiomatic constructions:

(9.23)   *I expect homage to be paid to the king.*
              I expect tabs to be kept on the protestors.
              I expect headway to be made against this problem.

While this exception could be represented in the grammar by the addition of a special note to the lexical entry of *expect* (and of every other verb in the same class), it is clear that to do this would be to miss the generalization: The "object" of *expect* in the infinitival complement case is precisely what we would expect if the complement of *expect* were an S.

Having established that the infinitive complement of *expect* is an S, let us now consider the statement of the rule of Equi-NP Deletion alluded to previously. The function of this transformation is to delete the subject of the complement S of verbs of the *expect* class under identity with the subject of the verb.

It is clear from the examples in (9.6–9.9) that Equi-NP Deletion cannot apply when the main verbs are *believe* and *force*. However, there is evidence that suggests that *believe* and *force*, while superficially similar, are fundamentally different.

Consider, first, the fact that the active and passive are essentially synonymous. From this, it should follow that the interpretation of a complex sentence does not depend on whether its complement is active or passive. This is in fact the case for *believe*, but not for *force*, as the following examples show:

(9.24)   a. *John believes the doctor to have examined Bill.*
          b. *John believes Bill to have been examined by the doctor.*

(9.25)   a. *John forced the doctor to examine Bill.*
          b. *John forced Bill to be examined by the doctor.*

Sentences (9.24a) and (9.24b) are synonymous. The two examples in (9.25) are not. The difference here has to do with who John's efforts are being exerted against. In the first case it is the doctor; in the second case it is Bill.

Since for many verbs the interpretation that some effort is being exerted on someone or something is represented by the presence of a direct object, one formulation of the difference between the active and passive complements of *force* is to assume the existence of an underlying direct object of *force* that is different in the two cases. Thus, when the direct object is different the interpretation of who is being acted on is different as well. This syntactic difference is illustrated in (9.26) and (9.27):

(9.26)

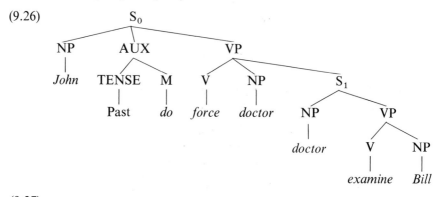

(9.27)

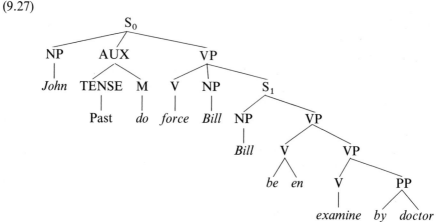

The direct object of *force* in (9.26) is *Mary*, and in (9.27) it is *Bill*. Notice that each structure contains two instances of the same noun phrase, and requires identity between the object of the main verb and the subject of the complement S. An additional condition on the rule of Equi-NP Deletion is therefore required in order to prevent the generation of the following sequences:

(9.28)   a. *John forced the doctor (for) the doctor to examine Bill.*
           b. *John forced Bill (for) Bill to be hit by Mary.*

It is important to note that the structure to which Equi-NP Deletion applies in (9.25) is **not** the underlying structure corresponding to *John forced Bill to be examined by the doctor*. Sentence (9.27) has undergone Passive on S$_1$ and, hence, is a derived structure. Equi-NP Deletion applies to derived subjects of infinitive complements; this raises a rather serious problem, which will be discussed in detail later in this chapter. We will simply observe here that if Passive did not apply in (9.27), the subject of the complement would be *the doctor*. Hence, Equi-NP Deletion would not apply. The result would be the ungrammatical **John forced Bill (for) the doctor to examine him/Bill*. This suggests that Passive must apply here, but the passive construction is optional and cannot be obligatorily derived in just these cases in a natural way.

The extension of Equi-NP Deletion for *force* is similar to that which applies in deriving sentences like *John expects to leave*. In both cases, the noun phrase that is deleted is the subject of the complement. The difference in the two cases is that the one for *expect* relies on identity between the subject of the complement and the subject of the main verb, while the one for *force* relies on identity between the subject of the complement and the direct object of the main clause. These two cases will be called, respectively, END(S) and END(0).

The range of possible infinitive complements is now definable in terms of the behavior of the subject of the complement.

Class A: complement subject **may** be deleted under identity with main subject (examples: *John expects to leave; John expects himself to leave*).

Class B: complement subject **must** be deleted under identity with main subject (examples: *John tried to leave; *John tried himself to leave*).

Class C: complement subject **must** be deleted under identity with direct object (example: *John forced Mary to leave*).

Class D: complement subject **may not** be deleted under any circumstances (examples: *John believes himself to have succeeded; *John believes to have succeeded*).

There are a number of difficult theoretical problems that emerge from this analysis; these will be taken up in a later section. The next section is concerned with the evidence for a rule of Raising, which causes the subject of the complement to become the direct object of the main S.

RAISING

The input to the rule of Raising is a tree like (9.29); its output is illustrated by (9.30):

(9.29)

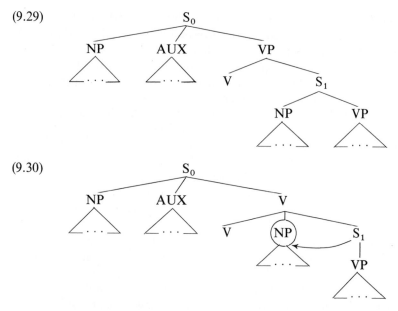

(9.30)

As can be seen, the effect of the transformation is to extract the subject of the complement and make it the direct object of the main verb. The syntactic evidence for the rule, then, must take the form of a demonstration that the subject of the complement actually functions like a direct object at some stage in the derivation. This section will present several of the arguments in favor of the rule, and will illustrate how it interacts with other transformations. An alternative approach to the same data is suggested in Chapter 10 in the context of certain theoretical considerations.

The Argument About There

In English, it is possible to have sentences that appear to have no subject but, rather, have *there* in the position that would normally be occupied by the subject NP, e.g.:

(9.31)   a. *There are two men in the living room.*
            b. *There seems to be some difficulty here.*
            c. *There arose a great clamor in the courtyard.*
            d. *There is a good reason for doing all this.*

The argument in favor of Raising that is based on *there* takes the following course: First, demonstrate that *there* must be inserted transformationally and cannot appear in underlying structure. Second, show that it can be inserted only as the subject of a sentence and not as an object. Then show that *there* functions as the direct object of verbs like *expect*. In order for this to happen, there must be a rule of Raising applying to verbs like *expect*. Certainly *there* cannot be the underlying direct object, and it is inserted as the subject of the complement when it appears by the first step of the argument.

The details of the argument are as follows.

There is clearly a surface subject, since it undergoes transformations such as Inversion and Tag Formation:

(9.32)   a. *Is there anyone in the room?*
             b. *There is someone in the room, isn't there?*

The distribution of *there* is not that of normal noun phrases, however, as examples like the following show:

(9.33)   a. **John was thinking about there.*
             b. **There makes me nervous.*
             c. **There hit John on the head with a magazine.*
             d. **I don't want there.*

Finally, in *there* sentences the verb agrees in number with the noun phrase to the right of it, not with *there*, which is to the left of the verb. The normal case, of course, is for the verb to agree with the noun phrase to the left of it:

(9.34)   a. *There is one man in the room.*
             b. **There is two men in the room.*
             c. **There are one man in the room.*
             d. *There are two men in the room.*

Since agreement is normally between the verb and the noun phrase to the right of it, and since it takes place between subject and verb, the noun phrase to the right of the verb must have been moved there by a transformation in these examples. This transformation, which is called *There* Insertion, is often formulated as follows.[3]

THERE INSERTION: X NP Y *be* Z
                     1   2   3   4   5 $\Rightarrow$ 1 *there* 3 4 + 2 5

Alternatively, the rule can be formulated as two transformations: One part moves the subject after *be* and leaves a dummy where the subject was, and the second part replaces the dummy by *there*. This alternative formulation has advantages over the one-rule version; these are discussed in Problem 3. For the sake of the exposition, we will assume the one-rule version here.

The agreement between subject and verb can be accomplished in two ways:

---

[3] This statement is only approximate. It is clear, for example, that *There Insertion* can apply in the contexts of verbs other than *be*, e.g., *There arose a great commotion*. In addition, it is necessary to specify that *be* does not have a noun phrase complement, e.g., *A man is a mammal* $\Rightarrow$ **There is a man a mammal*. Since what we are concerned with here is the fact that *there* is inserted rather than the precise conditions under which it is inserted, we will not pursue the many problems having to do with the formal statement of *There* Insertion here.

(i) Apply the agreement transformation before the application of *There* Insertion; (ii) insert a singular or plural *there* by *There* Insertion according to whether the subject is singular or plural. *There* Insertion can then be ordered before agreement. At a later point in this discussion, the second alternative will be shown to be correct.

It should also be noted that while *There* Insertion is similar to Inversion, it is a different transformation. While Inversion yields a structure in which the subject is to the right of the first verbal element in the verbal sequence, *There* Insertion moves the subject to the right of *be*, regardless of the number of verbal elements in the verbal sequence. E.g.:

(9.35) a. *There will be many problems with this.*
b. **There will many problems be with this.*

(9.36) a. *There has been considerable discussion of your problem.*
b. **There has considerable discussion of your problem been.*

(9.37) a. *There should have been some responses to his question.*
b. **There should have some responses been to his question.*

To continue with the argument, the crucial point that we have established thus far is that *there* is not an underlying direct object, and it appears in subject position by virtue of an insertion transformation.

Let us now compare a sentence containing *expect* with one containing *force*:

(9.38) a. *John expects there to be three men in the room.*
b. **John forced there to be three men in the room.*

We have already suggested that the underlying structure of sentences with *force* contains both a direct object NP and a sentential complement. This predicts that sentences such as (9.38b) will be ungrammatical. To see this, let us consider the following structure:

(9.39)

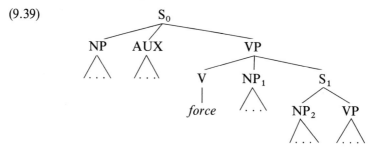

Force requires that its direct object NP_1 be identical to the subject of the complement sentence NP_2 in order for END(0) to apply. Hence, the only way in which sentences like (9.38b) could be derived would be if NP_1 could be *there*. However, it is quite clear that in general *there* cannot be a direct object. If *there* cannot be a direct object but must be transformationally introduced as a subject only, then this explains why it cannot appear as NP_1 in (9.39) and, hence, predicts why sentences like (9.38b) are ungrammatical.

On the other hand, let us consider a structure with *expect*, such as (9.40):

(9.40)

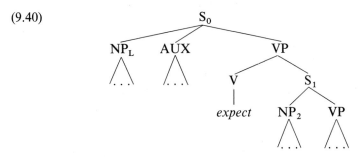

In this case, there is no requirement that the noun phrase that immediately follows the verb *expect* appear in the deep structure as its direct object. This predicts the grammaticality of sentences like (9.38a).

To conclude the argument, we must show that *there* behaves like a direct object in (9.38a). From this, it would follow that *there* was raised into object position, since it cannot be generated there in deep structure.

A rule that applies to direct objects is NP Preposing.

NP PREPOSING: X Δ Y V NP Z
                  1 2 3 4 5   6 ⇒ 1 5 3 *be en* 4 ∅ 6

NP Preposing moves the direct object into subject position when the subject is Δ. The following examples show that this rule applies when the NP immediately following the verb is *there:*

(9.41) Input $_{NP}$[Δ] *expected* $_S$[*three men to be in the room*]
        There Insertion $_{NP}$[Δ] *expected* $_S$[*there to be three men in the room*]
        NP Preposing $_{NP}$[*there*] *were expected* [*to be three men in the room*]

If, as we are assuming for the argument, NP Preposing can apply only to direct objects, then *there* must be a direct object in (9.41) at the point at which NP Preposing applies. Hence, it would follow that there must be a rule of Raising.

A small problem with this argument is that the verb *were* in (9.41) agrees with the noun phrase in the complement S. This is unusual because, as we have noted, verbs agree with their subjects. This problem is taken care of if *There* Insertion inserts a singular *there* when the original subject is singular, and a plural *there* when the original subject is plural. The derivation in (9.42) shows how this works for (9.41):[4]

(9.42)

Input	Δ *expected* ₛ[*three men* (pl) *to be in the room*]
There Insertion	Δ *expected* ₛ[*there* (pl) *to be three men in the room*]
NP Preposing	*there* (pl) *were* (pl) *expected* [*to be three men in the room*]

With this problem solved, the argument that there must be a rule of Raising based on *there* appears to go through.

However, as Chomsky (1973) has pointed out, the conclusion that there is a Raising transformation follows only if NP Preposing must apply to direct objects only. Notice that the formal statement of NP Preposing does not specify that the NP that is moved must be a direct object; all the rule says is that the NP must immediately follow the verb. In fact, the rule would have to be complicated by the introduction of labeled brackets if we wished to restrict its application to direct objects alone. Hence, on the face of it it would seem that the argument for Raising is without force.

There is a problem with letting rules such as NP Preposing reach down into complements, as Chomsky has also noted. When the complement is not an infinitive, that is, when it contains TENSE M, the subject cannot be extracted from the complement by NP Preposing. This is shown by (9.43):

(9.43)   a.   *John believes* ₛ[*Mary is in the next room*]
          b.   **Mary is believed by John* ₛ[∅ *is in the next room*]

---

[4] There is at least one alternative explanation. Suppose that *There* Insertion does not apply to the complement S, so that the complement subject remains *three men*. *Three men* is clearly not the direct object of *expect*, since the data about *there* show that *expect* does not take a direct object in deep structure. *Expect* nevertheless undergoes NP Preposing, as shown by (i):

i. *Three men were expected to be in the room.*

Then we apply *There* Insertion, moving *three men* after the second instance of *be*:

ii. *There were expected to be three men in the room.*

This analysis would also account for (iii):

iii. *There were three men expected to be in the room.*

However, it does not explain why only (ivb) is grammatical:

iv. a.   **There were forced to be three men in the room.*
    b.   *There were three men forced to be in the room.*

The ungrammaticality of (iv.a) would be inexplicable if *There* Insertion could move the subject of the main S into the infinitive complement. On the other hand, if *There* Insertion can apply only within the simple S, then the ungrammaticality of (iv.a) follows immediately: *There* Insertion does not apply in the complement, because if it did, the rule of Equi-NP Deletion would fail. *Force* cannot take *there* as its direct object, and if there is no match between the direct object and the subject of the complement, the derivation cannot go through.

The reason for the ungrammaticality of (9.43b) is that the subject of the complement *Mary is in the next room* has been incorrectly moved into subject position in the higher S. There are basically two ways to rectify this situation: (i) Restrict NP Preposing to direct objects, assume that there is a rule of Raising, and restrict Raising to subjects of infinitive complements; (ii) show that the application of NP Preposing to subjects of some complements and not others follows from general principles of rule application and need not be built into the particular transformations themselves. Approach (i) is taken by Postal (1974), and approach (ii) is taken by Chomsky (1973); I lean toward the second, and will present a tentative formulation of the general principles required by this approach in Chapter 10. For the sake of completeness and of full understanding of the issues involved here, the following section presents another argument commonly used to justify Raising.

The Argument Based on Reflexive and Passive

It has been noted that it is possible to paraphrase sentences of the form indicated by (9.44a) with those of the form indicated by (9.44b):

(9.44)   a. *John expects to vote for Dicky.*
                b. *John expects himself to vote for Dicky.*

The appearance of the reflexive pronoun is very suggestive. The reflexive is required when the subject and the object of a simple sentence are coreferential (cf. Chapter 8). The underlying structure of (9.44b) would therefore be (9.45):

(9.45)   *John expects* ₛ[*John vote for Dicky*]

The natural conclusion to be drawn from this in the case of (9.44) is that the subject of the complement, *John*, is functioning as the direct object of the verb *expects* with respect to the Reflexive rule. However, the fact that the subject of the complement may be a reflexive pronoun again does not prove this conclusively, since there is the possibility that the rule of Reflexive could be generalized to apply to subjects of complements as well as to direct objects. Still, the behavior of the reflexive in this context follows from the assumption that there is a rule of Raising.

Raising is stated as follows.

RAISING: X V NP Y
            1 2 3   4 ⇒ 1 2 + 3 ∅ 4

What this rule says is that if there is an NP immediately following the verb, then this NP ends up immediately dominated by the same node that dominates the V, as shown in (9.46):

(9.46)

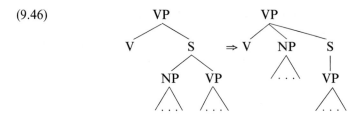

The result of applying Raising is to make the subject of the complement become the direct object of the higher verb, as intended. This predicts that the Passive and Reflexive rules will apply to this NP as though it were a direct object. Previous examples have shown that this is a correct prediction; the following sentences also support it:

(9.47)   a. *Mary expects John to visit George.*
          b. *John is expected by Mary to visit George.*
          c. *Mary expects George to be visited by John.*
          d. *George is expected by Mary to be visited by John.*

The derivation of (9.47d) involves multiple application of the Passive transformation. Sentence (9.47a) itself shows nothing about how the transformations apply; (9.47b) shows that Raising must apply before Passive applies, because otherwise it would be impossible for the rule of NP Preposing to move *John* to the subject position of the higher S. This leads to a contradiction of linear ordering, though, because in order to derive (9.47c) it must be the case that Passive applies to *visit* before Raising, since if Raising applied first, *visit* would have no subject for Passive to apply to.

Finally, (9.47d) shows that Passive must apply twice, both before and after Raising. Is this a further contradiction of the principle of linear ordering, or is some solution possible? The solution emerges from a closer examination of the derivation of (9.47d).

The underlying structure of this sentence is assumed to be (9.48):

(9.48)

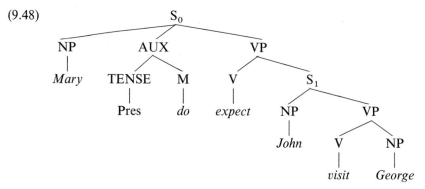

In order for *George* to become the superficial subject of this sentence by

Passive, it must at one time have been the direct object. In order for it to have been the direct object, it must have been raised. In order for it to have been raised, it must have been the subject of the complement when Raising applied. As can be seen from (9.48), the way to make *George* the subject of S_1 is to apply Passive to S_1:

(9.49)

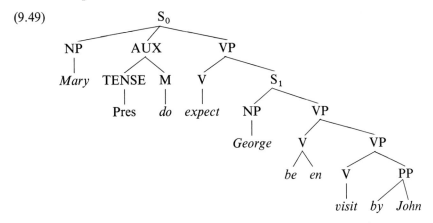

The conclusion, therefore, is that first Passive applies on S_1, then Raising applies between S_1 and S_0, and finally Passive applies on S_0.

The reason why this is not a contradiction of linear ordering is that it does not involve the application of Passive at two different times to the same level of the phrase marker. In fact, it appears that Passive applies first to the lower level of the phrase marker and then to the next S above it. Raising precedes Passive on S_0; it may also precede Passive on S_1, since at that level it cannot apply and, hence, does not affect the derivation. In other words, it appears to be possible to maintain the linear ordering of transformations if the transformations are applied in sequence first to the lowest S in the tree, then to the next highest, and so on. This method of applying transformations is called the **Cyclic Principle.**

CYCLIC PRINCIPLE: Given a sequence of transformations A, B, C, . . . that are linearly ordered on independent grounds, apply A, B, C, . . . in that order to the lowest S in the tree, then the next S in the tree above it, and so on, until the topmost S node in the tree is reached. At each S, each transformation may apply only to constituents dominated by that S.

What we have shown is that the linear ordering:

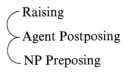

Raising

Agent Postposing

NP Preposing

can be maintained if the Cyclic Principle is adopted. Without this principle, the data constitute a strong counterexample to the principle of linear ordering. Furthermore, in adopting the Cyclic Principle we make the very strong claim that the applicability of a transformation to a particular S in the tree is determined only by properties of that S or of S's below that S; the principle embodies the claim that material above the S to which a transformation may apply is irrelevant. So far as is known, there are no counterexamples to this claim.

We have shown that sentences like *John expects himself to vote for Dicky* can be generated by application of Raising and Reflexive in that order. A sentence like (9.50) shows that Reflexive must apply both before and after Raising:

(9.50)   *John expects himself to vote for himself.*

This is another apparent contradiction to the principle of linear ordering that can be avoided by employing the Cyclic Principle. We order Raising before Reflexive, and apply both cyclically. The derivation of (9.50) is shown in (9.51):

(9.51)   Input $_{S_0}$[*John expects* $_{S_1}$[*John vote for John*]]
         Reflexive on S_1 $_{S_0}$[*John expects* $_{S_1}$[*John vote for himself*]]
         Raising from S_1 to S_0 $_{S_0}$[*John expects John* $_{S_1}$[*vote for himself*]]
         Reflexive on S_0 $_{S_0}$[*John expects himself* $_{S_1}$[*vote for himself*]]

It should be recognized that there are many transformations that need not be part of a cyclic sequence of transformations. Some of these transformations, such as Inversion, appear to apply only at the highest S node in the tree; hence, to say that they are cyclic is vacuous. There have also been arguments in the literature that there are transformations that must apply to the entire phrase marker before the application of cyclic transformations; these transformations are called **precyclic.** There are arguments that transformations exist that apply after all of the cyclic transformations have applied all the way to the top of the phrase marker; these are called **postcyclic.** The arguments for these kinds of transformations and others are quite intricate and will not be presented here. It should be emphasized, however, that much of the argument in favor of cyclic ordered transformations rests on the existence of the transformation of Raising. If there is no such transformation, then the subtle interaction between transformations that argues for the need for cyclic transformations substantially disappears.

In summary, then, the assumption that there is a rule of Raising accounts for the fact that the subject of the complement functions like a direct object with respect to the Passive and Reflexive transformations. The possibility exists that this property of the subject of the complement can be accounted for by stating the transformations that apply to it appropriately; however, the full details of such an analysis have not been provided to date.

PROBLEMS WITH THE ANALYSIS

There are a variety of problems associated with the analysis presented in the preceding sections. Only one will be dealt with here; briefly, it is that the transformations of Raising and Equi-NP Deletion do not apply freely to every verb in every context. Hence, there must be some way of specifying, for each verb, which transformation or transformations it undergoes and in what contexts.

To illustrate, the difference between *expect* and *believe* is that the former may undergo either END(S) or Raising, while the latter may undergo only Raising.

(9.52)　　a.　*John expects himself to be elected President.*
　　　　　b.　*John expects to be elected President.*

(9.53)　　a.　*John believes himself to have been elected President.*
　　　　　b.　**John believes to have been elected President.*

The problem here is to guarantee in some way that the rules will apply to derive just the grammatical sentences.

An interesting solution to this problem has been proposed by Bresnan (1972). One part of the solution is to motivate the expansion of S as COMP S', introduced tangentially in Chapter 8.[5]

PSR1a: S → COMP S'
PSR1b: S' → NP AUX VP

COMP identifies the position in the S into which *Wh* Fronting moves a constituent; it contains elements such as *as, than, before,* and *that* in examples such as the following:

(9.54)　　　　a.　*John is intelligent, **as** you can see.*
　　　　　　　b.　*Mary is smarter **than** she looks.*
　　　　　　　c.　*Look **before** you leap.*
　　　　　　　d.　*I believe **that** the world is a big, fat oyster.*

As Bresnan shows, assigning this constituent structure to the S captures a large number of generalizations with no more complication to the grammar than the addition of PSR1a.

Given this analysis of S (and S'), Bresnan shows that the difference between S and S' can be used to account for a variety of syntactic phenomena. One of these is the fact that some verbs undergo Equi-NP Deletion while others undergo Raising. Bresnan proposes that some verbs be assigned S complements

---

[5] Instead of S and S', Bresnan uses $\bar{S}$ and S, respectively. This notation is motivated by considerations that are not directly relevant to this discussion. See Chomsky (1970), Bresnan (1972), Jackendoff (1974), and Selkirk (1974) for the motivation for and applications of the so-called bar notation.

while others be assigned S′ complements, and that Equi-NP Deletion apply to S complements only.

To illustrate, consider *try*, *believe*, and *expect*. *Try* obligatorily undergoes Equi-NP Deletion; hence, it would appear in the structure shown in (9.55) according to this analysis:

(9.55)

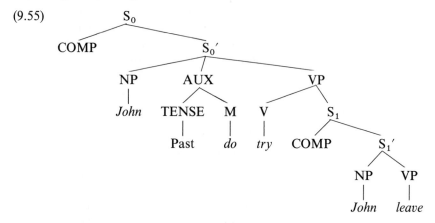

Believe cannot undergo Equi-NP Deletion. In the context of the analysis proposed here, *believe* will always take an S′ complement and, hence, will never be subject to Equi-NP Deletion.

This makes it possible to treat both Raising and Equi-NP Deletion as obligatory rules. By specifying which complement a verb can take, we automatically specify which rule will apply to it. This means that for a case such as *expect*, which appears to undergo both Equi-NP Deletion and Raising, it will be necessary to specify that both types of complement, S and S′, are possible. This leads to the following classification of verbs based on the behavior of their infinitive complements:

Class A: $+[\underline{\hspace{2em}} \left\{ \begin{matrix} S' \\ S \end{matrix} \right\}]$ (example: *expect*)

Class B: $+[\underline{\hspace{2em}} S]$ (example: *try*)

Class C: $+[\underline{\hspace{2em}} NP\ S]$ (example: *force*)

Class D: $+[\underline{\hspace{2em}} S']$ (example: *believe*)

The rules that apply are:

Class A: Raising (to S′), END(S) (to S)
Class B: END(S)
Class C: END(0)
Class D: Raising

Both of the rules are obligatory; furthermore, since neither can ever apply when the others are applicable, no unique linear ordering of them can be established (see Exercise 4).

Finally, consider the following problem, which arises in the formulation of this analysis. We noted that the function of Equi-NP Deletion is to delete the subject of a complement under identity with an NP in the higher S. If there is not such an NP in the higher S, the rule cannot apply. The result is not a grammatical sentence, however, as the following derivations show:

(9.56) a. Input   *John forced Bill $_S$[Bill leave]*
         END(0)   *John forced Bill $_S$[Ø leave]*
        b. Input   *John forced Bill $_S$[Mary leave]*
         END(0)   (blocked)
         Result   **John forced Bill Mary to leave.*

(9.57) a. Input   *John tried $_S$[John leave]*
         END(S)   *John tried $_S$[Ø to leave]*
        b. Input   *John tried $_S$[Mary leave]*
         END(S)   (blocked)
         Result   **John tried Mary to leave.*

A potential solution to this problem would be to require the complements of verbs such as *force* and *try* to have subjects that are coreferential with the appropriate NP in the S of which *force* and *try* are main verbs. The effect of such a requirement would be to ensure that the structural description of Equi-NP Deletion would be met when the structure of the sentence satisfied the rule in all other respects.

However, this does not solve the problem. Equi-NP Deletion does not necessarily apply to the deep structure subject of the complement, but may apply to the derived subject of the complement. For example, it applies after Passive has applied in the complement in the derivation of sentences such as the following:

(9.58) a. *John forced Mary to be examined by a doctor.*
        b. *Mary tried to be examined by a doctor.*

These sentences could not be derived if the subjects of the complements were required to be *Mary*. As can be seen, the underlying subject in each case is a *doctor*.

Furthermore, even if the underlying subject of the complement is coreferential with an NP in the higher S, this is no guarantee that Equi-NP Deletion will be applicable. By the cyclic principle, Passive may apply in the complement S before Equi-NP Deletion can apply between the two S's. Application of Passive will move the subject of the complement out of subject position, and will therefore block Equi-NP Deletion (unless, of course, the derived subject is also coreferential with the NP in the higher S). This is illustrated in (9.59):

(9.59) a. Input   *Bill forced a doctor* $_S$[*a doctor examine John*]
        Passive   *Bill forced a doctor* $_S$[*John be examined by a doctor*]
        END(0)   (blocked)
        Result   **Bill forced a doctor John to be examined by a doctor.*
     b. Input   *John tried* $_S$[*John examine Mary*]
        Passive   *John tried* $_S$[*Mary be examined by John*]
        END(S)   (blocked)
        Result   **John tried Mary to be examined by him.*

Thus, a deep structure restriction will not have the correct consequences for the application of Equi-NP Deletion.

A second potential solution to the problem would be to restate Passive so that it will apply obligatorily when (i) the underlying subject of the complement is not coreferential with the NP in the higher S and (ii) the underlying direct object of the complement is coreferential with the NP in the higher clause. In addition, Passive must be blocked from applying just in case it will remove a coreferential subject from subject position. Not only is it unlikely that such conditions can be stated, but even if they could be, they are so complicated that they would destroy the simplicity and elegance captured by our present formulation.

Furthermore, by the Cyclic Principle rules apply from the lowest S to the highest S and do not consider material in the S's above that to which they are applying. Hence, the Passive transformation could not even "know" whether the S to which it is applying is the complement of some higher S with certain specific characteristics.

The rule of Equi-NP Deletion is, thus, the one to be changed. What is required is a provision that states that if the structural description of the rule is met except for the lack of identity between NPs, then the derivation must be marked as unacceptable. Thus, Passive will be free to apply everywhere.

As can be seen, Equi-NP Deletion will have a **filtering** function. The notion of a filter was introduced in the discussion of relative clauses in Chapter 8. In that case, we found that we could formulate the filter as a deep structure condition; here, of course, we cannot. Whether deep structure filters and filters associated with particular rules are independently required by the theory is a complicated question that we will not pursue here.

It is important to emphasize that, in general, the introduction of filters into the theory of grammar constitutes a considerable extension of the power of the theory of grammar. Hence, filters should not be used unless there are no devices available that can do a better job, and continual efforts should be made to find more elegant alternatives. The fact that we find it necessary to assume filters in certain cases must be viewed as a failure of the theory to make available a deeper and more revealing account of the phenomena.

Since we are attempting to provide a **syntactic** analysis only, the failure of our syntactic theory to provide a satisfactory solution to a given problem may be perfectly appropriate, if the problem is in fact one that ultimately will receive a semantic rather than a syntactic solution. If filters are not permitted by our theory, then we must find solutions in semantics for the problems for which the filters provide solutions. This may very well be the direction in which to proceed, but to do so would take us far beyond the scope of this book.

SUMMARY

Infinitival complements may be either S or S′ in deep structure; the choice of complement depends on the lexical entry of each particular verb. Equi-NP Deletion applies to subjects of S complements only, while Raising applies to the subjects of S′ complements only.

Equi-NP Deletion is motivated primarily by the fact that infinitival complements possess many of the properties of sentences. Hence, we represent them as S in deep structure and delete their subjects in the course of the derivation.

Raising is motivated by the fact that in certain cases the subject of the complement functions as though it were the direct object of the main verb. It is possible to account for this without establishing a Raising transformation, as the discussion in the following chapter will show.

It is necessary to associate a filtering function with the rule of Equi-NP Deletion. The theoretical cost of filters is sufficiently high that this should lead us to seek elsewhere for solutions to the problems of specifying subjects for all infinitival complements. A promising alternative is provided by Jackendoff (1972).

Finally, in order to preserve the principle of linear ordering, it is necessary to apply transformations according to the Cyclic Principle. The transformations apply in a fixed linear order, and the sequence of transformations is applied first to the lowest S in the phrase marker, then to the next S above it, and so on until the topmost S in the phrase marker is reached.

SUMMARY OF RULES

Transformations

EQUI-NP DELETION:
  END(S): cf. Exercise 5
  END(0): cf. Exercise 5

RAISING: X V NP Y
$$1 \; 2 \; 3 \; 4 \Rightarrow 1 \; 2 + 3 \; \emptyset \; 4$$

THERE INSERTION: X NP Y *be* Z
$$1 \; 2 \; 3 \; 4 \; 5 \Rightarrow 1 \; there \; 3 \; 4 + 2 \; 5$$

(This is an approximate version; cf. Problem 2 for further refinement.)

Ordering of Transformations

Left as an exercise (cf. Exercise 4).

EXERCISES

1. Under what circumstances is it possible for a rule A to apply before a rule B in a derivation, yet follow rule B in the rule ordering?

2. Give all of the sentences that can be derived from the deep structure of the following sentence with both application and nonapplication of Passive:

a. *John believes Mary to have expected Bill to hit Susan.*

3. Derive the following sentences (give the deep structure and all intermediate terminal strings, and indicate the application of each transformation):

a. *John expected to leave.*
b. *John believed himself to be a genius.*
c. *Mary tried to force herself to eat the pie.*
d. *Susan ordered there to be a celebration in the park.*
e. *There was said to be a fire in the basement, wasn't there?*

4. Establish what the rule ordering relationships are between END(S), END(0), Raising, *There* Insertion, and the rules introduced in previous chapters.

5. State the rules of END(S) and END(0) as precisely as you can.

PROBLEMS

1. Sentences such as the following suggest that *order* is of the same class as *force* in terms of the types of complements they take:

a. *John ordered the doctor to examine Mary.*
b. *John ordered Mary to be examined by the doctor.*

In sentence (b) Mary is understood to be the recipient of the order; this is represented in the syntactic structure by generating *Mary* as the direct object of *order*.

    i. In light of this, what is the explanation for the fact that in (c) *Mary* is *not* the recipient of the order:

c. *John ordered Mary to be fired.*

Your explanation should be consistent with the framework for infinitival complements developed in this chapter.

    ii. How does the analysis of infinitival complements given in this chapter explain the ungrammaticality of (d):

d. **Mary was wanted to leave.*

    iii. Using the analysis developed in this chapter, explain the ungrammaticality of (e):

e. **Mary was hoped for to succeed by John.*

Notice, in this regard, that (f) is grammatical:

f. *Success was hoped for (but never achieved).*

  2. The italicized portions of the following sentences are **reduced relative clauses**:

    a. *The man **sitting in the park** was my brother.*
    b. *The woman **anxious to leave** finally left.*
    c. *The man **arrested by the police** was a citizen of Paris.*
    d. *The woman **in the park** was arrested by the police.*

(See Problem 4 in Chapter 8 for the transformation that derives these clauses.)
  The current rule of *There* Insertion will yield sequences that look remarkably like reduced relative clauses. For example:

    e. *A man was sitting in the park.*

THERE INSERTION :   *There was a man **sitting in the park**.*

There Insertion as now stated will also misapply and derive ungrammatical sentences such as (f):

    f. *There was a man a doctor.*

Note, however, that the sequence *a man a doctor* is also one that cannot be derived by relative clause reduction. E.g.:

g.   *A man who is a doctor is a credit to his nation.*
     *A man a doctor is a credit to his nation.

i. Beginning from these facts, show that there is a one-to-one correlation between the sequences that can follow the noun after *There* Insertion and those that can follow the noun after relative clause reduction. Suggest how this generalization should be captured by the grammar.

ii. Show that by capturing this generalization in this way *There* Insertion can be simplified so that it applies only when *be* is clause-final.

THERE INSERTION: X NP Y *be*
                      1   2 3 4 $\Rightarrow$ 1 *there* 3 4 + 2

3. In the text, it was suggested that a better way of formulating *There* Insertion would be to divide it into two rules. One rule would move the subject NP into the position following *be*, and the other would realize the dummy subject left behind by the first rule as *there*. Show that the first rule is independently required because of sentences like the following:

a. *In California is the only sixteen-lane freeway in existence.*
b. *On the next page will be a new problem to solve.*
c. *Under the table were eleven shoes.*

4. It is well known that *There* Insertion applies to verbs other than *be*, e.g.:

a. *There arose a great commotion in the courtyard.*
b. *Next door there are located a number of pleasant shops.*
c. *There appeared a distorted face in the window.*

Show that if the rule of *There* Insertion is revised as suggested in Problem 2 (ii) so that it applies only when the verb is in clause-final position, these other cases of *there* sentences can be accounted for simply by generalizing *There* Insertion from *be* to V.

5. In Problem 3, it is argued that the rule that moves the subject NP into position after *be* should be a separate rule from the one that inserts *there*. Problem 4 presents an argument that this rule that moves the subject NP should apply to all verbs, and not just *be*. Given the results of Problem 4, show that the following sentences provide further argument for this rule's being a separate transformation:

a. *Parked next door were forty-three Edsels.*
b. *Down the street walked Harold.*
c. *Into the room came the officials.*
d. *Sitting at the podium were the President and her husband.*
e. *Unable to attend were the three people that I told you about.*

SUGGESTED FURTHER READINGS

Equi NP Deletion

Bresnan, J. (1972), *Theory of Complementation in English Syntax*, Unpublished doctoral dissertation, MIT, Cambridge, Mass.
Jackendoff, R. S. (1972), *Semantic Interpretation in Generative Grammar*, MIT Press, Cambridge, Mass.
Postal, P. (1970), "On coreferential complement subject deletion," *LI*, **1,** 439–500.
Grinder, J. & Postal, P. (1971), "Missing antecedents," *LI*, **2,** 269–312.
Rosenbaum, P. S. (1967), *The Grammar of English Predicate Complement Constructions*, MIT Press, Cambridge, Mass.
Ross, J. R. (1967), *Constraints on Variables in Syntax*, Unpublished doctoral dissertation, MIT, Cambridge, Mass. Available from Indiana University Linguistics Club, Bloomington, Indiana.

Raising

Bresnan (1972).
Chomsky, N. (1973), "Conditions on transformations," in Anderson, S. R. & Kiparsky, P., eds., *Festschrift for Morris Halle,* Holt, New York.
Jackendoff (1972).
Kiparsky, P. & Kiparsky, C. (1971), "Fact," in Bierwisch, M. & Heidolph, K., eds., (1971), *Recent Advances in Linguistics,* Mouton, The Hague.
Postal, P. (1974), *On Raising*, MIT Press, Cambridge, Mass.

There Insertion

Kuno, S. (1971), "The position of the locative in existential sentences," *LI,* **2,** 333–378.

The Cyclic Principle

Grinder, J. (1972), "Cyclic and linear grammars," in Kimbal, J., ed., (1972b), *Syntax and Semantics* (Vol. 1), Seminar Press, New York.
Kimball, J. (1972a), "Cyclic and noncyclic grammars," in Kimball, J., ed., (1972b), *Syntax and Semantics* (Vol. 1), Seminar Press, New York.

Rule Features

Lakoff, G. (1970a), *Irregularity in Syntax*, Holt, New York.

10

Verb Complements II: *That* Clauses

INTRODUCTION

This chapter deals with *that* clauses of the type illustrated in the following examples:

(10.1)

$$
John
\begin{cases}
\textit{believes} \\
\textit{says} \\
\textit{knows} \\
\textit{hopes} \\
\textit{admits} \\
\textit{acknowledges} \\
\textit{guesses}
\end{cases}
\textbf{\textit{that the world is flat.}}
$$

(10.2)

$$
\textbf{\textit{That the world is flat}}
\begin{cases}
\textit{surprises me.} \\
\textit{is obvious.} \\
\textit{turns out to be true.} \\
\textit{proves nothing.}
\end{cases}
$$

(10.3)

$$
It
\begin{cases}
\textit{surprises me} \\
\textit{is obvious} \\
\textit{turns out to be true} \\
\textit{proves nothing}
\end{cases}
\textbf{\textit{that the world is flat.}}
$$

It will be assumed without discussion that the *that* in these clauses is a constituent of COMP and that the remainder of the clause is S'. Thus, the phrase *that the world is flat* is an S.

The position of the *that* clause in the examples in (10.1) will be called **object position,** and its position in (10.2) will be called **subject position.** The position of the *that* clause shown in (10.3) will be called **final position.** By adopting such a terminology, we leave open the possibility that object position and final position are syntactically distinguishable.

The two problems that this chapter focuses on are, first, the form of the transformation that relates the examples in (10.2) and (10.3), and second, the conditions on the transformation that optionally deletes *that* to derive sentences like *John says the world is flat.* There appears to be slight evidence in favor of a transformation that moves the *that* clause from subject to final position. A general constraint on the domain of applicability of transformations that will prevent this transformation from generating ungrammatical sequences also serves to constrain the rule deleting *that* in precisely the correct way.

MOVING THE *THAT* CLAUSE

Let us begin our discussion of *that* clauses by investigating the relationship between sentences such as those given in (10.4):

(10.4)   a. ***That the world is flat*** *is obvious.*
               b. *It is obvious **that the world is flat.***

There are two fundamental observations to be made about such pairs of sentences:

1. When the *that* clause is in final position, the subject of the sentence must be *it.*
2. For every verb phrase that can appear in a sentence in which the subject position is occupied by a *that* clause, such a verb phrase can also appear in a sentence with an *it* subject and an extraposed *that* clause.

The first observation is supported by the following examples:

(10.5)   *It is obvious that the world is flat.*
           *John is obvious that the world is flat.
           *That the world is round is obvious that the world is flat.
           *Is obvious that the world is flat.

The second observation is consistent with examples such as those in (10.6). It is important to note that there are some cases in which the *that* clause must be extraposed, i.e., where the *that* clause cannot appear in the subject position. These cases are illustrated in (10.7):

(10.6)

$$\text{a. } \textit{That the world is flat} \left\{ \begin{array}{l} \textit{is obvious.} \\ \textit{is ridiculous.} \\ \textit{offends me.} \\ \textit{bothers everyone.} \\ \textit{came as a great surprise.} \\ \textit{means nothing.} \\ \textit{strikes people as funny.} \end{array} \right\}$$

$$\text{b. } \textit{It} \left\{ \begin{array}{l} \textit{is obvious.} \\ \textit{is ridiculous} \\ \textit{offends me} \\ \textit{bothers everyone} \\ \textit{came as a great surprise} \\ \textit{means nothing} \\ \textit{strikes people as funny} \end{array} \right\} \textit{that the world is flat.}$$

(10.7)

$$\text{a. } *\textit{That the world is flat} \left\{ \begin{array}{l} \textit{seems.} \\ \textit{happens.} \\ \textit{turns out.} \\ \textit{appears.} \end{array} \right\}$$

$$\text{b. } \textit{It} \left\{ \begin{array}{l} \textit{seems} \\ \textit{happens} \\ \textit{turns out} \\ \textit{appears} \end{array} \right\} \textit{that the world is flat.}$$

There are three possible approaches to these data. One is that the *that* clause is moved from underlying subject position into final position. The second is the converse, that the *that* clause is moved from underlying final position into subject position. The third is that there is no transformational relationship between these sentences at all. In order to maintain the third approach, it would be necessary to demonstrate that there are rules of semantic interpretation that independently assign identical semantic interpretations to sentences regardless of whether the *that* clause is in subject position or in final position. While the possibility of such a demonstration is not denied here, none has been produced to date, and we will not attempt to produce one here. Hence, the subsequent discussion will be concerned with determining the form and applicability of a transformation that relates the examples in (10.6).

Extraposition

The first approach is called the Extraposition analysis. Here it is assumed that the underlying structure for both the final and initial *that* clauses is that illustrated in (10.8):[1]

---

[1] In the following trees, the *that* clause is immediately and exhaustively dominated by NP. An alternative approach, which appears frequently in the literature, is illustrated in (i):

(10.8)

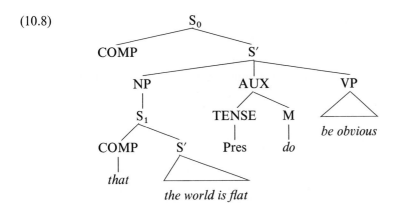

Thus, to derive the *that* clause in final position there must be a transformation of Extraposition (in this approach) that has the function of moving the *that* clause to the right and leaving an *it* behind. Such a transformation has roughly the following form.

EXTRAPOSITION: X S Y
                    1 2 3 $\Rightarrow$ 1 *it* 3 + 2

It can be seen immediately that the statement of this rule is too general. For example, it could apply to a relative clause, as in the following:

(10.9)   a.   *The man* s[*who you saw*] *was my brother.*
                b.   **The man it was my brother* s[*who you saw*].

What is required is that the extraposition apply just to an S that is exhaustively dominated by NP. To express this in the rule, it is necessary to introduce the labeled bracket notation into the structural description.[2]

(i)

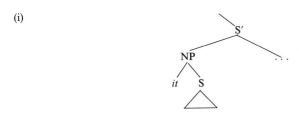

In either case, it is claimed that the complement S is also an NP. Rosenbaum (1967) provides considerable evidence to support this claim, while Emonds (1970) provides evidence that these complement S's are not in fact NPs. Higgins (1973) argues against Emonds' approach, and Emonds (forthcoming) adopts a version of the more traditional analysis represented in (i).

[2] The labeled bracket notation was introduced in Chapter 2 as a shorthand for representing tree structures in a linear form.

EXTRAPOSITION: X $_{NP}$[S] Y
$$1 \quad 2 \quad 3 \Rightarrow 1 \; it \; 3 + 2$$

Use of the labeled bracket notation restricts the S's that can be extraposed to just those that are exhaustively dominated by NP. The use of such a notation in the structural descriptions of transformations is of considerable importance, since the set of conditions under which transformations may apply is considerably augmented if this notation is introduced into the theory of grammar. Continued justification for the introduction of this notation is required if the power of the theory is to be increased in this way.

Besides requiring the use of labeled brackets, the Extraposition analysis has a number of other significant features. First of all, it appears to be the case that there are certain verbs for which the rule is obligatory, in spite of the fact that it is, in general, an optional transformation. Examples like (10.7a) show that verbs such as *seem, happen,* and so on cannot have sentential subjects in surface structure.

However, there is evidence that the complements in sentences like *It seems that the world is flat* are not in fact underlying subject complements but, rather, underlying object complements. We will return to this topic in the next section.

A second feature of the analysis is less obvious. Let us consider (10.8), and construct a phrase marker in which S_1 is the subject of some higher sentence, as illustrated in (10.10):

(10.10)

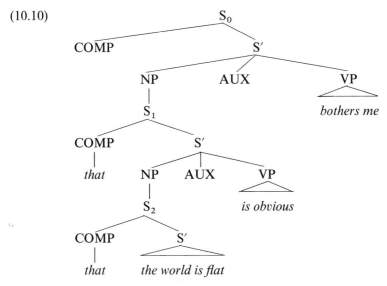

If Extraposition fails to apply to this structure at all, then we end up with the grammatical but somewhat awkward (10.11):[3]

---

[3] The awkwardness of (10.11) is due to a general processing limitation that is manifested when a constituent of a certain type has a constituent of the same type embedded in the center of it. The

(10.11)   *That that the world is flat is obvious bothers me.*

Extraposition may apply to (10.10) in two different ways: It may apply to S_2, extraposing it around *is obvious*, or it may apply to S_1, extraposing it around *bothers me*. If the rule applies only to S_2 it gives (10.12a), and if it applies only to S_1 it gives (10.12b) (in each case, the clause that is extraposed is in boldface):

(10.12)   a. *That it is obvious **that the world is flat** bothers me.*
               b. *It bothers me **that that the world is flat is obvious.***

However, since it is possible for Extraposition to apply to either *that* clause, it is also possible for it to apply to both clauses, giving (10.13):

(10.13)   *It bothers me that it is obvious that the world is flat.*

That is, the rule extraposes S_2 around *is obvious* and S_1 around *bothers me*.

The problem now is the following: Let us assume that Extraposition does not apply to S_2 when S_1 is being considered. The next stage of the cycle is S_0. At the level of S_0, there are now two ways in which the structural description of Extraposition may be met. These two possible analyses of the structure are illustrated in Figure 10.1.

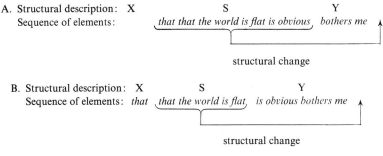

Figure 10.1   Application of Extraposition.

acceptability of **center embedding** decreases rapidly as the degree of center embedding increases. This is illustrated in the following sentences, first in the case of sentential subjects and then in the case of relative clauses:

 (i) *That that the world is flat is obvious bothers me.*
 (ii) *That that that the world is flat is obvious bothers me amazes Tom.*
 (iii) *That that that that the world is flat is obvious bothers me amazes Tom is surprising.*

etc.

 (iv) *The man that the dog bit screamed.*
 (v) *The man that the dog that the boy caught bit screamed.*
 (vi) *The man that the dog that the boy that my mother saw caught bit screamed.*

etc.

We treat the unacceptability of the more complex examples here to be a fact about performance and not about the competence of the native speaker. [Cf. Miller and Chomsky (1963) and Yngve (1960, 1961) for further discussion of performance considerations like this one.]

There are two analyses of the structure that satisfy the structural description of Extraposition. Thus, Extraposition should yield two grammatical sentences from the same input structure. The results of applying Extraposition in the two ways illustrated in Figure 10.1 are shown in (10.14):

(10.14)   a. *It bothers me that that the world is flat is obvious.*
            b. **That it is obvious bothers me that the world is flat.*

The result of moving the lower S, i.e., S_2, to the right of the verb phrase of S_0 is ungrammatical. In fact, it is possible to extrapose a *that* clause only to the right of the verb phrase of the sentence that most closely dominates it. Thus, S_2 can be moved only to the right of the verb phrase of S_1, and S_1 can be moved only to the right of the verb phrase of S_0.

It follows that Extraposition must be restricted. The logical alternatives are that the restriction appears as part of the statement of the rule itself, or that it is a more general constraint on the application of transformations that is part of the theory of grammar. As this and the next chapter will show, there is evidence that the restriction is part of the general theory, and applies to all transformations rather than to Extraposition alone.

The constraint on Extraposition alone would entail a complication of the statement of the rule. First, it would be necessary to change the structural description to mention the specific VP that the complement is to be moved to the right of.

EXTRAPOSITION (i):   X $_{NP}$[S] AUX VP
                         1   2   3   4 $\Rightarrow$ 1 *it* 3 4 + 2

By eliminating the variable between the S and the VP, we would prevent the S from being moved to the right of any VP but the one at the same level in the tree.

It can be seen that this statement of the rule would not be adequate, because it fails to mention the possible presence of *not* between AUX and VP and the possible absence of AUX. Extraposition clearly applies both in the presence of *not* and in clauses that lack AUX, as in *John believes it to be obvious that the world is flat*. Reformulation of the rule to take into account this and similar observations will not be attempted here because of the applicability in this case of the more general constraint on transformations to be developed. It should be kept in mind that adoption of the general constraint will permit us to maintain the more elegant formulation of Extraposition proposed originally.

The essential feature of the constraint to be developed is that transformations have a limited domain of application. More precisely, when the transformational cycle is operating at a certain node, transformations applied in that cycle are applicable to restricted portions of the phrase marker. Part of the task of restricting the domain of application of transformations is accomplished by the Cyclic Principle itself, since it prevents transformations from applying to nodes higher in the tree than the node on which the cycle is operating.

The effect of the constraint in the case of Extraposition will be to restrict the movement of an initial clause to the right of the verb phrase of which the clause was originally the subject, as noted previously. This is illustrated in (10.15):

(10.15)

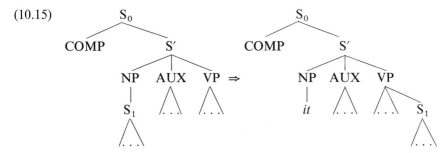

This constraint must be precisely formulated to accommodate a variety of transformational processes already encountered. It is clear, for example, that the constraint in its strongest form, i.e., that attachments can be made only to constituents of the same sentence from which the moved material originated, will be violated by the rule of Raising, which removes a constituent from an S′ dominated by VP and attaches it to the VP above. This is illustrated by (10.16):

(10.16)

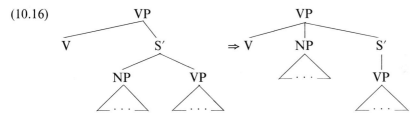

Another apparent violation consists of examples such as the following:

(10.17)   *Who did Mary believe Bill was going to marry?*

The interrogative pronoun *who* originates in the lower S as the direct object of *marry*. Yet in (10.17) it has clearly been removed from this lower S and attached to a constituent of the higher S. Hence, the strongest form of the constraint is too strong.

To weaken the constraint, we may assume that the fronting of *who* in (10.17) is accomplished in two stages: In the first stage, *who* is moved into the COMP of the lower sentence, and in the second stage *who* is moved from the COMP of the lower sentence to the COMP of the next-higher sentence. The two stages are illustrated in (10.18):

(10.18) Stage 1:

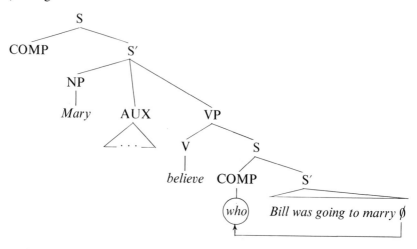

Stage 2:

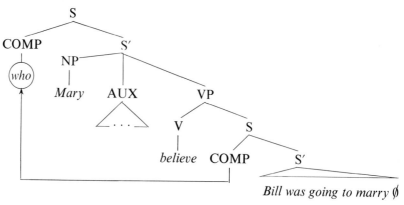

Given this assumption, it is possible to formulate the following tentative constraint on movement transformations.

ATTACHMENT CONSTRAINT: A moved constituent may be attached only to a constituent of the lowest S of which it was originally a constituent, or to the COMP of the next-higher S if it is moved from a COMP itself.[4]

This constraint will serve to limit Extraposition, and it will permit derivations of the kinds of sentences illustrated in (10.18). In addition, this constraint is consistent with the formulation of Raising given in Chapter 9, in which the

---

[4] The observation that Extraposition cannot move an S too far from its original location in the phrase marker was made by Ross (1967). Ross proposed that rules that move constituents to the right are **bounded** in the sense captured by the Attachment Constraint stated here. By comparison, rules like *Wh* Fronting appear to move constituents indefinitely far from their original position

raised constituent is moved out of an S′ and not out of an S. Thus, the subject of the complement that undergoes Raising is not in fact a constituent of a lower S, but is a constituent of a lower S′ only.

It should be recognized that the version of the Attachment Constraint just given is only a first approximation. In order to refine it further, we will have to consider substantially more data. A number of plausible refinements of the constraint are taken up later in this Chapter.

The formulation of the Attachment Constraint also bears on the question of whether there is in fact a transformational relationship between the extraposed and nonextraposed constructions. Recall that we began this discussion by observing that if there was an Extraposition transformation, then it would have to be constrained by the Attachment Constraint (or something similar to it). This constraint is not an ad hoc device whose only function is to save the Extraposition transformation, but has general applications quite independently of the data that led us to propose it in the first place. This will be shown in subsequent discussion. The fact that the general constraint also serves to account for distributions of grammaticality when the constraint is applied to the application of the Extraposition transformation itself serves to justify the position that what we are dealing with here is a body of data that can and must be analyzed transformationally.

As it turns out, the alternative transformational analysis in which the extraposed clause is moved into subject position is also consistent with the Attachment Constraint. All that can be concluded at this point, therefore, is that a transformational account is required in order to explain the ungrammaticality of examples like (10.14b) in a revealing way. As will be shown, the choice of Extraposition over the alternative approach is determined not by theoretical considerations but by empirical ones.

Intraposition

The alternative approach is called the Intraposition approach. The position that is adopted in this approach is that the underlying structure is roughly that of (10.19):

---

in the phrase marker (e.g., *Who does John believe that Mary said that Susan mentioned that . . . Harry saw?*), so that Ross was not able to extend the notion of bounding to all rules that move constituents to the left. See Ross (1967: Chapter 5) for discussion of this complicated question.

Chomsky (1973) argues that bounding can be generalized to all transformations if rules such as *Wh* Fronting are assumed to move constituents from the COMP of each S to the COMP of the next S above, as illustrated in (10.18).

The Attachment Constraint stated here is a simplified version of Chomsky's (1973) Subjacency Principle and the Binary Principle of Hamburger and Wexler (1975) and Wexler, Culicover, and Hamburger (1975). Later in this chapter, some further applications of this general notion are discussed. See Chapter 11 for some discussion of the role played by this constraint in the investigation of the conditions for language learnability.

(10.19)

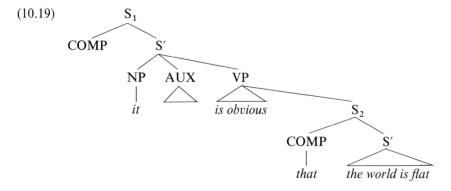

As can be seen, the deep structure in the Intraposition approach is the output of the Extraposition transformation, and vice versa. The two analyses are therefore converses of one another.

It is difficult to find strong arguments to choose between Intraposition and Extraposition. Since they are converses of one another, any generalization captured by one can be captured by the other, and any restriction on one can be formulated for the other. Most likely, the ultimate choice has to be made at the level of theory; that is, within the context of a particular theory, one analysis may require a type of movement that is impossible, or the transformation may interact incorrectly with other transformations.

An indication of the difficulty of finding internal evidence to choose between these two analyses is the following. It is possible to paraphrase certain *that* clauses by noun phrases, e.g.:

(10.20)

$$\text{a. } \textit{That Mary is here} \begin{cases} \textit{is obvious.} \\ \textit{bothers me.} \\ \textit{is apparent to all.} \end{cases}$$

$$\text{b. } \textit{Mary's presence} \begin{cases} \textit{is obvious.} \\ \textit{bothers me.} \\ \textit{is apparent to all.} \end{cases}$$

(10.21)   a. *John noted that Mary is here.*
    b. *John noted Mary's presence.*

While this paraphrase is not possible under all circumstances, the present discussion requires only that in *some* contexts an NP can be used to express the same thing as an S.

A difference between final position and subject position that we might find significant for deciding between Extraposition and Intraposition is that an S in final position can never be paraphrased by an NP. Compare the following with the examples in (10.20):

(10.22)

    a. *It* $\begin{cases} \textit{is obvious} \\ \textit{bothers me} \\ \textit{is apparent to all} \end{cases}$ *that Mary is here.*

    b. *It $\begin{cases} \textit{is obvious} \\ \textit{bothers me} \\ \textit{is apparent to all} \end{cases}$ *Mary's presence.*

We might seek to explain this fact by appealing to the transformations themselves. If *Mary's presence* is an NP, we could argue, then Extraposition will never move it to final position because Extraposition applies only to S.

Clearly, this explanation is not possible in the Intraposition analysis, where the constituent in final position is generated there in the base. However, the facts indicated earlier do not argue against the Intraposition analysis, because we can equally well specify in this case that final position may be occupied by an S only. This can be accomplished in the phrase structure rules, perhaps by a rule of the form VP → VP S. Hence, these facts do not constitute decisive evidence one way or the other.

One promising argument against the Intraposition analysis is also a good argument against the Extraposition analysis. It can be shown that there are certain cases in which it is implausible to generate a sentential subject in final position in the Intraposition analysis; rather, it appears most natural to generate such subjects in underlying subject position. This is an exception to the assumption of the Intraposition analysis that such subjects are transformationally derived.

There are certain verbs, e.g., *prove, imply, guarantee, suggest, mean,* and *indicate,* that may have a sentential subject and a sentential object:

(10.23)

    That the world is flat $\begin{cases} \textit{proves} \\ \textit{implies} \\ \textit{guarantees} \\ \textit{suggests} \\ \textit{means} \\ \textit{indicates} \end{cases}$ *that Galileo*

      was a genius.

Such verbs do not permit an S in final position unless there is no object complement S:

(10.24)

    *It $\begin{cases} \textit{proves} \\ \textit{implies} \\ \textit{guarantees} \\ \textit{suggests} \\ \textit{means} \\ \textit{indicates} \end{cases}$ *that Galileo was a genius that the*

      world is flat.

(10.25)

$$It \begin{Bmatrix} proves \\ implies \\ guarantees \\ suggests \\ means \\ indicates \end{Bmatrix} \text{ very little that the world is flat.}$$

These facts present a problem for the Intraposition approach, since it requires that the subject complement appear in final position in deep structure. Since Intraposition is optional, it need not apply, but if it fails to apply, ungrammatical examples like those in (10.24) will be derived. There are ad hoc ways of avoiding this situation, but there does not appear to be a natural explanation for these facts in terms of the Intraposition analysis.

In Emonds (1970, 1972), an attempt is made to motivate the Intraposition analysis. Emonds' solution to the problem of the *proves* sentences is to introduce a surface structure constraint that rules as ill-formed all derivations in which the two complement S's appear to the right of the verb. The ad hoc nature of this constraint is clear, and no further motivation for it has appeared, to my knowledge, since Emonds' original proposal.

Unfortunately, the situation is not more acceptable in the case of Extraposition. Here we find that verbs that normally permit Extraposition [cf. (10.25)] do not permit it just in case there is an object complement. Hence, it will be necessary to provide some restriction that will block outputs with two sentential complements to the right of the verb, precisely as in the case of Intraposition.

An argument that leans in favor of Extraposition relies on extrinsic ordering between Extraposition and another transformation. By ordering this transformation *before* Extraposition, we can guarantee that it will not apply to the output of Extraposition. Since the output of Extraposition is the input to Intraposition, to account for the same facts in the case of the latter analysis we would have to complicate the statement of this transformation. The argument is as follows.

It has often been observed that the relationship between the following sentences may be subject to a transformational analysis:

(10.26)   *I believe that the world is an oyster.*

(10.27)   *The world is an oyster, I believe.*

The phrase *I believe* in (10.27) is called a **parenthetical** expression. The general outlines of a transformation that derives the second sentence from the first are given in (10.28). Let us call this transformation Parenthetical:[5]

---

[5] Not all linguists agree that a transformation like Parenthetical is the appropriate way to derive parentheticals. Emonds (1974) argues that the structure that appears to the right of the arrow in (10.28) is in fact an underlying structure, in essence. It is not at all obvious that Emonds is correct, but if he is, the distinction to be drawn later between verbs that appear in parentheticals and those that do not must still be accounted for.

(10.28)

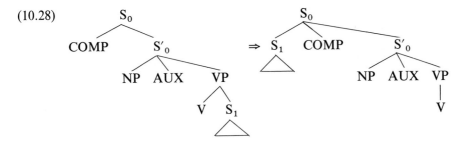

The details of Parenthetical are not important here; the essence of the transformation is that the complement sentence is moved from a position to the
right of the verb to the initial position in the sentence.

Consider, now, the Intraposition approach. It is assumed that extraposed
complements originate in the VP to the right of the V. It thus comes as a surprise to observe that none of these constructions permit the application of
Parenthetical, except for verbs like *seem, happen,* etc. (this will be explained
shortly):

(10.29)

   a. *It* $\begin{Bmatrix} \textit{is obvious} \\ \textit{bothers me} \\ \textit{is surprising} \\ \textit{matters} \end{Bmatrix}$ *that the world is an oyster.*

   b. **The world is an oyster, it* $\begin{Bmatrix} \textit{is obvious.} \\ \textit{bothers me.} \\ \textit{is surprising.} \\ \textit{matters.} \end{Bmatrix}$

By comparison, it appears that all verbs that take object complements permit
Parenthetical to apply:

(10.30)

   The world is an oyster, I $\begin{Bmatrix} \textit{believe.} \\ \textit{suspect.} \\ \textit{claim.} \\ \textit{admit.} \\ \textit{know.} \\ \textit{realize.} \\ \textit{hope.} \\ \textit{guess.} \\ \textit{.} \\ \textit{.} \\ \textit{.} \end{Bmatrix}$

The problem here is to explain why it is that the verbs that can undergo
Intraposition are those that cannot undergo Parenthetical, and the ones to
which Intraposition does not apply are those that do undergo Parenthetical.
This problem is eliminated, of course, if the Extraposition approach is adopted.

If Parenthetical is ordered before Extraposition, Parenthetical will never apply to the output of Extraposition.

By comparison, in the Intraposition approach it would be necessary to formulate Parenthetical in such a way that it could apply only to object complements and not to complements in final position. This is a complication of the transformation that is not required by the Extraposition analysis. Note, however, that if it should turn out to be the case that Parenthetical cannot be ordered before Extraposition, then the argument based on Parenthetical will be neutralized.

There is a special class of exceptions to the observation that extraposed complements do not undergo Parenthetical. These are given in (10.31):

(10.31)

$$\text{a. } It \left\{ \begin{array}{l} seems \\ happens \\ turns\ out \\ appears \end{array} \right\} that\ the\ world\ is\ an\ oyster.$$

$$\text{b. } The\ world\ is\ an\ oyster,\ it \left\{ \begin{array}{l} seems. \\ happens. \\ turns\ out. \\ appears. \end{array} \right\}$$

Remarkably, the verbs that are exceptions to Parenthetical are just those verbs that are exceptions to Extraposition. Note that we have already established that in order for a verb to permit Parenthetical it must take object complements, and not subject complements, in final position. For this reason, we are led to treat the complements of *seem, happen*, etc. not as subject complements but as object complements. But this is precisely what is required in order to explain why it is that *seem, happen*, etc. appear to require Extraposition: They do not in fact have anything to do with Extraposition, since their complements are not underlying subject complements but underlying object complements. This is a striking correlation that further justifies choosing Extraposition over Intraposition.

Finally, let us consider the fact that certain object complement verbs may take *so* instead of a sentential complement:[6]

---

[6] It should be noted that there are many verbs that take object complements but do not take *so*, e.g.:

$$\text{(i) } Mary \left\{ \begin{array}{l} mentioned \\ saw \\ heard \\ found\ out \\ regretted \end{array} \right\} \left\{ \begin{array}{l} that\ the\ world\ was\ an\ oyster. \\ *so. \end{array} \right\}$$

The argument presented here requires only that some object complement verbs permit *so*, not that they all do.

(10.32)   *Mary asked whether I thought that it would rain*

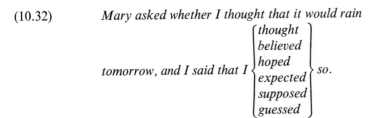

tomorrow, and I said that I $\left\{\begin{array}{l} thought \\ believed \\ hoped \\ expected \\ supposed \\ guessed \end{array}\right\}$ *so.*

By comparison, no verb that takes an extraposed complement may take *so* in place of the sentential complement:

(10.33)   *Mary asked whether I thought that it would rain*

tomorrow and I said that it $\left\{\begin{array}{l} *was\ obvious \\ *was\ uncertain \\ *was\ unlikely \\ *was\ probable \\ *was\ possible \\ *bothered\ me \\ *mattered \\ *didn't\ matter \end{array}\right\}$ *so.*

The only exceptions are those that give the appearance of obligatory Extraposition. The parenthetical argument suggested quite strongly that these verbs take object complements; the facts having to do with *so* confirm this:

(10.34)   *Mary asked whether it would rain tomorrow and I*

said that it $\left\{\begin{array}{l} seemed \\ appeared \end{array}\right\}$ *so.*

The fact that not all of these verbs take *so* is consistent with the fact that not all verbs that take object sentential complements also permit *so*. This is an independent question, it would appear, and probably one that is subject to semantic considerations.

The conclusion to be drawn from all this is that Extraposition is to be preferred over Intraposition, given the various empirical arguments cited. It must be specified, of course, that verbs like *seem*, *happen*, etc. cannot appear without *it* subjects, but provided that this is taken care of (presumably in the lexicon), the Extraposition analysis affords a somewhat more elegant account of the data.

AN ORDERING PARADOX

The conclusion that there is an Extraposition transformation is, however, not without problems. In this section, it will be shown that a complex argument leads to the further conclusion that there is a transformation that must apply both before Extraposition in some derivations and after Extraposition in others. This constitutes what is known as an ordering paradox. The paradox conflicts with the assumption that if there is an ordering of transformations, there is a unique linear ordering that is independent of the particular sentence that is to be derived. The ordering paradox again brings into question the validity of the transformation of Raising, since it is the Raising transformation that creates the paradox. As will be shown, we can eliminate the ordering paradox if we eliminate Raising and introduce a modified version of the Attachment Constraint discussed earlier in this chapter. The virtue of this is that the Attachment Constraint, appropriately refined, permits us to account for a diverse body of data. The ordering paradox that we will develop turns on the rule of *That Deletion*.

That Deletion

Consider the following evidence that there is a transformation that deletes the *that* complementizer in certain *that* clauses. As the examples given here show, *that* cannot be deleted when the *that* clause appears in subject position:

(10.35)   a. *John believes that the world is flat.*
                 John believes the world is flat.
        b. *It is obvious that the world is flat.*
                 It is obvious the world is flat.
        c. *It seems that the world is flat.*
                 It seems the world is flat.
        d. *John announced that the world was flat.*
                 John announced the world was flat.

(10.36)   a. *That the world is flat is believed by all.*
                **The world is flat is believed by all.*
        b. *That the world is flat is obvious.*
                **The world is flat is obvious.*
        c. *That the world is flat was announced by John.*
                **The world is flat was announced by John.*

The deletion of *that* is constrained in a number of other ways. For one thing, it cannot occur with every verb; for another, it cannot occur in every extraposed clause:

(10.37)

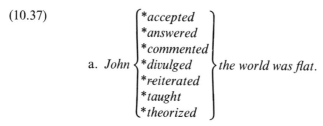

a. John
{
*accepted
*answered
*commented
*divulged
*reiterated
*taught
*theorized
}
the world was flat.

b. $\left\{\begin{array}{l}\text{*}It\ is\ believed\ by\ John \\ \text{*}It\ is\ accepted\ by\ everyone \\ \text{*}It\ was\ answered \\ \text{*}It\ bothers\ me \\ \text{*}It\ is\ a\ surprise\end{array}\right\}$ *the world is flat.*

Thus, it follows that the rule that deletes *that*, which we may call *That* Deletion, is a **governed rule**,[7] in that its applicability depends on there being a context in which certain verbs and adjectives appear. However, as may be seen from the following examples, there are also certain verbs that permit *That* Deletion in either the active or the passive, but do not permit *That* Deletion when there is a *by* phrase intervening between the verb and the *that* clause:

(10.38) a. *John believes (that) the world is flat.*
         b. *It is believed (that) the world is flat.*
         c. **It is believed by John the world is flat.*

Furthermore, there are constructions that contain verbs that permit *That* Deletion in which *That* Deletion cannot apply. Again, the reason appears to be that *that* does not immediately follow the verb in such circumstances. Consider the following examples:

(10.39) a. *John believes (that) the world is flat.*
         b. *John believes fervently that the world is flat.*
         c. **John believes fervently the world is flat.*

(10.40) a. *John says (that) the world is flat.*
         b. *John says frequently that the world is flat.*
         c. **John says frequently the world is flat.*

The generalization here appears to be that *That* Deletion may apply only when the *that* clause immediately follows the verb or adjective that governs the rule.

However, this is not simply a matter of *that* immediately following the verb. Let us consider a sentence in which a nonextraposed subject complement itself

---

[7] This term is due to Lakoff (1970), who develops an extensive theory of government. Lakoff proposes that no transformation is governed unless it mentions V in its structural description.

functions as the object complement of a higher verb:[8]

(10.41)   *Mary believes* $_{S'}$[$_{S}$[*that the world is flat*] *to be obvious*]

Here *believes*, which permits *That* Deletion, immediately precedes *that*. Hence, *That* Deletion should apply here, but it cannot:

(10.42)   **Mary believes the world is flat to be obvious.*

The reason for this might be that at the point at which *That* Deletion applies, the *that* clause is still the subject of *to be obvious* and has not yet been raised to be the object of *believes*. Then we might claim that the condition for the application of *That* Deletion cannot simply involve the linear order of the elements in the sequence, but must have to do with the structural relationship between the *that* clause and the verb that governs the rule. When the *that* clause is not the direct object of the verb that governs the rule, *That* Deletion will not apply.

However, (10.42) presents a problem, since it has already been established that there is a transformation of Raising that creates a direct object for the verb *believes* out of the subject of its complement. Hence, the rule of *That* Deletion must precede the rule of Raising, so that when *That* Deletion applies it will not be the case that the subject of the complement has already been raised into the higher sequence.

Constructing the Paradox

To review, an ordering paradox occurs when there are two transformations, A and B, such that there is evidence that A precedes B and that B precedes A. Occasionally such a paradox can be demonstrated by considering the derivation

---

[8] It must be the case that the peculiarity of this sentence is not a grammatical phenomenon but is due to something else. Note that there is no nonarbitrary way to prevent (10.41) from being generated by the grammar. Furthermore, (10.41) must be generated anyway if we are to derive sentence; like (i):

(i) *That the world is an oyster is believed by Mary to be obvious.*

Furthermore, examples such as (10.41) are considerably more acceptable when the possibility of mistakenly guessing the sentential subject of the complement to be the object of the main verb is avoided. This can be done by choosing a main verb that does not take a *that* complement:

(ii)   *Mary wants* $_{S'}$[$_{S}$[*that the world is flat*] *to be proven*]
(iii) **Mary wants that the world is flat.*

On this basis, we attribute the peculiarity of (10.41) to a processing error rather than to a grammatical violation.

Emonds (1970) suggests a different explanation. He adopts the Intraposition analysis and then argues that Intraposition cannot operate on embedded S's but only on the topmost or "root" S. In fact, in the theory that he proposes, this must be the explanation for (10.42), since Intraposition has certain properties that Emonds claims require it to be a root transformation. For further discussion, see Emonds (1970); for some problems with his analysis, see Higgins (1973).

of a single sentence; a paradox also occurs if there is a group of sentences such that in order to derive some of them A must precede B, and in order to derive others B must precede A. The paradox here is as follows.

We have already shown that *That* Deletion must precede Raising. In Chapter 9, it was demonstrated that Raising must precede Passive so that sentences can be derived in which the subject of the complement becomes the subject of the passivized higher sentence, e.g.:

(10.43)   *John was believed by everyone to be a crook.*

Hence, the ordering of rules must be:

$$\left\{\begin{array}{l} \textit{That}\ \text{Deletion} \\ \text{Raising} \\ \text{Passive} \end{array}\right.$$

Next, we can show that Extraposition follows Passive. In order to derive the following sentences, we apply Passive when the object is an S:

(10.44)   a. *That Mary had left early was suspected by the teacher.*
            b. *That the world was flat was claimed by Galileo.*
            c. *That the door was open was discovered.*

From these, we can derive the sentences in (10.45):[9]

(10.45)   a. *It was suspected by the teacher that Mary had left early.*
            b. *It was claimed by Galileo that the world was flat.*
            c. *It was discovered that the door was open.*

Hence, the ordering of rules must be:

$$\left\{\begin{array}{l} \textit{That}\ \text{Deletion} \\ \text{Raising} \\ \text{Passive} \\ \text{Extraposition} \end{array}\right.$$

On the basis of examples such as those in (10.46), it can be shown that *That* Deletion may apply to the extraposed *that* clause after Passive and Extraposition have applied:

(10.46)   a. *It is generally believed (that) the world is flat.*
            b. *It was claimed (that) Galileo was a genius.*
            c. *It was discovered (that) the door was open.*

---

[9] It should be recognized that in order to maintain this analysis it must be shown that, in general, Passive can apply to sentential objects. Either it will have to be demonstrated that the object complements are dominated by NP, or the Passive transformation will have to be revised to apply to S's as well as NPs. The latter is the less preferable solution, since it simply lists the constituents that Passive may apply to, with no explanation for why the list takes the form that it does. It would be the only solution, of course, if evidence could be found that showed that the object complements were not dominated by NP.

On this basis, the following rule ordering results:

$$
\left\{
\begin{array}{l}
\textit{That} \text{ Deletion} \\
\text{Raising} \\
\text{Passive} \\
\text{Extraposition} \\
\textit{That} \text{ Deletion}
\end{array}
\right.
$$

This is clearly a paradox, since for the same level in the phrase marker *That* Deletion must be ordered both before and after the other three rules mentioned.

The problem, of course, is that *That* Deletion cannot apply to the raised subject of the infinitival complement. This cannot be taken care of by the rule ordering, since a paradox arises. What is required is some other device that will block the application of *That* Deletion to the subject of the complement even when the linear order of constituents appears to satisfy the structural description of *That* Deletion.

Solving the Paradox

To solve the paradox, we first show that there are a number of respects in which the supposedly raised subject of the infinitival complement continues to behave like a subject. One of these is the fact that *That* Deletion cannot apply to it, as we have already noted. On the basis of these observations, we will hypothesize that Raising does not in fact apply to the subject of the infinitival complement, and that there is in fact no transformation of Raising at all. This will lead to a reformulation of the Attachment Constraint that will permit only certain rules to apply to the subjects of infinitival complements while blocking others. In particular, this constraint must permit the application of NP Preposing and Reflexive, while blocking *That* Deletion and *Wh* Fronting out of the subject complement.

The following example shows that it is possible to question the direct object of a *that* clause that is an object complement:

(10.47)
$$
\textit{Who did Mary} \left\{
\begin{array}{l}
\textit{believe} \\
\textit{say} \\
\textit{think}
\end{array}
\right\} \textit{that Susan would marry?}
$$

However, this cannot occur in cases that give the illusion, at least, that the direct object of the verb was originally the subject of the infinitive complement:

(10.48)   a. *Mary believes* ${}_{S'}$[${}_{S}$[*that Susan would marry who*]
                to be unlikely.]
           b. **Who does Mary believe that Susan would marry* $\emptyset$
                to be unlikely?
           c. *Who does Mary believe it to be unlikely that*
                Susan would marry $\emptyset$?

In fact, this observation is quite consistent with the fact that, in general, it is possible to question only out of object and extraposed *that* clauses, and not out of nonextraposed *that* clauses:[10]

(10.49)   a.   *Who is it obvious* ₛ[*that Susan will marry* ∅]?
             b.   **Who is* ₛ[*that Susan will marry* ∅] *obvious?*

The generalization here appears to be, then, that the *that* clause in (10.49b) is continuing to function like a nonextraposed subject complement, in contradiction to the predictions made from a consideration of the rule of Raising.

It should be clear that the restriction against questioning out of the *that* clause in (10.48b) cannot be attributed to the fact that the clause was once a subject, since the extraposed clause in (10.48c) was once a subject also, if a rule of Extraposition is assumed. The facts that have just been noted cast some doubt on the analysis that involves Raising, in spite of the fact that the subject of the infinitive complement appears to undergo Passive:

(10.50)   *That Susan would marry John is believed by Sam to*
             be unlikely.

In (10.50), the superficial subject was the underlying subject of *to be likely.*

The problem, therefore, is to arrive an analysis that (i) accounts for the fact that the complement of the subject can undergo Passive and (ii) either does away with Raising or else explains why Raising does not appear to apply in the case of examples like (10.48b).

The solution to be proposed here will involve an extension of the Attachment Constraint, repeated here for convenience.

ATTACHMENT CONSTRAINT: A moved constituent may be attached only to a constituent of the lowest S of which it was originally a constituent, or to the COMP of the next-higher S if it is moved from a COMP itself.

In order to extend this constraint to *That* Deletion, it will be necessary to extend it from movement transformations to transformations in general. Let us say as a first approximation that if a transformation involves two constituents of the phrase marker, then these two constituents must be either in the same S or in consecutive S nodes in the tree in order for the transformation to apply. This is a weaker constraint than the Attachment Constraint and, thus, permits both *That* Deletion and Extraposition. The application of the constraint to *That* Deletion is illustrated in (10.51):

---

[10] The earliest discussion of this phenomenon in the literature appears to be that of Chomsky (1964b).

(10.51)

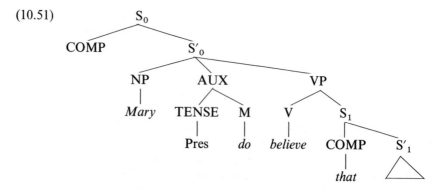

The *that* in S_1 may be deleted in the context of the verb in S_0, since the two are in consecutive S's in the tree.

By comparison, consider the structure of a sentence like (10.41) prior to the application of Raising:[11]

(10.52)

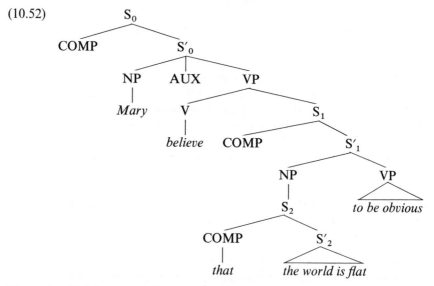

The verb which governs *That* Deletion, *believes*, is in S_0. The *that* that follows *believe* is in S_2. By the constraint that we are considering, a transformation cannot involve two constituents of the tree unless they are in the same or in consecutive S's. In this case, the two constituents are not; hence, the constraint will correctly block the application of *That* Deletion.

[11] Notice that in the tree in (10.52) the complement of *believe* is an S, while we concluded in Chapter 9 that it was an S'. This inconsistency will be eliminated as we arrive at a successful reformulation of the Attachment Constraint.

The following analysis is a variation of an analysis presented in Chomsky (1973). The major difference between the two is the hypothesis that S' is a cyclic node, which Chomsky does not entertain.

Let us consider, now, the application of NP Preposing to the subject of the complement. Compare the two phrases markers shown in (10.53):

(10.53)   a.

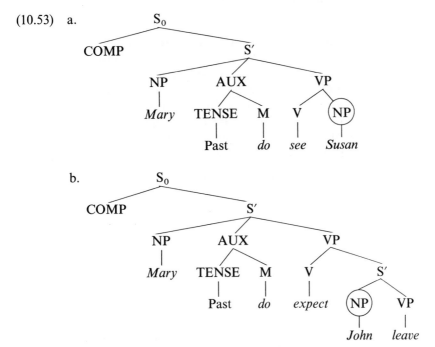

As can be seen from the structural description of NP Preposing, the NP immediately dominated by VP in (10.53a) is not distinguished from the NP dominated by the lower S′ in (10.53b).

NP PREPOSING: X Δ Y V NP Z
                            1 2 3 4 5 6 ⇒ 1 5 3 *be en* 4 ∅ 6

In order to restrict NP Preposing so that it would apply *only* to the direct object NP, it would be necessary to complicate the transformation. Chomsky (1972, 1973) has pointed out that the simplest statement of NP Preposing does not specify whether the NP that follows the V is located in the VP that contains the V or elsewhere. In order to provide this specification, the theory of grammar will have to be complicated by introducing labeled bracket notation into the structural descriptions of transformations. As noted before, this is a serious increase in the power of the theory and should be avoided unless there is no other solution to the problem.

Assume for the sake of argument, therefore, that NP Preposing applies to any NP that follows the V. This raises the question of why NP Preposing never applies to the subject NP of a *that* complement even when the *that* has been deleted. Compare the following examples:

(10.54)

    a. *John believes Bill to have left.*
    b. *John believes Bill has left.*
    c. *Bill is believed to have left.*
    d. **Bill is believed has left.*

In Chapter 9, it was proposed that Raising is restricted only to S' and does not apply to the subject of S. If we are to have a general constraint to do the work that was done by Raising, then we must formulate the constraint in such a way that NP Preposing can move the subject of an S' but cannot move the subject of a *that* clause because it is an S. For reasons that will be clear shortly, this constraint will be referred to as the **Binary Principle**

The way to formulate the Binary Principle is suggested by a comparison of the structures in (10.55) and (10.56). The first is the one that contains the infinitive object complement, while the second is the one that contains the *that* complement in object position:

(10.55)

(10.56)

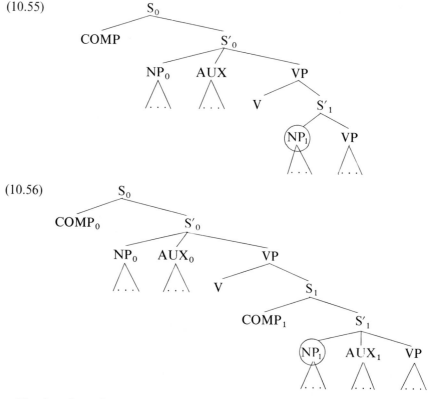

The function of the Binary Principle will be to permit the movement of the circled node in (10.55) into S'_0, while blocking a similar movement in the case of (10.56). In order to provide a precise formulation of the principle, it will be useful to have the following definitions.

DEFINITION: S, S', and NP are **cyclic nodes.**[12]

DEFINITION: Given two nodes, A and B, in a phrase marker, A is the **master** of B if and only if there is at most one cyclic node that dominates B and does not dominate A.

The tree in (10.56) provides an illustration of this definition. NP_0 and AUX_0 are both masters of $COMP_1$ and S'_1, since there is exactly one cyclic node that dominates $COMP_1$ and S'_1 and does not dominate NP_0 and AUX_0, namely S_1. All of the immediate constituents of S'_0 are masters of the others, since in this case there are no cyclic nodes that dominate any one of these without dominating the others. The same is true of the immediate constituents of S'_1.

As can be seen, the definition of **master** given here provides a difference between (10.55) and (10.56) with respect to the relationship between the subject of the complement and the subject of the main S. In (10.56), NP_0 is not the master of NP_1, since there are two cyclic nodes that dominate the latter but not the former—S_1 and S'_1. By comparison, in (10.55) NP_0 is the master of NP_1, since in this case there is only one cyclic node that dominates NP_1 but not NP_0.

This difference is incorporated into the statement of the Binary Principle.

BINARY PRINCIPLE: Given a phrase marker with constituents of type A and B and a transformation T that involves A and B, T may not apply to this phrase marker unless one of these two constituents is the master of the other, or they are both masters of the other.

In (10.55), when we are on the S'_0 cycle we will be able to apply transformations such as NP Preposing to the NP immediately dominated by S'_1. In (10.56), however, when we are on the S'_0 cycle we will only be able to have access to constituents in S_1 but not in S'_1. This will correctly predict that NP Preposing cannot apply to the subject of the *that* complement.

It should be emphasized that while we are using certain rather specific cases to formulate the Binary Principle, it is not possible to arbitrarily replace conditions on particular transformations with general constraints, or vice versa, unless doing so is supported by the empirical evidence. Extension of the Attachment Constraint into the form given as the Binary Principle is motivated by our attempt to avoid the ordering paradox caused by Raising and *That* Deletion; it is important to show that there is independent evidence that this is the direction in which to proceed.

In this regard, we note two further consequences of the Binary Principle. First, by treating S and S' as cyclic nodes we induce an ordering on certain

---

[12] Jackendoff (1972) argues that NP is a cyclic node. Chomsky (1973) shows how treating NP as a cyclic node accounts for a variety of facts with no additional theoretical machinery required. As Chomsky also indicates, however, there are certain related facts that are not explained even if NP is treated as a cyclic node.

transformations that otherwise would have to be extrinsically ordered. This is a consequence of the fact that S contains COMP while S' does not. Thus, if a transformation mentions COMP it will never be able to apply until all transformations that are applicable on S' have applied. This is discussed briefly in Wexler, Culicover, and Hamburger (1975).

Second, the Binary Principle is an essential part of the demonstration that a class of transformational languages is learnable. Without the Binary Principle, it appears to be difficult to constrain the class of transformational languages sufficiently so that they can be shown to be learnable by a reasonable (formal) language learning procedure.[13] This makes the possibility that the Binary Principle is an ad hoc constraint even less likely.

A number of other applications of the Binary Principle are taken up in the problems at the end of this chapter.

SUMMARY

A number of arguments suggest that a transformation of Extraposition is preferable to a transformation of Intraposition. Given that there are underlying sentential complements, however, a paradox arises in the ordering of Raising and *That* Deletion. In order to solve this paradox, we introduce the Binary Principle, which restricts the domain of application of transformations. The Binary Principle turns out to be an extended version of the Attachment Constraint on Extraposition, and accounts for a number of important differences between subjects of infinitival complements and subjects of *that* complements. It appears that by adopting the Binary Principle it is possible to get rid of the transformation of Raising, leading to an even greater simplification of the grammar.

SUMMARY OF RULES

Transformations

EXTRAPOSITION: $X_{NP}[S]\ Y$
$$1\quad 2\quad 3 \Rightarrow 1\ it\ 3 + 2$$

THAT DELETION: $X_{COMP}[that]\ X$
$$1\qquad 2\quad 3 \Rightarrow 1\ \emptyset\ 3$$

---

[13] For further discussion of this point, see the discussion in Chapter 11, Hamburger and Wexler (1975), and Wexler, Culicover, and Hamburger (1975).

EXERCISES

1. Provide a formal statement of the rule of Intraposition. Show that it satisfies the Attachment Constraint.

2. Give derivations for the following sentences, showing the deep structures, the intermediate terminal strings, and the transformations by which each stage in the derivation is related to the previous one:

 a. *It is believed by everyone that the world is flat.*
 b. *There arose a great commotion in the courtyard.*
 c. *Mary hopes that John will take out the garbage.*
 d. *Who do you expect to win the Kentucky Derby?*
 e. *Who was Mary believed to have visited?*
 f. *That John is a fink was believed by Mary to have been proven to be obvious to Sam by Ivan.*

3. Determine the ordering between Extraposition and the transformations introduced in previous chapters. Give examples that show what the ordering of the rules must be if an ordering can be established.

PROBLEMS

1. Provide a phrase structure analysis of sentences like the following:

 a. *The fact that Bill is a fink doesn't bother me.*
 b. *The claim that Mary is sick came from the hospital.*
 c. *I am amazed at Bill's belief that the world is flat.*

2. The analysis of *that* clauses suggested in this chapter does not account for the fact that it is impossible to question out of a sentential subject. E.g.:

 a. *Who is it likely that Mary will marry ∅?*
 b. **Who is that Mary will marry ∅ likely?*

Try to provide an explanation for this fact.

*3. Notice that it is always possible to question an object of an extraposed clause, but that it is possible to question the subject of an extraposed clause only after *that* has been deleted:

 a. *Who do you believe that John will marry ∅?*
 b. **Who do you believe that ∅ will marry Susan?*
 c. *Who do you believe ∅ ∅ will marry Susan?*

Notice, also, that it is never possible to question the subject of a sentential complement when the complementizer is *for*:

   d.   *Who will it be possible for Mary to see $\emptyset$?*
   e.   **Who will it be possible for $\emptyset$ to see John?*

Suggest an analysis that accounts for these facts.

   *4 A well-known transformation of English is Tough Movement, illustrated by the following sentences:

   a.   *John is easy to please.*
   b.   *It is easy to please John.*
   c.   *John is easy to give presents to.*
   d.   *It is easy to give presents to John.*

Provide a formal statement of this rule. Construct appropriate examples where necessary.

   *5. If the structural description of NP Preposing was X Δ AUX V NP Y it would not be sufficiently general to account for sentences like the following:

   a.   *John expects Mary to be arrested by the cops.*
   b.   *Mary wasn't arrested by the cops.*

(i) Why is this so? (ii) Show that our version of NP Preposing makes it possible for the grammar to derive sentences like (a) and (b). (iii) Show that the most general revision of NP Preposing cannot be maintained unless we adopt the Binary Principle also.

   6. Sentences such as the following suggest that Extraposition applies not only to *that* complements but to "*for–to*" complements as well:

   a.   *For John to smile at you would be surprising.*
        For Mary to hit Bill would bother me.
        For the world to explode would be a disaster.
   b.   *It would be surprising for John to smile at you.*
        It would bother me for Mary to hit Bill.
        It would be a disaster for the world to explode.

As in the case of the *that* complements, there is a difference between the complement of *seem* and that of the verbs that permit Extraposition just illustrated. This difference is shown by the following examples:

   c.   **For John to have broken his leg seems.*
        *For Mary to be ready to go appears.
        *For it to be true that the world is flat turns out.

d. *It seems for John to have broken his leg.
    *It appears for Mary to be ready to go.
    *It turns out for it to be true that the world is flat.
e. John seems to have broken his leg.
    Mary appears to be ready to go.
    It turns out to be true that the world is flat.
f. *John would be surprising to smile at you.
    *Mary would bother me to hit Bill.
    *The world would be a disaster to explode.

Show that these facts are accounted for with the following assumptions:
(i) The infinitival complement of *seem*, etc., like the *that* complement of *seem*,
etc., is an object complement; (ii) there is a transformation of Raising to Subject that moves the subject of an infinitival object complement into a dummy
subject; (iii) the lexical entry of *seem*, etc. requires that it take an underlying
it subject.

**7. The account of reflexives given in Chapter 7 does not tell the whole
story. It is possible for a reflexive to be coreferential with a noun phrase to the
right of it under certain conditions:

a. That picture of herself which was hanging on the wall made Mary nervous.
b. The story about herself which Mary told was excruciatingly funny.

Notice, also, that the reflexive may be coreferential with a noun phrase outside
of the simple sentence that contains the reflexive.

c. John said that those stories about himself are absolutely false.

There are also restrictions on the reflexive:

d. *This picture of himself proves that John is a football player.

Determine the conditions under which a reflexive may be coreferential with a
given noun phrase elsewhere in the structure.

*8. (i) Show that there is a problem in accounting for the relative clause in
the following sentence within the present framework of rules:

a. John, who you met yesterday, is my brother.

(ii) What is the difference between the two kinds of relative clauses in the following sentences:

b. The book which you told me about contains many errors.
c. The book, which you told me about, contains many errors.

The relative clause in (b) is said to be **restrictive,** while the relative clause in
(c) is said to be **nonrestrictive.** (The comma in (c) indicates a break in intonation.)

(iii) Formulate an account of the difference between restrictive and non-restrictive relative clauses. Observe that *That* Formation and *That* Deletion (Rel) cannot apply in nonrestrictive relatives:

d. *This book,* $\left\{\begin{array}{l} which \\ *that \\ *\emptyset \end{array}\right\}$ *you told me about, contains many errors.*

Notice, also, that nonrestrictive relative clauses may be used to modify sentences, while restrictive relative clauses may not be:

e. *Mary plays the violin* $\left\{\begin{array}{l} , which\ I\ find\ quite\ impressive. \\ *which\ I\ find\ quite\ impressive. \end{array}\right\}$

SUGGESTED FURTHER READINGS

Extraposition and Intraposition

Emonds, J. E. (1970), *Root and Structure Preserving Transformations,* Unpublished ditto, Indiana University Linguistics Club, Bloomington, Indiana.

Emonds, J. E. (1972), "A reformulation of certain syntactic transformations," In Peters, S., ed., (1972), *Goals of Linguistic Theory,* Prentice-Hall, Englewood Cliffs, N. J.

Emonds, J. E. (forthcoming), *A Transformational Approach to English Syntax: Root, Structure-Preserving and Local Transformations,* Adademic Press, New York.

Higgins, R. (1973), "On J. Emonds' analysis of extraposition," in Kimball, J., ed., (1973), *Syntax and Semantics* (Vol. 2), Seminar Press, New York.

Hooper, J. & Thompson, S. A. (1973), "On the applicability of root transformations," *LI,* **4,** 465–498.

Rosenbaum, P. S. (1967), *The Grammar of English Predicate Complement Constructions,* MIT Press, Cambridge, Mass.

Attachment Constraint (Bounding)

Ross, J. R. (1967), *Constraints on Variables in Syntax,* Unpublished doctoral dissertation, MIT, Cambridge, Mass. Available from Indiana University Linguistics Club, Bloomington, Indiana.

Binary Principle (Subjacency)

Chomsky, N. (1973), "Conditions on transformations," in Anderson, S. R. & Kiparsky, P., eds., (1973), *Festschrift for Morris Halle,* Holt, New York.

Hamburger, H. and Wexler, K. N. (1975), "A mathematical theory of learning transformational grammar," *Journal of Mathematical Psychology,* **12,** 137–177.

Wexler, K. N., Culicover, P. W. & Hamburger, H. (1975), "Learning-theoretic foundations of linguistic universals," *Theoretical Linguistics,* **2.**

COMP

Bresnan, J. (1970b), "On complementizers: Toward a syntactic theory of complement types," *FL*, **6**, 297–321.

Bresnan, J. (1972), *Theory of Complementation in English Syntax,* Unpublished doctoral dissertation, MIT. Cambridge, Mass.

Chomsky (1973).

Emonds (1970, forthcoming).

11

Constraints and Language Learnability

This chapter begins by surveying a number of constraints on transfor-formations that have been proposed in the literature. It then takes up the question of what the relationship is between syntactic constraints and the learnability of classes of grammars. It will be argued that if the notion of "possible grammar" is not sufficiently constrained, a learning device with certain specific capacities and limitations will be unable to guess which language it is being exposed to on the basis of a finite amount of information about that language. It is obvious that human beings do have the ability to learn language on the basis of finite information. Certain constraints on the form of grammars of human languages are claimed to stem from the condition that the grammars be learnable by human beings.

THE A-OVER-A PRINCIPLE

Chomsky (1964a, 1968) noted that sentences like (11.1a) and (11.1b) are ungrammatical:

(11.1)   a. *Who did Mary hit the man who likes?
           b. *Who is that Mary likes obvious?

He also noted that it is impossible to extract NPs in cases like the following:

(11.2)   a.   *John's refusal of* Wh + *something was surprising.*
          b.   **What was John's refusal of surprising?*

(11.3)   a.   *Bill told Mary about John's refusal of* Wh + *something.*
          b.   **What did Bill tell Mary about John's refusal of?*

Chomsky hypothesized that the cases in which *Wh* Fronting applies incorrectly and generates ungrammatical sentences are just those in which *Wh* Fronting extracts an NP that itself is a constituent of an NP. That is, he proposed that the structures corresponding to (11.1a). (11.1b), and (11.2b), respectively, are the following[1] (the circled nodes are those that stand in the relationship that Chomsky viewed as crucial here):

(11.4)   a.   (for 11.1a)

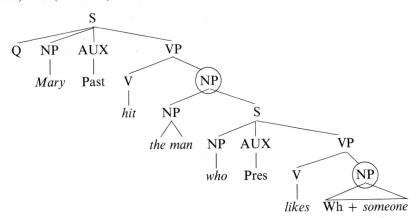

          b.   (for 11.1b)

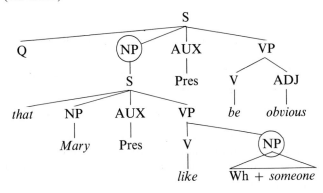

---

[1] Some details of the trees in (11.4) are not supported by the analyses presented in this book. For example, we have not given arguments for the abstract morpheme Q. The differences are not crucial to this discussion.

c. (for 11.2b)

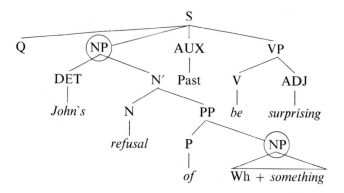

Chomsky proposed a principle according to which any extraction transformation must apply to the highest constituent that satisfies the structural description. Hence, by this principle, called the A-over-A Principle, in a structure of the form shown in (11.5) any rule that is formulated so as to apply to a constituent of type A must in fact apply to the highest A that meets the structural description:

(11.5)

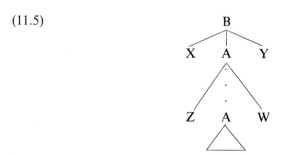

This principle rules out the derivation of (11.1a), (11.1b), (11.2b), and (11.3b), as desired.

Chomsky (1964b) noted that this constraint was too strong in that it ruled out grammatical sentences such as (11.6):

(11.6)   *Who would you approve of* $_{NP}$*[my seeing ∅]?*

(Ross (1967) proposed to replace the A-over-A Principle by a group of constraints that together would rule out all of the ungrammatical cases handled by the A-over-A Principle but would not rule out sentences that are in fact grammatical, such as (11.6).

ROSS' CONSTRAINTS

The Complex NP Constraint

Ross (1967), following Chomsky (1964a, b), observed that the statement of *Wh* Fronting (Chapter 5) makes incorrect predictions about the grammaticality of a variety of sentences. The statement of *Wh* Fronting appears as follows.

Wh FRONTING: X Q Y A Z
                   1 2 3 4 5 $\Rightarrow$ 1 2 + 4 3 $\emptyset$ 5

Condition: 4 dominates *Wh*

Notice that this formulation of *Wh* Fronting is the traditional one, in which a *wh* constituent is moved to the position in the phrase marker indicated by the abstract morpheme Q. Recent versions of this analysis treat the question morphene as a constituent of COMP, as illustrated in (11.7):

(11.7)

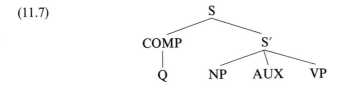

The rest of this discussion will take (11.7) as the underlying interrogative structure.[2]

As Ross noted, the fact that there is a variable Y between the Q to which the *wh* constituent is moved and the *wh* constituent itself makes the prediction that a *wh* constituent can be fronted from a position indefinitely far down in a structure to a COMP containing Q. Hence, for a structure that contains any number of embedded sentences it will be predicted that it would be possible to question a constituent in the lowest S by moving it to the front of the sentence if the highest S contained a Q. This prediction is verified by examples such as those given in (11.8):

[2] This is done for expository purposes only. It appears, in fact, that if the S is to be marked as an interrogative in deep structure, then this should be represented as a feature [+WH] on COMP. See Bresnan (1972) for discussion.

Also, it should be noted that Ross (1967) did not assume that there was a COMP constituent. I have rephrased the problem in terms of COMP in order to formulate it in terms more familiar to the reader; none of the essence of the problem is changed, however.

(11.8)   a. *Who does John like ∅?*
              b. *Who does [Mary believe [John likes ∅]]?*
              c. *Who does [Mary believe [Bill said [John likes ∅]]]?*
              d. *Who does [Mary believe [Bill said [Susan claimed*
                 [that John likes ∅]]]]?
              e. *Who does [Mary believe [Bill said [Susan claimed*
                 [that Harry knows [that John likes ∅]]]]]?

In principle, there appears to be no limit on the depth in the phrase marker of
S nodes from which a noun phrase may be extracted by *Wh* Fronting.

This generalization breaks down when the *wh* constituent appears in a relative clause. As Figure 11.1 shows, *Wh* Fronting should be able to apply in such
a way as to extract a *wh* constituent from a relative clause; however, this results
in ungrammaticality.

The obvious way to solve this problem would be to restate *Wh* Fronting in
such a way that it does not apply in cases such as that illustrated in Figure 11.1.
As Ross showed, this would not be an adequate solution to the problem for
two reasons. First, a descriptively adequate restatement of *Wh* Fronting would
entail complication of what is fundamentally a very simple and elegant transformation. Second, *Wh* Fronting is not the only transformation that cannot
extract a constituent of a relative clause. Any transformation that moves
constituents over a variable as *Wh* Fronting does is subject to an identical
restriction.

To see the first point, let us consider what a restatement of *Wh* Fronting would
involve. The function of this transformation is to move a *wh* constituent over
a variable of unbounded length, as shown by the examples in (11.8). The proper
restriction on this rule cannot be given in terms of a specification of the kinds
of syntactic structure over which the *wh* constituent may be moved, since,
because of recursion, there is no limit on the length of the intervening structure.
Hence, there is no way to express the structural description of *Wh* Fronting
except in terms of a variable.

We might consider a restriction on the rule in terms of a **negative** condition
on the form of the variable. That is, we might add a condition to the present
rule of *Wh* Fronting of the form "Y is not equal to . . . ," where the " . . . " is a
statement of the types of structures that a *wh* constituent *cannot* be moved over.
As our discussion thus far has indicated, this restriction would have to prevent
extraction out of a relative clause structure; hence, a first approximation of
this condition would be "Y is not equal to Z N $_S$[COMP W."[3] Note that the
sequence N $_S$[COMP is precisely that which is associated with the boundary
between a head noun and a relative clause on it.

This condition is too strong, however, since it rules out application of *Wh*
Fronting in cases such as (11.9).

---

[3] There is no closing bracket]$_S$ because Y represents the material between Q and A. A is in the
middle of the S with which the left bracket $_S$[is associated; the right bracket]$_S$ is part of the variable
Z to the right of A in the structural description of *Wh* Fronting.

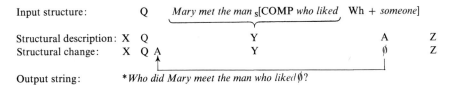

Input structure:		Q	*Mary met the man* ₛ[COMP *who liked*	Wh + *someone*]		
Structural description:	X	Q	Y		A	Z
Structural change:	X	Q A	Y		∅	Z

Output string: **Who did Mary meet the man who liked ∅?*

Figure 11.1 Extraction of an interrogative pronoun from a relative clause by *Wh* Fronting.

(11.9)

Input   Q *Mary told the police* ₛ[COMP[*that*] *John lost* Wh + *something*]
Wh Fronting *What did Mary tell the police that John lost ∅?*

As this example shows, the sequence N ₛ[COMP (represented here by *police that*) does not in itself block application of *Wh* Fronting. What is crucial is that the N and the S must be constituents of the same NP, as is the case in the relative clause structure.

A second approximation to the correct condition would explicitly incorporate the structure of a relative clause: "Y is not equal to Z′ ₙₚ[Z″ N ₛ[COMP] W." This is a very complex condition; furthermore, it does little more than state in formal terms what we have noted informally; *Wh* Fronting cannot extract a constituent of a relative clause.

It is important to show, therefore, that the condition on the application of *Wh* Fronting is not a property of the rule itself but is a constraint on the applicability of *all* movement transformations. If the restriction in fact applies to all transformations, then we would be missing a significant generalization by stating it individually on each transformation. We would also be able to avoid having to increase the descriptive power of the theory of grammar to permit individual transformations to have negative conditions associated with them as specific as the one formulated here.

Consider first the rule of Topicalization. This transformation moves constituents to sentence-initial position, as illustrated in (11.10). Note that there is no limit on this transformation, as in the case of *Wh* Fronting:

(11.10) a. *Nobody likes that man.*
         b. *That man, nobody likes.*
         c. *That man, John said that nobody likes.*
         d. *That man, Mary believes John said nobody likes.*
         e. *That man, the newspaper said Mary believes John said nobody likes.*

Like *Wh* Fronting, Topicalization cannot extract a constituent from a relative clause:

(11.11) a. *Nobody knowns anyone who likes **that man.***
         b. **That man, nobody knows anyone who likes ∅.*

(11.12) a. *I told Susan about the store where I bought this book.*
         b. **This book, I told Susan about the store where I bought.*

It is clear, therefore, that both rules share the same restriction.

Another transformation that is also subject to this restriction is *Though Attraction* (cf. pp. 166–167). The function of this transformation is to move an adjective or adjectival phrase to the left of *though*. This is illustrated in (11.13) (note that there is no limit on the length of the variable over which this movement may apply):

(11.13) a. *Though Fido is stupid, everyone likes him.*
b. *Stupid though Fido is, everyone likes him.*
c. *Stupid though John said Fido is, everyone seems to like him.*
d. *Stupid though Mary believes John said Fido is, everyone seems to like him.*
e. *Stupid though the newspaper said that Mary believes John said Fido is, everyone still reads it.*

Once again, the normally movable constituent cannot be moved out of a relative clause:

(11.14) a. *Though Fido bit a man who was stupid, everyone blamed the poor dog for the lawsuit.*
b. **Stupid though Fido bit a man who was, everyone blamed the poor dog for the lawsuit.*

(11.15) a. *Though I have seen lots of people who are tall, I have never seen anyone like Wilt.*
b. **Tall though I've seen lots of people who are, I have never seen anyone like Wilt.*

Thus, we find still another transformation that cannot extract a constituent of a relative clause.[4]

On the basis of considerations such as these, Ross proposed the Complex NP Constraint.[5] The term **complex NP** denotes noun phrases that contain a

---

[4] Many linguists believe that the transformation that derives the relative pronoun in initial position in the relative clause is not *Wh* Fronting but another transformation, called Relative Clause Formation. If this were the case, then Relative Clause Formation would be another rule that obeys the constraint against extraction, as shown by examples such as the following:

(i)   *I met **the man** ₛ[Mary saw the boy ₛ[**the boy** hit **the man**]]*

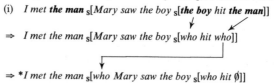

⇒ *I met the man ₛ[Mary saw the boy ₛ[who hit who]]*

⇒ **I met the man ₛ[who Mary saw the boy ₛ[who hit ∅]]*

See Ross (1967) for further discussion.

[5] Some, but not all, of these cases can be handled by the A-over-A Principle. In light of certain counterexamples to the A-over-A Principle, Ross chose to abandon it completely rather than to revise it to accommodate the counterexamples. This decision is particularly well motivated in the case of *Though* Attraction, where a violation occurs when an adjective is moved out of an S dominated by NP [cf. (11.14)]. There is no evidence to suggest that the A-over-A Principle, which is stated in terms of the categories of the various nodes, is relevant here.

relative clause, constructions like *the belief that the world is an oyster* (which does not involve a relative clause), and other constructions. The precise formulation of this constraint depends on the details of the structure of such constructions. Ross' constraint is not repeated verbatim here because his analysis of relative clauses differs from the one presented in this book in certain details that are crucial to the formulation of the constraint. The following is intended to be an informal statement of the constraint.

COMPLEX NP CONSTRAINT: No transformation may extract a constituent from a complex NP.

The Coordinate Structure Constraint

Ross (1967) noted that it is impossible to extract a constituent of a coordinate structure, that is, a structure of the type illustrated in (11.16):

(11.16)   a.

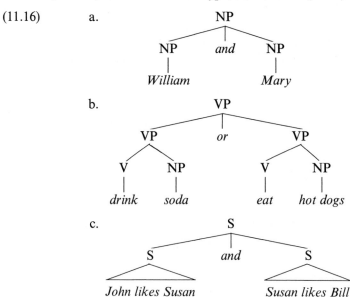

     b.

     c.

(11.17) a. Q *Mary likes John and* Wh + *someone*
   b. **Who does Mary likes John and* ∅?

(11.18) a. Q *Mary likes Bill and hates* Wh + *someone*
   b. **Who does Mary like Bill and hates* ∅?

(11.19) a. Q *Mary likes Bill and Susan hates* Wh + *someone.*
   b. **Who does Mary like Bill and Susan hates* ∅?

(11.20) a. Q *Mary likes* Wh + *someone and Susan hates Bill.*
   b. **Who does Mary like and Susan hates Bill.*

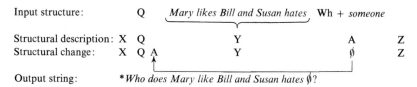

Figure 11.2   Extraction of an interrogative pronoun from a conjoined S by *Wh* Fronting.

(11.21)   a.   Q *Mary believes that Susan hates Bill and Sam likes*
              Wh + *someone.*
          b.   **Who does Mary believe that Susan hates Bill and Sam likes* ∅?*

It can be seen that structures of the type just illustrated also meet the structural description of *Wh* Fronting, and therefore *Wh* Fronting falsely predicts that the (b) examples should be grammatical. This is illustrated in Figure 11.2.

Again, it can be shown that there are strong reasons for formulating this restriction on *Wh* Fronting as a general constraint on transformations in the theory of grammar, and not as a condition on the rule itself. First, the condition on the rule would complicate the rule considerably, and second, all movement transformations are subject to the same restriction (cf. Exercise 2 for discussion). Hence, failure to state this restriction in the theory would fail to capture a general fact about transformations, and would require an increase in the descriptive power of transformations permitted by the theory of grammar.

The constraint proposed by Ross is called the **Coordinate Structure Constraint**. Again, an informal version is given here rather than Ross' original formulation.

COORDINATE STRUCTURE CONSTRAINT: Nothing may be moved out of a coordinate structure.

A precise formulation would presuppose an analysis of coordinate constructions far more detailed than that implicit in the structures in (11.16).

The Sentential Subject Constraint

As noted in Chapter 10, it is impossible to question a constituent of a sentential complement when that complement is the subject of a sentence:

(11.22)   a.   *Who is it obvious* ₛ[*that Mary likes* ∅]?
                 b.   **Who is* ₛ[*that Mary likes* ∅] *obvious?*

One again, the statement of *Wh* Fronting permits its application to structures that possess a sentential subject. This is illustrated by Figure 11.3. Again, it turns out that the condition that will block application of *Wh* Fronting here is required for transformations in general (cf. Exercise 3). On the basis of observations such as these, Ross proposed the following Sentential Subject Constraint.

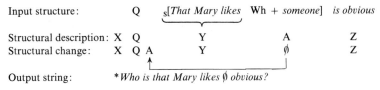

Input structure:		Q	ₛ[*That Mary likes*	Wh + *someone*]	*is obvious*
Structural description:	X	Q	Y	A	Z
Structural change:	X	Q A	Y	∅	Z

Output string: **Who is that Mary likes ∅ obvious?*

Figure 11.3   Extraction of a constituent of a sentential subject by *Wh* Fronting.

SENTENTIAL SUBJECT CONSTRAINT: No constituent may be moved out of an S that is itself the subject of an S.

The Internal S Constraint

Not surprisingly, there have been many other constraints proposed by linguists, since finding universal constraints is properly one of the major preoccupations of linguistics. Some of these constraints, such as Ross' three constraints noted previously, arose as a consequence of the fact that Chomsky's A-over-A Principle failed to capture certain phenomena and made incorrect predictions in a number of other cases. For example, the A-over-A Principle does not capture the facts that the Coordinate Structure Constraint accounts for, since extraction of an NP from a structure such as S *and* S is not ruled out by the A-over-A Principle.

Ross observed further that even when no rule of extraction has applied, it is impossible to form a question when the subject is sentential. Thus, note examples like those in (11.23) and (11.24):

(11.23)   a.   Q ₛ[*that the world is flat*] *is obvious.*
             b.   **Is* ₛ[*that the world is flat*] *obvious?*

(11.24)   a.   Q ₛ[*for Mary to climb the fence*] *would surprise Bill.*
             b.   **Would* ₛ[*for Mary to climb the fence*] *surprise Bill?*

Making the assumption that the sentential subject is exhaustively dominated by an NP, Ross proposed the following constraint.

INTERNAL S CONSTRAINT: Grammatical sentences containing an internal NP that exhaustively dominates S are unacceptable.

Noting that it is possible to analyze a **gerund** like *Mary's climbing the fence* as an S exhaustively dominated by NP, Ross (1967:251) revised this constraint as follows, in view of the grammaticality of (11.25):

(11.25)   *Would Mary's climbing the fence surprise Bill?*

INTERNAL S CONSTRAINT: Grammatical sentences containing an internal NP that exhaustively dominates an S are unacceptable unless the main verb of that S is a gerund.

Kuno (1973) points out that this constraint is too strong in that it rules out as unacceptable sentences that are in fact quite acceptable. Kuno assumes that the sentential complement of *believe* is an S that is exhaustively dominated by NP; then the constraint just stated incorrectly predicts that (11.26) is unacceptable:

(11.26)   *John believed that the world was flat when he was sixteen.*

On this basis, Kuno proposes that the Internal S Constraint be maintained, but that the notion of "internal NP" be formulated in such a way that the constraint makes the correct predictions for sentences like (11.26).

However, Kuno also points out that there are unacceptable sentences that apparently should be ruled out by the Internal S Constraint but are not; e.g.:

(11.27)   **How likely is ₛ[that the world is flat]?*

As can be seen, the sentential subject here is not internal under any reasonable formulation of what "internal" means. Kuno proposes, therefore, that the constraint be applied not to surface structures but to structures that precede the application of the rule that moves *be* into AUX, i.e., *Do* Replacement (or an essentially equivalent alternative). Hence, at this stage the structure for (11.26) would be roughly that of (11.28):

(11.28)   Q *how likely* ₛ[*that the world is flat*] *is?*

We have now discussed briefly a number of constraints on transformations. They are not entirely adequate as they stand, even for English, and there is not complete agreement at this stage as to their proper formulation. The discussion of Ross' constraints and Chomsky's A-over-A Principle shows that the same phenomena may be attributed by different linguists to different constraints. Just as when there is disagreement as to the rules of the grammar themselves, such alternative proposals must be evaluated.

Later in this chapter, we will consider the Binary Principle and another constraint on transformations. These constraints appear to improve on certain of the constraints that we have just reviewed. They are of particular interest because they contribute to a proof that the class of grammars required for the description of natural language are "learnable " As a basis for this discussion, we will now examine the concept of learnability of grammars and the relationship between learnability and constraints on the rules of a grammar.

FORMAL LANGUAGE LEARNABILITY: AN INTRODUCTION

A major goal of linguistic research is to uncover universal properties of human language. There are many properties that human languages have in common, not all of which can be attributed to the historical connections between languages. The deep universal properties of human language must be reflections of deep universal properties of the human mind. Of all the logically possible systems that could be used for communication, only some of these are of a kind that the human brain can learn and use.

The more constraints we can discover on what form a possible human language may take, the more internal structure we can attribute to the human language learner and user. From the point of view of the language learner, these constraints constitute, in effect, *innate knowledge* that the language that he is being exposed to is one of a relatively small class of possible human languages. Such knowledge will enable the language learner to pick out the *correct* grammar from the large (possibly infinite) number of grammars consistent with the data presented to him in the form of sentences from a particular language.

Common sense might suggest that a human being can learn anything, whether it is constrained or not. After all, English is English, and one learns it. However, the situation is not quite this simple, for it can be demonstrated that making certain assumptions about the language learning device has the consequence that certain classes of languages cannot be learned. In order to account for the fact that natural languages like English *are* learned, we must, therefore, either attribute more power to the learning mechanism that the child can employ or show that the class of languages from which the child is selecting is in fact restricted in such a way to make the class a learnable one. The former may indeed be both possible and necessary; but it appears that the latter, that is, restricting the class of languages, is also necessary, and this is our concern in this chapter.

Let us consider, now a very simple case in which it can be shown that a class of languages is not learnable by a particular type of learning device.[6] For the sake of illustration, let us assume a definition of a learning procedure (a "child"), a method of presenting data, a class of possible languages, and a definition of "learning." If these are carefully chosen, it can be shown that the procedure cannot learn the language that is being presented to it.

We will assume an infinite set of languages. Each language has a finite number of sentences in it except for one, which is an infinite language (like English). Naming each language as L_n for the numbers $n = 1, 2, 3, \ldots$, there is the following class:

L_1 contains the sentence *a*.
L_2 contains the sentences *a* and *aa*.
L_3 contains the sentences *a*, *aa*, and *aaa*.

.
.
.

L_k contains the sentences *a*, *aa*, *aaa* . . . all the way up to the sentence with
   k a's.

.
.
.

L_∞ contains every sentence with any number of *a*'s in it that we wish.

---

[6] The discussion here is based closely on that of Hamburger and Wexler (1973).

The problem for the procedure is very simple: When presented with a sentence, it must guess which language the sentence is coming from. Let us define "learning" as that situation in which the procedure always guesses the same correct language after a certain time, i.e., never changes its guess after that time. So, for example, let us suppose that the language is L_{10} and that the procedure is presented with a variety of sentences from L_{10} over a certain period. If at some time the procedure guesses that the language is L_{10} and then, for all further sentences with which it is presented, continues to guess that the language is L_{10}, then the procedure has learned the language in this sense.

It can now be shown that this procedure cannot in principle figure out which language its data are coming from, and so can never learn any language in the class. Let us pick a language, say L_5, and consider what the procedure would do.

L_5 contains the sentences a, aa, aaa, $aaaa$, and $aaaaa$. We assume that these sentences are presented to the procedure in any order, just as long as no sentence is systematically withheld, since this would involve withholding crucial information from the learning procedure and would clearly make it impossible for the procedure to learn the language.

What strategy should the procedure use? If it knows that L_∞ is a possible language, it must decide whether it should guess L_∞ or an L_n when presented with a new sentence. Assume that the procedure picks the strategy of choosing the L_n corresponding to the longest sentence encountered. So if aaa is presented first, the procedure will guess L_3. If aa is then presented, the procedure will not guess L_2 but will maintain L_3, since aa is also in L_3. If at some time $aaaaa$ is presented, then the procedure will guess L_5, and since all other sentences that could be presented to it are in L_5, it will never change its guess.

As can be seen quite clearly, this strategy will work only if L_∞ is not in the collection of possible languages. This is so because of the fact that if the language being presented is actually L_∞, and if the strategy followed by the procedure is to always guess an L_n corresponding to the longest sentence that it has encountered, then it will never guess L_∞.

On the other hand, if the strategy followed is to guess L_∞ always, then if the language from which the data are drawn is actually an L_n, the procedure will never guess that the language from which the data is drawn is L_n because every sentence is in L_∞. There will never be any reason to move away from L_∞ for any new sentence. Hence, it has been shown that given the particular collection of possible languages outlined here, and given a certain procedure and a definition of "learning," the procedure will never learn the language from which the data are drawn. No matter which strategy the procedure pursues, it is always possible to present data from a language in the collection such that the procedure that follows this strategy will not be able to identify the language from which the data are drawn.

Let us now consider what sort of constraint would have to be placed on the class of possible languages so that the procedure will be able to learn any language from the class, given data from the language. If a restriction is placed on the class of languages that it can contain no language such that it is an infinite language that contains every sentence that appears in all of the other languages taken together, this would yield a class of languages just like those in the preceding language with the exception that it does not contain L_∞. In such a case, a procedure can be established that will learn any language from the class, namely, the procedure that guesses L_k for any sentence containing exactly k a's that is not in the language currently guessed. The procedure is as follows: For each sentence presented, first see if that sentence is in the language that the procedure has guessed on the basis of previous data. If it is, do not change the guess. If it is not, guess L_k for k equal to the number of a's in the current sentence. At some point, the longest sentence in the language will be encountered; every subsequent sentence will be shorter than this sentence and, therefore, will be consistent with the language guessed by the procedure on the basis of this longest sentence. Hence, the procedure will learn the language from which the data are drawn.

This demonstration deals, of course, with a very simple and unnatural case. It illustrates, however, that it is possible to imagine a class of languages and a procedure such that the procedure cannot learn any language from the class of languages. In such a case, we say that the class is not **identifiable by the procedure** On the other hand, we have also seen that it is possible to constrain the class of possible languages so that it is identifiable by the procedure.

The problem for natural language is more complex, but comparable. Given some formulation of what the human language-learning procedure consists of, and given some idea of what kinds of linguistic data are presented to the child in learning language, one can in principle investigate the question of whether or not various classes of languages defined by the theory of grammar are learnable, or identifiable, by this procedure. Hence, it is worthwhile to consider whether there is evidence in natural language for universal constraints on what can constitute the grammar of a natural language, and whether it is possible, given such constraints, to show that the class of grammars so defined is learnable by a procedure that is a reasonable approximation of the human learning procedure.

Another way of approaching this question is the following: Obviously, one would only bother to test types of grammars that are plausible on the basis of the kinds of rules that appear in natural language. Now, suppose that we test a class defined by the constraints that we have already determined by examining natural languages, and suppose that we find that this class of languages is not learnable. Then, of course, we must look for more—or different—constraints to impose on the class. However, we need not look at random. We can sometimes determine what additional constraints would make that class learnable, and this will give us a clue about the sorts of constraints that we can expect to find in natural language.

THE LEARNABILITY OF TRANSFORMATIONAL GRAMMARS

An Unlearnable Class of Grammars

Chapter 2 introduced the notion that a theory of grammar that contains certain types of rules may be too powerful in the sense that it permits formulation of grammars that could not be grammars of natural languages. On the other hand, a theory of grammar may be too weak in the sense that it does not provide the formalism by which some phenomena occurring in natural language may be accounted for. For example, as has been argued at great length here and elsewhere (cf. Chomsky, 1957; Postal, 1964a, b), phrase structure grammars are too weak, and transformational grammars are required to provide the necessary descriptive power for natural language.

The question that must now be raised is whether the theory of transformational grammar is too powerful. Of course, in order to answer this question we must give a precise characterization of the notion of a transformational grammar. Depending on what operations we permit transformations to perform, how we permit them to be ordered with respect to one another, etc., this will make a difference in the class of grammars permitted by the theory. However, if it can be shown that even without certain kinds of rules a theory of grammar is too powerful, then it should also follow that the same theory augmented by one new type of rule will also be too powerful.

Naturally, the answer will also depend on the type of information presented to the learning procedure and the kind of procedure that is assumed. Hence, it is necessary to point out that any results that arise from an investigation of this question are reasonable only insofar as the assumptions are plausible, and true only insofar as the assumptions are verifiable.

The assumptions that we will make here about the learning procedure, called P, are the following: Whenever P encounters a sentence from the language that it cannot handle, it forms a new grammar by changing one rule of its old grammar so that the new grammar will account for this new type of sentence. If the sentence encountered can be accounted for by the old grammar, then P does not form a new hypothesis about what the grammar is, but maintains the old grammar. P cannot remember previous sentences that were presented to it but has available to it at any given time only the most recent grammar and the sentence that has just been presented to it.

We also assume that the data are presented to P in such a way that over time P encounters a sequence of grammatical sentences of the language, and that no sentence is systematically withheld from the sequence. Again, this assumption is made to ensure that there will be no information withheld from P relevant to the construction of the correct grammar of the language by P.

Consider, now, the most restrictive class of transformational grammars imaginable, which is the class of grammars that do not contain any transformations whatsoever. Each of these grammars will then in fact be context-free phrase structure grammars, since, in general, a transformational grammar is a grammar consisting of a set of context-free phrase structure rules and a set of transformations that apply to the trees characterized by these phrase structure rules.

Let us consider the question of whether this set of transformational grammars containing no transformations is learnable by P, given the method of presentation of data just outlined. The answer to this question, remarkably enough, is that it is not. That is, given data from one of the infinite set of languages corresponding to the set of possible context-free phrase structure grammars, P is unable to consistently guess which grammar characterizes the data from the language after some definite time. This result was shown by Gold (1967).

It follows, therefore, that if the class of transformational grammars containing even one type of transformation is considered, this class will also be unlearnable by P. Hence, the class of transformational grammars that linguists have proposed for natural language is also unlearnable. This class is the one permitting movement transformations, copying transformations, and deletion transformations, and initial phrase markers characterized by a context-free base component.

Thus, some way of constraining the class of transformational grammars must be found, assuming that P and the method of data presented are reasonable. On the other hand, if some assumptions are abandoned, it might turn out that the learnability of various classes of languages is changed. So, for example, Gold (1967) showed that if the procedure P is presented not only with grammatical sentences of the language but with sequences of words that are marked as ungrammatical in the language (with, for instance, a *), then the class of context-free grammars and the class of context-sensitive grammars are identifiable by P. However, the available evidence from the literature of language development suggests that the child who is beginning to learn language is not informed as to which sequences of words of the language are grammatical sentences and which are not (cf. Brown & Hanlon, 1970).[7] Hence, it appears to be reasonable to rule out this "informant presentation scheme" as the appropriate assumption to make about the kinds of data that the child is presented with.

Let us consider once again the class of context-free phrase structure grammars. It is easy to see that if there were only one possible context-free phrase structure grammar for all natural languages, then P would have no trouble learning the grammar of the language that it encountered. Since there would be only one possible grammar, this grammar would always be guessed. In other words, this grammar would be innate.

---

[7] Brown and Hanlon (1970) showed that when children were corrected they were corrected not for grammaticality but for truth value. At the earlier stages of language learning, at least, it appears that parents and other adults are more concerned that the child know the facts about his environment than that he know the facts about the language. Knowledge of the language seems to follow quite automatically as the child learns about the world.

It is not the case that all natural languages have context-free phrase grammars with no transformations; the evidence from English should be sufficient to show this. However, it has been argued that it might be reasonable to make the assumption that all natural languages have the same context-free phrase structure base to which language-specific transformations apply. This assumption is called the **Universal Base Hypothesis.** If it is correct, then the base does not have to be learned because it is innate. The question about learnability then becomes the following: Is the class of transformational languages with a fixed universal base learnable by P?

The answer to this question must depend, of course, on what is taken to be the class of transformational grammars. If it is assumed that the class of transformational grammars is too heavily restricted and is not learnable by P, then it would follow that the actual class of transformational grammars assumed by current linguistic theory will also not be learnable. And in fact, it is possible to show that even a heavily restricted class of transformational grammars is not learnable by P if P is presented only with grammatical sentences from the language.

The class of transformational grammars to be considered is the following. First, all transformations apply cyclically, and S is the only cyclic node. Second, the domain of applicability of all transformations is restricted by the Binary Principle formulated in Chapter 10. That is, if the transformational cycle is operating at S_1 in Figure 11.4, then transformations may not apply to the parts of the structure outside of the circled portion of the tree. The structural description of any transformation when the cycle is operating as S_1 may be met only by material in S_1 and S_2.

Third, there are no deletion transformations. Fourth, if a constituent of an S is moved out of that S and attached to a higher S (the next one up by the restriction of the scope of transformations), then this constituent may not be used to meet the structural description of later transformations. Finally, all transformations are obligatory, and at most one transformation may apply to any given S in the tree.

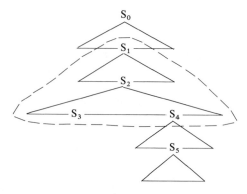

Figure 11.4 Scope of transformational analysis, by Binary Principle.

Given all of these constraints, the class of transformational grammars so defined is nevertheless not learnable by P, as proved by Wexler and Hamburger (1973). This is a remarkable result. It follows that the class of transformational grammars that have been found to be necessary for the description of natural language will also be unlearnable by P, unless some other constraints not yet discussed here are imposed. This is because the grammars that have actually been proposed for natural languages are less restricted than the class of grammars that Wexler and Hamburger examined. For example, it is necessary, for grammars of languages like English, to state deletion transformations and optional transformations. In addition, constituents that are moved out of an S may be operated on by later transformations, as in the case of Passive applying to the output of Raising and Raising applying to the output of Passive (cf. Chapter 9). Finally, as we have often seen, more than one transformation must be able to apply to a single S in the tree.

The Identifiability of a Class of Transformational Grammars

It is quite clear that transformational grammars are learned by children. However, the results of the preceding section suggest that unless we change our assumptions about the nature of the language-learning procedure, the class of transformational grammars themselves, or the method of data presentation, we will be in a poor position to formally account for this fact.

Hamburger and Wexler (1973) make the following proposal. Suppose that instead of assuming that P is presented with a sequence of grammatical sentences from the language, assume that P is presented with a sequence of pairs (b, s), the first member of the pair being the deep structure of the sentence and the second the grammatical sentence itself. Under this assumption, they prove that the class of transformational grammars outlined in the preceding section is learnable by P.

To summarize, then, the class of transformational languages is learnable by a procedure P under the following circumstances:

A1. P guesses at most one transformation when presented with a sentence not handled by its current grammar.

A2. The data presented consist of (b, s) pairs, where b is the deep structure of the sentence and s is the sentence.

A3. There are no deletion transformations.

A4. Transformations may analyze at most one cyclic node down (the Binary Principle).

A5. A raised constituent may not participate in any later transformations.

A6. All transformations are obligatory.

A7. At most one transformation may apply to any given S in the tree.

A8. Transformations apply cyclically (cf. Chapter 9).

A9.   The phrase structure base is universal.

A10.   S is the only cyclic node.

It is important, now, to note that these assumptions are sufficient to prove learnability of a class of transformational grammars, but they are not obviously necessary assumptions. Two of these assumptions appear to be substantially correct: Chomsky (1973) proposes a constraint similar to A4 on the basis of independent considerations,[8] and A8 is generally assumed to be correct.

On the other hand, A2 is clearly not correct. A more plausible assumption is that the procedure P is capable of inferring what the deep structure is from the sentence and the context in which it is uttered. What is crucial for the proof is that P have some way of determining the deep structure: The easiest way to satisfy this requirement is to present the deep structure directly, but obviously there are more plausible alternatives to this that will perform the same function.

A3 is also false, as even the evidence from English shows. A5 does not appear to be correct, either, regardless of whether Raising is a transformation. As shown in Chapter 10, the subject of the complement may in fact be raised into the subject position of the higher S either by Raising followed by Passive or by Passive alone, depending on which formulation one chooses. In either case, this raised NP is subject to later transformations.

A6 is clearly false, since we have motivated numerous optional transformations. A7 is also false, as we have seen. A9 is clearly too strong, and must be weakened at least to the extent that it allows different underlying constituent orders from one language to another. A10 should probably be extended to include at least NP, and possibly S'.

The next stage in the investigation is to bring these assumptions more in line with what is known about natural language and the language-learning environment while preserving learnability. It is demonstrable that the following assumptions also permit proof of learnability:[9]

B1.   Same as A1.

B2.   Same as A2.

B3.   There may be deletion transformations, movement transformations, raising transformations, copying transformations, and insertion transformations.

B4.   Same as A4 (the Binary Principle).

B5.   Certain transformational operations (to be defined later) cause the constituents on which they operate to be ineligible for the application of later transformations.

---

[8] Chomsky's constraint is formulated with the assumption that S and NP are cyclic nodes. It is called the **Subjacency Condition.**

[9] See Wexler, Culicover, and Hamburger (in preparation) for the proof. It should be noted that several minor assumptions are also required in addition to the ones mentioned here in order to rule out special cases that are logical possibilities but are of little linguistic significance.

B6.   All transformations are obligatory (same as A6).

B7.   Any number of transformations may apply to any given S in the tree and do not require extrinsic ordering.

B8.   Transformations apply cyclically (same as A8).

B9.   Either the base is universal, or there exists a universal procedure by which P can figure out what the deep structure of the sentence being presented is in terms of the context in which it is uttered.

B10. S is the only cyclic node (same as A10).

In connection with B6, it is not clear whether or not it can be shown formally that the class of transformational grammars with optional transformations can be learned, although given the evidence from natural languages like English, it appears that such a proof must certainly be possible. As far as B10 is concerned, extending the class of cyclic nodes to include S' and NP has not been investigated with regard to its consequences for the proof of learnability. There appears to be some empirical support for taking the class of cyclic nodes to be S, S', and NP, and it is not likely that this will affect the proof.

The only other assumptions here that require some empirical support are B4, B5, and B7, to which we turn now.

Two Hypotheses

THE BINARY PRINCIPLE

It is interesting to observe that a constraint that is similar to the Binary Principle is assumed by Chomsky (1973) on the basis of evidence internal to the grammar of English. Further linguistic evidence for such a principle was provided in Chapter 10. Since the Binary Principle can be shown to contribute to the learnability proof for natural languages, this suggests that we are indeed on the right track in relating constraints on grammars of natural languages to the problem of learnability. However, there are a number of phenomena that in current linguistic analysis are not consistent with the Binary Principle, and it is worthwhile to consider whether or not it is possible to provide an account of these phenomena that conforms to the principle.

These phenomena have to do with the rule of *Wh* Fronting. As observed earlier, there is some evidence that *Wh* Fronting operates in such a way as to extract a *wh* constituent from indefinitely far down in a tree from a COMP:

(11.29)   *Who did Mary believe that Susan said that . . . John likes $\emptyset$?*

Chomsky (1973) proposes the following alternative formulation. Suppose that whenever there was a sentence containing a *wh* constituent the rule of *Wh* Fronting applied in such a way as to move that *wh* constituent into the COMP node of that sentence. This is illustrated in (11.30):

(11.30)

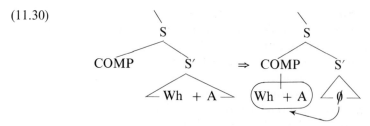

Assume, now, that *Wh* Fronting may also move a *wh* constituent from the COMP of the next S down. This is illustrated in (11.31):

(11.31)

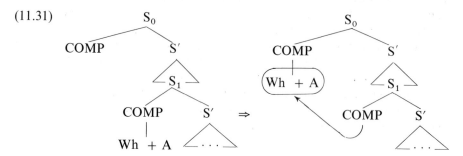

Clearly, this has the same effect as a rule of *Wh* Fronting that reaches indefinitely far down into trees to find *wh* constituents and moves them into higher S's.

Formulation of *Wh* Fronting as a successive cyclic transformation provides a possible explanation for some of the data handled by Ross' Complex NP Constraint. There is strong evidence (Jackendoff, 1972; Chomsky, 1973) that NP is a cyclic node. Given this, it is clear from the following structure that a constituent that has been moved into the COMP of the relative clause cannot be moved into the COMP of the next S above because of the Binary Principle:

(11.32)

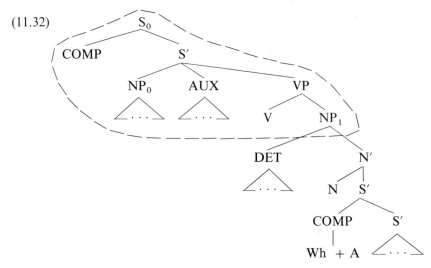

The domain of application of transformations applying on S_0 is shown by the broken line. Only nodes within the broken line may be applied to.

Similarly, it will be impossible to extract a constituent of the noun phrase NP_1, given the Binary Principle. This accounts for another observation of Ross (1967), which is that it is impossible to question the possessive pronoun of a noun phrase, as illustrated in (11.33):[10]

(11.33)   a.   *Mary ate* Wh + *someone's cheesecake.*
             b.   *Whose cheesecake did Mary eat $\emptyset$?*
             c.   **Whose did Mary eat $\emptyset$ cheesecake?*

The tree in (11.34) illustrates that only the noun phrase that contains the interrogative pronoun, and not the pronoun itself, is subject to a movement transformation such as *Wh* Fronting on the S_0 cycle:

(11.34)

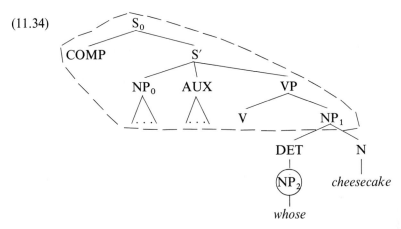

Next, note that the Binary Principle and the assumption that NP is a cyclic node together will block movement of the interrogative pronoun in cases such as the following:

(11.35)   a.   *John discussed Mary's refusal of* Wh + *something*
             b.   **What did John discuss Mary's refusal of $\emptyset$?*

The domain of application of the transformation in this case is illustrated in (11.36):

---

[10] The solution proposed by Ross takes the form of the following principle.

LEFT BRANCH CONDITION: No NP that is the leftmost constituent of a larger NP can be reordered out of this NP by a transformational rule.

Both the greater generality of the Binary Principle and its important role in the learnability proofs lead us to prefer it to Ross' more specific Left Branch Condition.

(11.36)

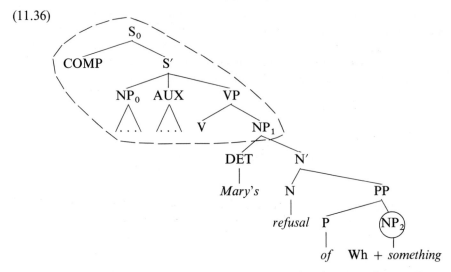

Finally, these assumptions permit us to account for the same data as Ross' Sentential Subject Constraint (cf. page 282), as well as data that are clearly related but not taken into account by this constraint. Consider, first, the case in which the subject is an S, and note the domain of application of a transformation at S_0 with respect to constituents of the sentential subject S_1:

(11.37)

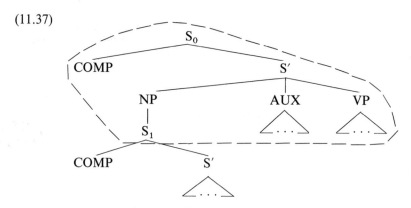

Note that by taking NP to be a cyclic node and applying the Binary Principle we will prevent any constituent of the sentential subject from being moved out of it. In particular, we can explain the ungrammaticality of the examples that motivated the Sentential Subject Constraint, e.g.:

(11.38)   *What did $_S$[that Mary said ∅] bother you?

etc.

The related phenomena have to do with the fact that the same restriction applies regardless of whether the subject is an S or an NP that dominates an NP. For example, if the subject is *Mary's refusal of* Wh + *something,* extraction of the interrogative pronoun yields the ungrammatical sentence given in (11.39):

(11.39)   *What did Mary's refusal of bother you?

This is not explained by the Sentential Subject Constraint, since the subject in this case is not sentential. It is accounted for by the Binary Principle, however, as the illustration in (11.40) makes clear:

(11.40)

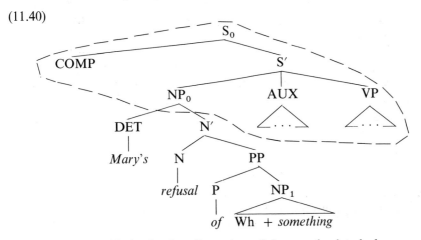

See Chomsky (1973) for further discussion of these and related phenomena.

The Binary Principle, taken together with the designation of S, S', and NP as cyclic nodes, permits us to account for several phenomena for which a number of independent and specific constraints had been proposed previously. The relative generality of the Binary Principle constitutes support for adopting it in the theory of grammar. This is particularly significant in view of the fact that the Binary Principle plays an important role in the learnability proof for grammars of natural languages.

THE FREEZING PRINCIPLE

As noted previously, an important aspect of the learnability proof for the class of transformational grammars needed for the description of natural language is the adoption of a constraint that restricts the extent to which transformations may apply to the output of other transformations. This constraint, which will be outlined here, is called the **Freezing Principle**

In order to state the Freezing Principle, it is helpful to first formulate the notion of **structure-preserving at a node**.[11]

---

[11] The term **structure-preserving** was originally used by Emonds (1970) in a somewhat different way then it is used here. The essential difference is that for Emonds an entire transformation is either structure-preserving or non-structure-preserving, while for us only individual operations performed by a transformation are structure-preserving. Hence, a transformation may perform two operations, one of each type, and so on. For an exposition of the role of the notion of structure-preserving transformations in a theory of grammar, the reader is referred to Emonds (1970, forthcoming).

DEFINITION: A transformation is **structure-preserving at a node** A just in case the structure immediately dominated by A after the transformation has applied to A is a structure that could have been generated immediately below A as a base expansion by the phrase structure rules.

The opposite of structure-preserving is **non-structure-preserving.**

To illustrate the meaning of these terms, let us consider a set of phrase structure rules that constitutes the base component of a grammar. Each phrase structure rule specifies what kinds of constituents may be dominated by each labeled node. For example, the rule S → COMP S′ specifies that the sequence COMP S′ may be dominated by the node S.

For the sake of illustration, let the base component contain the rule A → B C. Suppose that the base component does **not** contain a rule of the form A → B C D. Finally, suppose that there is a transformation whose function is to attach the node D to the right of the constituents dominated by A. The output structure of this transformation will look like (11.41):

(11.41)

$$
\begin{array}{ccc} & A & \\ \diagup & | & \diagdown \\ B & C & D \end{array}
$$

Since we have assumed that there is no phrase structure rule of the form A → B C D, the transformation that attached D to A is, thus, non-structure-preserving at A.

A node is **frozen** if a non-structure-preserving transformation has applied to it. We may now state the Freezing Principle.

FREEZING PRINCIPLE: No transformation may analyze a frozen node.

That is to say, no transformation may take into account the internal constituent structure of a frozen node. As observed earlier, this principle is a sufficient condition for learnability, given assumptions B1–B4 and B6–B10 (cf. pp. 292–293).

An extensive discussion of the kinds of evidence from natural language that are accounted for by this principle will not be provided here. The following section points to a number of cases in which the Freezing Principle appears to operate in natural language.

EVIDENCE FOR THE FREEZING PRINCIPLE

Complex NP Shift

In Chapter 7 there is a brief discussion of a transformational called Complex NP Shift. To review, this transformation derives sentences like (11.42b) from sequences like (11.42a):

(11.42)   a. *John gave a book about amphibians to Mary.*
              b. *John gave to Mary a book about amphibians.*

We may assume for illustration that there is a phrase structure rule of the form given in (11.43), and that the structural change of Complex NP Shift is as shown in (11.44):

(11.43)   VP → V NP PP

(11.44)

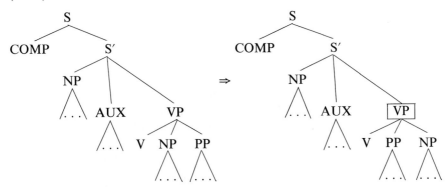

If a phrase structure rule of the form VP → V PP NP is not assumed for English, then it follows by the definition of non-structure-preserving that the VP in which Complex NP Shift applies will be frozen. The fact that a node is frozen is represented by a square around it, as in (11.44).

The prediction made by the Freezing Principle in this case is that it will be impossible to analyze this frozen VP. That is, no constituent of this VP may be taken to satisfy the structural description of any transformation that follows Complex NP Shift. To test this prediction, consider whether *Wh* Fronting may apply to the object of the preposition *to* either after Complex NP Shift has applied or before it applies:

(11.45)   a. *Who did John give a book about amphibians to ∅?*
              b. **Who did John give to ∅ a book about amphibians?*

As may be seen from these examples, if Complex NP Shift has applied, then *Wh* Fronting cannot apply. (Observe that we are looking here at the examples in which only the object of the prepositions is moved, and not the entire prepositional phrase. Since if the entire phrase is moved none of it will be left behind, we could not then determine whether the phrase had been moved from its position before Complex NP Shift has applied or after it had applied. Thus, such examples as *To whom did John give a book about amphibians?* or *What did John give to Mary?* do not test the correctness of the Freezing Principle.) Thus, the predictions made by the Freezing Principle prove to be correct if it is assumed that Complex NP Shift precedes *Wh* Fronting.

This ordering is an immediate consequence of the assumption that S and S′ are both cyclic nodes: *Wh* Fronting can apply only at the level of S, while

Complex NP Shift applies at S'. It is entirely possible that the Freezing Principle and the Cyclic Principle (with S' as a cyclic node) will permit all instances of extrinsic ordering to be done away with.

Dative

Observe that neither *Wh* Fronting nor any other movement transformation except NP Preposing may move an indirect object after Dative has moved it after the verb:

(11.46)   *John gave Mary the umbrella.*

(11.47)   a. **Who did John give the umbrella?*
                b. **Mary was easy to give the umbrella?*
                c. **Mary, I have given the umbrella.*
                d. **It was Mary that John gave the umbrella.*
                e. *Mary was given the umbrella by John.*

Wexler, Culicover, and Hamburger (1975) suggest the following analysis of Dative:

(11.48)

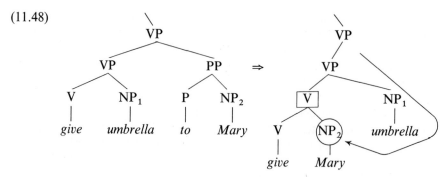

Since V → V NP is not a rule of the base, NP$_2$ is dominated by a frozen node after Dative and cannot be moved by later transformations. NP$_1$, on the other hand, may be moved. This accounts for the difference in grammaticality between the examples in (11.47) and those in (11.49):

(11.49)   a. *What did John give Mary?*
                b. *The umbrella was easy to give Mary.*
                c. *The umbrella, I gave Mary.*
                d. *It was the umbrella that John gave Mary.*

A remaining problem with this account of Dative is that it fails to explain why NP Preposing may apply in cases where the noun phrase immediately following the verb is dominated by a frozen node, as in (11.47e). It is conceivable that NP Preposing, being an obligatory transformation, must be exempted from the Freezing Principle. This is a question that clearly deserves further study.

Finally, note that the Freezing Principle eliminates the ordering paradox involved in deriving these examples that was pointed out in Problem 2 of Chapter 7.

NP Preposing

It is possible to formulate NP Preposing so that the output of the transformation is (11.50):

(11.50)

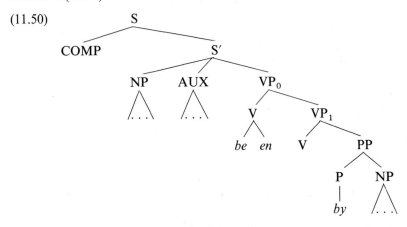

The *be en* that is introduced by NP Preposing is attached to a new VP node created between S' and the VP that dominates the main verb; the newly created node is indicated as VP_0 in the tree. This type of attachment is known as **Chomsky-adjunction.**

The structure of (11.50) is generable by the phrase structure rules VP → V VP and VP → V PP, both of which can be motivated as rules of the base component. By this analysis NP Preposing is structure-preserving and does not cause freezing. This is a correct prediction in view of the fact that a passive sentence behaves just as though it were an underlying structure with respect to a wide variety of transformations, including Raising, *Wh* Fronting, Inversion, Equi-NP Deletion, and Extraposition. Not surprisingly, it is this state of affairs that makes it appear that there might not be any transformational derivation of the passive in the first place, since it is difficult to find syntactic evidence to distinguish between a deep structure analysis of some construction and a structure-preserving transformational analysis of that construction.

SUMMARY

1. The Freezing Principle accounts for a variety of grammatical phenomena.
2. The Binary Principle accounts for the data for which the A-over-A Principle, the Complex NP Constraint, the Sentential Subject Constraint, and the Left Branch Condition were proposed. It also subsumes the Attachment Con-

straint for Extraposition, and blocks the application of Reflexive and Passive to the subjects of embedded S nodes (but not of S′ nodes), as discussed in Chapter 10.

3. S, S′, and NP are cyclic nodes. This, together with the Freezing Principle, may permit us to eliminate extrinsic ordering completely.

4. The Binary Principle and the Freezing Principle are the cornerstones of a proof that the class of transformational grammars required for the description of natural languages is learnable.

5. It appears probable that the Coordinate Structure Constraint and the Internal S Constraint cannot be replaced by these constraints and must therefore be independently maintained.

EXERCISES

1. For each of the following cases, indicate which of Ross' constraints will predict the ungrammaticality:

    a. *Who did the fact that Mary married ∅ surprise?
    b. *What were you amazed at John's refusal to give ∅ to Susan?
    c. *What did John meet Susan before George found ∅?
    d. *What did Susan meet a man who gave ∅ to Bill?
    e. ***Blazing Saddles** is a movie which I laugh every time I see ∅.
    f. *What did Susan give ∅ to George and a magazine to Harry?
    g. *Who does Mary believe that for George to visit ∅ would be ridiculous?
    h. *Would for John to leave early bother you?
    i. *What did John's refusal of ∅ surprise you?

2. Give examples that show that the Coordinate Structure Constraint is a general constraint and is not specific to *Wh* Fronting.

3. Give examples that show that the Sentential Subject Constraint is a general constraint and is not specific to *Wh* Fronting.

PROBLEMS

1. Show that, given the Freezing Principle, if there is a transformation A that is structure-preserving at a node and a transformation B that is non-structure-preserving at the same node, then it will always appear that A is ordered before B, even if the two rules are in principle permitted to apply in either order.

2. Discuss the relationship between the following examples and the Katz–Postal hypothesis:

a. *John doesn't love anyone.*
    *Anyone is not loved by John.
b. *It is not easy to fool all of the people.*
    All of the people are not easy to fool.
c. *You may now examine me, Dr. Caligari.*
    I may now be examined by you, Dr. Caligari.
d. *John should have fed the baby.*
    The baby should have been fed by John.
e. *All of the women expect all of the women to leave.*
    All of the women expect themselves to leave.
    All of the women expect to leave.
f. *Each of the men saw one of the women.*
    One of the women was seen by each of the men.

3. (i) The words *and* and *or* are **conjunctions.** Constituents of the same category may be linked with a conjunction to form another constituent of the identical category; e.g.:

a. ***John and Mary*** *ate dinner* (NP and NP).
b. *John* ***washed and ironed*** *his underwear.* (V and V).
c. *Mary* ***read the book and took notes.*** (VP and VP).
d. *Harold found some dirt* ***behind and under the chair.*** (P and P).
e. *Harold found some dirt* ***behind the chair and under the rug.*** (PP and PP).
f. *Mary swam* ***quickly and quietly.*** (ADV and ADV).

In many cases, sentences with conjoined constituents may be paraphrased by conjoining sentences:

g. *John ate dinner and Mary ate dinner.*
h. *John washed his underwear and ironed his underwear.*

etc. What does this suggest about the status of a transformational relationship between conjoined sentences and sentences containing conjoined constituents? Is this relationship motivated? Are there any counterexamples? Try to state the transformation that would capture such a relationship.

(ii) What do sentences like the following suggest about the transformational relationship discussed in the first part of this problem:

i. ***John and Mary*** *are very much alike.*
j. ***John and Mary*** *ate dinner together.*
k. ***John and Mary*** *slugged each other.*

Provide a phrase structure analysis of conjoined structures and compare it to the transformational analysis.

(iii) Does the phrase structure analysis handle all the cases that would be handled by a transformational analysis, or vice versa? Justify your answer.

**4. Generally, pronouns may be coreferential with noun phrases in other clauses in the sentence, but need not be. E.g.:

    a. *John thinks that he will win.*
    b. *Before he came home, John called up his mother.*
    c. *That he is going to win is obvious to John.*

However, there are constructions in which the pronoun *cannot* be coreferential with any other noun phrase in the sentence:

    d. *He thinks that John will win.*
    e. *John gave the books to him.*
    f. *Next to John he found a snake.*

What generalizations can be made about the circumstances under which a pronoun may and may not be coreferential with another noun phrase in the sentence?

5. (i) Show that there is a problem in deriving the following sentence if the Binary Principle is adopted and if S′ is a cyclic node:

    a. *Who did John expect Mary to visit?*

Show that it makes no difference whether there is a rule of Raising or not.

(ii) Show that the problem in (i) is eliminated if there is a rule of Raising and if nonbranching nodes that arise by virtue of a transformation are "pruned" (Ross, 1969a). That is, the node is erased, and the material that it dominated is attached to the node that immediately dominated it:

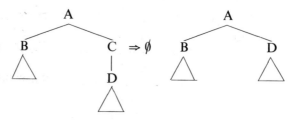

(iii) Show that the problem indicated in (i) applies to Equi-NP Deletion unless there is a pruning convention.

6. Show that the Binary Principle blocks *That* Deletion in the subject of the infinitival complement even if there is a rule of Raising.

SUGGESTED FURTHER READINGS

The Need for Constraints

Chomsky, N. (1965), *Aspects of the Theory of Syntax*, MIT Press, Cambridge, Mass.

Ross, J. R. (1967), *Constraints on Variables in Syntax*, Unpublished doctoral dissertation, MIT, Cambridge, Mass. Available from Indiana University Linguistics Club, Bloomington, Indiana.

Constraints on Rules

Chomsky, N. (1973), "Conditions on transformations," in Anderson, S. R. & Kiparsky, P., eds., (1973), *Festschrift for Morris Halle*, Holt, New York.

Emonds, J. E. (1970), *Root and Structure Preserving Transformations*, Unpublished ditto, Indiana University Linguistics Club, Bloomington, Indiana.

Emonds, J. E. (forthcoming), *A Transformational Approach to English Syntax: Root, Structure-Preserving and Local Transformations*, Academic Press, New York.

Hankamer, J. (1973), "Unacceptable ambiguity." *LI*, **4**, 17–68.

Kuno, S. (1973), "Constraints on internal clauses and sentential subjects," *LI*, **4**, 363–386.

Ross (1967).

Other Constraints

Perlmutter, D. (1970), "Surface structure constraints in syntax," *LI*, **1**, 187–255.

Perlmutter, D. (1971), *Deep and Surface Structure Constraints in Syntax*, Holt, New York.

Schwartz, A. (1972), "Constraints on movement transformations," *JL*, **8**, 35–85.

Pruning

Ross, J. R. (1969a), "A proposed rule of tree-pruning," in Reibel, D. & Schane, S. A., eds., (1969), *Modern Studies in English*, Prentice-Hall, Englewood Cliffs, N. J.

Identifiability and Learnability

Gold, E. M. (1967), "Language identification in the limit," *Information and Control*, 10, 447–474.

Hamburger, H. & Wexler, K. N. (1973), "Identifiability of transformational grammars," in Hintikka, K. J. J., Moravcsik, J. M. E., & Suppes, P., eds., (1973), *Approaches to Natural Language*, Reidel, Dordrecht, Holland.

Hamburger, H. & Wexler, K. N. (1975), "A mathematical theory of learning transformational grammar." *Journal of Mathematical Psychology*. **12**, 137–177.

Wexler, K. N., & Hamburger, H. (1973), "On the insufficiency of surface data for the learning of transformational languages," in Hintikka, Moravcsik and Suppes (1973).

References

Akmajian, A. (1970), "On deriving cleft sentences from pseudocleft sentences," *Linguistic Inquiry*, 1, 149–168.

Akmajian, A. (1975), "More evidence for an NP cycle," *Linguistic Inquiry*, 6, 115–129.

Akmajian, A., & Heny, F. W. (1975), *Introduction to the Principles of Transformational Syntax*, MIT Press, Cambridge, Mass.

Akmajian, A., & Jackendoff, R. (1970). "Anaphora and stress," *Linguistic Inquiry*, 1, 124–126.

Anderson, S. R. (1971), "On the role of deep structure in semantic interpretation," *Foundations of Language*, 7, 387–396.

Arbini, R. (1969), "Tag-questions and tag-imperatives in English," *Journal of Linguistics*, 5, 205–214.

Bach, E. (1967), "Have and be in English syntax," *Language*, 43, 462–485.

Bach, E. (1971), "Questions," *Linguistic Inquiry*, 2, 153–166.

Bach, E. (1974), *Syntactic Theory*, Holt, New York.

Bach, E., & Harms, R. T., eds. (1968), *Universals in Linguistic Theory*, Holt, New York.

Baker, C. L. (1970), "Notes on the description of English questions: The role of an abstract question morpheme," *Foundations of Language*, 6, 197–219.

Baker, C. L., & Brame, M. (1972), "'Global rules': A rejoinder," *Language*, 48, 51–75.

Bar-Adon, A., & Leopold, W., eds. (1971), *Child Language: A Book of Readings*, Prentice-Hall, Englewood Cliffs, N. J.

Bierwisch, M., & Heidolph, W., eds. (1971), *Recent Advances in Linguistics*, Mounton, The Hague.

Bolinger, D. (1970), "The imperative in English," in *To Honor Roman Jakobson*, Mouton, The Hague.

Borkin, A. (1973), *"To be* or not *to be,"* in Corum, C., Smith-Stark, T. G., & Weiser, A., eds. (1973), *Papers from the Ninth Regional Meeting*, Chicago Linguistic Society.

Bresnan, J. (1970a), "An argument against pronominalization," *Linguistic Inquiry*, **1**, 122–133.

Bresnan, J. (1970b), "On complementizers: Toward a syntactic theory of complement types," *Foundations of Language*, **6**, 297–321.

Bresnan, J. (1971), "On sentence stress and syntactic transformations," *Language*, **47**, 257–281.

Bresnan, J. (1972), *Theory of Complementation in English Syntax*, Unpublished doctoral dissertation, MIT, Cambridge, Mass.

Brown, R. (1973), *A First Language*, Harvard University Press, Cambridge, Mass.

Brown, R., & Hanlon, C. (1970), "Derivational complexity and the order of acquisition in child speech," in Hayes, J. R., ed., (1970), *Cognition and the Development of Language*, Wiley, New York.

Burt, M. K. (1971), *From Deep to Surface Structure*, Harper, New York.

Carden, G. (1970), "On post-determiner quantifiers," *Linguistic Inquiry*, **1**, 415–428.

Chomsky, N. (1957), *Syntactic Structures*, Mouton, The Hague.

Chomsky, N. (1963), "Formal properties of grammars," in Luce, R. D., Bush, R. R., & Galanter, E., eds. (1963), *Handbook of Mathematical Psychology* (vol. 2), Wiley, New York.

Chomsky, N. (1964a), "The logical basis of linguistic theory," in Lunt, H. (ed.), *Proceedings of the Ninth International Congress of Linguistics, Cambridge, Mass., 1962*. Mouton, The Hague.

Chomsky, N. (1964b), "Current issues in linguistic theory," in Fodor & Katz (1964).

Chomsky, N. (1964c), "On the notion 'rule of grammar'", in Fodor & Katz (1964).

Chomsky, N. (1964d), "A transformational approach to syntax," in Fodor & Katz (1964).

Chomsky, N. (1965), *Aspects of the Theory of Syntax*, MIT Press, Cambridge, Mass.

Chomsky, N. (1966), *Topics in the Theory of Generative Grammar*, Mouton, The Hague.

Chomsky, N. (1968), *Language and Mind*, Harcourt, New York.

Chomsky, N. (1970a), "Remarks on Nominalizations," in Jacobs, R., & Rosenbaum, P., eds., (1970), *Readings in English Transformational Grammar*, Ginn (Blaisdell), Boston, Mass.

Chomsky, N. (1970b), "Deep structure, surface structure, and semantic interpretation," in Jakobson, R., & Kawamoto, S., eds., (1970), *Studies in General and Oriental Linguistics* (Commemorative Volume for Dr. Shiro Hattori), TEC Corporation, Tokyo.

Chomsky, N. (1972), "Some empirical issues in the theory of transformational grammar," in Peters, S., ed., (1972), *Goals of Linguistic Theory*, Prentice-Hall, Englewood Cliffs, N. J.

Chomsky, N. (1973), "Conditions on transformations," in Anderson, S. R., & Kiparsky, P., eds., *Festschrift for Morris Halle*, Holt, New York.

Chomsky, N., & Halle, M. (1968), *The Sound Pattern of English*, Harper, New York.

Chomsky, N., & Miller, G. A. (1963), "Introduction to the formal analysis of natural languages," in Luce, R. D., Bush, R. R., & Galanter, E., eds. (1963), *Handbook of Mathematical Psychology* (Vol. 2), Wiley, New York.

Corum, C., Smith-Stark, T. C., & Weiser, A., eds., (1973), *Papers from the Ninth Regional Meeting*, Chicago Linguistic Society.

Culicover, P. W. (1971), *Syntactic and Semantic Investigations*, Unpublished doctoral dissertation, MIT, Cambridge, Mass.

Culicover, P. W. (1973), "On the coherence of syntactic descriptions," *Journal of Linguistics*, **9**, 35–51.

Dale, P. S. (1972), *Language Development*, Dryden Press, Hinsdale, Ill.

Davidson, D., & Harman, G., eds. (1972), *Semantics of Natural Languages*, Reidel, Dordrecht, Holland.

Delorme, E., & Dougherty, R. C. (1972), "Appositive NP Constructions," *Foundations of Language*, **8**, 1–28.

Dingwall, W. O., ed. (1972), *A Survey of Linguistic Science*, University of Maryland Press, Baltimore.

Dougherty, R. (1970), "A grammar of coordinate conjoined structures: I," *Language,* **46,** 850–898.
Dougherty, R. (1971), "A grammar of coordinate conjoined structures: II," *Language,* **47,** 298–339.
Emonds, J. E. (1970), *Root and Structure Preserving Transformations,* Unpublished ditto, Indiana University Linguistics Club, Bloomington, Indiana.
Emonds, J. E. (1972), "Evidence that indirect object movement is a structure-preserving rule," *Foundations of Language,* **8,** 546–561.
Emonds, J. E. (1972), "A reformulation of certain syntactic transformations," in Peters, S., ed., (1972), *Goals of Linguistic Theory,* Prentice-Hall, Englewood Cliffs, N. J.
Emonds, J. E. (1974), "Parenthetical clauses," in Rohrer, C. & Ruwet, N., eds., (1974), *Actes du Colloque Franco-Allemand de Grammaire Transformationelle,* Niemeyer Verlag, Tübingen, Germany.
Emonds, J. E. (forthcoming), *A Transformational Approach to English Syntax: Root, Structure-Preserving and local Transformations,* Academic Press, New York.
Ferguson, C., & Slobin, D. I., eds. (1973), *Studies of Child Language Development,* Holt, New York.
Fillmore, C. (1963), "The position of embedding transformations in a grammar," *Word,* **19,** 208–231.
Fillmore, C. (1965), *Indirect Object Construction in English and the Ordering of Transformations,* Monographs in Linguistic Analysis 1, Mouton, The Hague.
Fillmore, C., & Langendoen, D. T., eds. (1971), *Studies in Linguistic Semantics,* Holt, New York.
Fodor, J. A., & Katz, J. J., eds. (1964), *The Structure of Language: Readings in the Philosophy of Language.* Prentice-Hall, Englewood Cliffs, N. J.
Fraser, B. (1970), "Idioms within a transformational grammar," *Foundations of Language,* **6,** 22–42.
Freidin, R. (1975), "The analysis of passives," *Language,* **51,** 384–405.
Fromkin, V., & Rodman, R. (1973), *An Introduction to Language,* Holt, New York.
Gleason, H. (1961). *An Introduction to Descriptive Linguistics,* (Revised edition), Holt, New York.
Gold, E. M. (1967), "Language identification in the limit," *Information and Control,* **10,** 447–474.
Grinder, J. (1971), "Chains of coreference," *Linguistic Inquiry,* **2,** 183–202.
Grinder, J. (1972), "Cyclic and linear grammars," in Kimball, J. ed., (1972b), *Syntax and Semantics* (Vol. 1), Seminar Press, New York.
Grinder, J., & Elgin, S. (1973), *Guide to Transformational Grammar,* Holt, New York.
Grinder, J., & Postal, P. (1971), "Missing antecedents," *Linguistic Inquiry,* **2,** 269–312.
Gumperz, J., & Hymes, D., eds. (1972), *Directions in Sociolinguistics,* Holt, New York.
Halle, M. (1964a), "On the bases of phonology," in Fodor & Katz (1964).
Halle, M. (1964b), "Phonology in a generative grammar," in Fodor & Katz (1964).
Hamburger, H., & Wexler, K. (1973), "Identifiability of transformational grammars," in Hintikka, K. J. J., Moravcsik, J. M. E., & Suppes, P., eds., (1973), *Approaches to Natural Language,* Reidel, Dordrecht, Holland.
Hamburger, H., & Wexler, K. (1975), "A mathematical theory of learning transformational grammar," *Journal of Mathematical Psychology,* **12,** 137–177.
Hankamer, J. (1973), "Unacceptable ambiguity," *Linguistic Inquiry,* **4,** 17–68.
Harms, R. (1968), *Introduction to Phonological Theory,* Prentice-Hall, Englewood Cliffs, N. J.
Harris, F. W. (1974), "Reflexivization I" and "Reflexivization II," Unpublished ditto, Indiana University Linguistics Club, Indiana University, Bloomington.
Harris, Z. (1964) "Co-occurrence and transformation in linguistic structure," in Fodor & Katz (1964).
Hasegawa, K. (1968). "The passive construction in English," *Language,* **44,** 230–243.
Higgins, R. (1973), "On J. Emonds' analysis of extraposition," in Kimball, J. ed., (1973), *Syntax and Semantics* (Vol. 2), Seminar Press, New York.
Hintikka, K. J., Moravcsik, J. M. E., & Suppes, P., eds., (1973), *Approaches to Natural Language,* Reidel, Dordrecht, Holland.
Hockett, C. (1958), *A Course in Modern Linguistics,* Macmillan, New York.

Hooper, J., & Thompson, S. A. (1973), "On the applicability of root transformations," *Linguistic Inquiry*, **4**, 465–498.

Huddleston, R. (1970), "Two approaches to the analysis of tags," *Journal of Linguistics*, **6**, 215–222.

Hyman, L. (1975), *Phonology*, Holt, New York.

Jackendoff, R. S. (1968), "Quantifiers in English," *Foundations of Language*, **4**, 422–442.

Jackendoff, R. S. (1969), "An interpretive theory of negation," *Foundations of Language*, **5**, 218–241.

Jackendoff, R. S. (1971), "Gapping and related rules," *Linguistic Inquiry*, **2**, 21–35.

Jackendoff, R. S. (1972), *Semantic Interpretation in Generative Grammar*, MIT Press, Cambridge, Mass.

Jackendoff, R. S. (1974), "Introduction to the · X̄ · Convention, Unpublished ditto, Indiana University Linguistics Club, Bloomington, Indiana.

Jackendoff, R. S., & Culicover, P. W. (1971), "A reconsideration of dative movement," *Foundations of Language*, **7**, 397–412.

Jacobs, R., & Rosembaum, P., eds. (1970), *Readings in English Transformational Grammar*, Ginn (Blaisdell), Boston, Mass.

Jakobson, R., & Kawamoto, S., eds. (1970), *Studies in General and Oriental Linguistics* (Commemorative Volume for Dr. Shiro Hattori), TEC Corporation, Tokyo.

Jespersen, O. (1961), *A Modern English Grammar on Historical Principles*, Allen and Unwin, London.

Jespersen, O. (1964), *Essentials of English Grammar*, (Reprint), University of Alabama Press, Montgomery, Alabama.

Katz, J. J. (1972), *Semantic Theory*, Harper, New York.

Katz, J. J., & Fodor, J. A. (1964), "The structure of a semantic theory," in Fodor & Katz (1964).

Katz, J. J., & Postal, P. (1964), *An Integrated Theory of Linguistic Description*, MIT Press, Cambridge, Mass.

Kimball, J. (1972a), "Cyclic and noncyclic grammars," in Kimball, J., ed., (1972b), *Syntax and Semantics* (Vol. 1), Seminar Press, New York.

Kimball, J., ed. (1972b), *Syntax and Semantics* (Vol. 1), Seminar Press, New York.

Kimball, J. (1973a), *The Formal Theory of Grammar*, Prentice-Hall, Englewood Cliffs, N. J.

Kimball, J., ed. (1973b), *Syntax and Semantics* (Vol. 2), Seminar Press, New York.

Kiparsky, P., & Kiparsky, C. (1971), "Fact," in Bierwisch, M., & Heidolph, K., eds. (1971), *Recent Advances in Linguistics*, Mouton, The Hague.

Klima, E. S. (1964), "Negation in English," in Fodor & Katz (1964).

Koutsodas, A. (1973), "Extrinsic order and the complex NP constraint," *Linguistic Inquiry*, **4**, 69–82.

Kuno, S. (1971), "The position of the locative in existential sentences," *Linguistic Inquiry*, **2**, 333–378.

Kuno, S. (1973), "Constraints on internal clauses and sentential subjects," *Linguistic Inquiry*, **4**, 363–386.

Kuno, S., & Robinson, J. (1972), "Multiple wh questions," *Linguistic Inquiry*, **3**, 463–488.

Kuroda, S.-Y. (1969), "English relativization and certain related problems," in Reibel, D. & Schane, S. A., eds., (1969), *Modern Studies in English*, Prentice-Hall, Englewood Cliffs, N. J.

Labov, W. (1969), "Contraction, deletion and the inherent variability of the English copula," *Language*, **45**, 715–762.

Labov, W. (1973), *Sociolinguistic Patterns*, University of Pennsylvania Press, Philadelphia.

Lakoff, G. (1970a), *Irregularity in Syntax*, Holt, New York.

Lakoff, G. (1970b), "Global rules," *Language*, **46**, 627–639.

Lakoff, G. (1971), "On generative semantics," in Steinberg, D., & Jakobovits, L. P., eds. (1971), *Semantics: An Interdisciplinary Reader in Philosophy, Linguistics, and Psychology*, Cambridge University Press, London.

Lakoff, R. (1968a), *Abstract Syntax and Latin Complementation*, MIT Press, Cambridge, Mass.

Lakoff, R. (1968b), "Some reasons why there can't be any some-any rule," *Language*, **45**, 608–615.

Langacker, R. (1968), *Language and Its Structure,* Harcourt, New York.

Langacker, R. (1969, "On pronominalization and the chain of command," in Reibel, D. & Schane, S. A., eds., (1969), *Modern Studies in English,* Prentice-Hall, Englewood Cliffs, N. J.

Langacker, R. (1972), *Fundamentals of Linguistic Analysis,* Harcourt, New York.

Langacker, R. (1974), "The question of Q," *Foundations of Language,* **11,** 1–37.

Langendoen, D. T. (1969), *The Study of Syntax,* Holt, New York.

Lees, R. (1960), *The Grammar of English Nominalizations,* Mouton, The Hague.

Lees, R., & Klima, E. S. (1969), "Rules for English pronominalization," in Reibel, D. & Schane, S. A., eds., (1969), *Modern Studies in English,* Prentice-Hall, Englewood Cliffs, N. J.

Luce, R. D., Bush, R. R., & Galanter, E. (1963), *Handbook of Mathematical Psychology* (Vol. 2), Wiley, New York.

McCawley, J. D. (1971), "Tense and time reference in English," in Fillmore, C., & Langendoen, D. T., eds. (1971), *Studies in Linguistic Semantics,* Holt, New York.

McNeill, D. (1970), *The Acquisition of Language,* Harper, New York.

Menyuk, P. (1969), *Sentences Children Use,* MIT Press, Cambridge, Mass.

Menyuk, P. (1971), *The Acquisition and Development of Language,* Prentice-Hall, Englewood Cliffs, N. J.

Miller, G. A., & Chomsky, N. (1963), "Finitary models of language users," in Luce, R. P., Bush, R. R., & Galanter, E. (1963), *Handbook of Mathematical Psychology* (Vol. 2), Wiley, New York.

Montague, R. (1973), "The proper treatment of quantification in ordinary English," in Hintikka, K. J. J., Moravcsik, J. M. E., & Suppes, P., eds. (1973), *Approaches to Natural Language,* Reidel, Dordrecht, Holland.

Perlmutter, D. (1970), "Surface structure constraints in syntax," *Linguistic Inquiry,* **1,** 187–255.

Perlmutter, D. (1971), *Deep and Surface Structure Constraints in Syntax,* Holt, New York.

Peters, S., ed. (1972), *Goals of Linguistic Theory,* Prentice-Hall, Englewood Cliffs, N. J.

Pope, E. (1971), "Answers to yes-no questions," *Linguistic Inquiry,* **2,** 69–82.

Postal, P. (1964a), *Constituent Structure: A Study of Contemporary Models of Syntactic Description,* Mouton, The Hague.

Postal, P. (1964b), "Limitations of phrase structure grammars," in Fodor & Katz (1964).

Postal, P. (1970), "On coreferential complement subject deletion," *Linguistic Inquiry,* **1,** 439–500.

Postal, P. (1972), "A global constraint on pronominalization," *Linguistic Inquiry,* **3,** 35–60.

Postal, P. (1974), *On Raising,* MIT Press, Cambridge, Mass.

Quirk, R., Greenbaum, S., Leech, G., & Svartvik, J. (1972), *A Grammar of Contemporary English,* Seminar Press, New York.

Reibel, D., & Schane, S. A., eds. (1969), *Modern Studies in English,* Prentice-Hall, Englewood Cliffs, N. J.

Ringen, C. (1972), "On arguments for rule ordering," *Foundations of Language,* **8,** 266–273.

Rodman, R. (1972), "The proper treatment of relative clauses in a Montague grammar," in Rodman, R., ed. (1972), *Papers in Montague Grammar, Occasional Papers in Linguistics,* No. 2, UCLA, Los Angeles.

Rohrer, C., & Ruwet, N., eds. (1974), *Actes du Colloque Franco-Allemand de Grammaire Transformationelle,* Niemeyer Verlag, Tübingen, Germany.

Rosenbaum, P. S. (1967), *The Grammar of English Predicate Complement Constructions,* MIT Press, Cambridge, Mass.

Ross, J. R. (1967), *Constraints on Variables in Syntax,* Unpublished doctoral dissertation, MIT, Cambridge, Mass. Available from Indiana University Linguistics Club, Bloomington.

Ross, J. R. (1969a), "A proposed rule of tree-pruning," in Reibel, D. & Schane, S. A., eds., (1969), *Modern Studies in English,* Prentice-Hall, Englewood Cliffs, N. J.

Ross, J. R. (1969b), "On the cyclic nature of English pronominalization," in Reibel, D. & Schane, S. A. eds., (1969), *Modern Studies in English,* Prentice-Hall, Englewood Cliffs, N. J.

Ross, J. R. (1969c), "Auxiliaries as main verbs," in Todd, W., ed. (1969), *Studies in Philosophical Linguistics* (Series 1), Great Expectations Press, Carbondale, Ill.

Ross, J. R. (1969d), "Adjectives as main verbs," in Reibel, D. & Schane, S. A., eds., (1969), *Modern Studies in English*, Prentice-Hall, Englewood Cliffs, N. J.

Ross, J. R. (1971), "Gapping and the order of constituents," in Bierwisch, M., & Heidolph, W., eds. (1971), *Recent Advances in Linguistics*, Mouton, The Hague.

Ross, J. R. (1972), "Act," in Davidson, D., & Harman, G., eds. (1972), *Semantics of Natural Languages*, Reidel, Dordrecht, Holland.

Ruwet, N. (1968), *Introduction à la Grammaire Générative*, Librarie Plon, Paris.

Sapir, E. (1921), *Language*, Harcourt, New York.

Schane, S. (1972), *Generative Phonology*, Prentice-Hall, Englewood Cliffs, N. J.

Schwartz, A. (1972), "Constraints on movement transformations," *Journal of Linguistics*, **8,** 35–85.

Searle, J. R. (1969), *Speech Acts*, Cambridge University Press, London.

Selkirk, E. (1974), "French liason and the $\overline{\text{X}}$ notation," *Linguistic Inquiry*, **5,** 573–590.

Smith, C. S. (1969), "Determiners and relative clauses in a generative grammar of English," in Reibel, D. & Schane, S. A., eds., (1969), *Modern Studies in English*, Prentice-Hall, Englewood Cliffs, N. J.

Steinberg, D., & Jakobovits, L. A., eds. (1971), *Semantics: An Interdisciplinary Reader in Philosophy, Linguistics, and Psychology*, Cambridge University Press, London.

Stockwell, R., Schachter, P., & Partee, B. (1973), *The Major Syntactic Structures of English*, Holt, New York.

Thorne, J. P. (1966), "English imperative sentences," *Journal of Linguistics*, **2,** 69–78.

Todd, W., ed. (1969), *Studies in Philosophical Linguistics* (Series 1), Great Expectations Press, Carbondale, Ill.

Wexler, K., Culicover, P. W., & Hamburger, H. (1975), "Learning-theoretic foundations of linguistic universals," *Theoretical Linguistics*, **2.**

Wexler, K., Culicover, P. W., & Hamburger, H. (in preparation), *Formal Principles of Language Acquisition*.

Wexler, K., & Hamburger, H. (1973), "On the insufficiency of surface data for the learning of transformational languages," in Hintikka, K. J., Moravcsik, J. M. E., & Suppes, P., eds. (1973), *Approaches to Natural Language*, Reidel, Dordrecht, Holland.

Yngve, V. H. (1960), "A model and an hypothesis for language structure," *Proc. Am. Phil. Soc.,* **104,** 444–466.

Yngve, V. H. (1961), "The depth hypothesis," in Jakobson, R., ed. (1961), *Structure of Language and Its Mathematical Aspect: Proceedings of the 12th Symposium in Applied Mathematics*, American Mathematical Society, Providence, R. I.

Subject Index

A

ADJ, *see* Adjective
Adjective, 11
Adjective phrase, 163
Affix, 52
Affix Hopping, 52, 58, 195
  multiple application of, 53–55
  order of, 94ff
  in questions, 65–67
Agent Postposing, 161, 171
A-Over-A Principle, 276, 280, 284
AP, *see* Adjective phrase
ART, *see* Article
Article, 9, 80
Attachment Constraint, 250–251, 262–263
AUX, 47–51
[+AUX], 58
Auxiliary verbs, 39

B

Base component, 29
Binary Principle, 266–268, 292, 293–298
Bottom-up procedure, 16

Braces notation, 13
Branching node, 19

C

Chomsky-adjunction, 302
Cleft construction, 207–208
Common noun, 11
COMP, 199–200, 233, 268, 277
Competence, 4–5
Complex NP Constraint, 280
Complex NP Shift, 154–156, 299–300
Constraints, *see Individual constraints*
Context sensitive phrase structure rule, 67n, 123
Contraction, 128–131
Coordinate Structure Constraint, 282
Coreference, 145
Cyclic node, 267, 291, 293–296
Cyclic Principle, 231–232, 236, 249

D

Dative, 155, 159, 300–301
  ordering of, 155, 156, 159–160, 165

Deep structure, 29, 40
DEM, *see* Demonstrative
Demonstrative, 184
Derivation, 28, 90
Descriptive adequacy, 19, 24, 32–33
DET, *see* Determiner
Determiner, 80
Direct domination, 20
Do, 69–71, 105–114
    in imperatives, 150–152
Do Deletion, 70, 96–97
    and *Do* Support, 107–114
    ordering of, 70, 94–98
Do Replacement, 71, 100, 124
    ordering of, 100
Do Support, 105–107
    and *Do* Deletion, 107–114
Dummy modal, 112–113

E

Echo question, 73n
En, 40
En/Ing Hopping, 50
END(0), 223
END(S), 223, 233
Equi-NP Deletion, 218, 221–223, 233–236, 302
Exhaustive domination, 20
Expansion, 20
Explanatory adequacy, 19, 98
Extraposed relative, 202–203
Extraposition, 244–251
    bounding of, 246–251
    ordering of, 261–263
Extraposition from NP, 156–157
Extraposition of PP, 156–157
Extrinsic ordering, 93

F

Filter, 196, 236–237
Free relatives, 203–205
Freezing Principle, 298–302

G

Gapping, 130n
[GEN], 81–82
Generate, 18, 90
Generative grammar, 19

Grammar, 2, 19
Grammatical sentence, 3

H

Head noun, 195

I

Identifiable (class of grammars), 287
Idiom, 167–168
Immediate constituent, 20
Immediate domination, 20
Imperatives, 147–153
Indirect questions, 203–205
Infinitive, 215
    subject of, 217–223
Ing, 40
Input (to transformation), 53
Intermediate phrase marker, 90
Internal S Constraint, 283
Interrogative NP, 26
Interrogative pronoun, 77
Intransitive verb, 15
Intraposition, 251–257
Intrinsic ordering, 93
Inversion, 67ff, 73, 99, 101–104, 302
    ordering of, 70, 99–102
    in tags, 134

K

Katz-Postal Hypothesis, 115–116

L

Labeled bracket, 20–21, 246
Learnability, 268, 284–293
Left Branch Condition, 295
Lexical entry, 56, 215
Lexicon, 2
Linear ordering, 98

M

M, *see* Modal verb
Markers, 40
Master, 267
Modal verb, 23, 39, 47–48
Morphology, 55–56

N

N, *see* Noun
Neg Contraction, 129–130
Neg Placement, 124–126, 218
Negation, 120–131
Node label, 19
Nonlexical category, 13
Noun, 9
Noun phrase, 13
NP, *see* Noun phrase
NP Preposing, 161, 171, 227, 262, 265, 301–302

O

Optionality of constituents, 13
Optionality of transformations, 90
One, 80–82
One Substition, 80, 185–188
Output of a transformation, 53
Overgeneration, 197

P

P, *see* Preposition
Parentheses notation, 13–14
Parenthetical, 254–257
Passive, 160–172, 220–223, 230–231, 236, 261–262, 291, *see also* Agent Postponing; *see also* NP Preposing
Passive participle, 163
Path, 20
Performance, 4–5
Phonological representation, 55
Phonology, 2
Phrase marker, 17
Phrase structure grammar, 22
Phrase structure rule, 10, 15
Phrase structure tree, 16
Power, 24–25, 30–33, 169
PN, *see* Proper noun
PP, *see* Prepositional phrase
Preposition, 76
Prepositional phrase, 76
[PRO], 82–85
Pronouns, 76–78
Proper noun, 11
Pseudo-cleft construction, 126–128, 205–207

Q

Q, 277

QUAN, *see* Quantifier
Quantifier, 79–80, 184

R

Raising, 223–237, 261–264, 291, 302
Recursion, 27–28, 179–183
Reflexive, 146, 218–219, 229, 262
    ordering of, 159–160
Reflexive pronouns, 144–147
Relative clause, 178, 187–201
Relative Clause Filter, 197
Relative pronouns, 191–195
Rule ordering, 89–107; *see also Individual transformations*
    and order of application, 99

S

Semantic component, 3
    relationship to syntactic component, 114–116
Sentential Subject Constraint, 282
Simplicity, 98
Sister-adjunction, 52
some, 78–79
Structural change, 53
Structural description, 53
Structure-preserving at a node, 298
Surface structure, 29, 40
Syntactic category, 9–16
Syntactic component, 2–3
Syntactic features, 56–59
Syntax, 2

T

Tag formation, 133–139
Tag question, 131–139
Tense, 40–46
    and time, 43–46
TENSE, 47–52, 149
That clauses, 242–265
That Deletion, 258–264
That Deletion (Rel), 201
That Formation, 200
That (relative), 198–201
Theory of grammar, 2–3, 8, 29, 89
There Insertion, 224–229
Though Attraction, 166–279
To be Deletion, 166
Top-down procedure, 18

Topicalization, 279
[TRANS], 57
Transformation, *see also Individual transformations*
  constraints on, 274–305
  formal statement of, 53
  function of, 28
Transitive verb, 15
Truncated passive, 170–172

U

Universal Base Hypothesis, 289
Universals, 2, 25

V

V, *see* Verb
V$_I$, *see* Intransitive verb
V$_T$, *see* Transitive verb
Variable, 51

Verb, 9
Verb complement, 214–237, 242–257
Verbal sequence, 39–55
  in questions, 63–71
Verb phrase, 15
VP, *see* Verb phrase

W

Wh Fronting, 73–76, 100–102, 104, 195–196, 199, 262, 275, 277–279, 281–282, 294–297, 300
  ordering of, 100–102
Wh question, 72–76
Wh words, 74, 76–85

Y

Yes-no question, 63–67
You Deletion, 148–150, 152